Performing Ethnomusicology

Performing Ethnomusicology

Teaching and Representation
in World Music Ensembles

EDITED BY

Ted Solís

UNIVERSITY OF CALIFORNIA PRESS

Berkeley   Los Angeles   London

University of California Press
Berkeley and Los Angeles, California

University of California Press, Ltd.
London, England

© 2004 by the Regents of the University of California

Library of Congress Cataloging-in-Publication Data

Performing ethnomusicology : teaching and representation in world
  music ensembles / edited by Ted Solís.
      p.   cm.
  Includes bibliographical references and index.

  ISBN 978-0-520-23831-2 (pbk. : alk. paper)

  1. Ethnomusicology.   2. World music—Instruction and study.
3. Folk music groups.   I. Solís, Ted.

ML3798.P47   2004
780'.89—dc22   2004043967

Manufactured in the United States of America

13   12   11   10   09   08
10   9   8   7   6   5   4   3   2

The paper used in this publication is both acid-free and totally
chlorine-free (TCF). It meets the minimum requirements of
ANSI/NISO Z39.48–1992 (R 1997) (*Permanence of Paper*).

CONTENTS

ACKNOWLEDGMENTS

I wish to express my gratitude to Mary Francis, of UC Press, for her faith in the project and invaluable insights; Katherine Hagedorn and R. Anderson Sutton for extensive and constructive manuscript criticism; J. Richard Haefer for innumerable acts of technical assistance and many years of collegiality and comradeship; my students Sezen Ozeke, Kristina Jacobson, Tony Dumas, and Eun-Jung Young for help with the bibliography; Ayala Solís for editing assistance; Kathleen Hood for invaluable help with Arabic orthography; Julie Codell for positivity, encouragement, and her rich scholarly perspectives; Colette DeDonato and Lynn Meinhardt, of UC Press, for cordial and patient professionalism; copyeditor Sharron Wood for her amazing eye and ear; David Harnish for staying on my back; Roger Vetter, the first to whom I broached the idea, for his irreverent encouragement; Philip F. Nelson for long ago helping me make the cultural connection; Barbara B. Smith for "specificity," taking a chance on me, and so much else; Bruno Nettl, for being a *mensch* and exemplar of clear and insightful expression; Ricardo D. Trimillos for offering me my first chance to teach a world music ensemble, decades of friendship and support in our field, and help at every stage of this project; and my distinguished contributors for the pleasure of their enthusiasm and stimulating interactions.

I dedicate my work on this book to Max, Hazel, Rick, Maile, Gabbi, and Aya Solís. *Performing Ethnomusicology* began long ago, as I made music with them.

Introduction

Teaching What Cannot Be Taught

An Optimistic Overview

TED SOLÍS

"ENSEMBLE ENCOUNTERS"

It is rather remarkable that, in spite of the proliferation of world music performance programs and the importance of such activities in ethnomusicologists' professional lives, so little has been written about the academic world music ensemble. We aim to fill that lacuna. My fellow contributors and I, in the words of Anne Rasmussen, "hope that this volume, by problematizing our performance in the language of the academy, will provide models for our colleagues and their institutions who are trying to make a place for world music performance and its evaluation."

The Ethnomusicological Dilemma Manifest in Our Ensembles

During a break in a graduate seminar on ethnomusicological issues, I put on a venerable Nonesuch LP, *Javanese Court Gamelan*. After a couple of minutes, mildly irritated that few of the students were paying attention to the music and most were gabbing animatedly with one another, I rhetorically asked why no one was listening. Randy, a bright choral DMA candidate, pointed out to me that they were, by my own description, responding to gamelan music "as Javanese might." They were not listening quietly and reverently, as would an American concert audience, but rather accepting the music as a pleasant background for social interaction while awaiting a subsequent lively musical event upon which to concentrate. Feeling amiably hoist by my own petard, I admitted that our exchange nicely illustrated some issues very germane to the volume I was beginning to edit, on ensembles in ethnomusicology. It struck me that his observation encapsulated perhaps the foremost dilemma that faces ethnomusicologists: how do we represent the rich cultures we revere while we acknowledge and deal with the cultural distance between us and our students, and between both of us and these cultures?

In no sphere of ethnomusicological academia do we enter this contested space more unequivocally and richly than through the world of the ensemble, with its formidable diversity of cultural relationships: the director and each of the ensemble members, each of the members to every other, and one and all to the represented cultural tradition. The emotions engendered and engaged through the act of ensemble creation and participation are profound and volatile. Throughout the development of this volume, from its genesis as a panel for the 1999 Society for Ethnomusicology meeting in Austin, Texas, to its final form, I was struck by the quick and enthusiastic responses to the proposal by a large number of already oversubscribed scholars. At the 1999 conference, the panel attracted perhaps the largest audience of any conference session, in spite of the early hour. Enthusiastic audience commentary after we presented our papers went on for about an hour. It was thus clear from the beginning that the subject was very exciting to all concerned. Why so?

This subject seems to hit us directly where we live. Many of us seem to feel that performing in or teaching an ensemble that stems from our primary research embodies more of what we are professionally, and reflects why we do what we do in more ways and more directly than nearly anything else. We bring the field with us to every rehearsal, constantly reassessing our theories and competencies. We may apply to the ensemble James Clifford's words on "participant observation [which] obliges its practitioners to experience, at a bodily as well as an intellectual level, the vicissitudes of translation. It requires arduous language learning, some degree of direct involvement and conversation, and often a derangement of personal and cultural expectations" (Clifford 1988: 24). In teaching ensembles we subject and resubject ourselves and our students to such "vicissitudes of translation," combining pedagogy, constant self-assessment, feedback that happens both in the moment and in semesterly and yearly evaluations, and the constant creative resynthesis of life experience. This happens in classroom teaching as well, but *here,* creating music (a notoriously evocative catalyst), we explicitly draw our students into the process as active collaborators at every level.

As Benjamin Brinner states, "More aspects of competence are foregrounded in ensemble than in solo performance" (1995: 4). Certainly, these aspects include emotional and social competence. We overtly expose, in a highly visible venue, our ability to function in another cultural and aesthetic world. In the ensemble, unlike in the lecture/discussion, in which instructors can control the discourse to their advantage, "rights" and "wrongs" actually *do* exist. In a Cuban-style *inspiración,* for example, you need to stay "in clave," not be thrown off by the *montuno* anticipated bass, and get everyone through the *cierres* (complex unison passages separating major structural units of the piece) together. Hardja Susilo recounts in his chapter how a Javanese gamelan piece performed by those without competence and "correctness" turned into a sort of comic round of endless pursuit without closure. If you've trained your students well enough, they will expect competent and satisfying group collaboration. Dropping the train of thought in a class discussion can always be masked with a quip or a clever aside, but "dropping the (musical) baton" is a much more serious betrayal of mutual obligation.

Structure of the Book

Each of our contributors engages many of the common paradigms explored by the others, as well as ideas appropriate to their unique backgrounds and current situations, thus providing a rich variety of reinforcing and complementary perspectives. Our overarching preoccupation is intercultural and intergenerational transmission; the interlocking pedagogical relationships linking a number of the authors vividly illustrate this process. After the Introduction and Part One, consisting of an overview and personal perspectives, the book is organized around three principal challenges arising from this transmission process. Part Two addresses the challenges of working within the academy, Part Three the challenge of representing cultures to students and to the public, and Part Four the challenge of undertaking pedagogical negotiations in the interest of the preceding endeavors. The titles of these parts draw partly upon authors' felicitous key phrases.

Challenges of "Learning" and "Knowing"

The essays of Hardja Susilo, Ricardo Trimillos, Sumarsam, and Gage Averill provide rich historical perspective on the discourse that ultimately led to the present prominence of world music ensemble performance. The trajectory of this discourse is predictable, given contemporary ethnographic philosophies: reflecting current emphases on objectivist and dualistic ethnography, we appropriately find in earlier ethnomusicological studies analysis of product; during the last thirty years or so emphasis has, rather, increasingly been on person (note Ali Jihad Racy's call for a study of "the teacher as text") and process. One challenge to the earlier methodology—a clear harbinger of change—was posed by Leonard B. Meyer in 1958:

> Ethnologists try to have their cake and eat it too when they claim they are relativists, because at the same time they work from all kinds of absolute assumptions. If you were really a relativist you would not pretend to analyze a tune from another culture. You claim a universal you can "understand." No linguist would dare take a tape of an unknown language and try to analyze it. The

point is, it is not how we analyze but how they, the native speakers and singers, analyze it, that counts. (" 'Whither Ethnomusicology?' " 1959: 103)

If carried to its ultimate implication, this admonition to shed cognitive distance between ourselves and our "subjects" leads us to "do what they do," and perhaps even "be what they are." Susilo speaks to this quest, so endemic to the ethnomusicological condition:

> You couldn't hear these different thoughts in the mind of the players during a concert, except when they get out of synch. It's at that time when you hear the result of the wrong thoughts. Learning a culture, in this case a music culture, is not just learning how the natives physically do it, but also how they think about it.

Another paradigm with profound implications is Charles Seeger's oft-stated reminder of the importance of both ways of "knowing" music: through speech, and in terms of itself. Jihad Racy recounts student reaction, in rehearsal, to the ineffable. "Certain students are particularly interested in verbalizing the experience. Some ask me, 'How do you play that ornament? Can you explain it?' And oftentimes I say, 'Well, I wish I knew how to.'" We aspire to move in our performance and representation of these musics from what Paul Stoller calls the "intellectualist vision" (1989: 4) to one in which we integrate "the play of personalities, the presentation of self, and the presence of sentiment," and in which "one cannot separate thought from feeling and action" (ibid.: 5). We persevere in exploring ways to understand, channel, and "express the inexpressible" to our students.

SQUARE PEGS AND SPOKESFOLK: SERVING AND ADAPTING TO THE ACADEMY

As academicians, most ethnomusicologists operate within traditional academic institutional frameworks: job searches generated by committees; periodic reviews, from first-year evaluations to the "up or out" tenure decision; and, increasingly, forms of post-tenure review. We serve on the usual committees. We are obliged, like everyone else, to justify ourselves and our activities according to legislative, institutional, and unit mandates du jour.

The Academic Other

Yet we ethnomusicologists often flatter ourselves that we are somehow different, countercultural multiculturalists more attuned to the wider world than many of our compatriots, ethnocentric, monolingual folks who always "order it mild" (whereas *we* always ask for it "spicy"). We perceive ourselves as different from those in many other disciplines who seem library- and computer-bound; from some music department colleagues who teach what seem to us deracinated, noncontextual, reproduction-bound performance traditions; and even sometimes from our historical musicology colleagues (themselves often marginalized within music departments)[1] with whom, as departmental "academics,"[2] we are conventionally and nominally allied within divisions and subunits of music history and musicology. The traditional divide between ethnomusicologists and historical musicologists (indisputably narrowing in recent years) is reflected in the former's espousal of E. B. Tylor's "pervasive" definition of "culture" versus the latter's allegiance to Matthew Arnold's "elite" view; differing views on "the typical" and "the masterpiece"; the importance of oral materials; fieldwork; and other fundamental issues.[3]

Ethnomusicologists, although champions and sometime inhabitants of worlds known by few others, nonetheless usually find their academic homes in the music department, which "in some ways . . . functions almost as an institution for the suppression of certain musics" (Nettl 1995: 82). Such "suppression," however, is much less common now than twenty and certainly thirty years ago; multicultural and global curricular requirements have led to regularly offered popular and world music classes, and many universities and colleges now include ethnomusicologist faculty.

How do we justify the maintenance of our ensembles specifically? Anne Rasmussen reminds us of the dual roles that ensembles play: her Middle Eastern ensemble represents both "the university and their respect for diversity" and Middle Eastern "culture and community." The latter sort of function is particularly important and advantageous to urban universities in locales with large—and especially politically active—self-consciously "ethnic" populations (for example, Hawai'i, Los Angeles, New York, and Pittsburgh). Community good will is vital to public institutions, which increasingly find themselves under legislative scrutiny and financial pressure. Ensembles also provide vehicles for students and community members to "act out" their perceived and chosen heritages, however constructed and reconstructed. They provide performing opportunities for nonspecialist, non–music major students from around the campus, thus also attracting a significant number of credit hours. They act as badly needed interdisciplinary nexuses between music departments (notoriously isolated and autonomous) and other university departments and area studies centers.

And how do ethnomusicologists, who consider themselves among the most alternative of academicians, fit themselves and their performing ensembles into the often conservative academic framework of the music department? A number of this volume's contributors (including Hardja Susilo, David Harnish, Michelle Kisliuk and Kelly Gross, Roger Vetter, and

Ted Solís) comment on the logistical and psychic difficulties of adjusting to the academy's organizational paradigms (thus Vetter's "A Square Peg in a Round Hole") and recount their negotiations of these strictures.

Public Vindication in the Concert

Especially problematic is the semesterly formal evaluative concert. Although authors recount their often fruitful and educational efforts toward alleviating what they perceive to be sterile and unbecoming presentation environments, few have apparently found a way to completely bypass the institution of the concert itself. It is axiomatic in musical academia that one shows in public what one can do, and that this is the primary proof of one's *bona fides*.[4] The less presentational study group model (see Sumarsam, Susilo, and Trimillos) of the early days of Mantle Hood's Institute of Ethnomusicology at UCLA appears less feasible nowadays. University arts units are now obliged to be more self-sustaining and depend on good public relations through public performances.[5]

Mounting a substantial semesterly concert in the face of constant turnover and eternally green student musicians with little or no prior exposure to either the instruments or the sound provides our eternal challenge. Our difficulties are compounded by the fact that as directors we do it all: we are obliged to represent all the instrumental, vocal, and choreographic abilities required within a complex, multitasking performance ensemble. Western university orchestra conductors, on the other hand, are not required to teach, for example, flutter tonguing or the *col legno* technique; students have already learned such things and can consult with their studio teachers about difficult score passages. A few world music ensembles are exceptions. These include university mariachi bands, which draw their personnel largely from those already somewhat competent. Many mariachi vocalists, violinists, trumpeters, and guitarists[6] have played in high school groups and are familiar with mariachi aesthetics. J. Lawrence Witzleben's Chinese ensembles in Hong Kong also draw mainly upon students already adept on their instruments.

This suggests two academic ensemble schemas. The first we might call "realization ensembles"; students enroll in them not primarily for mind-opening cultural experiences, but rather to realize preexisting musical skills. Vetter refers to these groups as "canonic ensembles": concert band, orchestra, choir, etc. He summarizes the modus operandi of such ensembles, writing, "In general, ensemble rehearsal time is dedicated to musical matters; any cultural contextualization of the works being prepared is typically relegated to printed program notes. [Goals are] a high standard of musical presentation in public performance and the honing of the performers' technical skills and expressive potential." We might somewhat waggishly refer to the typical world music group, on the other hand, as an "experience ensemble"; students here embrace a second (cultural) child-hood, akin to the sort of entirely new musical experience most musicians underwent as children with their first piano lessons or sixth-grade band. Mark Slobin speaks of affinity groups, "charmed circles of like-minded music-makers drawn magnetically to a certain genre that creates strong expressive bonding" (Slobin 1992: 72). Certainly most world music groups (and, of course, many "canonic ensembles") can be described this way.

Ensemble Choices and Hegemonies

A list of typical academic world music ensemble types is certainly shorter than one would imagine, given the great range of interests reflected in general ethnomusicological scholarship. Clearly, certain ensembles are emerging as canonic. These ensemble choices partly reflect historical trends in ethnomusicological investigation since the early 1950s. Befitting Mantle Hood's profound influence, gamelans abound[7] as glittering sonic and visual symbols of "the Other."[8] Perhaps second to these in number have been West African percussion ensembles.[9] Previously Ghanaian Ewe (see David Locke's comments on Ewe ethnomusicological hegemony) with an admixture of Ghanaian Ashanti—the study of whose musical culture Hood embraced as his "second area"—predominated. Now *djembe* drums of Senegal abound. These percussion ensembles offer a more technically accessible and there-fore "democratic" medium that has proliferated worldwide across many class and ethnic categories.[10] Antillean steel bands may be next in number, but these are directed somewhat less frequently by ethnomusicologists[11] than by percussion faculty, who often make little effort to contextualize their world music activities.[12]

Middle Eastern ensembles, although well represented in this volume, are less common, probably because Americans (unlike Europeans) paid relatively little attention to the music of that area until the late 1960s and early 1970s. Increased interest in the Middle East results partly from the fortu-itous intersection of Bruno Nettl's Iranian research with the recruitment of Jihad Racy, a committed and professional Arab music performer, as a University of Illinois graduate student in 1968. This confluence helped expand the discourse to a more general exploration of Middle Eastern modal procedures. Racy also began a performing tradition lineage that by now has developed several branches.

Some other ensembles, such as Hankus Netsky's klezmer groups and Ricardo Trimillos's Filipino ensembles, are location-specific phenomena. They arise from synergies among the ethnomusicologist's personal ethnic heritage, research predilections, and proximate populations (Jews of the northeastern megalopolis and Filipinos of Hawai'i, respectively). Academic mariachi ensembles abound in heavily Hispanic Texas, the Southwest, and California, but are much less common elsewhere.

The Shona *mbira* of Zimbabwe appears to be quietly emerging as a new academic ensemble, established first by the work of Paul Berliner and later by that of Thomas Turino. It offers a useful variety of performance roles for students with different capabilities and shares "high art" characteristics with many other ethnomusicology ensemble musics: an indigenous theoretical framework, relatively high prestige within traditional society, and a rich body of associated scholarly literature.

The more common ensembles also tend to belong to "great traditions" with clear familial links across broad regions. Gamelans, for example, are clearly related historically and in performance practice to other Southeast Asian percussion ensembles; music makers in Arab, Turkish, Persian, and even to some extent Balkan traditions can jam together. West African percussion ensembles share basic structural and communicative elements. On the other hand, relatively few ethnomusicologists have built ensembles upon limited "local" traditions, regardless of their personal research allegiances. (I am not aware, for example, of any academic Melanesian panpipe counterpart for Dale Olsen's or Thomas Turino's pan-Andean panpipe ensembles.) Most likely the desire for "cost-effectiveness"—the ability to communicate with as many as possible in a recognized musical *lingua franca* rather than a more local language—is the overriding factor.[13] Thus, for example, one might teach Central Javanese gamelan, rather than the Sundanese[14] or Dayak tradition on which one has written a dissertation.

PATCHWORKERS, ACTORS, AND AMBASSADORS: REPRESENTING OURSELVES AND OTHERS

The Long Funnel: Constructing and Representing Ourselves

From the first, I intended that one important contribution of this book be the reflexive examination of ethnomusicologists' personal learning and teaching continua, including their formative influences before succumbing to the blandishments of ethnomusicology as a field per se. Although we see the importance of pedagogical lineages and the procedural philosophies of particular teachers (however subsequently adapted and evolved),[15] it is also clear that the formation and teaching of ethnomusicology ensembles has not yet reached any sort of canonic stage, in which methodologies and procedures have become standardized. No "proper" way to develop and lead, for example, a West African drum ensemble exists. Even some who teach ensembles connected to some aspect of their perceived ethnic heritage have come to that point rather circuitously, through a process of mediated recapture.[16] Thus, in the contemporary spirit of academic reflexivity, an awareness of what Rasmussen calls "a patchwork of experience" in each specific case is an indispensable tool for understanding our product and process:

> A musician's musicality is the result of a patchwork of experience [and] collections of encounters and choices: pastiches of performances they have experienced, the lessons they have taken, the people with whom they have played, the other musicians they admire, other musics that they play or enjoy, and the technical and cognitive limitations of their own musicianship.

The pedagogical means by which we achieve these goals are as much a part of the patchwork as our musicianship. As Harnish says, "Ethnomusicologists who teach non-Western ensembles are neither instructed by professors at academies nor by their master teachers in the field how to teach the music to students at universities. . . . The degree of compromise a director negotiates tells a great deal about his or her identity and overall plans and goals." This can be as true for "native" teachers as for foreigners. Racy had never taught his ensemble, and Susilo had little experience doing so, before coming to America; they formed methodologies largely in response to the American *tabula rasa*. Sumarsam, on the other hand, who formally trained in the gamelan conservatory tradition, adapted those methods at Wesleyan.

The continuum encompassing learning and teaching is a long curve, or narrowing funnel. In Witzleben's words,

> As a graduate student, learning to play Chinese and Indonesian music was a natural part of my studies and life. The typical scope of my vision was from lesson to lesson, performance to performance; the larger picture related this learning and music making to things such as research papers, thesis topics, and chances to study performance abroad, either as an end in itself or as a component of research-oriented fieldwork. Even if a course in "world music ensemble pedagogy" existed, it would have held little interest for me, since the idea of teaching such ensembles myself was not even on the horizon.

One "enters the funnel" long before graduate school, and perhaps long before focused musical engagement of any sort. Descriptions of the particular means by which ethnomusicologists gravitate to their ultimate foci provide stimulating reading throughout this volume. More than that, of course, these means literally delineate the terms of their negotiations with these cultures and the performative artifacts with which they interact. Inducing contributors to engage in this sort of autobiographical revelation was, however, not always easy; some equated self-revelation with egotism and even exhibitionism. This, although certainly none believed themselves born fully formed, like Athena from the head of Zeus, as world music ensemble directors. I believe that the resulting volume provides unique insights into the structuring of ethnomusicologists' careers and methodologies.

Hopeful Antiorientalists: Representing Others

As ethnomusicologists, we embrace a trope that challenges orientalism and facile essentializations of multifaceted and fluid cultural systems. Racy speaks to this "cultural encapsulization":

> We used to recognize our "native" teachers as embodiments of specific performance traditions: We brought this woman from Korea; we've got Korea here; we brought this gentleman from West Africa; we've got West Africa here. . . . We may have done that at a time when we viewed our field informants as individuals who have somehow internalized the essence of their respective cultures.

He elaborates at length on his desire to balance analytical verbal or written discourse and his resistance to categorization as "merely" an implicit, intuitive culture bearer.

However, both experience and simple logic teach us that without at least some encapsulization and abstraction we cannot transmit cultural information. Furthermore, no "pure, unadulterated essences," untouched by human hands, can be conveyed or are even possible. In the words of Lila Abu-Lughod, "Even attempts to refigure informants as consultants and to 'let the other speak' in dialogic . . . or polyvocal texts—decolonizations on the level of the text—leave intact the basic configuration of global power on which anthropology, as linked to other institutions of the world, is based" (1991: 143). We may engage most closely with the politics of race, power, and representation through our performances, which (appropriating Clifford's words on ethnographic texts) are "orchestrations of multivocal exchanges occurring in politically charged situations" (1988: 10). David Locke accordingly notes that

> World music ensembles inexorably are affected by the world's imperial, colonial past. This is the condition of all ethnomusicological action, but the very nature of performance calls it forcefully into debate. . . . Music studies, unlike less performative modes of cross-cultural inquiry, encourage nondominant relationships. But like anthropology, ethnomusicology came into being during the period of Euro-American colonialism, so we are complicit despite well-intended efforts to redress its aftermath of social injustice.[17]

Clearly, then, the influences and methodologies themselves become for us an important scholarly preoccupation. Edward Said states that

> Everyone who writes about the Orient must locate himself vis-à-vis the Orient; translated into his text, this location includes the kind of narrative voice he

adopts, the type of structure he builds, the kinds of images, themes, motifs that circulate in his text—all of which add up to deliberate ways of addressing the reader, containing the Orient, and finally, representing it or speaking on its behalf. (1978: 20)

We are, of course, almost always perceived as "speaking on behalf" of the cultures we "perform." As Harnish says, "For those of us teaching in geographic areas of little diversity, we are charged with—*or charge ourselves with*—the task of representing the music and culture of the ensemble" (emphasis mine). Finding ourselves perforce in this role (even in geographical areas with considerable diversity), we become mired in the question of how "authentically" to pursue public presentation. Barbara Kirshenblatt-Gimblett considers

> the artfulness of the ethnographic object . . . an art of excision, of detachment, an art of the excerpt. Where does the object begin and where does it end? . . . Shall we exhibit the cup with the saucer, the tea, the cream and sugar, the spoon, the napkin and placemat, the table and chair, the rug? Where do we stop? Where do we make the cut? (1991: 388)

Try as we may, we will never really make our gamelan performances "Yogyanese," or our marimba events "Chiapanecan." Apology is futile; should one apologize for not being what one can never be? We profit more from accepting and examining our inevitably shaping roles. Timothy J. Cooley, in his introduction to *Shadows in the Field* (a book to which the authors of this volume are considerably indebted), states that "we wish . . . to consider more meaningfully the aspects of the ethnographic process that position scholars through their fieldwork as social actors within the cultures they study" (1997: 4). Ethnomusicologists have all in this way found themselves actors during their fieldwork. Moreover, we who conduct world music ensembles also write screenplays based upon our experiences, produce, do the casting and costuming, and, of course, direct our productions. We are, in other words, interpreters, creators, re-creators, and molders of those cultures in the academic world. If, however, we are thus auteurs, we are often very nervous ones, mentally looking over our shoulders at those from whom we learned. Many ethnomusicologists so strongly identify with their chosen cultures through extended fieldwork, ethnicity, acquired language facility, and shared musical and other deep experiences that they resemble "halfies," Abu-Lughod's term for "people whose national or cultural identity is mixed by virtue of migration, overseas education, or parentage" (1991: 137). She writes of the heightened and compounded sense of accountability weighing upon "halfie" anthropologists:

> As anthropologists, they write for other anthropologists, mostly Western. Identified also with communities outside the West, or subcultures within it, they are called to account by educated members of those communities. More

importantly, not just because they position themselves with reference to two communities but because when they present the Other they are presenting themselves, they speak with a complex awareness of and investment in reception. (Ibid.: 142)

Clearly, an angst born of serving as ambassadors (or at least local consuls) for cultures to which they only equivocally belong has stimulated the thoughtful reflexivity of many of our contributors.

Most ethnomusicologists can be said to have entered a sort of no-man's-land (or is it "every-man's-land"?) in which we examine our ethno-cultural allegiances not only during foreign research summers, winter sessions, sabbaticals, and grant-generated leaves, but several times a day, when confronted by our books, writings, slides, videos, class notes, and class presentations. Our personal doubts and insecurities elicited when we direct ensembles usually lie more in the sphere of cultural heritage—our not quite bicultural credentials—rather than race per se. In racially absolutist America,[18] however, this emphatically does not hold true for African ensembles. Locke states,

> leading an African ensemble at a university in the United States means working within a racialized discourse. Courses about the music cultures of Africa often become a setting where young people work through their views on race prejudice, ethnic and gender stereotypes, international economic equity, the legacy of slavery, and right action in the present. Race, conceived as a bipolar black/white condition, is an ever present issue. The African ensemble is a rare setting in which nonblack participants may seem racially out of place.

Far from being apologetic for his "faulty phenotype," however, Locke defends his position as African ensemble director by emphasizing his strong commitment to honest presentation and the inculcation of respect for the tradition among the students and audience. He also emphasizes the positive aspects of playing against type in the racial makeup of ensemble personnel, writing, "Performances of world music by born-in-the-tradition musicians reinforce comfortable categories, but anomalous presentations of the other by nonothers confound expectations." Kisliuk and Gross express similar sentiments about a nearly all-white BaAka ensemble, writing, "by way of our undeniably non-pygmy visual impression (race and movement style), we in fact prime our audiences to expect interpretation instead of a representation. We also play with costume as a means of bridging this gap. The result is a fundamental challenge to racial and ethnic essentialisms." Rasmussen notes the widespread practice of inviting "native" guest artists to participate in concerts:

> That our guests are all visibly and audibly of Middle Eastern heritage may constitute an act of reverse discrimination in which many of us engage. In my

search for guest artists of Middle Eastern heritage, I may well be considering more than issues of musicianship, for example, the almost sacred position of the musical insider / native musician as well as the attraction of such an "authentic" performer for students and audiences.

Harnish notes the double bind of (doing rural Ohio the service of) "creating Bali" where none exists, while experiencing discrimination in being denied participation in an Asian festival. He writes, "The booking agent explained that the Asian Chamber of Commerce, which sponsors the festival, did not think that a gamelan consisting almost exclusively of Caucasians and directed by one could properly represent an Asian culture. We did not appear 'authentic,' and could therefore not truly 'speak for Bali or Indonesia or Asia.'" Trimillos, on the other hand, notes what we might call "misplaced approval" of his right to perform and teach Japanese koto, based upon his "Asian appearance" (although he is of non-Japanese ancestry).

He also refers to a special sort of ex officio credibility, even a cachet, accruing to ethnomusicologists in their representations of cultures:

> The ethnomusicologist brings to the study group a constructed form of credibility different from that of the native teacher. Field research carries credibility; the ethnomusicologist can relay personal experiences and insights about general culture and the specifics of the tradition. Authority for the music devolves less from the lineage of the teacher and student and more from the academic degree and its research exercise, the dissertation, supplemented by performance competence. For the ethnomusicologist, credibility as a teacher derives largely from Western criteria and structures that are brought to bear upon a native Other.

This prestige associated with ethnomusicological activity can also affect the tradition itself. Netsky and Witzleben both attest to heightened interest in, and greater approval of, klezmer and Chinese orchestral musics once they were presented to members of the heritage community in academic contexts.

WHAT'S THE "IT"?
PEDAGOGICAL GOALS AND COMPROMISES

In the end, whether we choose or reject the role of ambassador, whether we are ascribed culture bearers or not, the realities of professional necessity render us representatives and intermediaries of these cultures. Those directing ensembles drawn from traditions with substantial ethnic populations in the places we teach—Middle Eastern performance in Southern California, for example—face the challenge of satisfying eager audiences often consisting of local community culture bearers. The fact that Middle Eastern folk, popular, and art genres share many basic concepts of mode, form, improvisation, and performer-audience interaction ensures the strong probability of relatively high connoisseurship at most concerts.

We may, however, be the *only* representatives of these cultures in the areas where we teach. Those involved with musics of ethnic groups not strongly represented in the U.S. population (Javanese and Balinese gamelans and BaAka ensemble, for example) tend to present public performances almost exclusively before nonheritage, potentially less critical audiences. Directors thus find themselves relatively free to present to their students (who, as Witzleben starkly states, are "absolute beginners with no knowledge of gamelan music and no direct aural experience of the tradition other than hearing themselves") and audiences any type of repertoire, played at nearly any level of competency. The sonic and visual novelty is often enough, initially, to sustain interest and to entertain for reasons entirely at odds with "authentic" aesthetic criteria.

Moving the ensemble toward a level of achievement commensurate with the director's hopeful expectation is often problematic. World music ensembles often undergo considerable turnover. Unlike those in "major" ensembles such as concert band, concert choir, and symphony orchestra, most students in world music ensembles are not the recipients of renewable performance scholarships. They often cannot reenroll due to class conflicts or the class credit limitations imposed by their major. Ensembles may thus remain for semesters or years at frustratingly basic levels of expertise.[19] Directors are thus challenged to negotiate for themselves zones of satisfaction. They generally know what music they would produce absent constraints. They must, however, *pace* their principal teachers and field research collaborators, make aesthetic and ethical compromises with which they can live. Without the connoisseurship of audience and performers they may be relatively free, within the constraints of their own consciences, to determine those compromises for themselves. Vetter, for example, describes how his goals have changed. Early in his career, he idealistically hoped that his gamelan students would emerge with near-Javanese musical and sociocontextual competency. His more recent and much more modest goals, however, include introducing others "to a significantly different form of musical expression" and sharing his "enthusiasm for and perspective on Javanese culture."

Another goal of Vetter is to "provide students with a face-to-face, long-term interactive exercise." All the ensembles represented here proceed via intragroup cues, markers, and mutual stimulation rather than via the central authoritative model exemplified by the Western conductor. Thus, a desire for such interaction is a goal shared by most of our contributors. One of the things Rasmussen finds exciting about Arab music is "the musical texture produced by the interaction between musicians." Kisliuk and Gross and Solís, among others, find satisfaction and motivation in creating vibrantly interactive and creative relationships within the greater group, encompassing both ensemble and audience. Harnish and Solís search for natural and relaxed performative states in Balinese *gamelan gong kebyar* and Latin marimba through, respectively, such culture-specific concepts as *guru pang-gul* ("the mallet [as a] teacher," guidance through kinesthetic memory) and "Latin groove."

Most ethnomusicologists share a background of intensive and extensive practical language study, which inevitably informs their pedagogy. Vetter likens ethnic ensemble learning "in the paradigm of the academy" to classroom language training: "In my teaching of gamelan I do such things as articulate underlying structure, present melodic and rhythmic vocabularies as building blocks of more complex musical utterances, and impart abstracted principles of musical syntax." Both Locke and Solís employ nontraditional abstractions—musical versions of language pattern drills—in teaching basic rhythmic structures prior to tackling a complete piece. Susilo brings his Western university–acquired knowledge of phonetics to the task of teaching Javanese singing.

Some have transferred modes of analysis and pedagogical techniques from one tradition to another. Note Kisliuk's adaptation of David Locke's Ewe teaching techniques to the demands of her very different BaAka pygmy ensemble, and Solís's eclectic pedagogy, which draws upon the gamelan, among other sources.

INWARD AND OUTWARD GAZES

In the final analysis, how do we make this music "our own"? Gage Averill wonders "whether mimesis can constitute an adequate rationale for ensemble praxis." David Hughes, in a similar vein, states that "if our students do not aspire to and achieve some degree of creativity, then world music ensembles lay themselves open to the potential charge of doing little more than producing bad copies of Zimbabwean/Japanese/Javanese/Indian musicians." He muses, however, that "most students are having enough trouble keeping up with the basics without being creative." The disorienting challenges of learning, performing, and responding are great enough that ethical problems of imitation and appropriation are usually of much greater concern to directors than to the others involved. Averill, Netsky, and Hughes all refer to the historical, sometimes uneasy coalition between world music and the avant-garde, which unite in their ability (if not always intent) to *epater les bourgeois*.[20]

Certainly most of us fall somewhere between mimesis and radically creative adaptation (see Hughes's discussion of the SOAS gamelan composition group). We maintain our allegiances to the source as best we can; try as we may, however, we inescapably shape the medium to our conceptions.

Our common tendency, for example, to valorize older, more traditional repertoire (Trimillos notes this as one way ethnomusicologists establish credibility, acting "more Catholic than the Pope," as it were) partly reflects the persistent ethnological desire to maintain Paradise Lost in the face of inevitable change. It may also, of course, indicate our "marginal retention" of older repertoire simply due to spatial and temporal distance from the cultural centers of repertoire production.

Much of our activity involves the presentation, negotiation, and/or creation (using Hobsbawm's schema) of both "'traditions' actually invented, constructed and formally instituted and those emerging in a less easily traceable manner within a brief and dateable period—a matter of a few years perhaps—and establishing themselves with great rapidity" (Hobsbawm 1983: 1). Note the widespread embrace of the relatively modern Balinese *gamelan gong kebyar,* the genesis in Bali of which is clearly documented; Hankus Netsky's creative synthesis of an academic klezmer tradition; and Solís's construction of a decontextualized Latin marimba instrumentation and performance practice.

Other important shaping influences include the homogenization of styles and genres, as well as the incorporation and synthesis of traditions that in the home culture are perceived as very different and performed separately. Note, for example, the Middle Eastern ensembles of Jihad Racy and Scott Marcus. The former incorporates a wider variety of styles from across the Arab world—including art, folk, and cabaret dance music—than would have been the case in the Cairo conservatory ensembles he used as a model. Marcus goes even further, including material from non-Arab and even Balkan sources.

Marcus's synthesis is one example of directorial activism, as he uses the ensemble to further social goals. He heuristically promotes amicable performative interaction among various West Asian cultures that, politically speaking, refuse to communicate. Averill advocates involving student ensembles

> in the discourse about representation . . . [using] our rehearsals and performances as platforms for raising questions . . . [and] musical performances as spaces of dialogic encounter . . . to use ensembles to provoke, disrupt, and challenge complacency. In this way, we can make the ensemble encounters a part of a student's intellectual, personal, aesthetic, *and ethical* transformation.

Locke's and Kisliuk and Gross's challenges to assumptions of "racially correct" African performance have already been noted. Kisliuk and Gross, bringing Kisliuk's performance studies background to bear, refer to "embodied experience," which can "facilitate an understanding, or at least an awareness, of both macro- and micropolitics. In learning to dance and sing in new ways, one becomes vitally aware of issues of self and other, and of 'here' and 'there,' challenging the distancing that takes place in much disembodied scholarship." They, like Averill, Solís, Locke, Rasmussen, and others, also use the ensemble to challenge Western concert conventions of audience passivity, audience-performer distantiation, and inhibition.

Ultimately, it is our personally conflicted relationship to tradition itself that provides our greatest anxieties and profoundest self-examinations. As Westerners, or even as Western-employed non-Westerners, we are vulnerable to accusations of cultural appropriation and misrepresentation. We fall between Scylla and Charybdis in that the more self-consciously we embrace "authenticity," and the more earnestly we attempt to present what we perceive to be "accurate" cultural context and practices to our audiences, the more likely we are (with the tacit acquiescence of supporting administrations) to fall into a sort of benevolent, essentializing, and (in the words of Harnish) "domesticating orientalism." In the end, whether we adhere fiercely to what we perceive as orthodoxy, or shed all pretexts to "accurate" reproduction, we know we may be charged with either neocolonialism or irresponsible cultural squandering.

Each author is a sort of Noh drama *shite,* undertaking and recounting a journey between worlds full of symbolic encounters. This journey, still in progress for us all, results in emotional and cognitive growth and conflict. We are strongly committed to the overarching mandate of our profession: "grow yourself so that others may also grow." All have undergone the exquisite agonies of cultural transplantation to the field, and the equally traumatic act of leaving it. In the field, our friends and research collaborators have unselfishly given us gifts we know we cannot repay; we know that whatever fees or presents or help we offered in exchange were nothing compared to the worlds revealed to us. Thus we labor mightily to engage our students and to convey at least something of what we felt and feel, re-creating the field a little at each rehearsal. We know we cannot replicate the experience, yet we are determined to create a meaningful and coherent performative world. In *Performing Ethnomusicology* we share the lessons of our journeys and the challenges of our engaging, vital, bittersweet, and exhilarating task.

NOTES

My thanks to Gage Averill, Julie F. Codell, Katherine Hagedorn, Ellen Koskoff, Henry Spiller, R. Anderson Sutton, Ricardo Trimillos, Roger Vetter, Andrew Weinstein, Sean Williams, and Deborah Wong, who provided helpful commentary on passages or all of this introduction.

1. "To be sure, they are hardly the pariahs they sometimes see themselves to be, but most students and teachers are ambivalent about musicologists, sometimes seeing them as a 'requirement police'" (Nettl 1995: 100).

2. Note the absurd but common practice of differentiating "'academic' aca-

demics" (music historians, ethnomusicologists, those in music education) from "nonacademics" (studio performance faculty) within "the academy."

3. See Lieberman 1977 for an important discussion of these perceived differences at that time. More ethnomusicologists are also likely to combine "teaching" and "doing" (performance) (Nettl's dichotomy) than do many (but by no means all) historical musicologists. See Nettl 1995: 57 for statistics on musicologists' performance.

4. Hardja Susilo jokes that he considered suggesting "I Have to Play a Concert in Three Months or I Lose My Job" as a title for this book.

5. One second-hand comment relayed to me concerning my request for support for a non–publicly performing Karnatak "study group" at my university: "Why should we provide them with a room if they're not going to give a concert?"

6. Preexisting Spanish guitar skills also aid in learning the Mexican regional folk guitars: the *vihuela, guitarra de golpe,* and *guitarrón.*

7. Gamelans are rather heavily represented in this volume due to a combination of circumstances. However, our gamelan contributors represent a broad spectrum of generational and cultural perspectives. The contributors include Hardja Susilo and three of his students teaching in very different circumstances: Javanese gamelan in a small private Midwestern liberal arts college, Javanese gamelan in Hong Kong, and Balinese gamelan in a Midwestern state university. We also find striking contrasts between Sumarsam's Surakarta- and conservatory-influenced pedagogical methodologies and Hardja Susilo's primarily Yogyakarta-derived and somewhat more empirical and eclectic approach.

8. In Trimillos's words, "The acquisition of a gamelan as part of a 'proper' ethnomusicology program in the United States appears as iconic as the establishment of a national airline for a 'proper' nation!"

9. Lois Anderson's early Ugandan *amadinda* xylophone groups at the University of Wisconsin apparently never caught on elsewhere.

10. In Paris I once saw a line of white *djembe* players stretching along the length of a quay on the Seine, and on the same day, a *djembe* group of Francophone West Africans demonstrating for working papers in the Place de la Bastille. Eric Charry notes the Guinean musicians' search for new sources of patronage after the death of President Sékou Touré as one of the reasons for the upsurge in *djembe* popularity (Charry 2000: 193).

11. The steel band ensembles of Gage Averill (at his former institution, Wesleyan), Shannon Dudley (University of Washington), and T. M. Scruggs (University of Iowa) are among the exceptions.

12. Some other ensembles exist as semiacademic "asteroids" floating among the "gravitational fields" of academic departments, ethnic student associations, and local communities. These include Japanese *taiko* drum groups, Brazilian style *samba batucada* percussion ensembles, and Balkan music and dance troupes.

13. A linguistic analogy: It often makes more sense for an Indonesianist to learn Bahasa Indonesia, spoken and understood, with its nearly identical sister language Malay, throughout Malaysia and the Indonesian archipelago, than, for example, Batak, a language group limited to North Sumatra.

14. This sometimes depends on whether one inherits or establishes a gamelan program. Because Central Javanese and Balinese gamelans are more common, even those who have specialized in the musics of outlying areas may find themselves teach-

ing on a Central Javanese or Balinese gamelan obtained by a predecessor. They usually are quite capable of doing so, having likely been trained in institutions emphasizing those hegemonic traditions. If, on the other hand, they are given free rein and budget, they may teach the "outlying" tradition.

15. Note the ways Marcus's and Rasmussen's conceptions of a Middle Eastern ensemble both draw upon and diverge from those of their teacher Jihad Racy, and from each other's; how Michelle Kisliuk and Kelly Gross's ideas compare to those of Kisliuk's West African ensemble teacher David Locke; and how Harnish's and Vetter's conceptions relate to those of their gamelan teacher Hardja Susilo.

16. As we see, old recordings served both Netsky and Solís in their constructions of klezmer and Latin marimba performance, and Susilo's work with recordings partly compensated for his youthful departure from Java.

17. The small number of women contributing to this volume may indicate that even in academic ethnomusicology we clearly have not escaped that "past," nor the politico-academic realities of the present. In spite of the rather equal numbers of women and men in ethnomusicology graduate programs and beginning faculty positions in recent years, it would seem that a surprisingly small number of the women relative to the men direct ensembles. Neither Michelle Kisliuk and Kelly Gross nor Anne Rasmussen make mention here of gender-derived obstacles. Can it be that the same set of societal mechanisms that more broadly limits the participation of women in positions of public authority—whether in the Rose Garden, boardroom, film director's chair, or at the symphonic and even high school band podium—operates also among ethnomusicologists, by our own self-satisfied assertion among the most "liberated" of academics? Can one reason be that many of these ensembles are traditionally associated with male performers, teachers, and directors? Is another that the ensemble often seems an unappreciated "extracurricular" activity not perceived to lead toward tenure and promotion for those hired as "scholars"? (Note Anne Rasmussen's fight for recognition of "nonload" ensemble activities in her tenure application package.) The disparity is, at any rate, too striking to be mere coincidence.

18. Note anthropologist Marvin Harris's use of the term *hypodescent* in connection with the nonrational, nonbiological designation of anyone in the United States with even "a drop" of African blood as "Black" (Harris 1970: 75).

19. Sumarsam notes that U.S. gamelan directors confront this problem by availing themselves of the large national gamelan network, bringing competent performers from other institutions to assist in major performances.

20. Clifford's statement on the "ethnographic surreal" applies as well to the effects of world music ensemble presentation on the uninitiated: "Reality is no longer a given, a natural, familiar environment. The self, cut loose from its attachments, must discover meaning where it may" (1988: 119).

PART ONE

Sounding the Other

*Academic World Music Ensembles
in Historical Perspective*

Chapter 1

Subject, Object, and the Ethnomusicology Ensemble

The Ethnomusicological "We" and "Them"

RICARDO D. TRIMILLOS

This chapter is both subjective-personal and objective-general. It is my opportunity to reflect upon more than four decades of personal involvement with world music ensembles, initially as a student, then as a (sometimes reluctant) teacher, and finally as an ethnomusicologist overseeing such projects. Although I focus here upon the ensemble within an American academic setting, we should acknowledge and appreciate similar activities outside academe, such as at the Naropa Institute (Boulder, Colorado), the World Kulintang Institute (Los Angeles, California), and Gamelan Sekar Jaya (El Cerrito, California), as well as outside the United States, including at the Chinese University of Hong Kong, La Cité de la Musique (Paris), Osaka University (Japan), the School of Oriental and African Studies (London), and the Tropen Museum (Amsterdam). Although I intend my observations to have wider application, my immediate purview is circumscribed by institution and by nation: I examine world music ensembles as found at colleges and universities in the United States.

The comments and observations following draw upon past and ongoing experiences at a number of American institutions, including the University of Hawai'i at Manoa, UCLA, U.C. Santa Cruz, U.C. Santa Barbara, Oberlin College, the University of Miami, and Beloit College. They are further informed by sojourns overseas, including to the University of Cologne (Germany), the University of the Philippines (Quezon City), the University of Malaya (Kuala Lumpur), Institut Seni Indonesia (Yogyakarta), Musashino College of Music (Tokyo), and the Australian National University (Canberra), as well as other locations specifically cited in the chapter. They are also influenced by my interests in the pedagogical developments of ethnomusicology, world music, and multiculturalism in the American academy (Trimillos 1988b, 1990; Volk 1998).

It is my intention to attempt a self-reflexive critique of ourselves and our field. The willingness to interrogate subject as well as object is a relatively recent and welcome development encouraged by cultural studies and recent developments in anthropology. There has always been a need to locate ourselves and our own agency within the domain of study, which has clearly undergone change. The American world music ensemble at the beginning of the twenty-first century operates in a different space than it did in the 1960s. We will briefly revisit that earlier space.

SOUNDING THE OTHER: A PARADIGM FOR THE ACADEMY

The world music ensemble, an innovation by Mantle Hood at UCLA in the late 1950s, began as a study group. It originated as a means for understanding the music of another culture, that is, accessing the musical other. Its purpose was explicit in its original designation as study group, which emphasized understanding rather than presentation in intent. The study group is my point of reference for the term *ensemble*.

Charles Seeger, Hood's colleague at UCLA, provides an elegant statement of the original purpose and value of the study group. It became a quasi-credo during the reductionist debates between "Hood-ites" and "Merriam-ites" at the end of the 1960s. In his introduction to Hood's seminal work *The Ethnomusicologist*, Seeger historicizes the study group within the then-current apparatus of ethnomusicological inquiry:

> The distinguishing mark of the second epoch [that of Mantle Hood] is the learning to *make* music, that is, becoming reasonably participatory in, the music one is studying. We have realized that to the speech knowledge of music—that is, the knowledge sought and expressed in terms of a language— there must be added the music knowledge of music. Where speech knowledge fails, music knowledge can be gained only by the making of it. (Hood 1971: vii)

However, Seeger does not stop with the argument that performance can enhance reflexive, word-based scholarly inquiry. He advances a corollary notion: learning (and, by implication, teaching) through performance commands parity with, if not superiority to, the logocentric processes of conceptualization, reflection, and analysis, which he characterizes as "armchair study." The primacy of these processes he assigns to the first epoch of the field. The corollary to the above argument is that "Precept and objectivity have their place in learning, but there is more than one reason to believe that it is *second* to example. And in all example, the subjective element—at least in the humanities—is as important as the objective" (ibid.; emphasis mine).

It could be argued that during the ensuing three decades this corollary has become a second and independent tenet of the "credo," evidenced by the significant number of non–ethnomusicology students who populate study groups and, remarkably, by the presence of world music ensembles in institutions without ethnomusicology programs. A notable model is the World Music Center at West Virginia University (Morgantown), an institution that supports Caribbean, African, and Asian music performance ensembles but has no resident ethnomusicology faculty to provide broader contextualization or scholarly reflexivity about these genres.[1] Neither world music nor ethnomusicology is featured in the university's curriculum. The center's 2001 mission statement claims, "The philosophy behind the World Music Center is to help students gain a better understanding of people and traditions that are different *from our own* Western culture" (www.wvu.edu/~music/special.htm; emphasis mine).

Barbara B. Smith certainly recognized the intrinsic worth of music as performance when she began the University of Hawai'i ethnomusicology program in the 1950s. Equally importantly, she realized music's potential to validate cultural identity. At least a decade before proponents of ethnic studies emerged to press for minority and alternative voices in the academy, she was concerned about relevance for a multicultural Asia-Pacific student population:

> I wondered if the musics being taught in the schools . . . were contributing to conflicts between students' perceptions of their ethnic identity and their cultural identity [operating in an American mainstream] and if, instead, music could help bridge the gap. I concluded that in Hawaii, it was important that the music education program . . . acknowledge value in the students' ancestral heritage. (Smith 1987: 210)

She acted upon that concern. Rather than seeking performance teachers from abroad, she drew them from the multicultural Asia-Pacific communities of Hawai'i, a decision she considered an "important step in integrating the community-at-large into the ethnomusicology program" (ibid.: 211). The study groups not only brought music of the Other to the academy; they also served as a mainstream validation for these musics, an important statement for ethnic minorities in the throes of assimilation to American society. Barbara Smith organized study groups for both musical and social reasons, a pedagogical stance that parallels the major interests of our discipline.

Thus a forty-year trajectory reveals development from a single academic rationale to multiple ones responding to concerns of multiculturalism, alternative modes of knowledge acquisition, cultural and ethnic advocacy, aesthetic and artistic pluralism, and community outreach, to name a few. In my view, the multiplicity constitutes a synchronic continuum between two contrasting polarities concerning the academic value of the study group, 1) as adjunct to scholarly inquiry, and 2) as a self-contained, independent, aesthetic and expressive activity.

THREE SOCIAL ISSUES IN CURRENT ACADEME

The multiplicity of rationales certainly reflects a change in the American social environment since the 1960s, with an expanded civil rights movement, the social issues raised by the Vietnam war, the specter of ethnic cleansing, and global electronic linkages. The present teaching environment itself is informed by at least three major developments. The first is the trope of the pluralistic, multicultural America. The second is the concern for academic relevance, that is, how the study group supports notions of academic goals and priorities. The third is a higher level of public essentialist rhetoric, part of a current mood of political correctness that carries serious implications for our field. All three developments comprise subtexts for this discussion. Therefore, I give each some consideration here.

Pluralism is both a reality and an aspiration. Demographic studies and census data attest to its statistical significance. The vision of the American multicultural heterotopia has been a theme in education since the 1970s, and it is a major part of educational debate today (Nussbaum 1997). Given America's history of racism, the vision has not yet been fully achieved as social reality. To its credit, ethnomusicology as a multicultural enterprise predates this educational vision. When multiculturalism was articulated nationally in the 1970s, ethnomusicology stood ready to provide musical content, to fill in the cultural world map, as it were. Performance of world musics as an experience of the Other validates and empowers, both goals of multicultural education. For some, the ensemble provides an avenue for actualizing a pluralist vision and contributing to the multicultural reality.

Relevance is a central theme for institutional justification and pedagogical rationale. The study group, like every component of a curriculum, is continually challenged to demonstrate long-term relevance and usefulness to the academy. Justification is particularly critical at sites where ensembles are staffed by part-time or non–tenure track faculty or when financial resources are limited. Although Hood's original intent was satisfactory for the 1960s, at the onset of the twenty-first century it may no longer be sufficient. The contemporary rationale needs to reference diverse aspects of the experience. For example, the study group certainly resonates with current music learning theory, including Gardner's multiple intelligences (1999), with general critiques of the academy (Kingsbury 1988), and with national priorities for the arts in education (Down 1993). However, the case for its raison d'être rarely employs an expanded rationale. Granted, the study group is only one of the identities for the world music ensemble at present. As evident by the West Virginia program, it may no longer exist solely as the handmaiden to ethnomusicology and its exercises in reflexivity.

Essentialism presently commands a national foreground beyond academe. The awareness of cultural pluralism and the hope for multiculturalism raise the difficult issues of entitlement and authenticity. The term *authenticity* applied to the object is problematic; I have discussed this issue elsewhere (1995). However, I use the word without qualifiers[2] here to mark the spectator position advanced by Balme (1998), that is, the authoritative or the credible from a consumer viewpoint. For our purposes the student, the personnel committee member, and the concert series director are all part of the academy's consumership.

The appropriateness of any individual speaking for a culture or a people has come under intense scrutiny, bringing greater attention to the identity of the messenger. Widely discussed in academe (see, for example, Brunner 1998; Roof and Wiegman 1995; Spivak 1988), essentialism has been identified as a means for empowerment, often for people of color. Such discussions have been notably absent from ethnomusicological forums. Although essentialism was raised almost four decades ago in reference to African-American music,[3] a serious debate on essentialism in our field has yet to emerge. Any essentialist position has far-reaching implications for the study group, and particularly for its teacher, whose persona comprises a major theme of this chapter.

Consideration of the teacher suggests provocative parallels with the relationship of message and messenger. The teacher is the critical link for the study group, the individual who delivers musical and cultural knowledge of the Other to the American student. As one who has been both part of the study group's historical development and one of its messengers, I consciously conflate subject and object, the "we" and "them," the "ours" and "theirs," in the course of this discussion. Multiple positionalities are unavoidable in the cross-cultural work we do. Invoking them here is an attempt to convey the complexity of this work. I begin with a most essentialist conflation of subject and object, my gaze upon myself as study group teacher. In the first scenario, I analyze my own agency within two variant locales for Philippine music. In the second, I problematize myself, koto musician and teacher, as the object of gaze by various populations in Hawai'i.

THE PHILIPPINE ENSEMBLE:
TEACHING WHICH HERITAGE TO WHOM?

In this first narrative, I contrast teaching the Philippine Ensemble in two different locales during the 1980s: the University of Hawai'i and the University of California, Santa Cruz.[4] The format and content of the ensemble were the same at both campuses. The study group focused upon the Lowland repertory of the *rondalla* string band, which functions de facto as the national folk music.[5] The *rondalla* references the Spanish colonial heritage of the Philippines, both in its material culture and musical styles. Although the ensemble concentrated on instrumental repertory, I also taught songs with texts in Tagalog, the national language. A source for my knowledge of the *rondalla* and its repertory is my personal background, as I come from an emigrant Filipino enclave in the then-agrarian environs of San Jose, California. It was the music I heard and played as part of a Filipino-American family, and the music has personal significance as part of my cultural heritage.

The *kulintang*, a gong-chime ensemble of six to seven players from the Muslim south of the Philippines, served as a Southeast Asian contrast to the Hispanicized *rondalla*. It has stylistic and organological connections to the more elaborate gamelan orchestras of Indonesia. Musical ties of the *kulintang* to insular Southeast Asia include: a tuning system not based upon equal temperament or upon a system of standard pitches, a praxis that requires improvisation, and a repertory unfettered by an indigenous notation system. Other ties are contextual: *kulintang* represents Filipinos who successfully resisted Spanish and American colonization and, like its people, has been subjected to exploitation and misrepresentation by a Lowland Filipino hegemony. My source for this knowledge is my study of Tausug *kulintang* and its repertory as part of graduate field research in the Sulu archipelago of the southern Philippines between 1963 and 1968. The ensemble has personal significance as part of my first fieldwork experience.[6]

In both Santa Cruz and Hawai'i my major goals for the study group were the same: performance competence in Filipino musics, experience with standard repertory, and an entrée for cultural understanding. I found, however, that the two sites required different approaches.

THREE EDUCATIONAL GOALS IN TWO SETTINGS

For this discussion of the three goals, I focus upon the *rondalla*, leaving an extensive consideration of *kulintang* for another opportunity.[7] The learning environments were different in Hawai'i and Santa Cruz, in part because of contrasting social histories. In Hawai'i with its multicultural and plantation history, there was already general recognition of Filipino culture and an aural familiarity with the *rondalla*. Within the racial hierarchy of the Hawaiian Islands, Filipinos have historically ranked below Japanese, Chinese, Koreans, and Caucasians *(haole)*, and, like the Portuguese and Samoans, they have often been subject to negative racial stereotyping. Most Hawai'i-reared students (self-identified as "local") in the ensemble came with this history, although they reflected diverse ethnicities: they were Japanese, Korean, Hawaiian, Vietnamese, Chinese, and *haole* as well as Filipino. Nonlocal students, primarily mainland Americans, foreign students, and military dependents, were generally ignorant of the island racial hierarchy and considered Filipino culture simply another culture with which to become familiar.

In Santa Cruz I found a general ignorance of Filipino culture, in spite of the existence of a significant resident community. None of the study group students came from the Santa Cruz area; they had minimal contact with the region's cultural diversity or its ethnic minorities. Unlike Filipinos in Hawai'i, those in California are subsumed in the general category of Asian American, a construct that arose from the civil rights and related activist movements of the 1960s. The number of students of Filipino heritage on campus was small; I had none in the group. Diversity was represented by one student of Jewish background. Gender diversity was completely lacking; I found it a novel (and singular) experience to teach a music class that was completely male and white.

Among the Hawai'i students, I found uncritical acceptance of the *rondalla* as Filipino and an aural attraction to *kulintang* as a Filipino but exotic Other. Filipino music and dance are regularly part of multicultural public presentations; a number of Filipino performance troupes exist in the community, and the music is frequently presented on radio and television broadcasts. For Hawai'i students, then, the identity of *rondalla* music as Filipino was reinforced in the general community. In Santa Cruz, however, no wider soundscape for *rondalla* existed; the study group constituted the students' principal, if not only, point of contact with the tradition. Its "Mediterranean" quality coupled with the students' unfamiliarity with the genre occasionally led to questions about its authenticity as an Asian music. "It's too Western to be from Asia," one remarked.

Attitudes about *kulintang* were generally reversed. Local students in Hawai'i were less familiar with the gong ensemble as "really Filipino"; it wasn't part of their experience. A student of Filipino heritage expressed a widely held attitude about identity with the observation that *kulintang* "doesn't sound Filipino; it's Moro [a historically derogatory term for Muslim Filipinos]."[8] The Santa Cruz group, in contrast, considered the *kulintang* a more satisfying representation of the Philippines as a musical Other. The Santa Cruz campus already had a well-established West Javanese gamelan, a gong ensemble with which students could make comparisons. Because of its considerable volume, pervasive timbre, and the physical effort required, the *kulintang* came across as a more "muscular" music than the *rondalla*. This appeared to be an additional source of satisfaction for my all-male class.

These contrasts in student background called for different teaching strategies in order to achieve the stated goals. Performance competence, the first goal, was valorized equally by the students and by the teacher. It is the most observable of goals, and the most useful in the academic setting. For the student, it is a gauge of his mastery and, by implication, the effectiveness of the teaching. For the teacher, it provides a means for evaluating student progress and translating it into a grade. Given the broad array of competencies possible, I had to choose which ones were to be concentrated upon. My choices were different in the two settings.

The *rondalla* generally employs staff notation. In some regions of the Philippines a full score with all parts notated is employed. In other locales only the melody is written, and other parts (normally six parts, including guitar and bass) are realized or "improvised" from it.[9] In some rural areas, however, performance is still entirely *oido,* the prescribed melody learned and performed by ear, without notation. Most good *rondallistas* can both read and play by ear.

The Hawai'i group learned how to derive parts from a set melodic line readily, because they were somewhat familiar with the musical style. The Santa Cruz students had no preexistent sound model, although they occasionally referenced Russian balalaika or Puerto Rican *orquesta* genres. To strengthen their aural model, I used a portion of initial sessions to play recordings of *rondalla,* to get its sound "in the ear." I did not anticipate the aural analyses that emerged during these listening sessions. Students articulated a number of features they considered notable or significant, including alternation of the melody between higher range and lower range instruments, the replication of brass band figures such as "French horn off beats," and chromaticisms in the countermelodies. They incorporated melodic figures and harmonic combinations heard in the recordings. When improvising countermelodies or descants, they sometimes resorted to solutions from jazz. I would admonish them that jazz licks were not "in the tradition" and did not "sound Filipino." In actual practice, many *rondallas* in the Philippines and in Hawai'i do use jazz stylings as a novelty. In Santa Cruz, however, I was concerned about presenting the core characteristics of the tradition to students who knew little about Philippine culture. Lacking any other basis for comparison, they accepted my "no jazz" pronouncement as authoritative, at least initially.

The general absence of sound models in Santa Cruz influenced my teaching and the performance competencies achieved. My idiosyncratic style, especially in improvisation, became the primary model, so that the students tended to duplicate the way I played. All were music majors, and their ability to replicate my playing was excellent. I found it novel (and occasionally disconcerting) to hear my improvisations and melodic gestures reproduced literally and without change. The local students in the Hawai'i group, however, tended not to copy. For them my improvisations represented general parameters; for example, the countermelody should proceed in even quarter notes for a specific section, from which they fashioned a melodic line within the style rather than reproducing my version note for note. Although students occasionally strayed from the style, such departures were not frequent, nor did they reference other musical styles, such as jazz. In Hawai'i my teaching was more nonverbal. I found it productive to demonstrate a correct or acceptable version or to work out a musical problem by playing rather than discussing. During rehearsal I often signaled an individual error or acknowledged a well-played phrase by facial expression or glance rather than verbal comment. The Hawai'i students tended to interact with one another visually as they played rather than remaining fixed upon the notation. The group in Santa Cruz, on the other hand, tended to discuss errors or details that didn't quite work. Part of the verbal exchange inevitably included a defense of or rationale for a mistake. Members of ensembles in the Philippines generally do not feel the need to explain themselves, and this behavior occurred only occasionally among the Hawai'i students. In Santa Cruz verbalization occupied a significantly larger part of the teaching and learning process. As the course progressed and the students became more confident, they began to question some of my statements, including my proscription of jazz!

The learning curves of the two groups differed. The Hawai'i students grasped the feeling and the dynamics of ensemble quickly, often before achieving mastery of notes or virtuosic playing techniques. Even when concentrating upon their individual parts, students were aware of the others, using "peripheral hearing." This ensemble awareness allowed me as leader to "edit" during performance, perhaps repeating a section or modulating to another key, without the *rondalla* falling apart. In contrast, the Santa Cruz players learned their individual parts more quickly and, in the case of notated pieces, committed their parts to memory in one or two sessions. Achieving an ensemble sensibility, however, was more of a challenge. When a mistake required stopping and restarting, resumption was inevitably delayed by discussion about who made the mistake. A frequent rejoinder was, "well, I can play *my* part." The level of individual mastery allowed me to introduce more virtuosic pieces earlier in the term at Santa Cruz. The group could perform the challenging "Pandango sa ilaw" (Fandango with Lamps) at a blistering pace after the eighth week; at Hawai'i the same piece required at least two semesters to negotiate at a comfortable tempo. As teacher, I assessed the collective personality and predisposition of each group, adjusting instruction strategies and repertory to optimize the results. This strategy not only built on each group's specific strengths, but it also ensured that the groups would complete sufficient repertory for the end-of-term program, a public "proof" of performance competence.

The second goal, to present significant repertory, was shaped by my personal and family experiences with Filipino music. Although the pieces carried historical and sometimes personal associations for me, the students' attitude toward the music was generally noncommittal and, in some instances, nonchalant.[10] Tunes familiar to most Lowland Filipinos constitute an unofficial but functioning canon for *rondalla*. I felt it was important for students to be familiar and comfortable with this repertory. Some iconic tunes reference Filipino identity, such as the folksong "Leron-leron sinta" (Dear Little Leron), and others refer to national historical events, such as the composition "Bayan ko" (My Country) by Corazon de Guzman, which marks resistance to the American occupation of the Philippines (1898–1946) and to the Marcos dictatorship (1972–86). Performance of repertory from the canon won instant recognition and approval from Filipino and Filipino-American audience members, who often sang or clapped along. The canon encompasses a range of dance rhythms adapted by Filipinos from European forms—the waltz, march, fandango, *paso doble, habañera,* schottische, and polonaise—as well as native innovations such as the *polkabal,* a combination of polka and waltz. The rhythmic variety was an attractive feature and a ready point of entrée to the music for the non-Filipino student and for non-Filipino audiences. Emphasizing the canon was a conscious pedagogical decision on my part, although I did include one or two contemporary pieces.[11]

The third goal, to provide entrée to the culture, readily engaged the students. They found aspects of Filipino culture interesting and were eager to crack the codes of Filipino folkways. For example, in the Philippines, raising the eyebrows as a means of communication involves a complex protocol in which timing, duration, degree, gender, and context are all variables. Both study groups gave this gestural system a great deal of attention, with varying degrees of individual success. As with the previous goals, validation of cultural learning often occurred during performances where Filipinos were present. Filipinos in the audience responded readily to the eyebrow gestures, usually with laughter of recognition.

American education valorizes individual merit and initiative, which challenges a traditional Filipino preference for collective accomplishment. A central Filipino value is *pagkapwa,* the continual awareness of others (Enriquez 1985). As part of a social dynamic, it emphasizes identity of an individual in relation to a group rather than the individual as a social isolate. This value has direct relevance for music making; it governs the ensemble sensibility discussed above. Each musician, through "peripheral hearing," is constantly aware of the totality of the ensemble and able to adjust to any changes or developments, whether caused by design or by chance. In the Philippines, *rondalla* musicians often observe that a mistake only occurs when the performance comes to halt, when it cannot be "saved" through the ability of the group's members to adjust to one another. Those who ascribed to the *pagkapwa* mindset would not respond, "well, I can play *my* part."

I felt that experiencing collective identity as a manifestation of *pagkapwa* was important for American students and an appropriate goal of the study group. I devised various activities, mostly extramusical, that required cooperative effort. For instance, the class had to prepare Filipino food for the informal performance at the close of the term. Cooking constituted such a cross-cultural extramusical element. Each class learned to make *adobo,* a popular marinated meat dish. The fact that all members could prepare the same dish contributed to a sense of *communitas*. Even in this mundane exercise, *pagkapwa* came into play. Although *adobo* can be made with either chicken or pork or a combination of the two, the classes used chicken only in deference to two members, the Jewish student in Santa Cruz already mentioned and a Muslim in Hawai'i. Did this culinary selectivity represent a distortion of tradition? Quite the opposite: it reinforced the principle of *pagkapwa*, here an awareness of dietary restrictions within the group.

Group identity was reinforced by close social interaction. Both groups toured to surrounding communities. The Santa Cruz group, numbering six, played for Filipino communities in the Central Valley and the Bay Area, and the Hawai'i group, usually ten, performed on the neighbor islands. I was able to arrange home hospitality, usually in sleeping bags on the living room floor of one host family. The tour experience, including sleeping, eating, and grooming in close quarters, reinforced *communitas*. In this intense collectivity, *pagkapwa* was frequently invoked, such as by looking after the habitually late member, pitching in to replace a string broken at the last minute, or adjusting quickly to a cramped or ill-equipped performance space. On both campuses, the opportunity to tour set the Philippine Ensemble apart from other ensembles, further solidifying ensemble identity and collectivity. The internal dynamics of identity in the Hawai'i group approximated the traditional Filipino *barkada*, a close-knit association of primary social interaction (Dumont 1993; Lapuz 1981: 28–30). The quasi-*barkada* nature of the ensemble was manifested at the wedding of two Hawai'i members of the group, where the entire ensemble showed up to perform during the reception.

In the foregoing narrative I have indicated the importance of place. I have suggested that teaching a study group is site-specific, especially vis-à-vis a universal set of educational goals. Variables of demography, local soundscape, cultural perspective, and musical background determine how, and sometimes what, the teacher presents. For this narrative I positioned myself as culture carrier and examined my own agency.

THE KOTO ENSEMBLE: CONSTRUCTING CREDIBILITY

In the second narrative I consider the persona of the teacher. I examine my role as teacher of the koto study group at the University of Hawai'i.[12] My qualifications and therefore my credibility derived from a completely different set of criteria than those for the Philippine Ensemble. I had no claim on koto through cultural heritage, and I had carried out no fieldwork in Japan. My personal sources for koto knowledge represented at least three degrees of separation from a Japanese original. My teacher was Kay Mikami, a *kibei*[13] who studied in Japan with the Ikuta School master Miyagi Michio.

She returned to Honolulu and established a private teaching practice within the local Japanese community. I studied with her only at the university, and not in the traditional diasporic setting, during lessons on weekends at her house. I have taught koto at the University of Hawai'i only, and always as an ensemble class. I established no private studio in the Honolulu community. Thus I did not learn the instrument in a traditional Japanese or diasporic setting, nor have I taught in such a setting. Upon her retirement from the university, Mikami-*sensei* recommended that I assume responsibility for koto instruction. Although my qualifications for teaching koto might represent an idiosyncratic construction of credibility, they are somewhat similar to those of other ethnomusicologist colleagues with study groups.

Koto ensemble students, unlike those in Western ensembles, often entered without prior training in the instrument. The beginning class, consisting of rank novices, presented the greatest contrast to the indigenous teaching setting. Advanced ensemble classes, on the other hand, consisted of students who had a level of musical competence comparable to that in the university orchestra or band.

Although I am a koto performer, I didn't feel comfortable representing Japanese culture writ large, or providing entrée to the culture, the third goal described above in the *rondalla* discussion. I felt most secure teaching about the world of koto and traditional music, and I used these as major themes for cultural insight. In retrospect I realize that my construction of Japanese traditionalism was selective and biased toward Otherness, that is, that which was different from the students' normal experience. For example, the class was conducted in *seiza,* with the students kneeling on the floor, even though in Japan today koto lessons frequently occur with the students seated in chairs and the instruments raised on stands. At the University of Hawai'i music department we are fortunate to have a *zashiki,* a Japanese room with tatami mats. Playing in *seiza,* that is, kneeling, establishes a specific physical relationship between koto and player. For certain physical movements, such as pressing a string to raise the pitch, the locus of physical energy is different when sitting on the floor (the shoulder and torso) as opposed to sitting in a chair (principally the upper arm). Sitting in chairs is a recent development; therefore, less traditional Japanese nationals pointed out the present use of chairs in Japan and commented on the difficulty of learning while sitting in *seiza.* At formal and public concerts in Japan, however, musicians perform in *seiza.* Thus it is still part of current practice, although it is no longer the only mode of sitting. *Seiza* for the Hawai'i study group was an opportunity to experience another aspect of culture in addition to its sound organization. Another feature outside the normal American experience involved a peripheral, nonmusical practice, the application of egg white to the interior of the plectra rings *(tsume no wa)* to prevent slippage. When this practice was presented during the second lesson, it seldom failed to evoke a reaction from the students.

I felt that there should also be some experience in rote learning, even though it reflected historical rather than present practice. The first few lessons, which included orientation to the instrument and playing techniques, were conducted without notation, as was the introduction of the first piece, "Kurokami" (Black Hair). The balance of repertory and koto exercises came from the Miyagi lineage, using its published method books. A goal for the fifteen-week session was to learn part of "Rokudan No Shirabe" (Six Variations), one of the best-known pieces of the canon. I discovered that expecting beginning students to sing while playing was unrealistic, although through commentary and demonstration I reinforced that this ability was required of the "complete" koto musician.

The reperformance of tradition, selective as it was, had to be adapted to limitations of the American academy. Unlike the *sensei* in Japan, I had no *deshi,* or assistant. Normally the *deshi* prepares the instruments and tunes them before the teacher arrives. The teacher is not ordinarily involved in such mundane preparations, and students are certainly not entrusted with them. However, in the study group the students were responsible for unpacking the instruments, putting in the bridges, and setting the general tuning *(choshi).* I adjusted and corrected the tuning for the eight to ten instruments before instruction could begin. The Hawai'i ensemble evolved its own distinctive protocols: half the group was responsible for preparing the instruments before class, and the other half for putting everything away at the close of each session. In traditional learning a group of students is present at each lesson, although the group does not constitute an ensemble as described here. Each student works with the teacher individually for a short but intensive period of time, while other students in the group watch and listen. This mode of learning entails both observation and active playing. In the Hawai'i koto study group all the students played together while I scurried from one student to the next, correcting, explaining, and encouraging.

In each class my students formed four different groups according to their background and reasons for studying koto music. Some were of Japanese ancestry but had minimal knowledge of the culture. Others were non-Japanese, often Caucasian, who had an academic interest in Japan and were studying or were already competent in the language. Still others were Western music majors exploring an alternative music. Those of the fourth type, the ethnomusicology majors, were familiar with the broader musical and cultural settings of koto music. This diversity of student types was a challenge for me; each had different problems and perceptions in approaching this musical Other. The issue of intonation illustrated the differences. In traditional *choshi* (tunings) the interval of the semitone is slightly smaller than the tempered semitone.[14] For those who weren't music majors, achieving the correct intonation meant replicating or matching the intervallic relationships of *choshi* as presented by the teacher. For music majors, however, achieving the correct intonation meant adjusting to pitches that did not match previously learned notions of absolute pitch and interval size. The ethnomusicologists tended to overcompensate: they often tuned the semitone intervals smaller than the Japanese norm. For the *sensei* in Japan neither tuning nor intonation would be an issue, since the instruments are tuned by the assistant, not by each individual student. Similarly, tuning accuracy would not be contested by a neophyte invoking the authority of concert pitch and equal temperament.

As the ethnomusicologist, I felt that these differences and adjustments presented opportunities for making theoretical points and analytical observations germane to social context or to music as sound. However, as the teacher, I felt that reflexivity was not the pedagogical thrust of the study group, and it was rarely the interest of the students. I tried to keep explanations to a minimum in an attempt to provide a "more traditional" learning experience for the beginning class. I emphasized demonstration and repetition, which sometimes meant discouraging student questions during the session. So much for the teacher's gaze upon the ensemble and the student.

What were the gazes upon me as the teacher? What kinds of credibility and entitlement to teach koto did I bring to the study group? In this regard the perceptions of students (which I usually received as feedback well after the semester was over) and the local Japanese community are informative. The criteria for credibility were mixed, drawing in an ad hoc manner upon qualifications within the koto tradition itself, from the academy, and from what might be best described (with a nod to Ben Anderson) as an imagined universe. My principal qualification related to tradition was the recommendation of my teacher, Kay Mikami. With reservations, I agreed to teach until another teacher could be found, some two years later. In effect I inherited the position from my *sensei*, a process familiar to and normative within the Japanese community. Another factor grounded in tradition that contributed to my credibility was my reputation as a koto performer. I initially performed with my teacher, then with visiting artists from Japan, and finally with other musicians from the Honolulu community (not all of whom were Japanese). So for both students and community, I possessed credentials as a performer.

Although armed with the imprimatur of my teacher, I still had some reservations about my own entitlement regarding the project. Unlike in the Philippine study group, in the world of koto I embodied an Other. I am not of Japanese ancestry, nor am I fluent or literate in the language. These shortcomings could be (and often generously have been) overlooked because I possess another set of credentials, those of the academic. In the

Japanese community I was always referred to as *hakase* (professor) from my first year of appointment as assistant professor. At the university I taught classes about Japanese music and often lectured on Japanese performance for the general public. Members of the Japanese community observed that as a native speaker of American English I made Japanese culture more easily understood to non-Japanese as well as to their own third- and fourth-generation offspring. In Hawai'i, a society in which many communicate using a number of Asian and Pacific languages as well as its own indigenous creole, fluency in "standard English" conveys cultural, political, and economic status. Such criteria for credibility were external to the domain of Japanese music and represented incursions from a Western hegemon. They nevertheless informed my reception in the academy, in the Japanese community, and in the larger cultural community.

The third factor that influenced my credibility had little to do with competence in music or status as an academic. It concerned my Asian physical appearance, part of an imagined universe of ethnic and racial typology. As phenotype I am Filipino with a prominent admixture of Chinese; however, dressed in a kimono and kneeling before a koto, I might easily be interpreted as Japanese, or occasionally Okinawan. When asked, I point out that I am not Japanese. Rather than foreground my non-Japanese heritage, however, I prefer to emphasize performance values. To my surprise and continued amusement, people often ascribe a Japanese heritage to me. For the audience member my perceived ethnicity increases the "authenticity" of my performance, which makes the individual's concert experience more "authentic" and in turn makes me more credible as practitioner and authority for koto. A performer with such authority would certainly be qualified to teach at the university!

This focus upon the teacher serves as pivot to move from the subjective-personal to an objective-general discussion, although I acknowledge the permeability of the two categories. The foregoing personal narratives, I feel, are relevant to larger concerns for the world music ensemble in the American university. I suggest that these narratives provide illustrative material for a general consideration of the study group and its teacher, which follows.

THREE ARCHETYPES OF ENSEMBLE TEACHER

I posit that there are three major categories of instructor at the American university: the culture bearer (indigenous artist), the ethnomusicologist, and the foreign practitioner.[15] Each of these personae "fits" the academic environment differently. In the academy, the category sometimes carries implications for the type or duration of employment; for example a culture bearer will often be employed for the short term and an ethnomusicologist for the long term, while a foreign practitioner is likely to work for the university part

time. I suggest that the first two archetypes, the culture bearer and the ethnomusicologist, are the most highly contrastive in terms of cultural background, identity politics, and teaching strategies. The foreign practitioner
occupies a medial position. The type is exemplified by the American who
goes to India to study tabla with a master for ten years, tours with his teacher
for two years, and returns to the United States to teach and perform.[16] The
foreign practitioner shares some of the characteristics identified for the previous two. We shall consider the teacher in terms of five themes: kinds of
authenticities, delivery of musical and cultural knowledges, personal relationship to the tradition, styles of teaching, and institutional imperatives.

The Culture Bearer and Staged Authenticity

Staged authenticity is a term borrowed from the literature on cultural tourism
(MacCannell 1992). It denotes a conscious, often idealized re-presentation
of a cultural setting, in this case music learning. Its notions of credibility and
ethnographic purity outside the native setting are relevant to the project of
the music ensemble and the Other. It provides a dialogic relationship between musics of the Other and musics of the Self, for example, the greater
efforts expended to bring a Thai master teacher from Bangkok for *piphat*
than a vocal coach from Oslo for the art songs of Grieg. From the point of
view of the institution, one of the consumers identified earlier, the culture
bearer as study group teacher embodies immediate authenticity, an insider
who "culturally knows." However, as has been argued elsewhere,[17] culture
carriers have different degrees and areas of expertise concerning tradition.
In some cases, the native musician is known for playing a particular instrument or perhaps even knowing a specific genre. When he comes to the
American university to teach, however, he becomes a resource for an entire
tradition—all instrumental and vocal parts; any associated dance, costuming, and decorations; and architectural requirements of the performance
space—and it is presumed that he possesses both the knowledge and
authority to carry out relevant ceremonies.

A second aspect of authenticity concerns the phenotypic; the culture
bearer looks the native.[18] Visual credibility figuratively colors the reception
of the knowledge delivered and performances mounted. There is an often
unarticulated assumption that performance supervised by a culture bearer
will be closer to the original, more authentic. Conversely, performances
supervised by the foreign ethnomusicologist or practitioner may be slightly
suspect, subjected to more questioning and closer scrutiny. The experienced observer searches for additional markers of authenticity, such as types
of repertory, specific stylistic characteristics, or subtle details of protocol.

The relationship of the native teacher to his tradition inevitably changes
in a foreign context. One change relates to what he may be allowed to

teach. Is a Japanese *gagaku* musician who specializes in playing *sho* qualified to teach the other two melodic instruments *(ryuteki, hichiriki)*, the stringed instruments *(gakubiwa, gakuso)*, the percussion instruments *(kakko/san-no-tsuzumi, odaiko, shoko)*, and *gagaku*-related dance? In the homeland the question would probably never arise; no individual is responsible for teaching the entire ensemble. In a foreign setting, however, the culture bearer is frequently expected to teach all aspects of the tradition, as well as serve as an icon for the totalized culture.

What are the elements of tradition that the native teacher brings to the study group? Primarily these center upon the potential interaction for the American (Western) student with an Other. The native teacher occupies a position of leadership and relative authority. Not only may the musical material be unfamiliar to the student, but strategies of teaching can embody Otherness. The teacher may use elements of traditional instruction that are different from but that nevertheless do not challenge basic American notions of teaching and learning. For example, the kabuki drumming teacher uses a fan and a wooden block to visually indicate the strokes and rhythms for the two drums, *otsuzumi* and *kotsuzumi*. These are simultaneously reinforced by mnemonics recited by the teacher. The learning is principally kinetic and aurally selective; the student plays a single part, although the teacher presents the two drum parts as a gestalt. The student learns to distinguish the mnemonic and visual prompts for his individual part. However, not all traditional teaching practices are acceptable in a university setting; some run counter to American practice. In Japan the teacher of kabuki drumming might strike a student who is inattentive or does not maintain focus during the lesson. In America striking a student, whether to reinforce a musical point or to express displeasure, is not countenanced. Nor is it deemed appropriate for the teacher to give advice concerning personal relationships, finances, or leisure time. Indigenous teaching practices are necessarily reframed within and subjected to established Western norms of teaching, learning, and teacher-student relationships. They contribute toward the construction of a staged, if not managed, authenticity.[19] It is assumed that the native teacher is better qualified to provide cultural knowledge than a foreigner. To teach gamelan it is necessary to know more than just the various pieces of repertory, how to "fit" rehearsed improvisations, and how to effect transitions from one section to another with a minimal understanding of drum signals and their meanings. The culture bearer also knows the array of pieces appropriate for specific occasions and the satisfactory sequence of pieces that can constitute a presentation.[20] In addition he provides authority for such extramusical concerns as the *selamatan* (ceremonial meal), protocol for the *kris* (dagger) worn by male performers, and appropriate kinds of decoration for the gamelan and stage.

Although valorized as the "real thing" by his students, the native teacher is nevertheless expected to accommodate institutional structures of the university, including finite and short periods for instruction and the necessity of providing individual evaluations—the letter grade—for each student, even though the music may traditionally valorize collectivity and coordinated effort. The native teacher as embodiment of the authentic negotiates at least four perceptions of authenticity: his authenticity as a purveyor of the Other; the students' authenticity as clients within the American university; the teacher's perception of his students' authenticity; and the students' construction of the authenticity of their teacher.[21]

As an example of the latter perception, the beginner student may be surprised to find that his master Burmese *saingwaing* drum circle teacher is equally "hot" on an electronic keyboard and records pop-based fusion CDs at home. Can a traditional musician from Burma also be competent in international pop styles? He can. Such a revelation can unsettle reductionist assumptions of authenticity, purity, and traditionalism that often shape an external gaze upon the native teacher. In the future a detailed examination of these four relationships should provide insight into the internal dynamic of the study group as a microsociety and its nature as a medium for the cross-cultural transfer of skills and knowledge.

I have described some of the features of the culture carrier as native teacher for the study group. Although the descriptive strokes have been deliberately broad, these features provide a matrix against which the two remaining, "outsider" archetypes can be considered. The first is the ethnomusicologist as ensemble teacher.

The Ethnomusicologist Mediating Tradition

The ethnomusicologist who is an established performer and the ethnomusicologist who is only knowledgeable about performance may be viewed as belonging to two different categories. For both, performance training may come from various sources or experiences. The ethnomusicologist may have developed performance ability as part of field research, learning within an indigenous context.[22] Alternatively, he could have learned from a native teacher within an American university context, such as described in my personal narrative. A third possibility is that the teacher has been taught by another outsider, perhaps another ethnomusicologist or a foreign practitioner. What are the kinds of knowledge an individual ethnomusicologist can transmit to his study group? How can he best deliver these knowledges? We focus initially upon the first category, the ethnomusicologist who is an established performer.[23]

The ethnomusicologist brings to the study group a constructed form of credibility different from that of the native teacher. Field research carries credibility; the ethnomusicologist can relay personal experiences and insights about general culture and the specifics of the tradition. Authority for the music devolves less from the lineage of the teacher and student and more from the academic degree and its research exercise, the dissertation, supplemented by performance competence. For the ethnomusicologist, credibility as a teacher derives largely from Western criteria and structures that are brought to bear upon a native Other.

The ethnomusicologist teacher tends to use verbal explanation and conceptualization to communicate both musical and cultural knowledge. Although his knowledge derives from sources generally considered to be "authentic," that is, research in the field, the medium of delivery is biased toward Western strategies of teaching. For example, it seems less "natural" in Japanese music lessons to bow and intone "onegaishimasu" ("please do me the favor [of teaching me]") to an American ethnomusicologist than to a visiting Japanese *sensei.*

The ethnomusicologist brings several pedagogical strengths to a study group. His learning experience, as cultural outsider, more closely approximates that of the student. Although the cultural baggage of the ethnomusicologist and the student are not identical, they are frequently similar. In addition, each is familiar with the folkways of academe. For example, the ethnomusicologist knows how to accommodate musical content to fit a fifty- or ninety-minute instructional period and can assess implications of a twelve- or fifteen-week term for the learning curve. In terms of music skills, both student and teacher are grounded in a Western (but not always classical) musical sensibility. The ethnomusicologist teacher can anticipate which aspects might confuse or confound students steeped in a homophonic and heptatonic heritage. The reflexive predispositions of academe can make learning performance more efficient. A theoretical explanation can serve as a shortcut to traditional rote repetition. Prompted by the nontraditional reflexive explanation, which is conceptual rather than experiential, the student may successfully master the gestalt of a musical style in a shorter period of time, albeit at the expense of the loss of other details of the tradition. For example, improvisation in Javanese gamelan can be explained as meeting the basic melody *(balungan)* at intervals of fourths, fifths and unisons. Such a principle gives the student a conceptual guide for creating a workable improvisation without halting performance flow. However, the subtlety of alternative solutions or the limits of musical risk taking, which develop through multiple repetition and rote experience, are not always communicated in such a linear, stripped-down transmission process.

How does the ethnomusicologist as performance teacher communicate broader aspects of the culture? Although the native teacher can "perform" his own culture in the study group, the outsider ethnomusicologist has no recourse but to present it. The non-native who attempts to perform another's culture immediately confronts issues of entitlement and reception, as well as suspicions of "going native" or "playing ethnic." For the out-sider, performing another culture is almost always the result of conscious code switching. If one decides to do this, the challenge is to switch without appearing exploitative, condescending, or colonial. For example, when a South Indian touches his fingertips to his eyes as a kinetic, nonverbal apol-ogy for inadvertently touching another's foot, the observer recognizes it as a traditional gesture and a cultural reaction. However, when a Westerner performs that same gesture, it may be interpreted as "playing Indian" or making claims to a more complete understanding of Indian culture. Is the Westerner entitled to engage in this gestural system, especially if he does not subscribe to the deeper belief system that considers the touch as more than a temporary invasion of personal space? Without hoping to be prescriptive, I suggest the most effective means for the outsider to bring understanding of these broader cultural aspects to the student is through discussion, taking advantage of the reflexivity of the academy.

For the ethnomusicologist teacher, authority is not a matter of cultural entitlement. It devolves from a current Western construction of status based upon work rather than ethnicity, although the heritage of one's teacher can be a factor, as discussed below. The paradigm of work assumes field re-search, presumably relevant to the study group. Status ascription assumes authentication through a system of peer review that valorizes specific knowl-edge bases and musical skills, that is, hiring and promotion and tenure processes. The scholar-teacher seldom embodies the Other; rather, he more frequently serves as mediator for the Other (or at least the Other's music). His authority devolves from a process of acquiring it, which contrasts with the authority of the native teacher as one who "culturally knows." The eth-nomusicologist's authority is earned rather than inherited.

Like the native teacher, the non-native teacher (here the ethnomusicol-ogist) also carries visual baggage both when teaching and performing pub-licly. As I have suggested earlier, the native teacher (or ethnomusicologist) with appropriate (or near-appropriate) indigenous phenotype assures the learner and the observer that the material delivered is authentic and credi-ble, even though that may, in fact, not always be the case. The physical char-acteristics of the non-native teacher can engender a variety of meanings. At present the majority of ethnomusicologists are white, reflecting the domi-nant culture of the academy in the United States.[24] As a non-native, the teacher can convey a positive message to the American student: it is possible for an outsider to become competent in a music tradition. Although the beginning student may initially find this musical Other baffling or incom-prehensible, the non-native specialist stands as physical testimony to its learnability; the ethnomusicologist's skill suggests that through commit-ment, diligence, and hard work mastery of another music is possible.

As an outsider, the non-native teacher has to address issues of credibility, authenticity, and integrity. Because he cannot embody the cultural credibility of the native teacher, he must establish his credibility in other ways. One strategy is to emphasize older repertory and recognized aspects of "tradition," a problematic notion. Innovation and the performance of newer compositions tend to be secondary.[25] In this strategy, the teacher presents what he has learned rather than extends the repertory through composing or expanding the musical style through innovation, both of which are options for the native teacher. By doing so, the ethnomusicologist teacher reinforces a standard repertory or canon for the study group and valorizes a specific musical style. In koto instruction, a canon may include the instrumental pieces "Rokudan No Shirabe" (Six Variations), an arrangement of the *shoga* "Sakura" (Cherry Blossoms), Miyagi Michio's twentieth-century duet with *shakuhachi* "Haru No Umi" (Spring Sea), and, if singing is taught, the *tegotomono* "Chidori No Kyoku" (Sand Plover).

This preoccupation with tradition colors attitudes toward an Other, a value that may be promulgated through the study group. Brian Singleton critiques this predisposition, claiming that "tradition . . . is a powerful ruling weapon on which colonialism depends, on which the post-colonial world feeds, but which is ultimately a fabrication, and which blocks the formation and emergence of new narratives" (1997: 95). His pronouncement certainly challenges study group practice and a dominant ideology. Although not as overtly critical, Judith Becker similarly problematizes the role of the study group, indirectly critiquing the academy as well. She writes, "Those ensembles which remain dedicated to imitation and repetition of this past rather than innovation and adjustment to the 20th Century context have their own importance, as do innumerable other instances of preservation in American universities" (Becker 1983: 88). The shift from a traditional learning setting to an overseas, academic one is fraught with challenges and adjustments that should be a part of planning or assessing a study group.

Does the relationship of the researcher to the culture studied change when he begins to teach performance? I suggest that it does. When the ethnomusicologist's performance skills are limited or below the standards for public performance in the home culture setting, should he be expected to teach the tradition? For example, the ability to document and analyze drumming signals for Thai *piphat* does not necessarily transfer to competence in deploying those drum signals during real-time performance. Thus an ethnomusicologist teaching a study group may find himself in a curious position, in which his competence in the tradition is not comparable to that of colleagues supervising Western ensembles. In some cases the ethnomusicologist may be uncomfortable leading a study group, and even more so presenting its performance in a public setting. Nevertheless, both have become institutional expectations for the ethnomusicologist–*cum*–study group teacher.

Why should an ethnomusicologist with limited performance skills lead a study group? Frequently encountered is the "only resource" argument: "there is no one else to lead the group, and at least I know something about it." Such a rationale would not be acceptable for choosing the leader of a jazz ensemble or a collegium musicum. Why would it be it acceptable for a non-Western musical tradition? Would a faculty member whose entire orchestral background consisted of playing four semesters in the second violin section and two courses in string technique be entrusted with a university symphony orchestra? The qualifications for the ethnomusicologist as performance teacher should be subject to the same queries. These queries are not intended as a criticism of the admirable intent to provide a broader musical experience for the student, but are rather meant to raise issues of pedagogical intent and ideology that should not go unexamined by ethnomusicologists leading study groups.

Yet another set of queries shifts the focus away from the music tradition and toward the ethnomusicologist and his perception of the music in question. There exists an apparent tension between two conflicting perceptions of the musical tradition of the Other: 1) its complexity requires a lifetime of research, but, at the same time, 2) it can be taught well enough in sixteen to thirty weeks to be presented in public performance. The beginner's concert, widespread among study groups in the United States, generates mixed signals for the student and for the general public. On the one hand it suggests that the Other is simple. On the other it suggests that the nature of the American student or the Western academy enables a faster learning curve. Both raise uncomfortable images of musical ethnocentrism: notions of superiority, domestication of a foreign Other, or both. A third implication of instruction by the non-native teacher is that a cultural experience through music need not involve individuals native to that culture, in effect a counterstatement to essentialist claims. In a society where racial tension and inequality are still public issues, this implication is problematic. The question, of course, is less troublesome if the study group remains just that, a group that studies music as performance. However, when the study group takes on the identity or the behavior of a performance group, the stakes are raised. The gamelan as study group does not necessarily engender musical expectations on a par with the university orchestra mentioned earlier, for example. The gamelan as performance group, however, does carry such expectations. The reality is that in most American universities the gamelan is considered a performance group; it has become a major showpiece for ethnomusicology and world music programs.[26] Undeniably, the gamelan has great lay appeal, given its size, appearance, and compelling sound.

In the consideration of the ethnomusicologist I have deliberately raised the intensity of the critique. As the subject "we," we need to address our complicity in the maintenance and proliferation of the study group, as well as in the formation of its pedagogical and institutional intent. Aspects of pedagogy and institution often represent challenges for the third type, the non-native practitioner.

The Foreign Practitioner and Cultural Entitlement

The third and final type of teacher is the foreign musician, whose primary experience with the host culture has been training and living as a performer. His background is similar to that of the ethnomusicologist teacher. The modus vivendi of the foreign performer, however, is more completely subject to indigenous ways of learning, evaluation, and integration in contrast to the external construct of ethnomusicological fieldwork, especially in that the decision to end the interaction more often lies with the foreigner rather than with members of the host culture. It is the rare non-ethnomusicologist, foreign neophyte who can dictate the way in which he learns and for how long, especially where there are formal means of transmission, such as the *iemoto* system of Japan or the *halau* system of Hawai'i. At the same time, the foreigner is recognized as coming from outside the culture, and adjustments to his normal routine are inevitable. Adjustment can affect learning expectations. The novelty of a foreigner performing can sometimes lead the audience to forgive shortcomings in musicality or performance technique. To compensate for this effect, foreigners are sometimes intentionally separated from indigenous students. For example, there are annual national competitions exclusively for foreign students of Korean music in Seoul and Japanese music in Tokyo. With or without such compensation, the performer subjects himself to indigenous systems of training and evaluation in ways that the field researcher does not. The latter uses music learning as one means toward a research end. The performer, in contrast, has entered more completely into the host community, learning and, in some cases, establishing a career within it.[27]

Recently "authentic" learning need not be acquired abroad, that is, outside the United States. For example, it is possible to study classical Indian music for an extended period in a traditional manner with Indian masters in California. A network of diasporic Indian communities in the United States and Canada enables occasional bookings for the foreign performer, who may be engaged to perform with a native artist, usually his teacher or native artists from the same school of performance *(gharana)*.

Cultural credibility for the foreign performer can be achieved in different ways, singly or in combination. The most credibility can be achieved by studying and establishing a performance career within the host society. Some musics have an indigenous means of accreditation, such as the *iemoto* and *halau* systems previously mentioned. In the U.S. setting, appearing as a co-performer with recognized native artists strengthens the foreigner's reputation. The status of the performer's teacher is another factor influencing credibility. The individual who has studied with a native teacher rather than a foreign one certainly has more cachet as performer. Although status among native teachers may be hierarchical and often factionalized, the foreign performer trained by a renowned native teacher nevertheless enjoys greater credibility then one who was not. Increasingly, a reputation can also be built through sound recordings. The CD can represent material validation for the foreign artist. The nature of artistic credibility is presently in a state of change. The fields of Japanese and Indian music, for example, are becoming globalized. The 1998 World Shakuhachi Festival in Boulder, Colorado, included many prominent non-Japanese artists; the Ali Akbar College of Music, located in San Rafael, California, includes non-Indian instructional staff.

The foreign practitioner category includes the heritage performer, someone from the relevant ethnic group born or socialized in the diaspora. For example, Japanese Americans performing Japanese music are not considered native performers by the arts community in Japan. Within the academy, however, the heritage performer may become part of the native teacher archetype. Visual authenticity—appropriate phenotype—adds to his credibility. The current essentialist climate may be a factor in reinscribing the identity of this subgroup of foreign practitioners as native in the university setting. This is a notable instance in which heritage might advantage rather than disadvantage a minority in America.

The foreign practitioner is subject to a third type of relationship to the academy and institutional practices. I suggest that this relationship entails the greatest personal challenges. In cases where this tradition is the foreigner's only or first performing medium—this is, he had no previous music training, Western or otherwise—accommodation to the university can be problematic. The university assumes familiarity and agreement with institutional practices, especially if the practitioner is American. This may not, in fact, be the case. Like the visiting native teacher, the foreign practitioner may encounter difficulties in pacing, accommodating the learning curve, and accessing the musical background of his students.

The ability of the foreign performer to communicate cultural context is another area of concern. Somewhat disadvantaged in this regard, he does not possess the "cultural knowing" or the entitlement of the native teacher, nor is he as well equipped as the ethnomusicologist to mobilize theory and analysis. However, his position does entail advantages. His bicultural (but not necessarily bimusical)[28] background can contribute to an efficient and student-appropriate delivery of instruction. Further, he has been exposed to a culture's traditional ways of learning in more depth than is usual for the ethnomusicologist. It is my experience that the foreign teacher concentrates more upon knowledge and mastery of a specific genre than upon general cultural understanding. His expectations for the level of student performance may be different. While the indigenous teacher may be more forgiving concerning musical conceptualization or attention to detail, the foreign practitioner may be more critical, expecting a higher level of mastery commensurate with his own experience in the home culture. One American teacher of the drumming of Ghana observed, "We have to be careful about how we present this music to the outside, especially because we aren't natives. . . . We have to be better [than a Ghanaian group] because it isn't ours."

The concerns encompass representation as well as presentation. Currently representation—especially representation of minority groups—is a contested issue. An essentialist view posits limitations to cultural representation by the non-native. Is it sufficient for the non-native instructor to handle performance as a self-contained domain with techniques, repertory, and ensemble protocols to be mastered rather than as a vehicle for insight and broader understanding of a host culture? Is a bicultural or bimusical state actually approachable within the classroom setting? For the foreign practitioner this balance—and how it is tipped—has implications for his artistic reputation, as well as for his livelihood.

This chapter has been an opportunity to examine the study group, a high-profile component of our field. In conclusion, I present questions intended both to challenge our present perception of the study group and to advance arguments for its value within the academy. These questions also shift my discussion into the realm of advocacy.

The question "is the ensemble a good thing?" has been asked and answered in the affirmative. In my opinion, this question needs be replaced by a more pressing query for the twenty-first century: what is the ensemble good *for?* This question has implications not only for American ethnomusicology, but also for such emergent subject categories as World Music and the internationalized fusion music industry,[29] as well as for broader humanistic concerns about multiculturalism, processes of identity, and the consequences of globalization. It also suggests that in a future that includes the West Virginia model, the study group may no longer be the purview of ethnomusicology alone. The gestalt of our field, as well as the nature of its messengers, may undergo major changes.

What is the study group good for? I feel that a principal pedagogical value is the presentation and valorization of alternative systems and approaches to creativity. As alternative, a musical system from another culture is more compelling than one developed by an individual: for example, the systemization of *gagaku* reflects an established and ongoing consensus developed over time, while the Western avant-garde more frequently represents reaction, resistance, or challenge by an individual to his own musical heritage. Viewed in the broadest terms, the availability of culturally identified alternatives in the institution gives students choice and agency, humanistic themes that transcend the inevitability of the plagal cadence, the fixity of *tihai,* or the consensus of *jo ha kyu.* How do we reinforce this argument to an academy that continues to foreground the hegemonic, providing only limited space for alternatives?

Certainly a principal argument we must make addresses the aesthetic. American ethnomusicology and its study groups are located primarily in music departments, which themselves steward the arts (that is, aesthetic) domain.[30] Should the affective nature of a genre be a primary criterion for study group status? We may be subjecting ourselves to (or perhaps be guilty of) an institutional "descriptive chauvinism" (Nussbaum 1997: 118), in which we read another culture's music using the paradigm of our own culture, that is, the primary raison d'être of music in the Western academy is aesthetic rather than religious, political, or economic. Do we select genres for study groups that fit more easily into a mainstream paradigm? To argue the reverse, shouldn't the aesthetic experience, whether indigenous or "chauvinistic," be part of an educational encounter? For students a music they find "arresting" or "beautiful" is certainly more memorable.[31] It may initially evoke a personal aesthetic experience or process. Must the student be delivered to a culturally authentic aesthetic experience, or is a spontaneous, unmonitored affective experience equally valid? For the academy, an affective reaction to music is a reasonable expectation. For the study group leader, a concern for the nature and quality of that aesthetic experience should also be a reasonable expectation. Is there a risk in privileging the aesthetic?

A second argument is the cultural one, that we gain understanding of an Other through its cultural expressions. Ethnomusicology is not the only field to advocate this position. Using cultural studies as a frame, Brunner, citing bell hooks, suggests that the arts can enable such cultural understanding (Brunner 1998: 76). In my reformulation specific to the study group:

1. The study group distills a culture's notion of how to be in the world, through defining representations within a particular "order of things."

2. It represents a place in a society where assumptions are questioned and critiqued.

The first point resonates with my decision to teach koto in *seiza* (kneeling position), and the second, with the importance for *rondalla* students to know the song "Bayan ko" and its historical significance. Do our study groups accomplish these cultural understandings? Do we regard them as part of our pedagogical mission?

As part of a philological reflection on teaching about other cultures in general, Nussbaum presents five points that she feels characterize "good teaching of non-Western cultures":

1. Real cultures are plural, not single.
2. Real cultures contain argument, resistance, and contestation of norms.
3. In real cultures, what most people think is likely to be different from what the most famous artists . . . think.
4. Real cultures have varied domains of thought and activity.
5. Real cultures have a present as well as a past. (Nussbaum 1997: 127–28)

Although I find her use of the terms *non-Western* and *real* problematic, this does not in my mind diminish the centrality of the five points to cross-cultural representation. In what ways does a study group address them? In what ways does it fall short? In my construction of the Philippine Ensemble in Santa Cruz, my decision to ignore point two was deliberate. In our study groups is the frequent silence on points four and five a deliberate strategy or an instance of benign neglect? As pedagogical rationale, can (or do) we claim that the study group is an effective means of understanding culture per the Nussbaum paradigm? In constructing our rationales for the study group, we must be aware of the multiplicity of conversations about cultural representation and understanding. Those voices constitute potential allies, and their discussions broader support for both the need for alternatives and the efficacy of the study group. Apropos of alternatives, different study groups may fulfill different goals, depending upon the mission of the host institution, the nature of its student population, and its peculiar relationship of "town to gown." For example, a mariachi group in Tempe, Arizona, would differ in reception, intent, and motivation from one in Honolulu; similarly, a koto class in Honolulu would contrast with one in Mount Vernon, Iowa.

After each institution has determined its primary goals, then the question of who teaches becomes paramount. As I suggested in the discussion of archetypes, the type of teacher profoundly influences the kind of knowledge and experience transmitted. In some instances hiring a native teacher is absolutely key. In others, hiring a performer-ethnomusicologist is more appropriate. Hypothetically, the selection of the teacher should receive at least as much thought and discussion as that invested in choosing the Bösendörfer concert grand instead of the American Steinway for the new recital hall. Although the choice is necessarily program-specific, the process should derive from a clear articulation of programmatic priorities and strengths rather than from circumstances of immediate availability or the fortuitous grant.

Finally, what is the value of the study group to the community at large? This final issue references my initial discussion of the term *study group* in contrast to "ethno-" or "world music ensemble." It also revisits my reservations about the tradition of public performance by beginning students. When and why does the study group become a performance ensemble? At a time when academe is fending off accusations of ivory tower isolation and proactively reaching out to its local communities, public performance undeniably presents an irresistible opportunity for high-profile (and nonthreatening) contact with a community at large. The public concert becomes iconic for a university that both "gives back" to its community and supports multiculturalism, that is, that provides spaces for alternative cultural expressions. It benefits the institutional image.

However, does it benefit the culture from which the genre comes (another community at large, often overlooked)? As I suggested earlier, there is both possible benefit and damage to the genre through its presentation by "single-semester artists." Many of us feel there are important benefits to this type of performance, for example, introduction of the genre to American audiences, opportunities for students to perform and to validate learning, and the groups' achievement of parity with other ensembles such as the symphony orchestra and the collegium musicum. However, how do we avoid distorting or misrepresenting the genre through its reperformance by our students, whose mastery of the tradition is, to be charitable, incomplete? This concern is particularly problematic in a performance environment inevitably informed by descriptive chauvinism, in which the dominant paradigm is aesthetic, harboring expectations of technical mastery and virtuosic performance. Do we diminish an American audience's appreciation or damage its respect for a genre through the repeated performance of simple repertory? Of greater personal concern, does the practice do damage to the teacher, native or not, who is fated to teach his tradition's counterpart of "Für Elise" to each new class, with little hope of ever reaching the monuments of the repertory, his genre's *Diabelli Variations*?

At the onset of a new century, it behooves the "ethnomusicological we" to have at the ready a set of clearly articulated rationales for the study group within the academy. To be effective, they should embrace the pedagogical, social, aesthetic, and experiential. We must be able to communicate them convincingly to—and realize them for—our students, colleagues, institutions, and communities.

NOTES

1. The center's 2002 web site lists Mantle Hood as ethnomusicologist, although he does not teach regularly at this institution.

2. It also differs from the forms *staged authenticity* as used by MacCannell and *"authenticity,"* which denotes an ascription whose validity may be questionable.

3. See the early 1963 critique and essentialist argument by Amiri Baraka [Leroi Jones] (1968).

4. In the interests of comparison, I have selected two cases delimited by location and time. Although treated synchronically, the Santa Cruz data are from 1984 and the Hawai'i data are from around 1982.

5. The *rondalla* is a plucked string band of Spanish origin consisting of flat-backed lutes with strings arranged in courses. Related to Latin American ensembles such as the Puerto Rican *orquesta*, it is described in Trimillos (1988a) and Cultural Center of the Philippines (1994).

6. See Trimillos 1965 and 1972. Two related *kulintang* traditions from the island of Mindanao are the focus of *Asian Music* 27, no. 2.

7. For a discussion by an indigenous teacher of American learning experiences in *kulintang*, see Cadar (1996).

8. The term *Moro* is part of Spain's colonial heritage, and in the Philippines referred to Filipino Muslims, located mainly in the south. It is most familiar to Hawai'i-born Filipinos through its use in folkloric dance theater, for example Bayanihan, as a programming category.

9. The term *improvisation* is used by *rondallistas* to denote parts that are not fixed either by notation or by consensus. The actual process reflects many of the aspects described by Sutton on the question of improvisation in Javanese gamelan (1998), which are also applicable to *kulintang*. Paraphrasing his final observation, "*rondallistas* improvise, but *rondalla* music is not improvisatory."

10. The notable exception in Hawai'i was the occasional foreign or emigrant student from the Philippines.

11. As part of the national project, composers have created contemporary works for *rondalla*. For example, Jerry Dadap's pieces explore atonality and minimalism. Others have arranged European works for the ensemble. Juan Silos Jr. produced transcriptions of opera overtures for his "symphonic *rondalla*." There is also a considerable body of commercial music that has crossed over to *rondalla*, including the classic film song "Dahil sa iyo" (Because of You), by Velarde.

12. Koto classes at the University of Hawai'i were begun by Barbara Smith in 1957 and then continued by my teacher, Kay Mikami, in 1959. For an account of these beginnings, see Smith (1987: 210).

13. *Kibei* denotes a youth sent back to Japan for a traditional education; the practice was common for *nisei*, Hawai'i-born offspring of immigrant Japanese.

14. During my four decades of contact with the tradition, there has been a noticeable movement toward employing the tempered semitone for traditional performance. For contemporary and pop repertory tempered tuning and concert pitch are already standard.

15. I use the term *foreign* in relation to the homeland of the tradition and not from the point of view of the United States. The archetypes are constructions selected for the present discussion and are not intended as exclusive categories. For example, variants—such as the native ethnomusicologist, the foreign performer who later becomes an ethnomusicologist, or the foreign performer ethnomusicologist resident abroad who occasionally teaches at an American university—are not addressed here.

16. Although I acknowledge both female and male participation in most traditions discussed, I use the masculine form for all third-person singular pronouns.

17. See, for example, the exchange about difference in native expertise presented by Moyle (1993) and Kaeppler (1994).

18. As noted earlier, visual authenticity can be misleading.

19. I distinguish between the two: in the former the culture carrier has agency and initiative; in the latter he is subject to externally imposed structures. Certainly complicity is an element in both.

20. University of Hawai'i colleague Hardja Susilo points out that this knowledge for gamelan is nevertheless subject to change in order to conform to the format of the Western concert (1990: 9).

21. Javanese dancer F. X. Widaryanto describes negotiating these identities and diverse educational expectations as a visiting teacher (1984).

22. Of course, this characterization does not apply to the native performer/ethnomusicologist leading a study group in his performance tradition.

23. He exhibits some similarities with the third archetype, the foreign practitioner. Some shared aspects are reserved for that discussion.

24. One notable exception is the late Gertrude Rivers Robinson, an African-American ethnomusicologist specializing in Balinese music ("Ethnomusicology" 1963).

25. Goldsworthy makes similar observations about gamelan in Australia (1997).

26. The acquisition of a gamelan as part of a "proper" ethnomusicology program in the United States appears as iconic as the establishment of a national airline for a "proper" nation!

27. Notable are the American *shakuhachi* artists Christopher Yohmei Blasdel and John Kaizan Neptune, whose performance careers are based in Japan.

28. As an example, the American who has studied only Indian music and has no training in Western musics.

29. Interestingly, the term *world music* in Europe denotes commercial music reflecting fusion and globalization. The American usage as a subject category in music education is less familiar outside the United States.

30. The early expectation that ethnomusicology would additionally be part of most anthropology departments was not fulfilled.

31. Other genres we offer up may not be immediately attractive, in which case we often advance an ethical rationale: it is useful or valuable for the student to experience the particular genre.

Chapter 2

"A Bridge to Java"

Four Decades Teaching Gamelan in America

INTERVIEW WITH HARDJA SUSILO
BY DAVID HARNISH, TED SOLÍS,
AND J. LAWRENCE WITZLEBEN

This interview took place on February 25, 2001, at the University of Hawai'i.

JAVANESE ENCULTURATION
AND AMERICAN ACCULTURATION

TED SOLÍS: We wanted to talk to you about your experiences, which are extensive in this country and also in Java. How did your journey to UCLA begin?

HARDJA SUSILO: Yes, that was rather interesting. First of all, I got interested in gamelan music early in life, although I didn't have a chance to learn it until I was eleven. I became instantly attracted to it the first time I heard it in the palace, and in the princely residence across the street from my house in Yogyakarta. It was so elegant. I wanted to be in some ways involved in that. My father did not encourage me. Later I learned that being a professional gamelan musician is no way to make a living. . . . It's an invitation to poverty. Unlike dancers, not too many gamelan musicians live comfortably. So, when I was at Gadjah Mada University in Yogyakarta, during my freshman year, I decided to be an English teacher in the daytime and a gamelan musician at night. I would be a gamelan amateur in the best sense of the word. With regards to arts, being a gamelan amateur was preferable at that time largely due to the reputation of professional gamelan players. I prepared for that goal by studying English and learning to play gamelan seriously. At the same time I also practiced *macakandha*, that is, reading the narration in the Yogyanese style *wayang wong* (Javanese dance drama). I had studied Old Javanese, or Kawi, for three years in high school, and I continued on to learn literary Javanese at the teacher training school. I danced and played gamelan whenever there were opportunities. The music and musical treatment that I learned were mostly for dance, Yogyakarta-style dance accompaniment. Solo was very far away then. . . .

TS: Could you elaborate on that dance background?

HS: Before coming to America I was a student and member of the teaching staff of the now defunct Krido Bekso Wiromo [KBW, the first private traditional dance school in Yogya, founded in 1918]. I was the gamelan director for a couple of their major productions. Otherwise I taught gamelan at the teacher training school once a week to pay for my college tuition. For about forty years KBW was the only Yogyanese-style Javanese dance school in Indonesia. I was trained as a "refined" dancer rather than a "strong" dancer because of my small build. Because I didn't (and still don't) have what might be considered a face with delicate features, I was often cast as refined *sabrangan* [foreign] characters, such as Wibisono, Rawana's youngest brother, or Sarpokenoko, Rawana's younger sister [Rawana is the demon king in the *Ramayana* epic]. Sometimes I was cast as a character whose physical appearance had not been strictly prescribed by the tradition, such as Raden Sakso or Ronggolawe, from the dance repertoire drawn from the Javanese history. I would never be cast as Lesmono [Lakshmana, Rama's brother] or Romo [Rama]. Unlike today, in the past they were quite picky about casting. In any case, in my search for an appropriate part for myself I learned to do different characters such as clowns, a robber demon, a monkey—a Mongolian general, even. Once I did Subali in a Javanese opera *[langen mandra wanara]* produced by Radio Republik Indonesia. It was an honor. So I was trading doing one type of dance perfectly for doing different characters, but not perfectly. I did that because of, shall we say, my physical imperfection. But as it turned out, my dance experience was helpful when I had to choreograph Sendratari, a dance drama involving different characters. Clare Holt [an ethnologist] saw me dance in Java, then she saw me dance again in America. She told me that I danced better in America than when I was in Java. Maybe so. Frankly, in America I try harder, both in *karawitan* [traditional gamelan and related performing arts] and dance. Being the first Javanese dancer/musician in an American university I had the feeling like a salesman. I didn't want to be the cause that American audiences didn't like Javanese performing arts. Americans might not know good Javanese dancing from bad. But they would know that a wobbly dancer could not be considered good. That much they know. . . .

Anyhow, while at Gadjah Mada University, I practiced my English with some visiting Americans. I would teach them gamelan and in return I would practice English with them.

And then I saw this book *[The Nuclear Theme as a Determinant of Patet in Javanese Music]* by Mantle Hood [Hood 1954]. At that time I was very baffled by the idea of *pathet* [a modal classification system], because Javanese musicians usually, when I asked them about it, would say, "well, it's a feeling.

If you don't feel it, maybe you just are not old enough to feel it And if you're old enough to feel it and still don't feel it, maybe your artistic mind doesn't go that far." That was unsatisfactory to me. So, although I could not understand the writing I was very impressed by Mantle Hood and his book. Now, here was an American who could propose a rational explanation of this baffling idea.

Then a few months later he came to Yogya . . . in late 1956, I think it was. So I decided "forget college for a while. I'll help him somehow . . . because he must have studied a lot to be able to explain *pathet*." With that decision I stopped going to lectures at Gadjah Mada in order to assist him voluntarily. When he found out that I stopped going to lectures to help him he insisted that I resume my classes. I worked hard on my English classes. I was a rather rare bird then, a person who spoke English but who also knew something about Javanese traditional performing arts.

Anyway, Mantle Hood thought that I might enjoy training in ethnomusicology in America. To make a long story short, I came to UCLA in 1958, to have training in ethnomusicology and to teach Javanese gamelan. The plan was for a year with a possible extension for a second year. When I finished the second year Pak Hood thought that I should stay for another year and get my B.A. in music in three years. I worked hard and got my B.A., with honors, even. Then he suggested that I try the master's degree. That took me a while. UCLA insisted that I take a foreign language, either French or German. English wasn't foreign to them, of course, but it was still very foreign to me. Indonesian and Javanese, well, I was told that there were not enough research papers written in those languages; in short, they were unacceptable foreign languages. I chose German. So to get my M.A. I had to translate an article in German into English. The way I felt then, well, this might just as well be translating Sanskrit to Chinese. That is an exaggeration, of course. Anyway, after taking longer than I care to remember, I got my M.A. I have no regrets, because while working on my M.A. I learned more about Western music. I attended symphony rehearsals and joined the chamber singers and various ethnic music study groups. One of the most memorable was the mariachi study group. We played around town, and people thought I was a Mexican. Unfortunately, the immigration officers often mistook me for a Mexican, too. That was no fun. I guess I played my part too well. Anyway, the original plan was a year or two in America, but forty years later here I am, still in America, talking to you.

"BIMUSICALITY" IN ITS ACADEMIC INFANCY

HS: At that time it was quite novel for ethnomusicology students to learn to play instruments in order to enhance their understanding of the musical tradition under study. But by and by, in the gamelan study groups we had two groups of people, people who like to talk about gamelan—the ethno-musicology students—and people who liked to play gamelan. It is understandable that ethno students could not be expected to know in depth the practical aspects of every musical culture they are studying. We need twenty-five people in the gamelan and at any given time there were never twenty-five ethno students specializing in gamelan study. So, the gamelan performance group survived owing to students and community members who just liked the sounds of the gamelan.

About the methodology of teaching, that was interesting. People memorized their parts, then we put them together, and boom, we had Javanese ensemble! It was incredible, but it sounded stiff. Furthermore, it would only sound acceptable as long as nobody missed a note, or added notes, which would cause them to go out of synch with the rest of the ensemble. The problem was that when they got out of synch, they didn't know how to return to the ensemble, because they only knew their parts and not their relationship with the other instruments. One time the ensemble had to play without me, because I had to prepare to dance in the next number. Unknown to them, several instruments got out of synch. I don't know, maybe they left out some notes, or added one or two. . . . . Of course, this meant that people reached the terminal note at different times. So, some reached the last gong tone, but they didn't want to stop because the others had not gotten there. And when the others got there, there were stragglers who were still in the middle of their phrase. And this went on and on like a round, a catch. There was no way I could fix it because I was in the wing trying to put on my Yogyanese headdress and monkey mask, which required some concentration. Boy, that was the most helplessly frustrating moment I had ever had! Finally, one musician decided to stop at the terminal point and was followed by others. It sounded like they arrived at that terminal point one by one, ending up with a single, lonely sound of the *gender* [metallophone played with two beaters]. The audience loved it. They applauded wildly. I guess it must have sounded like the most profound music they had ever heard. Debussy would have loved it, too.

DAVID HARNISH: Now the group can recover after getting lost.

HS: Yes, they can come back. Most of the time anyway.

There was another time when I danced Yogyanese *klana gagah* [Javanese strong male dance]. In this dance I, the dancer, would proceed to the next section of the dance when the music would go to *ngelik* [a contrasting section moving to the upper register]. The drum was supposed to signal the change at a certain point in the music, but he missed the mark. So when he gave the signal nobody heard it. It's like placing a detour sign on a straight road. The ensemble just ignored the signal, because it was placed at the wrong spot. This results in repeating that section of the music over and over and over again, and I repeating that portion of the dance over and over and over again. I was so frustrated my face must have looked so stern. I was so upset, and there was nothing I could do about it except repeat my dance sequence. Finally the drummer realized the mistake, and the music went back on track. When the dance finished the audience applauded wildly. Later some came up to me telling me how they loved my dramatic facial expression.

People knew that even if the music is not totally improvised, it is at least varied from one repetition to the next or one performance to the next. But when I gave them parts that were different from my earlier lesson they were not happy. So I learned not to alter the part. Today I change my strategy. I emphasize relationships. I also give the students playing *gambang* [a xylophone played with two beaters], *gender*, and *bonang* [a set of horizontal gongs played with two beaters in melodic elaboration], etc., different options so as not to sound stale.

Also, learning from the past, I recall back in the early 1960s how I felt when after dancing hard, and getting off the stage, there was not even a cup of tea. How ironic: here I was dancing in one of the richest countries in the world and they didn't even have tea for the dancer. I felt the concert was too audience-oriented. Everything was for them, nothing for the performers, except for the five minutes of applause. So, around 1967, when we staged the second all-night *wayang kulit* [shadow puppet theater performance] in the United States [the first one was at Wesleyan] I had *slametan* [a ritual feast held to wish for good fortune, or to celebrate or commemorate important events]. We cooked the food ourselves. Today I always have a *slametan* before our concert, and make sure that there are beverages during the night for the performers.

TEACHING STUDENTS TO "THINK AS JAVANESE MUSICIANS"

HS: There is something else that I have learned from teaching gamelan abroad for so many years, namely, just as important as learning to do it is learning to think the way the Javanese musicians think. Admittedly, even just learning how to play correctly is very challenging. Because to do it right one must know how to interrelate with the other parts and with other concurrent events. I can teach a total novice to play a piece in an hour. But learning to be reactive, proactive, flexible . . . that takes years. More than that, though, the students should learn to feel or think the way a native thinks when playing gamelan. I don't mean just emphasizing beat eight instead of beat one, but actually *feeling* that a gong signals the end of a phrase, rather than the beginning. It is true that I cannot hear whether the musicians are thinking one way or the other in a concert. So, insofar as the product is concerned, "it don't make no never mind" how you think about it. The only thing that confirms my suspicion that there has not been much change in the way some people think about or hear the music was when I heard them sing the piece "Bendrong": 3G 5 3 5 2 5 2 5. It *must* be 5 3 5 2 5 2 5 3G. In other words, you don't just count 8G 1 2 3 4 5 6 7 instead of 1G 2 3 4 5 6 7 8. To a Javanese this would feel hanging. You know, like striking dominant seven without continuing on to the tonic. Wherever you start counting you have to *end* on 3G.[1] Actually, if you want to be really authentic you don't count at all. You would recite the colotomic structure, *"dhoot, goong, dhoot, tho,"* or *"thuk, pul, thuk, nong,"* to represent *kethuk, kempul, kethuk, kenong.*[2] Dancers or dance teachers, however, do count: they would recite the numbers *"siji, loro, telu, papat"* [Javanese], or, after the establishment of the National Dance Conservatory, *"satu, dua, tiga, empat"* [Indonesian], or, as is taught in America, "one, two, three, four." The teachers may instead recite some basic leg movement, *"junjung, tekuk, nggejojor, seleh"* (lift, bend, stretched, down). *Seleh,* the end of the dance motif, coincides with "four," the end of the musical motif. So, if you don't finish your count with four or eight, the dancer will end up with one foot suspended in the air.

This is true in learning Balinese music as well. When you play the piece "Baris," for example, it has to be *"dang ding dong deng dong deng ding dong dang,"* or "translated" into cipher notation, 6G 1 2 3 2 3 1 2 6G. You have to end on 6G. Not to do so, especially while the dancer is walking, you might force him to keep one of his feet hanging. Also, still about . . . Balinese music, sometimes I am amazed how one can learn a *sangsih* [one of the two interlocking parts] alone, without having any idea how the *polos* or complementary interlocking part sounds. To me it is like reading a book every other word. You might make some kind of sense out of it, but it's probably not the sense that the writer intends. You have to hear both parts even if you only play half of a pattern.

As I said, you couldn't hear these different thoughts in the mind of the players during a concert, except when they get out of synch. It's at that time when you hear the result of the wrong thoughts. Learning a culture, in this case a music culture, is not just learning how the natives physically do it, but also how they think about it. Maybe this way of thinking owes to my orientation in culture learning. If your orientation is to use these foreign implements to create something new, to employ them detached from their cultural context, well, that's a different story, of course. You can think any way you want.

Unfortunately the university setting, the setting that I have been associated with, limits your learning period. This is why a community gamelan is good and helpful, because it has no limit as to how long you want to learn. Community gamelan provides continuity, as well as a pleasant and somewhat stress-free learning environment. It simulates the learning environment found in Javanese and Balinese community groups.

CREATING AN ACADEMIC GAMELAN COMMUNITY

TS: Would you say something about the kinds of communities that grew up around and within the gamelan at UCLA and here in Hawai'i?

HS: Like many other groups, the UCLA and Hawai'i groups began with music students or students who, out of curiosity or need for easy credits, take the gamelan ensemble course. At the end of the semester some of these folks want to know more. They do so by either repeating the course or auditing it. By doing so they form a layer of musicians in the community group. So, to simplify the explanation, if you have a ten-semester-old community group, you might have ten layers of musicians with different abilities to play. In the process some of the members will drop out. My challenge is that I have members who have been with us since 1972, 1974, and 1980, and some from last semester. The challenge is how to provide a musical challenge for each of them. So far I can still challenge them. This is important; otherwise you don't have a group for very long. Both at UCLA and Hawai'i I have been blessed with interest from the community. Gamelan has been one of the large groups among our ethnic music ensembles. Unlike the other ensembles, whose members are largely people from that particular ethnic group, most members of our gamelan ensemble are non-Javanese, non-Balinese. They are mostly Americans of different ethnic extractions. The few Indonesians that we have had in the group have not been the backbones of the group, except when they are invited guest teachers.

DH: So when you have *gagaku* [a Japanese court orchestra] here, you have many Japanese?

HS: Yes, and in the Korean group there are a lot of Koreans. The Javanese and Balinese groups have one or two Indonesians, and they are not necessarily playing the most important instruments. The American students, when they want to play important instruments, they work hard to conquer them. Most of them are very tenacious. Their determination is admirable. This is something that I tell my Javanese audience when I give lectures in Indonesia. The Javanese, those who care to learn, usually feel that the music is their heritage, so they don't have to work hard on it. They are not as committed as their American counterparts.

TS: Well, you've had a group here since 1971 and you still, I believe, have a few people who have stayed on from the beginning. So do you feel that some of those people are approaching the kinds of proficiency that you expect of a good Javanese group in Java, and do your pedagogical methods reflect that?

HS: I think they, the long-term players, hear the music better than some of the newer players. Whether they are better players or not, that depends on how much they continue their learning. But thinking of myself, as a musician you need to socialize musically. That's what I miss in the United

States as opposed to in Java. We practice only once a week. There is no other musical socialization. The group is good, but of course they are not as proficient as if they were in Java, involved with Javanese musicians. Some of our old members who have gone to bigger and better things have had this socialization in Java. And they, of course, are very proficient.

TS: What kind of socialization do you mean? Interaction?

HS: Interaction, yes, hearing, following, making spontaneous change. Or even just being exposed to such practice as interaction between a *dhalang* [*wayang* puppeteer/narrator] and his musicians, a drummer and his ensemble; hearing all these subtle signals, hints, musical suggestions, musical jokes, etc. That is hard to achieve. We try, but our time is limited. And when there is a concert event coming up those two hours would go to concert preparation.

TS: So for more than forty years you've been feeling a certain lack of, as you say, socialization among musicians. . . . ? You have never been quite satisfied?

BUILDING A BRIDGE TO JAVA

HS: About 85 percent satisfied, but you know . . . I think my function here is to be a bridge. I think I know about being a bridge better than a lot of musicians in Java. So, you know, it's a tradeoff. A long time ago I asked myself, "Would I want to be the best gamelan drummer?" And I found that that was not what I wanted. If I wanted exclusively to be a gamelan teacher I could have stayed at UCLA. But I found teaching *lancaran*[3] one semester after another, with no other academic activities, would be a bit too much for me. It would be like teaching "Twinkle Twinkle Little Star" semester after semester after semester. I wanted more than that. And here in Hawai'i I was given the opportunity to become a bridge. I taught academic classes and nurtured a community group, while servicing the novice. Being a bridge is perhaps where I am most useful. If they [the students] were going to Java, it was easier if they passed through me.

DH: So you are saying that a lot of your methodology is geared toward students getting ready to go to Java?

HS: To Indonesia. I always have such feelings. If students do the best they can with me, by the time they go to Java they are ready to learn. When they get to Java they don't have to learn to handle the beaters, or to make different sounds on the drum. They can go directly learn to play *gender,* or *gambang,* or drum, whatever. They have precious little time in Indonesia, and they don't need to squander it on learning how to hold the beaters, how to damp the keys. They can do those things here. You know, like an Indonesian language teacher, by the time a student finishes the course in the United States, he won't be speaking perfect Indonesian, but he would be ready to learn Indonesian in its cultural context. I think I'm more patient than a lot of Javanese teachers in Java. Because for one thing, I don't have any choice; if I am not patient, I don't have students.

IMPRINT OF THE TEACHER
AND PEDAGOGICAL RESPONSIBILITY

DH: You said that you actually improved as a performer from teaching. . . .

HS: And from performing. Definitely. I made a lot of improvement both in playing and dancing, which probably I would not have made in Java. You would find out that when you make a mistake in teaching somebody, that mistake is perpetuated. And if there were ten students, your mistake would be multiplied ten times. Did I make mistakes in teaching? You bet I did. And I am sure I still do occasionally. . . .

Here in America I have access to excellent recordings by some of the best musicians, some subtle, rich *gender* playing, nice elaboration, all kinds of things. When I pass these materials to the students I would ask myself, would I really want him to play the same pattern every time? Maybe not. You see, sometimes fancy playing is like a loud batik shirt. You should wear it sparingly. If you can only afford to have one shirt, don't acquire a loud one. People will soon notice that that's the only one you have.

Oh, I'll tell you an interesting anecdote pertaining to this learning by tape. I was in Solo. I wanted to record Pak Martopangrawit's *rebab* [two-stringed spiked fiddle] playing. So I played the *gender* as he played the *rebab*. We played a heavy-duty piece, *Lala Kalibeber*. After we finished the piece he asked, "Where did you learn your *gender* playing?" "I learned it from you. I listen to your recordings." He looked amused and said, "No wonder some of the variations are like mine." "Do you mind if I perpetuate it?" "Of course not." I felt that my *gender* playing was certified. As he observed correctly, I didn't copy everything he did. In the world of *wayang* I am Bambang Ekalaya, so observed the late Pak Banjaransari [one of the vocalists of Radio Republik Indonesia Yogyakarta from the 1950s to the mid-1970s]. Bambang Ekalaya is a character in *Mahabharata* [one of the two major Hindu epics], a young man who wanted to study very much with Durno, the great teacher. But he was rejected. So he carved a statue in the image of Durno. So fervently did he want to learn that he actually learned from this image of a teacher. So, I owe a great deal of what I know to recordings, the images of teachers. This is a perfectly valid method of learning. After all, in music most of our learning is aural, rather than oral. I don't know how Pak Banjaran figured me out on that. . . .

As a teacher, my job is just making a rough figure, chiseling the first shape of a statue. If the person is sufficiently interested he or she will have to go to Indonesia. I don't teach my students to copy me exactly.

TS: But they have to start off playing like you.

HS: Oh sure. But I think it's the ultimate of arrogance to say, "I want you to play just like me." Maybe while they are in phase one. But they have got to move on. In Java I'll point my finger and say, "you study with him, he's a good teacher."

AURALITY AND NOTATION IN PEDAGOGY

J. LAWRENCE WITZLEBEN: I'm interested in what you said about how American students are eager to show that they can play things from memory. You make it sound so natural, but is that something that you found hard teaching in a music department, getting people to learn things by ear rather than writing it down and reading it?

HS: Reliance on what is written seems to be very much ingrained in this culture. You hear people say "Here it is, in black and white," as they point to a written document, much more often here than in Java. In Java when one is angry one might say *"Nek cangkeme ora kena digugu, sing arep digugu apane."* Incidentally, in Javanese this is quite a rude statement, although if translated into English the harshness does not carry over as strongly. In English it simply means, "If we can't trust his mouth, what part of his body can we trust?" In other words, oral and aural orientation is important. So, yes, quite often I have a hard time persuading people to abandon their notation when they play. For one thing, what is written is incomplete information. It does not tell you when and how to accelerate, to stop, to get soft, to get loud, to drop off, to make transitions, etc. Secondly, it hinders your playing; it makes you less sensitive to interrelationship, less perceptive to signals, oblivious to concurrent events, etc. So, some people do their best to memorize their part, which makes them more sensitive to what's going on around them. Others insist on having notation around for a security blanket. The truth is that playing by memory is not such a weird thing in Western music tradition either, as, for example, when they play a concerto.

JLW: But they don't go into a lesson and say, "we are going to learn this concerto, play this phrase, play that phrase." The learning process by ear is different from the process in Java.

HS: Yes, true. But the end result is the same, i.e., playing without notation. In the West, playing without notation would give a musician more freedom to add or to express appropriate feelings. . . . Playing without notation, by memory or by improvisation, allows the musician to be creative, interactive, and sensitive to the concurrent events. . . .

JLW: It seems that all of your students that I know of who are teaching are very much stressing learning orally.

HS: Yes.

JLW: Learning to hear and learn very deeply. And in a sense that's preserving a certain spirit of the tradition. I'm thinking that in the conservatories in Java, they're getting more and more into writing out *gender* parts and things like that.

HS: That's true among students. But among their teachers and professionals, they very rarely read while playing. At the radio station in Yogya there was one guy who read notation while playing. *Gerong* [male chorus] and *sindhen* [female vocal soloist] are different. You often find them reading their song texts.

At the Konservatori Karawitan, the high school for *karawitan* studies in Solo, back when Pak Wiranto was the director, he supported the idea of the students submitting a *kerja nyata,* which was a work on a specific traditional piece, usually one that is rare and has not been previously presented. In this *kerja nyata* students are required to provide written formulaic parts for all of the instruments. No musician worth his salt would play the parts as written, of course. These are guidelines. To play them as written would be as stale as last week's bread.

INNOVATION, COMPOSITION, AND "AMERICAN GAMELAN" STYLE

TS: Thinking in terms of evolution: plants or animals separated by a body of water eventually evolve into separate species. Do you think there's such a thing as "American gamelan," an American gamelan style that is evolving as a whole separate world?

HS: I would say so. As early as the mid-1960s one of Bob Brown's gamelan students, I believe it was Dennis Murphy, made his own gamelan. As I understand it, it did not look like a Javanese or Balinese gamelan, but it sounded like gamelan. Later, in the Bay Area, Daniel Schmidt, Bill Colvig, and Sita Wulur of Holland also created homemade gamelans. Bill's gamelan does look like an authentic set. Several others followed. That's the hardware. The gamelan-type composers are, among others, Lou Harrison, the late Gertrude Robinson, Robert Kyr, Jody Diamond, and many, many more. I am talking about composers who actually use gamelan. Colin McPhee is a different breed. Of course, this phenomenon is no longer restricted to America. You can find Western gamelan composers in Canada, Holland, England, Germany, Japan, Australia, New Zealand, and elsewhere.

The presentational aspect of gamelan, I mean the way the gamelan is performed by American students in America, is also slightly different from the way it is presented in Indonesia. As those of you who have been in Indonesia have seen, more often than not gamelan is presented in conjunction with other events, such as rites of passage, various dramatic and theater presentations, temple festivals, etc. In Java, the idea of having a gamelan concert in which the gamelan is performed for its own sake, with the audience attending for free or paying admission specifically to watch gamelan being played, is rarely done. And when it is done, it is often ceremonial in nature, like with *Sekaten* [a special set of Javanese court gamelan to be played primarily one week every year to commemorate the birth of the prophet Mohammed]. Otherwise, the idea of a concert is relatively foreign to the Javanese. Pak Cokro and his excellent musicians did such paid concerts in Yogya; as I recall, it was in the early 1950s. It only drew a handful of audience members. I was told that Pak Nartosabdo did a similar thing in Jakarta and it was not a financial success. The closest thing to that idea of a concert is perhaps the Indonesia radio station broadcasting of this "concert," in which people would listen to it often as background music. What is more common with regards to gamelan presentation is the idea of *uyon-uyon* or *klenengan*. This is a gamelan presentation, usually in conjunction with a celebratory event, sponsored by a person or an institution. Guests are invited, free of charge of course, and served dinner, munchies, and a beverage, which sometimes include something that is stronger than tea. In other words, it's a party with live background music. Such a party can easily last until 1 or 2 AM. Sometimes, somewhere in the middle of the presentation, one of the beautiful *pesindhen* [female vocal soloists] would stand up and dance *gambyong* [a flirtatious Javanese dance].

Another non-Javanese practice in the Javanese concert in the West is the idea that musicians exchange places after each piece. It's true that in Java musicians can play several instruments, but they don't play all the instruments that they know how to play all in one night. They would not exchange places unless there was a need to do so. For example, in the middle of the night the *kempul* [tuned vertical gong about fifteen inches in diameter] player needs to be excused for a while, then maybe one of the *saron* [metallophone played with a single beater] players would fill the spot. In America this practice is to give different experience to the students, so that they are not stuck to one instrument for the whole semester. The choice and the order of the pieces might not follow the traditional prescription, for example by beginning the evening with an austere big piece in *pelog pathet lima,* and gradually moving to the more lively music in *pelog barang* and *slendro manyura.*[4]

LEARNING IN A BROAD CULTURAL CONTEXT

DH: Do you think it's important that students also learn aspects of Javanese culture by playing the music? I mean not only the behavior around the music, but also behavior toward each other and other ideas of Java?

HS: I think so. As I said elsewhere, for me, learning gamelan is only part of culture learning. That's my background, because I learned gamelan at a princely house, which adhered very faithfully to the court tradition. I cannot teach it any other way. You don't go *nyaknyakan,* walking without showing any reverence to anything or anybody, *nganyur*, standing straight in a situation where you should sit down or at least bend your knees, following *tatakrama*, behaving with adherence to common courtesy. One might be able to play gamelan without observing these practices, but I know that my students, who adhere to these norms, are very much appreciated by their hosts. When they compliment you they do so in Javanese, softly and among themselves. I know.

Ultimately, what is the aim of learning music and dance? It's like I said in that video [*Gamelan Music of Java,* 1983]: to be a better member of the society. That's the higher goal. So I am not terribly impressed by somebody who's a top-notch musician but very rude. I don't need it. I'd rather have a good human being.

DH: Gamelan does not create egotistical superstars.

HS: Right. When our Hawai'i gamelan group played in Indonesia for the first time in 1973, one of the best compliments was about "the evenness of your group; nobody is showing off." The goal is that everyone sounds good.

DH: The senior musicians help with that, too. I remember some comments from somebody who was listening to me play. Just saying a few words that I still remember about maybe playing too many "flower" patterns (melodic flourishes that alternate with interlocking *imbal* patterns on the *bonang*). You don't have to play a different pattern every time you go to pitch three. You can play the same one once in a while or you can let it go. Because that was sort of my attitude. I always wanted to play different patterns, but sometimes that's not appropriate.[5]

ADAPTING TO THE INDIVIDUAL STUDENT

JLW: I guess one thing that, in retrospect, I find really amazing was that you knew what they were going to be able to do as musicians and dancers several months before they were going to do it. In other words, if you have to put on the *Ramayana,* and you have people coming out of one semester of dance or one semester of something else, you know this person will be able to do that. And . . . this person has studied in Java but is still reading the notes too much . . . and we have got to get somebody else to play *bonang,* and so on. Knowing what potentials are there and what limitations are there. I find that that's something very amazing and very moving, that you have the sense of realizing what people can do. And also having to make the decisions, but do it in a way that keeps the social harmony. That's very sensitive.

HS: Yes, I used to have different levels of dancers. Some, after one semester, can only walk. Okay, that's what he will do in this dance drama, walk. I found out later that that's kind of like the Suzuki method. You know, when they have a concert every student plays according to their level. If all they can do is play "Twinkle Twinkle Little Star," then that is what they are going to do. If a student can only play the rhythm of "Twinkle Twinkle Little Star," let him just play the rhythm of the piece. If he can't even play the rhythm, well, at least he can learn to bow to the audience while having a violin under his armpit. It's just assigning people according to what they can do. . . . You want to do it so that everyone is involved. In the course of learning, you observe how conscientious and responsible the person is. I have to know how much time he has so I don't overload him. In other words, don't put him in a position where he might do damage to the ensemble. . . .

TS: So how do you decide who plays what?

HS: After learning the basics, playing *saron* and understanding the colotomic structure, I would let them learn whatever they want. But interestingly, my good *gender* students have been mostly gentle but stubborn individuals. So now I know how to choose a *gender* player. . . .

DH: I can remember that you had some frustration teaching singing, because people kept hearing Western diatonic scales, the approximation, and they would sing those intervals, but they didn't fit the gamelan. Did you ever figure out a way to deal with that?

HS: I think so. I am getting better sound now. Rather than thinking about pitches, I try to get them to think about intervals. I used to correct a wrong note by saying "your six is flat, raise it." Now I am more likely to say "your interval between five and six is too narrow." I learned that if I just tell them to raise the six, in their mind they also raise the five. So when they go to five, the five is sharp.

Of course correcting the pronunciation is important, too. The pitches might be correct, but the pronunciation might betray them. I am glad I took phonetics when I was in college. So I have some ideas how to correct pronunciation.

CULTURAL APPROPRIATION AND "OWNERSHIP"

TS: One of the things that has come up in a lot of writing and a lot of people's remarks . . . is the idea of appropriation. The idea that we're colonizing—appropriating—by what right are we doing these kinds of things? Do such things ever occur to you?

HS: Yes, to me that is political talk. I am frankly honored that you guys are studying the gamelan, that you think it is a worthy subject. A lot of Indonesians don't think so, you know. So, appropriate all you want. You see, it isn't like "if you take it then I don't have it anymore." This is a case where if you take it then we have two, you see. If other people take it, too, then we have three of whatever it is that you are supposed to take. So, it isn't like a flute; if you take it, than I don't have it. If this music culture is lost, that is not because you take it, but because they, the Javanese, are neglecting it. They lose it. If the Javanese lose the art of playing gamelan, I assure you it's not because you "appropriate" it and teach it in Hong Kong, or you're teaching it in America.

Now, copyright is something else. I remember reading Oscar Brand's *Ballad Mongers* [1962], where he talks about the first recording of American folk song. The recording became so popular that the recording company made a lot of money. They felt guilty, so they announced "whoever wrote the song, please come forward to receive the royalties." Ten people stepped forward claiming to be the rightful owner of the song, causing a great deal of legal problems. Ever since then recording companies don't want to record anything unless somebody claims it, in order to avoid a similar problem. So, people claim the right to some folk songs, with the excuse "well, if I don't do it, somebody else will." Charles Seeger's reaction to that was, that's the rationale of robbing a bank. So I too have some objection to laying claims on public property. I recall that when UCLA was recording the Javanese gamelan played by UCLA students, Columbia Masterworks didn't want to release it unless the tunes in the recording were claimed. UCLA had to claim them if the recordings were to be released. Theoretically, then, whenever I wanted to perform those pieces on the record I had to have permission from UCLA. That gave me some discomfort for many years. I guess, having been more than thirty-five years, the right has expired. *That* is like taking a flute.

TS: It's a big thing now, intellectual property rights—a big thing at universities . . .

HS: Yes, my feeling is you can appropriate all you want as long as it does not lead to any kind of restriction.

POSTLUDE

TS: So any last sweeping thoughts about your forty-five years in America?

HS: Yes, yes, August 19 . . . no, September 6, 1958.

DH: You remember the date?

HS: Well, how many Javanese dancers/musicians came to America those days, flying on a propeller-driven plane for a couple of days? It was very special. I am honored that you guys, university professors, came back to interview me. I am of course thankful for my experience. I think I've had it both ways. I still play gamelan and live in a milieu that allows me to broaden my mind . . . not to mention that because of my being here I am married to a beautiful wife, and have three beautiful children. I thank God.

NOTES

1. In *karawitan* compositions that adhere to quadratic meter, the most heavily accented beat is marked by a stroke on a big gong. The melodic pitch coinciding

with the stroke of the gong is called the "gong tone" (indicated in the examples above by "G"). An argument exists as to whether the gong begins a musical phrase or ends it. Native musicians feel that it ends a musical phrase. Even the first stroke upon which the different instruments enter at the beginning of a piece is in fact the end of an introduction. This is supported by the fact that important dance phrases, which often coincide with the landing of a dancer's foot, coincide with a gong tone. It can be assumed that the music and dance of a given culture share the same system. Thus, in *karawitan,* to withhold a gong tone is to require a dancer to halt his or her movement just when one foot is a few inches from the floor. In most instances this is not possible; even when possible, it is extremely unnatural for the dancer.

2. Colotomic structure is the tonal accentuation pattern in *karawitan* usually performed on horizontally and/or vertically mounted tuned gongs. The most common among the colotomic/accentuating instruments are the *kethuk* (small horizontal), *kempul* (medium vertical), *kenong* (large horizontal), and *gong* (largest vertical). Teachers represent these instruments orally by reciting the syllables *"thuk," "pul,"* *"nong," "gong,"* or *"thuk," "gung," "tho," "gong,"* respectively. These instruments may be represented in writing by different symbols or different letters in the alphabet: "t, P, N, G," respectively. In addition, there is a colotomic rest, or *wela* (W), which is the absence of a colotomic instrument stroke where one might reasonably be expected. As an example, here is the colotomic pattern of a *ladrang* form.

t W t N
t P t N
t P t N
t P t NG

3. This Javanese musical form has eight beats per large gong stroke, according to the following colotomic structure.

1   2   3   4   5   6   7   8
t W t N t P t N t P t N t P t NG

4. In the *pathet* modal system disagreements still exist about the modes of the seven-tone *pelog* tuning system. Traditionally, a *karawitan* "concert" would adhere to the above order of *pathet,* lest major disorientation result among the musicians.

5. In adhering to one of the themes of Susilo's interview, Harnish is referring here to restraining oneself while playing *bonang* and instead listening to the other musicians while deciding what to play. For further discussion of this idea see Harnish's article in this book and Sutton 1998.

Chapter 3

Opportunity and Interaction

The Gamelan from Java to Wesleyan

SUMARSAM

It has been more than four decades since gamelan performance was first incorporated into the ethnomusicology program at UCLA. Today, interest in studying gamelan performance remains strong in American colleges and universities: discussion of various gamelan topics and announcements of gamelan events appear almost daily on gamelan@listserve,[1] and the falling value of the Indonesian currency since 1997 has encouraged many institutions and individuals to buy gamelan instruments.[2] An announcement that preceded the 2000 Music Teachers' National Association (MTNA) conference calling for the development of a David Letterman–style top ten list of reasons for establishing gamelan study also indicates a continuing fascination with gamelan among music educators.[3]

There is a long historical precedent for Western fascination with the gamelan and its music. Throughout much of Indonesian history Java was the center not only of power, but also of local and international commerce. Since the seventeenth century European traders (and, later, colonists) had to maintain relations with the state and dynasty of Mataram. By the eighteenth and nineteenth centuries, Java was the regional headquarters of the colonial government. This close relationship made it possible for Europeans to have long-standing exposure to the Javanese. Consequently, European interest in Indonesian cultures was first focused on the island of Java. More importantly, such exposure to Europeans and European cultures resulted in the articulation of Java, by both Javanese and Europeans, as a world of difference, especially in her court arts and literature (Pemberton 1994: 23). Pemberton locates this articulation of Java in the content of Javanese court manuscripts written by Javanese courtiers from the early eighteenth century onwards, and subsequently in the writing of Dutch scholars in collaboration with their

Javanese informants in the early twentieth century (ibid.: 22–24); he characterized it in terms of a discursive logic that "occurred in contradistinction to the invasively constant, yet only partially incorporated, presence of the Dutch" on the island (ibid.: 24).

In any event, this cultural articulation contributed to the fame of Javanese arts. For example, gamelan ensembles appeared in Western exhibition halls and at early world's fairs, such as the 1889 Paris Exposition Universelle and the 1893 Chicago Columbian Exhibition. One important reason for holding such expositions was commercialism. As a display of exotica, gamelan performance was meant to attract the audience to visit the exposition.

A group sent to these expositions consisted of Sundanese musicians and dancers from a plantation in the foothills of the West Javanese mountains. Closer inspection reveals, however, that a few dancers and perhaps also musicians from the court of Surakarta were invited to join the group.

When Indonesia achieved her independence from the Dutch in the 1940s, a plural society of hundreds of different ethnic groups was formed. Thus, maintaining Java's world of difference became problematic. Some scholars and political leaders thought of elevating Javanese gamelan into a "national" music (Sumarsam 1995). Their opponents attempted to design national Indonesian arts that would represent Indonesia as a whole, and that could be enjoyed by all of Indonesia's people, regardless of their ethnic background. For example, in the 1940s, a genre of Indonesian popular music, *kroncong*, whose origin and development can be traced back to Portuguese music introduced in the sixteenth century, was promoted as a new form of Indonesian national music. The rationale was that *kroncong*, with its modern, Western diatonic scale, was popular and enjoyed by many Indonesians throughout the archipelago. A Sumatran-based social dance called *serampang dua belas* (a social dance in which men and women dance together with equal status) was similarly promoted as a national dance in the 1960s by the Sukarno regime (Murgiyanto 1991: 53–54).[4] Nonetheless, attempts to create a single national cultural performance did not have any significant impact.

In spite of the plurality of the modern Indonesian nation-state, the long Javanese dominance in state political life made it possible for Javanese culture to receive more prominence than other regional cultures. In this regard, the "New Order" regime perpetuated a view of Java as a world of difference. The common use among Javanese political leaders of the adjective *adi luhung* (beautiful and glorious) (Sumarsam 1995) to legitimize the status of Javanese art and literature, and pointed references to the importance of *nilai-nilai traditional* (traditional values) and *warisan kebudayaan* (cultural inheritance) (Pemberton 1994) in discussing cultural development, have reinforced the retention of Java's world of difference. In one instance, the need for bureaucratic uniformity resulted in the use of the Javanese word *karawitan* (a word referring to gamelan or gamelan and its related arts) to name schools of traditional music both in and outside Java, thus adding to the feeling of Javacentrism and to the resentment of non-Javanese people. Another example of Javacentrism was the distribution of a number of Javanese gamelan to Indonesian embassies and consulates around the globe. In a few cases, the government even presented sets of gamelan instruments as gifts to selected Western institutions. For example, the Javanese gamelan set in Seattle was a gift from the mayor of Surabaya, as an appreciation for the formation of the Seattle Surabaya Sister City Association. The Indonesian government gave to the University of Montreal a set of Balinese gamelan after its use in the 1986 World Exposition in Vancouver (Catra 2002). The Javanese gamelan set from the same exposition was given to Simon Frazer University in Vancouver (ibid.). The New Order regime also gave scholarships to foreign students to study in Indonesia; many ended up studying gamelan in Yogyakarta and Surakarta.

All in all, colonial and contemporary political forces have directly or indirectly encouraged the spread of gamelan around the globe. It is worth noting, however, that other elements also contributed to the interest in gamelan in the West. The physical appearance of gamelan instruments, and especially the impressive carved and painted wooden frames and stands, is quite attractive to Western eyes.[5] Gamelan is also often described as the largest percussion ensemble in the world, so much so that nonpercussive instruments and singing, which often have important roles in the ensemble, are often deemphasized by Westerners. Gamelan enthusiasts do not seem to be bothered by the peculiarity of gamelan *sléndro/pélog* tuning systems, that is, their incompatibility with the Western diatonic tuning system. Perhaps these unique gamelan features have even made the music more attractive to Westerners.

It is commonly thought that the structure of the music makes gamelan suitable for musical education. Consisting of several melodic layers, each with a different density, gamelan has aptly been described as an ensemble with melodic stratification (Hood 1963b: 452). In general, the lower the register of an instrument, the lower its rhythmic density level and the simpler its playing technique. A common learning strategy is for beginning students to start learning instruments from the lower to middle strata of the ensemble, as they require less challenging playing techniques. Gradually, the student proceeds to the study of instruments in the higher strata, whose playing techniques and melodies are more complex and challenging.[6]

JAVANESE GAMELAN AND ETHNOMUSICOLOGY

In his discussion of small musical units (micromusics) within big music cultures, Slobin (1992: 72) proposed two types of ensembles: "*bands,* that is, performing units of professional or semi-professional musicians that play for the pleasure of paying customers, and *affinity groups,* charmed circles of like-minded music-makers drawn magnetically to a certain genre that creates strong expressive bonding." Furthermore, Slobin characterizes affinity groups as locating "themselves at a determined point and [perhaps even building] walls around their musical strongholds. They serve as nuclei for free-floating units of our social atmosphere, points of orientation for weary travelers looking for a cultural home" (ibid.: 73). Gamelan performing units in the West fall easily into this affinity group category, but the context of the rise of gamelan activity in the West deserves mention here. Usually micromusics develop in response to the needs of a local and/or diasporic community. In the case of gamelan performing ensembles in the United States, however, the community is academic, not Javanese.

The study of Indonesian music, particularly gamelan music, was directly linked to the initial development of ethnomusicology during the post–World War II period. This was largely thanks to Jaap Kunst, a musician/lawyer/musicologist/Dutch colonial civil administrator, who, after spending fifteen years in Indonesia, returned to Holland in the 1940s and began to promote the study of Indonesian music. Kunst contributed to the definition and development of a new academic discipline that he named "ethnomusicology." This new discipline spread and developed further in Europe, North America, and beyond. Kunst's American student, Mantle Hood, introduced gamelan studies in the United States. After completing his degree at the University of Amsterdam and carrying out postdoctoral research in Java, Hood established the Institute for Ethnomusicology at UCLA in the mid-1950s. Subsequently, graduates of UCLA's ethnomusicology program were responsible for the dissemination of gamelan study and the establishment of performing ensembles in many university ethnomusicology programs throughout the United States and abroad.

Since the 1970s, the benefits of the presence of gamelan in North America and Europe have been many: the increasing number of Western gamelan scholar-musicians, the "explosive" development of gamelan theory,[7] and the increasing body of new music written for gamelan by composers in North America and Europe. In light of these developments, it is worth reviewing the activity of performing gamelan ensembles in the West. As a practitioner and observer of gamelan study in the United States over the last three decades, I would like to offer my views on the study of gamelan in university ethnomusicology programs in the United States with special attention to gamelan in the World Music Program at Wesleyan University.

It is well known that in the 1960s, Mantle Hood advocated practical musical experience as a requirement for students of ethnomusicology; this led to the incorporation into the curriculum of non-Western performing ensembles. Hood referred to these ensembles as "performance-study groups"

(Hood 1960: 55). The mission of such groups was to facilitate the development of what he called "bimusicality." In this regard, Hood recognized the importance of requiring Western students of non-Western musics to acquire some practical experience of the music in question in order to better comprehend it (ibid.: 58). The active participation of one or more native teacher-musicians was an important component of the performance-study group. The native teacher-musician was not only a teacher or teaching assistant for the performing ensemble, but also a research resource. In return, native teacher-musicians were given the opportunity to enroll as students of ethnomusicology.

During this same period fieldwork and participant observation became vogues in ethnomusicology. That is, it was thought that a student must study the music in its home country, carrying out an intimate observation of the lives of musicians and people in a particular community and learning to play or sing the music he or she was studying.

In the 1960s and 1970s, a handful of universities established ethnomusicology programs incorporating performing ensembles such as gamelan. Perhaps because of economic, organizational, or administrative reasons, interest in the participation of native teacher-musicians was declining somewhat (Wesleyan and UCLA were notable exceptions, and see below for a new development in gamelan performing ensembles in the United States). Having more than one native teacher seemed to be a standard practice at UCLA and Wesleyan in those decades.[8] It seems that subsequently the difficulty of finding university funding made it impossible to invite even one native teacher, let alone to establish long-term residencies. Consequently, some universities occasionally sought outside funding for temporary residencies of native teachers.

A fundamental reason debated among ethnomusicologists is also worth mentioning here: some argue that having only one or two long-term non-Western performing ensembles would not give students enough exposure to the variety of musical traditions of the world. In order to achieve this goal, programs should rotate performing ensembles and musicians from different cultures. Thus, the idea of the long-term presence of a certain musical tradition in the program is not an option.

Some ethnomusicology programs, including the program at Wesleyan University, stood on the other side of the debate, preferring to support a long-term gamelan performing ensemble with or without the participation of native musicians. At Wesleyan, a modification of the native musician's position took place in 1976, when the temporary, part-time position of native teacher-musician (at that time called "visiting artist") was changed to a long-term, closer to full-time position with a new name: "artist-in-residence." I will return to this topic later.

It is safe to say that the presence of native musicians in a program inspires a certain kind of dynamic. In the first place, for Western students, joining a non-Western performing ensemble is

> an effort of the will to transcend one's physical and mental limitations. . . . The physical movements are not ones you grew up with. The relationship to the instruments—for example, the need to step around rather than over them as a sign of respect—automatically pushes you outside your cultural frame of reference. (Slobin 1996: 23)

The presence of a native musician in such ensembles may enhance students' experience of learning music outside their tradition.

I should point out that the native teacher who teaches abroad on a long-term basis is not only a passive transmitter of his or her musical tradition. In addition, as Slobin explains in defense of the long-term residency of native musician-teachers at Wesleyan,

> The teachers and their teaching methods blend Javanese and American ways of thinking and acting, at many levels. Under Wesleyan's program of long-term residence of instructors from other cultural backgrounds, the gamelan instructors have had long experience with inflecting their tradition in ways appropriate to the transmission of that tradition to American students. Several M.A. theses have been written at Wesleyan on the question of local teaching methods. The pedagogical means that have developed on this American campus are the fruit of thirty-five years of moving towards convivencia. The careers of Adjunct Professors of Music T. Viswanathan and Sumarsam exemplify the Wesleyan approach. Both grew up in very traditional communities (in India and Indonesia respectively), and came to America as "culture bearers" of foreign musical heritages. Over the decades, each has acquired an American Ph.D. degree and has evolved teaching methods appropriate to Wesleyan. Based firmly on the need for intense discipline and achieving a state of flow, these pedagogical approaches make use of small, flexible stages of development that move towards the students' feeling natural in an intercultural space of action and knowledge. (Ibid.)

I mentioned earlier the lack of interest in the residency of native gamelan teachers in ethnomusicology programs in the United States. This does not mean that the interest in gamelan performing ensembles is in decline, however. On the contrary, in the late 1970s and the 1980s, the number of gamelan performing ensembles increased.[9] This is because many students who were originally exposed to gamelan during their college years have continued to be involved in or to form their own gamelan performing ensembles. Secondly, a number of ethnomusicology graduate students specializing in Indonesian music have gotten teaching positions in colleges (for many of these students, fieldwork and participant observation have borne much fruit). In turn, they have maintained their interest in Indonesian gamelan, for example, by instituting gamelan performing ensembles and incorporating the teaching of gamelan music into their programs. Gamelan teaching in Java and its transformation in the United States will be the focus of the remainder of my discussion.

GAMELAN LEARNING IN JAVA

When Europeans introduced notation for Javanese music in the 1870s, they assumed that each Javanese song had one correct standard melody. "But Javanese teachers cannot use notation," one complained, "thus Javanese teachers teach their students without pre-existing standard sound [melodies]" (*Layang Wuwulang Nut* 1874). Relative to the publication of notations of Javanese songs, he goes on to say, "That is why [songs are] always incorrectly sung, since they teach aurally. And [each teacher] has his own melody. If this teaching method continues, the publication of [the notation] of *Sekar Kawi* songs will be useless, and there will be many different melodies for each song; the correct melody will not be known" (ibid.).

The above quotation reflects the late-nineteenth-century perception of the power of printing technology and Western scientific method, not to mention the author's lack of understanding about the art of variation in Javanese song. What can be written down is scientific and can be codified and objectified. Certainly this view alters the perspective of a tradition that depends on aural transmission. Nonetheless, the impact of modern ideology and technology on the modern Indonesian nation-state was inevitable. The ideal aural transmission of gamelan cannot be kept separate from the influence of print technology. The question is, how far and in what way has print technology penetrated into the fabric of the gamelan tradition?

Traditionally, when someone, often a very young child, wanted to become a gamelan player, he would have to spend much time listening to and observing gamelan playing.[10] He would observe how the mallets are handled and how the keys are damped. He could choose any instrument that fascinated him (though usually not soft-sounding, elaborating instruments, whose playing technique and melodies cannot be learned in a brief encounter). When ready to play, he would try to reconstruct melodies on his instrument as well as he could. If he had difficulty, he would imitate or listen to other players' parts in order to approximate his own part. His skills reinforced by endless listening to and observing gamelan performances, he would ultimately become a musician.

My early experience in learning gamelan reflects this traditional process. As a six-year-old village boy, I used to get together with my friends to play gamelan at the neighbor's house across the street from my house. A small *sléndro* iron gamelan, a type commonly found in small villages in East Java, provided enough excitement for us to play a number of short pieces such as "Puspa Warna" and "Srepegan." Occasionally, one or two professional musicians in the village dropped by to give us guidance. A year later, I found myself informally joining a professional village gamelan group. It happened when I watched an all-night *wayang* (shadow puppet) performance. A *saron* (a metallophone played with a single beater) player was too tired to play and was sleeping with his head resting on the *saron*'s keys. Noticing that the *saron* should be played to accompany the next scene, the *kendhang* (drum) player asked the *saron* player to go for a walk and invited me to play the unoccupied instrument. It was fortunate for me that I knew some of the *gendhing* (gamelan composition) being played. But even if I did not know the piece well, I could still approximate my part by imitating or listening to other instruments. After that first performance, the group often asked me to play with them. The head of the musicians even paid me. Most likely I was paid much less than other members, because I was only a child. But as a seven-year-old boy, I was happy for the opportunity to play music, regardless of how much money I received.

During my teenage years, academic success became the top priority in my life, since I felt that academically I was not a strong student. Thus, I played gamelan only occasionally. In fact, in the last year of junior high school, I did not play gamelan at all. I was able to pass my final junior examination with impressive grades, even though it took me an extra year to complete junior high. Perhaps being away from gamelan had something to do with my academic success. To celebrate the completion of junior high, I joined a commercial *kethoprak* troupe, which performed a form of professional folk dance drama whose stage and auditorium are modeled after the European proscenium stage. I played gamelan almost every night for a whole month. Mostly I played *slenthem* (a metallophone with a single beater) and *bonang* (a set of two-row *gong*s with two beaters). It was in this *kethoprak* troupe that I was able to build my *gendhing* repertoire, because every night the musicians had to play a different piece to accompany the *gambyong* dance (a group female dance performed as an introduction to the play). My *kethoprak* experience ended when the troupe completed its run in my village, which coincided with my departure in 1961 to Surakarta to begin formal gamelan training at the gamelan conservatory (Konservatori Karawitan Indonesia, or KOKAR, now SMKI, or Sekolah Menengah Karawitan Indonesia).

In my village gamelan tradition, *bonang* and *gambang* (xylophone) were the only two elaborating instruments present in the ensemble (for a general description of gamelan instrument functions, see below). I learned other elaborating instruments, especially *gendèr* and *rebab* (two-stringed bowed instrument), when I began formal study at the conservatory. Because of the complex melodies played on these instruments and their demanding playing techniques, learning these soft-sounding, elaborating instruments takes longer than learning the simpler instruments. Let us consider learning the *gendèr* (a metallophone played with two padded mallets) as an example. In the first place, the *gendèr* student would usually already know how to play other instruments, for example, *saron, gong* (large hanging *gong*), *kempul* (small hanging *gong*s), *kenong* (a large standing *gong*), *kethuk-kempyang* (a pair of small standing *gong*s), or *bonang*. Therefore, his initial observation of *gendèr* playing is done while he is simultaneously playing another instrument. Sometimes he might also listen in particular to the *gendèr* in gamelan concerts. Eventually, when this future *gendèr* player feels ready to try to play *gendèr* for a short composition, he tries to play as much as he can, or as much as he can remember, approximating what he has heard and observed. If in some sections of a composition he really does not know what to do, he might try to reconstruct the part as well as he can. An experienced *gendèr* player might occasionally correct him if he makes mistakes or does not know a particular section of a composition. The experienced player could correct him by singing the vocal melody of the phrase that the inexperienced player cannot figure out. These vocal parts usually have exciting melodies and are given attractive names such as *ayu kuning* ("pretty yellow," meaning a pretty, light-skinned girl) or *jarik kawung* (a batik cloth of *kawung* design). Unfortunately, not all phrases used in *gendèr* playing have vocal melodies related to them, nor does every phrase have a name, and the names in use are far from standardized. Thus, the experienced *gendèr* player cannot always help the inexperienced one: he can do so only if the phrase that is troubling the inexperienced player can be sung or has a name. Even this guidance is given only offhandedly. Therefore, the success of the future *gendèr* player will depend on his independent study. In addition, his experience in playing other instruments will help him understand the relationship between the *gendèr* and the rest of the ensemble. Gradually, he will also feel that the melodies of other instruments in the ensemble guide his *gendèr* playing or remind him of the proper *gendèr* melody.

Notation, from the time of its introduction in the mid-nineteenth century to the beginning of the twentieth century, was used mostly for documenting the music; it was only minimally used for learning the music. Out of a handful of experimental notations, cipher notation gained the widest use. The use of notation for learning gamelan became increasingly common in the mid-twentieth century. A handful of books containing notation of *balungan* (the melodic "skeleton") of *gendhing* became accessible throughout Java. Known in Central Java (especially in Surakarta) as *kepatihan* notation, it was used extensively for teaching gamelan and vocal music at the government-sponsored gamelan conservatories and academies.

The most commonly used notation at such gamelan schools then and now is notation for *balungan* of *gendhing*. Typically, gamelan ensemble class starts with one of the teachers writing down the *balungan* notation on a blackboard. After a brief explanation of the use of notation, the sequencing of the *gendhing*'s sections, and the playing techniques of particular instruments, one teacher guides the students in playing the piece by pointing at the *balungan* notation written on the blackboard. Another teacher assists *bonang* and *kendhang* students. If the piece requires the playing of elaborating instruments, especially the *rebab* or *gendèr*, students may use notation written in their notebooks, notations given for the particular instrument in classes designed for individual instruction (see below).

Notation is also used to teach elaborating and leading instruments, especially *rebab*, *gendèr*, and *kendhang*. Each of these instruments is taught in a class for individual instruction. Other elaborating instruments, for example the *gambang*, *suling* (a bamboo flute), *gendèr panerus*, and *celempung* (a plucked-zither-like instrument), are not taught in either ensemble or individual instruction (see below). These instruments are considered less essential, dispensable elaborating instruments that interested students may learn on their own time. In any event, the nontraditional instruction at the conservatory required gamelan teachers to create a new method of teaching appropriate to a classroom setting. I will discuss briefly the teaching method of *rebab* and *gendèr* at the conservatory.

In a class of individual instruction on *rebab,* three teachers are present. The classroom has several *rebab,* a set of *gendèr*, and a set of *kendhang.* For the beginning *rebab* students, the class begins with a teacher explaining how to play the *rebab* (for example, how to hold the instrument and bow, certain finger positions, and the use of notation). This is followed by the playing of a short melodic passage, the notation of which is written on the blackboard. During this time, the teachers make necessary corrections, for example in the accuracy of intonation, the position of fingers, and the direction of the bow. Eventually, students play the piece in its entirety, guided by notation for the whole piece. One teacher guides the whole class by pointing to the notation on the blackboard or moving around, making necessary physical corrections for each student. The other teachers accompany on *gendèr* and *kendhang.*

The same process operates in classes of individual instruction on *gendèr.* The classroom has a dozen or more *gendèr*, a *rebab,* and a set of *kendhang.* After explaining and demonstrating technical matters such as how to hold the mallets, damping techniques, and the use of notation, a teacher writes down a *gendèr* melodic pattern and teaches students to play it. The teacher then introduces and teaches other patterns. When enough patterns have been introduced for the entire piece, the teacher writes down a sequence of patterns that constitute the *gendèr* part for an entire piece. Then students play the patterns together, while two teachers accompany on *rebab* and *kendhang;* the lead teacher makes necessary corrections.

In the past, each *gendèr* pattern was identified with a letter (S L T M N G P), taken either from the Javanese name for the ending note of the pattern *(sèlèh)* or from the name of the pattern itself. For example, a pattern ending on pitch one *(siji)* is identified as S, a pattern ending on pitch two *(loro)* as L, G for *gantungan* (sustained note) pattern, etc. This form of naming patterns was proposed by the *gendèr* teacher Pandji Sutopinilih, familiarly known as Pak Pandji.

Subsequently, R. L. Martopangrawit (known as Pak Marto) developed another method of teaching *gendèr* when he was appointed gamelan teacher at the gamelan academy in Surakarta in 1965. To identify each *gendèr* pattern, Pak Marto used names associated with vocal parts of the piece. As I mentioned earlier, this way of naming *gendèr* patterns is based on a traditional learning practice, although not all phrases used in *gendèr* playing have vocal melodies related to them, nor does every phrase have a name. This limitation led Pak Marto to expand the system of naming and classifying *gendèr* patterns.

In any event, the methods of *gendèr* teaching described above are one solution for teaching a group of students to play a single elaborating instrument, that is, by fragmenting the *gendèr* melodies. It is a reasonable way of teaching the *gendèr,* considering the difficulty of the playing technique that requires the player to coordinate two hands, each playing an independent melody and each damping the keys. However, a new method for teaching *gendèr* has developed that classifies the instrument's melodic phrases. Students who learn *gendèr* (and also *rebab,* for that matter) at the conservatory have an advantage: when students play the entire piece on *gendèr,* other instruments *(rebab* and *kendhang)* are played with them, hence, a sense of ensemble prevails.

No one has undertaken an extended examination of the impact of using notation on the music and musicians using it.[11] I should point out that not all conservatory graduates become accomplished *gendèr, rebab,* or *kendhang* players, in spite of the requirement that they must learn all elaborating instruments. Those students who do become accomplished players rarely use notation in performance. However, it is common for a student to own a small notebook containing hundreds of handwritten *balungan* notations and, when the situation demands it (for example, members of the group want to play a rarely performed, structurally expansive *gendhing*), the student may occasionally need to consult the notebook.[12]

For the most part, I have had personal experience learning and teaching music both at gamelan schools and outside the formal classroom. As I mentioned earlier, I started gamelan training at KOKAR in 1961, but my previous village musical experience helped make my gamelan lessons much easier. I already knew not only the basics of gamelan, but also a certain number of *gendhing.* Playing *pélog* gamelan and learning the *gendèr* and *rebab,* however, were new to me, since these instruments were not found in my village. In learning *kendhang* I also had to make a major adjustment. In my East Javanese village gamelan tradition, the drum's large head was played by the left hand, the small head by the right hand; the opposite is the case in the

Central Javanese gamelan tradition. In spite of the necessity of making this adjustment, *kendhang* became one of my favorite instruments. I also focused my study on *gendèr*. Like other students, I began my *gendèr* lessons following Pak Pandji's "letter pattern" teaching method. By my second year, I was able to learn *gendèr* and other elaborating instruments (as well as *kendhang*) without notation, except for consulting the *balungan* notation whenever we learned a new *gendhing*.

Extracurricular gamelan activity also had a strong impact on the development of my musicianship. At the end of my first year at KOKAR, I discovered some students with a musical background like mine; some were already advanced gamelan players. We became close friends and formed a gamelan group that performed outside the school, with or without pay. In other words, for our group, learning activities were not limited to the classroom at the gamelan conservatory. In fact, these extracurricular gamelan activities were crucial to the development of my musicianship and the formation of my *gendhing* repertoire. In this regard, Sutton rightly points out that "learning *karawitan* relies now, as it has in the past, very heavily on individual initiative outside of any 'class' or 'lesson' context" (Sutton 1992: 17). The success of my study of gamelan performance and my modest academic achievement earned me the rank of second-best graduating student from KOKAR in 1964. As a reward, I received a tie from the director of KOKAR. My first teaching job was at the Kasatriyan junior high school, a private school originally founded by the Kasunanan court of Surakarta. In the following year, KOKAR appointed me as a full-time teacher, teaching individual lessons on *kendhang,* in a gamelan ensemble class of Solonese and Yogyanese style. A year later, I was also assigned to teach a course on the theory of gamelan playing to first-year students.

Coincidentally, in the year of my appointment as a gamelan teacher at KOKAR, a college-level gamelan school, Akademi Seni Karawitan Indonesia (Gamelan Academy of Indonesia), or ASKI, now Sekolah Tinggi Seni Indonesia (Indonesian Institute of the Arts), or STSI, was founded. I was one of the first students to enroll in ASKI. Many of my teachers at KOKAR also entered ASKI; they became my classmates. In addition to being a student, in 1966 I was appointed *asisten dosen,* assisting Pak Marto to teach gamelan performing ensemble and knowledge of gamelan to first-year students.

At that time, ASKI students had the choice of majoring in either performance *(kesenian)* or scholarly research *(keilmuan)*. I choose the *kesenian* major. After three years of course work, the final requirement for the *kesenian* major was to compose two *gendhing* (one in each tuning system) and to write a brief essay about them. I composed *gendhing Panggayuh* (Aspiration) in *pélog Nem* and *gendhing Wulan Sih* (Moon and Love) in *sléndro Nem*. For my essay, I wrote on aspects of performance practice of my *gendhing*. The final examination had two parts: performing my *gendhing* and an oral exam. I graduated from ASKI in 1968.

Another activity in which many students and faculty of KOKAR and ASKI hoped to participate was government cultural missions abroad. Such missions involved sending a performing group, usually comprising performing artists from a number of different ethnic groups, to perform abroad. In the mid-1960s, I was selected for two cultural missions, but both of them were canceled because of the 1965 political turmoil in Indonesia. In 1970, however, I did participate in a seven-month cultural mission to the World Exposition in Osaka, Japan. On our way back to Indonesia, we performed in Manila for a week.

After returning from my first experience of performing abroad, I spent a year in Solo, resuming my post at KOKAR and being both a student and assistant lecturer at ASKI. In 1971, the Indonesian Department of Foreign Affairs invited me to teach gamelan at the Indonesian embassy in Canberra, Australia. The procedure for getting a leave of absence from the Department of Education and Culture (the department that included KOKAR) was unclear and led me to resign my post as a government employee. Although my job at the Indonesian embassy did not give me enough stimulation in my gamelan activity and intellectual development, I gained invaluable experience from teaching Indonesian employees and their wives and local Australian junior high school students. A timely invitation to teach at Wesleyan University came in 1972. This came about through personal rather than institutional connections. Some Wesleyan graduate students had noticed my teaching experience in Solo. In addition, a handful of American students, including Martin Hatch, a recent M.A. graduate of Wesleyan, had studied gamelan with me in Solo in 1970. In August 1972, I left my job at the Indonesian embassy in Australia and came to Wesleyan.

GAMELAN AT WESLEYAN UNIVERSITY

No comprehensive study of teaching and learning gamelan in the West exists.[13] The following discussion will be limited to the gamelan program at Wesleyan University. I hasten to add that it is not my intention to boast about the program with which I have long been associated. I hope, however, to show what we can learn by examining the long-term existence of a non-Western performing ensemble in one American institution of higher education.

At the outset, I should mention two general points. The first regards the status of gamelan performance in ethnomusicology curricula in the United States. Each university places gamelan class (and all music performance classes, for that matter) in one of the following categories: 1) an extracurricular activity for which students do not get grades; 2) a course for which students can receive partial credit; 3) a course for which students receive full credit if it is taken in conjunction with another, academic class related to gamelan; or 4) a course for which students receive full credit when taken alone (Wesleyan follows this last model).

Second, to some degree gamelan teaching in the United States is an adaptation of modern gamelan teaching in Java. This means that cipher notation is commonly used and individual lessons on elaborating instruments or singing are offered if the teacher is capable of teaching them. I have observed, however, that the absence of a gamelan teacher, or the limited time a teacher can be provided for the students, tends to encourage greater use of notation.

When I started teaching at Wesleyan University in 1972, the gamelan program there had existed for almost a decade. Wesleyan's World Music Program traced its beginnings to liberalism embraced by the university's president Victor Butterfield, who in the 1960s challenged departments to search for new pedagogical visions (Slobin 1996).[14] The gamelan program was founded in 1962, under the direction of Robert Brown, a recent graduate of the UCLA ethnomusicology program. The program used a small iron village gamelan lent by the late Harrison Parker, then a USAID employee stationed in Jakarta, and a patron of Javanese gamelan and dance. In 1964, the university bought from the Indonesian government a complete gamelan displayed at the 1964 New York World's Fair. After 1964, several visiting artists were invited to teach and perform at the university. These included dancers (Theresia Suharti, Soedarsono, and Ben Suharto), a musician (Prawoto Saputro), lecturers (Surya Brata and [now] Dr. R.M. Soedarsono), and a *dhalang* (puppeteer) (Ki Oemartopo).

On my arrival at Wesleyan, I learned that in 1971 a change in faculty had taken place. Robert Brown, one of the founders of the Wesleyan World Music Program, who had been responsible for supervising gamelan and other non-Western music performing classes, had left for the California Institute of the Arts in Valencia, and later for a more ambitious program at the American Society for Eastern Arts (ASEA). A number of Wesleyan gamelan students had gone with him, which meant that when I arrived, there was no ethnomusicologist whose area of study related to Indonesia. With the help of a handful of previous gamelan students, I had to figure out how to teach my gamelan class.

Initially, I taught gamelan in the same way I had taught at the conservatory in Solo, where each student had to learn all the instruments, because the conservatory graduates were themselves training to become gamelan teachers. I soon realized, however, that requiring each student at Wesleyan to learn all the gamelan instruments was a very slow process and was educationally unnecessary. Since then, we have had no fixed requirement specifying how many instruments a student must learn beyond at least two instruments from two different instrumental groups. In addition, students who want to learn elaborating instruments or *pesindhèn* (female vocal soloist) singing are taught individually; each is given a weekly one-hour lesson and is expected to find extra time to practice individually.

In my first year at Wesleyan there was only one gamelan class, consisting of about fourteen students. The class always consisted of a mixture of advanced and new students. This condition created a close working relationship among themselves: the advanced students gave guidance to the new students and helped me familiarize myself with evaluation procedures. Like all performance courses at the time, the class employed the pass/fail system. Instead of receiving a letter grade, students received written evaluation noting their ability and the progress they had made on their instrument(s).

At the end of each semester, a performance was given. Gamelan students themselves organized and handled the publicity for these performances. As the performance approached, extra rehearsals and individual lessons were to be expected. In addition, a kind of *slametan* (ritual meal) was prepared before the performance, a practice that was established by the previous gamelan teacher. In this *slametan*, the preparation of the food often fell on the shoulders of the gamelan teacher's wife. In other institutions, Indonesians who happen to be in residence often help with this task. For logistical reasons, the Wesleyan *slametan* has changed over the years, from Indonesian food prepared by the teacher's family, to a potluck, and finally to simply ordering food from a local Chinese restaurant.

In 1973, with the completion of the Center for the Arts (CFA) complex, a major organizational change took place. The performing activities of four departments (art, dance, music, and theater) were centralized in the CFA building complex and were professionally administered by the CFA administration. At this time, the gamelan was allocated its own permanent building, called the World Music Hall. The gamelan stage consists of three graduated tiers, a nontraditional design that ensures that the gamelan instruments are attractively displayed but causes a bit of a problem in hearing each other play.[15] In order to minimize the difficulty of hearing each other play during both teaching and performing, I requested that the first tier be extended, adding more space for other instruments. (The request was granted.) In addition, a temporary riser for *kendhang* was added in the back center of that tier, positioning the drum higher than other instruments; hence, the drum can be heard better by players in the second and third tiers. In front of the gamelan stage is an area for dancers or other performers. For nongamelan events, a large screen can cover the gamelan stage. The audience sits crosslegged on the carpeted floor of several tiers at the opposite end of the hall.

The number of students enrolled in gamelan classes has increased steadily. To accommodate these students, we now have advanced and beginning classes. To cope with the changes in class size, the grading system was modified. With an average of forty students per semester, it became too difficult to track each student's progress in the class, and writing evaluations for each student became an overwhelming task. To resolve this problem, a mixed grading system was offered: students could choose between a pass/fail option and a letter grade. Most students choose the latter.

The increased enrollment also brought about the appointment of a second gamelan teacher, I. M. Harjito, who filled the position from 1974 to 1976. He was my classmate at both KOKAR and ASKI. Between 1976 and 1983, my teacher from KOKAR, R. M. Sukanto Sastrodarsono (familiarly known as Pak Kanto), filled the position. Upon Pak Kanto's return to Indonesia, the music department invited I. M. Harjito back in 1984.

Two years of academic exposure at Wesleyan and close relationships with a number of my students had an impact on my own intellectual development. In 1974, I enrolled in the master of arts program in world music at Wesleyan, while teaching gamelan. I was able to complete my degree in 1976. I remember vividly the daunting task of writing my thesis. I felt that Western scholars had written so much about gamelan that I could only ask myself what else could I write, and I faced the difficulty of writing the thesis in English. In any event, with a lot of help from my advisor, my colleagues, and my students, I was able to write a thesis entitled "Inner Melody in Javanese Gamelan." Harold Powers (1996: 9, n. 12) later accurately described this thesis as my most distinctive personal contribution to Javanese theory. It grew out of many questions my students asked me and discussions I had with them on the structure of gamelan *gendhing*. Part of the thinking behind the thesis also came from my collaborative work with Vincent McDermott, a composer and one of the Americans I had taught in Solo in 1971. We wrote about some aspects of gamelan modal practice *(pathet)* as seen in *gendèr* playing (McDermott and Sumarsam 1975). (To be honest, he did most of the writing; I only supplied the ideas.) We also touched on the question of the "true" *balungan* (melodic skeleton) of *gendhing*, which became the point of departure for my thesis.

In the mid-1970s, the Wesleyan music department, with its progressive graduate students, had a series of discussions on the nature of the World Music Program. The discussions included an attempt to improve the status of visiting artists. As a result, the artists' contracts were changed from a part-time, annually renewed position to a multiple-year contract, closer to full-time status. The name of the position was also changed, from "visiting artist" to "artist-in-residence."

This change in status brought about an improvement in benefits, including eligibility for sabbaticals. I took my first sabbatical after my sixth year of teaching. I used the one-year sabbatical to begin the doctoral program at Cornell University in 1983. Beginning my pursuit of the highest academic degree was not an easy decision in light of my age (I was in my late thirties). Under the umbrella of ethnomusicology, my program consisted of courses in music and Southeast Asian Studies. I completed the course work in three semesters and two summers. In the spring semester of 1985 I returned to teaching at Wesleyan. During my second sabbatical, the summer and fall semester of 1987, I returned to Cornell to research and write my dissertation. Under the guidance of Professors Martin Hatch, William Austin, and Benedict Anderson, I completed and defended my dissertation, "Historical Contexts and Theories of Javanese Music," in the fall of 1991. In 1995, the University of Chicago Press published my dissertation with minor revisions under the title *Gamelan: Cultural Interaction and Musical Development in Central Java.*

While I was working on my dissertation, the reevaluation and discussion of the aims and definition of Wesleyan's World Music Program resumed in the 1980s. This coincided with a required evaluation of the department's graduate program by a team of external experts. In the course of this assessment, matters relating to the duty and position of the artists-in-residence were discussed. It was noted that a few artists carried out work beyond teaching music performance. To remedy this situation, an adjunct professor position was established;[16] artist-in-residence positions could now be converted into adjunct professorships. In addition to teaching ensembles, adjunct professors are also responsible for classroom teaching, for departmental and university administrative work, for serving as major advisors, and for carrying out research (though the result of such research is not necessarily subject to formal evaluation). In practice, these criteria are a guide rather than a requirement.

In 1987, a number of artists-in-residence became adjunct professors. My junior status in terms of age and length of stay at Wesleyan earned me the rank of adjunct associate professor. After I received my doctoral degree in 1992, however, my status was upgraded to that of adjunct professor. It is a privilege for me to have obtained such a special status. As far as I know, Wesleyan is the only place where an adjunct professorship was created to accommodate the status of performing artists and was available to non-Western performing artists.[17]

It is worth noting that the search for a suitable format and content for our gamelan class has been an ongoing process over the many years of my tenure at Wesleyan. Essentially, the spirit of the "performance-study group" conceived at UCLA, which I mentioned earlier, has been maintained. It is worth mentioning that the term *study group* was commonly used in the 1960s at Wesleyan.

Having two gamelan teachers and one or two graduate assistants running a gamelan class is certainly an advantage in teaching a large gamelan ensemble.[18] The increased individual attention makes it possible to start teaching students challenging pieces sooner. Instead of starting with a piece in a short *gongan* structure, such as the sixteen-beat *lancaran* (for example, *lancaran Ricik-Ricik,* a standard piece for beginning gamelan), the beginning class starts with a piece in the thirty-two-beat *ladrang gongan* structure. As much as possible, the teaching begins without notation, making sure that students focus their attention on familiarizing themselves with gamelan sound and tuning. When students begin to have a hard time remembering the piece, then notation is introduced.

Typically, the class begins with the teaching and demonstrating of each group of instruments. (Gamelan instruments can generally be categorized into different groups according to their functions. The interplay between the instruments' register and their density levels may define their functions.) The instruction begins with the first group of instruments (all *gong*s), whose function is to delineate the formal structure *(gongan)* of *gendhing: gong, kenong, kempul,* and *kethuk-kempyang.* These instruments play the lowest density level in the ensemble. The second group (*slenthem, demung,* and *saron,* all metallophones) comprises instruments that play *balungan* within their limited octave range, playing in medium level of rhythmic density. The elaborating instruments comprise the next group (that is, horizontal *gongs bonang barung* and *bonang panerus,* and *peking*), playing a high level of density. *Kendhang* (drum), whose function is to supervise the temporal aspect of *gendhing,* is the last instrument to be explained. By the end of the class, the students should (hopefully) have a basic understanding of how a gamelan piece is put together.

Reading and listening also became an integral part of class assignments, as well as a midterm exam and a brief report at the end of the semester. Typically the report consists of the student's experience in his or her semester of gamelan learning. These assignments are another way to track students' progress in the basic understanding of gamelan, although class participation in music making is the primary factor in evaluating the students' work. Most of the time, discussion is held at the same time as teaching students to play. Occasionally, a class is devoted to discussion or to the showing of documentary films on gamelan and other related arts. Although the beginning class is not geared toward formal performance, the class's final assignment consists of an informal presentation in which the class performs two pieces: a welcoming piece and a piece for accompanying the beginning Javanese dance class. To widen their experience in performance, the beginning class often plays a piece or two in a performance given by the advanced group.

The advanced gamelan group operates with different expectations. The group, which meets twice a week for four hours, is oriented toward performance. Students who have taken the beginning class may join the advanced group. Graduate students in music and music majors may join the advanced group without taking the beginning class only if they cannot take beginning class because of a scheduling conflict. Many students also stay in the class for several semesters. A few spaces are available for Wesleyan faculty and staff and members of the Middletown community and its vicinity.

One of the challenges in teaching gamelan in the United States is maintaining enough students to play the elaborating instruments and to sing *pesindhèn* (female solo). Most of the time, this need is fulfilled by a handful of ethnomusicology graduate students concentrating on Indonesian music. In some cases, other ethnomusicology graduate students with a strong interest in playing the elaborating instruments regardless of their area of studies (or graduate students in composition or undergraduate music majors) also help out. In any event, any student may learn to play the elaborating instruments as long as he or she has time for an individual lesson on the instrument in question (one hour per week) and extra time to practice.

Even with this kind of effort, there is no guarantee that the group will have enough players of elaborating instruments at the end of the semester when they are needed for a performance; one semester is not always enough time for a student to master his or her instrument. To fill the need for players for elaborating instrument for concerts, the group invites gamelan teachers from other universities. The network of gamelan teacher-players is an important aspect of university-affiliated gamelan activity in the United States.

One of the goals of gamelan study is to expose students to wider aspects of gamelan music. This includes introducing students to other art forms related to gamelan, especially *wayang* and dance. This goal is dependent on the availability of resources in the institution. Fortunately, since the beginning of its gamelan program, Wesleyan has had a part-time slot for a Javanese dance teacher.[19] Also since the beginning of the program, Wesleyan has had a complete set of *wayang* puppets and stage equipment.[20] With the availability of these resources, the gamelan program can routinely offer not only music, but also musical accompaniment for dance and *wayang*.

I should mention another gamelan activity at Wesleyan. Once a month on Saturday there is a *klenèngan* (gamelan "jam session") held at Wesleyan. The event was initiated in the mid-1970s by a former artist-in-residence, the late Pak Kanto, and his advanced students. They got together periodically to play pieces beyond the repertoire taught in regular classes. After Pak Kanto's retirement, the *klenèngan* continued under the direction of Mr. Harjito. In its present form, the *klenèngan* is attended mostly by advanced players from the New England area (a number of them former Wesleyan gamelan students), although it is open to any gamelan enthusiast.

It seems obvious from the foregoing discussion that opportunity and interaction on many different levels are key to the gamelan journey, experience, and learning in both Java and the West. We learn that colonialism was responsible for the early introduction of gamelan in the West through early world expositions, such as the 1889 Paris Exposition and the 1893 Chicago Columbian Exhibition. Moreover, the interaction between the Javanese and European colonial culture brought about the articulation of Java as world of difference in its arts and literature. This led to the opportunity for gamelan to be heard and studied in Western countries, first in Europe, and then in the United States and beyond. Colonialism also influenced the introduction of gamelan notation and helped change the perspective of the Javanese elite toward their music in accordance with the notion of "high art" in European culture.

To Indonesians, interaction with European colonial culture resulted in the Indonesian national movement and, in the 1940s, Indonesian independence. This nationalism in turn brought about the institutionalization of government-sponsored gamelan schools and academies in Central Java in the 1950s and later in West Java, Bali, and other regions. The presence of the Western-style gamelan conservatory strengthened the use of notation for learning the music. Although it is true that in gamelan schools notation plays an important role for learning and analysis, I have also observed that a mixture of aural and written learning tends to produce more successful students.

Government-sponsored gamelan schools have also played an important role in facilitating the continuing interaction between Western scholars and their Indonesian colleagues, an interaction that started during the colonial period. As part of the development of ethnomusicology, this interaction has resulted in the incorporation of gamelan in many university and college curricula in the United States and beyond. The commonly required "field study" for students in ethnomusicology, with an emphasis on "participant observation," has created Western ethnomusicologists capable of performing and teaching the musics they study; some of them have even become accomplished musicians.

It is safe to say that the majority of Indonesian gamelan teachers who land teaching positions abroad were educated at gamelan conservatories and/or gamelan academies. This has lead to the adoption of modern gamelan conservatory teaching methods, with some adaptation, at institutions in the West. In particular, the use of notation is almost universal. The opportunity to study ethnomusicology in the West is also available to some Indonesian students and faculty. Mutual exchanges between Javanese gamelan theorists and their Western colleagues have brought about more active gamelan performing ensembles abroad and rigorous development of gamelan theory. They have also had a measure of influence in shaping ethnomusicological study in Indonesian art institutions.

Opportunity and interaction also brought me, born and raised in a small village in East Java, to the regional, national, and transnational world of gamelan. The opportunity to play with a professional group in my village, to play music for commercial *kethoprak* dance drama, and to experience modern school systems in Java and the United States have shaped my life as a gamelan musician, teacher, and thinker. Anyone who believes in musical inheritance will be disappointed to find out that so far I have not been able to discover my own musical ancestry. My late father was a cow cart driver, and later the chief of our village; he disappeared during the Indonesian revolution. As far as I know, my great-grandfather was a farmer with a special devotion to the Javanized form of Islam. My recent attempts to trace my musical ancestry have yielded an interesting story that I like, although I cannot confirm it: it is said that my ancestors, who came from the town of Kediri in East Java, had to flee from warfare. Disguised as street musicians, they played gamelan along the north coast of Java. I like this story not because of its truth, but because of its fictional qualities. In any event, the development of my musicianship and my career can only be explained in terms of the opportunity for me to advance and my interaction with others.

For me, to be a card-carrying member of the Society for Ethnomusicology (SEM) means to have ample opportunity to advance my intellectual development so as to interact with other like-minded scholars. I was in the audience at a panel discussion on "the 'ethno' ensembles" at the 1999 annual meeting of the SEM. At the end of the day, the chair of the panel approached me and, on behalf of the panel, invited me to write an essay on the topic the panel had just presented, to be included in the present publication. I am grateful for this opportunity to tell my story.

AFTERWORD

I would like to tell a story that Richard Winslow recounted in his talk for a gathering of Wesleyan alumni in 1994. As a young student at Juilliard School of Music, he always had reservations about his music teachers' use of the term *masterpiece* to refer to musical works by European composers such as Brahms, Beethoven, and Bach. "What about other cultures? Don't they also have masterpieces?" he pondered. His question was given an immediate answer after he attended the performance of Balinese music and dance by a group from Peliatan, Bali, in New York in 1952. To him the Balinese music he saw and heard earned the description of "masterpiece" as much as the works of Brahms, Beethoven, and Bach. He was convinced that there must be many other masterpieces around the globe.

Winslow was instrumental in almost all aspects of the development of Wesleyan's World Music Program: developing the curriculum, raising funds, hiring, and buying a Javanese gamelan set from the Indonesian representative to the 1964 New York World's Fair. In justifying the proposal for a grad-

uate program in ethnomusicology, he explained that the reasons for studying non-European music are no different from those of other disciplines:
"There's wisdom in 'them thar hills,' there are neighbors to know, there are
great cultural systems and there is beauty. There are answers to known questions and there are new questions" (Winslow [1967]: 4). He was also very
much aware that modern communication, transportation, and technology
have made it possible for Westerners to see that "music from other cultures
is not only interesting, but often dazzling and sometimes built on structural
concepts which make western musicians, such as Debussy, catch their breath
in wonder. And all this art is a form of ready access to a cultural viewpoint.
Should not this access be welcomed?" (ibid.: 5).

His vision of the melting down of East and West, "foreign" and "native,"
deserves full mention here.

> Fundamental to the question of the wisdom of teaching "foreign" music is
> probably the question of what happens to "our" music. (It could possibly give
> one a jolt to realize that what is meant by "our" classical music is mostly Aus-
> trian, German, French, Italian and Russian. There is very little American
> music implied.) Actually what is happening, I believe, is that our traditional
> music study and performance is being strengthened at Wesleyan. . . . We con-
> tinue to teach everything that was taught before; we have, in fact, added to the
> department rather than replace elements of the department. . . .
>
> Which brings me again to the concept of *World Music* when compared with
> *Ethnic Music*. We would like to allow the feeling of *native vs. foreign* to wither
> away. (Is the reader amused or irritated to realize that he is "ethnic" when
> viewed by a foreigner?) Even that poet laureate of Empire, Rudyard Kipling,
> foresaw such a desirable breakdown of oppositions: His famous phrase about
> east and west, "never the twain shall meet," is taken out of context, for the
> poem goes on to speak of a final merging of east and west. The modern world,
> whether we like it or not, is a physical unit. (Ibid.: 5–6)

It should be mentioned that Winslow's collaborations with David McAllester,
who offered a course on non-Western music in the psychology department
long before the World Music Program was instituted, and with Robert Brown
were fundamental to the early development of the program. For Winslow
himself, the opportunity to hear and watch Balinese music in New York, the
opportunity to respond to President Butterfield's challenge for creative pedagogical vision, his interaction with fellow musicologists and ethnomusicologists, and his views of modernity all sparked his vision and the formation of
Wesleyan's World Music Program.

NOTES

I would like to thank Professor Margaret Sarkissian of Smith College and Professor
Mark Slobin, who read a draft of this chapter. They made invaluable suggestions and

made my English prose clearer. I would also like to thank Professor Ted Solís, the volume's editor, who showed me the importance of self-reflexivity to enhance the significance of the essay.

1. Created in 1994, gamelan@listserve.dartmouth.edu is sponsored by the non-profit American Gamelan Institute, founded by Jody Diamond and Kent Worthy. Presently, it has about four hundred subscribers worldwide.

2. The economic crisis in Asia in 1997 hit Indonesia very hard. It led to political turmoil, beginning with the downfall of Suharto's "New Order" and the rise of the Reformasi period. The economic hardship continues today.

3. Here is an excerpt from the announcement: "I am planning to put together a top ten list of why one should establish or encourage the establishment of a gamelan center. Do send me your ideas and I will compile / take the best ten. The resulting list will definitely never be selected by David Letterman for his audience. . . . Secondly, I thought that it might be more encouraging if there is advice on how to go about starting a gamelan studies center. Therefore, those of you who have been pioneers, do share the steps that you had taken to realize your dream" (gamelan @listserve, March 14, 2000).

4. One of the aims of promoting this dance was to counter the spread of Western rock and roll music and dance, which was ultimately banned by the Sukarno regime because it was contradictory to Indonesia's cultural identity (Murgiyanto 1991).

5. Sometimes one may also find an amusing description regarding the shape of the metallic body of gamelan instruments from which sound is produced, such as "gamelan is a collection of frying pans and kettles."

6. This manner of learning gamelan, however, is by no means the standard in Java. Traditionally, Javanese children could start learning whichever instruments they were interested in playing.

7. With regard to the development of gamelan theory, Harold Powers (1996: 8–9) notes the active participation of Javanese theorists. He writes, "With Western as well as Javanese practitioners of gamelan music taking active roles, Javanese musical theory has evolved explosively, especially since the 1970s, and is now a highly sophisticated explanatory and analytical tradition resting on a completely indigenous practical base, as may be seen most recently in Sumarsam's just published comprehensive book, *Gamelan*."

8. Wesleyan continues to have two gamelan teachers and a part-time Javanese dance instructor today. The other institution that maintains the presence of more than one gamelan teacher is the California Institute of the Arts in Valencia.

9. A survey conducted in 1983 (Benary 1983) showed the total number of gamelan sets in the United States as close to one hundred, consisting of Central Javanese, Sundanese, Balinese, and American homemade gamelan. More than 50 percent of these gamelan were owned by colleges and universities; the rest were privately owned or were found at Indonesian embassies and consulates.

10. The discussion on learning gamelan in Java is based on my personal experience as a gamelan student and teacher at the gamelan conservatory in the 1960s. On learning *gendèr*, I draw from my manuscript on learning to play *gendèr* (1979). A short version of the manuscript appeared in *Seleh Notes* 7, no. 1 (Nov. 1999): 4–6, entitled "Learning and Teaching Gender: Recounting My Experience."

11. See Sutton (1992) and Supanggah (1992) for a brief discussion on this topic.

12. My colleague I. M. Harjito, an accomplished *rebab* and *gendèr* player, says that he really has to know the piece by heart, especially when he plays *rebab*. For him, looking at *balungan* notation in the performance is not helpful (personal communication, spring 2000).

13. For some discussions on this topic, see Susilo (1986) and Sumarsam (1986) in *Proceedings of the First International Gamelan Festival and Symposium,* papers presented at the first Gamelan International Festival in Vancouver in 1986.

14. Certain individuals had particularly important roles in responding to this challenge. Richard Winslow, choral and orchestral conductor, professor of theory and composition, and department chair, was one of them. See the Afterword for an account of his activities in helping initiate the Wesleyan World Music Program.

15. Recently Robert Brown told me that the stage was modeled after the gamelan stage in the Indonesian pavilion at the 1964 New York World's Fair.

16. I should mention that the positions of artist-in-residence and adjunct professor at Wesleyan are not limited to non-Western artists only. Currently, besides three adjunct positions for the non-Western music program (Indian, Javanese, and African music), there are three adjunct positions for each of the following music programs: Western music (i.e., conductor of the orchestra), African-American music, and experimental music.

17. University of Hawai'i is the only institution that has granted a full-time professorship to a gamelan teacher and professor of ethnomusicology, the now retired Professor Hardja Susilo, a UCLA graduate.

18. Each semester we have two gamelan classes, the beginning and the advanced. Each averages twenty students.

19. In the beginning, Javanese dance and other non-Western dances (e.g., Indian and African dance) were part of the World Music Program. A reorganization took place in the 1980s, in which non-Western dances were integrated into the curriculum of the dance department.

20. Every other year, our program focuses on *wayang*. Not only invited guest *dhalang*s (puppeteers), but I too often perform *wayang* at Wesleyan and elsewhere. My *dhalang* training came very late in my life. It started with required *wayang* classes I took at KOKAR and ASKI in the 1960s. With some independent training outside the schools, I became a keen *dhalang* amateur. Knowing my interest, some of my friends invited me to perform *wayang* (without pay) in their homes or their communities, for events such as wedding ceremonies and Indonesian independence day celebrations.

Chapter 4

"Where's 'One'?"

Musical Encounters of the Ensemble Kind

GAGE AVERILL

The ultimate goal is personal and social transformation: music-making must
be used to enhance personal consciousness and experience in community.
JOHN BLACKING, 'A Commonsense View of All Music'

LAISSEZ LES BON TEMPOS ROULER:
WESLEYAN CARNIVAL, FEBRUARY 14, 1992

Carnival bunting, glitter, banners, and fringe cover the spare modernist limestone
walls and stage of Wesleyan's Crowell Hall. With a conch shell blast and a call to
"laissez les bon temps rouler," I begin to throw beads into the audience as a New
Orleans–style brass band descends into the auditorium playing a wailing funeral
number that quickly morphs into a raucous parade jazz beat. Video cameras trained
on the audience members project their own image back to them on monitors arrayed at
the side of the stage and in the aisles. Whatever they do—whether they dance or sit
passively—their actions will become part of the performance. Above the stage in the
organ loft, students from my "Carnival and the Carnivalesque" class are dancing in
the costumes they prepared on the theme "Cyborgs and the humanity-devouring poten-
tial of technology" (their choice). Their own spectacular participation in dance and
masquerade—they are perched above the stage as though on a carnival reviewing
stand—is intended as a model of audience immersion in Carnival.

All of these layers of "performativity" were intended to call into question
the boundaries and the tensions between participatory revelry and specta-
cle in Carnival.[1] This may seem a bit heady for a carnival concert, but its connection to my style of ensemble pedagogy will, I hope, become a little
clearer by the end of this chapter. Other performances that night challenged the right of the performers, most of whom were North American by
birth, to speak for and represent the cultures on display. The most obvious
infraction of this sort was the "Three Carmen Mirandas," a trio of singers
dressed in the exaggerated, sexualized "Baiana" image that Carmen
Miranda adopted in some of her Hollywood movies. I had just read a won-

93

derful piece in the *New York Times* by the Brazilian tropicalist singer Caetano Veloso, "Caricature and Conqueror, Pride and Shame," exploring the politics of third world representation through the contested image of Miranda. The "Three Carmen Mirandas" was our extension of this debate into the arena of performance. Were we enacting an objectionable, sexist, and even colonialist caricature? Were we attempting to recoup the carnivalesque zeal and fashion embodied by Carmen? Or were we performing a metacommentary on forms of touristic voyeurism directed at subaltern festivities?

The brass band is followed by a Rio-style samba batucada, two steelbands, a Haitian community dance troupe, a Cuban-style carnival comparsa band (and rumba group), a visiting Brazilian capoeira group, and a Haitian-style rara band; each of these groups has dancers, a chorus, percussionists, singers, and other instrumentalists. They follow each other without a break or intermission, often overlapping in acoustic spheres. Names of my own bands purposely accentuate the sense of something out of control: "Rara Blan Fou Yo" (Rara of the Crazy Foreigners), "Pandemonium Steelband," and "Con-Fusion Brass Band," for example.

We purposefully drew Carnival texts and songs that confronted issues of race, class, representation, and cultural difference, and, indeed, these kinds of texts are not in short supply in Caribbean and Latin American Carnivals, where politics are habitually danced, sung, and paraded. With more than a hundred performers and lasting more than three hours, the concert was designed to exhaust the audience; I wanted the experience to feel vivid, tiring, and provocative, full of all of the sensory bombardment, surplus signifiers, and playfulness of Carnival as it is celebrated throughout the African Americas. I also wanted the performances to challenge the audience to cross the divide between spectatorship and involvement, to throw themselves into the transformative and life-affirming power of Carnival, regardless of the political and representational issues we were trying to raise. Is there a space for critical *and* sensual involvement that doesn't reproduce exoticist voyeurism?

With the lights of the auditorium off entirely, our rara band enters through the back door singing a song lamenting the lack of "spiritually advanced people/elders in the 'courtyard.'" As the group processes through the audience, the vaksins (single-note bamboo trumpets) sound the basic ostinato while the conch shells, drums, bells, and whistles accompany. I am playing "colonel" and I carry the whip that clears the space of spiritual danger and helps to direct the band. I also blow the command whistle, and I use it and the whip to move the band forward to the crossroads (in front of the stage) to hold a ceremony honoring the deity of the crossroads. The only light is from the candles and lanterns we carry. Then I notice the university president and his wife in the front row. What would a rara band do in Haiti if it encountered a powerful person? I advance on the couple, wrap them with my whip, blow a foula or spray of rum in the four cardinal directions, sing an honorific ochan song, and put out my hat to request payment. At that moment, having consumed a good portion of the Haitian *rum myself, I begin to wonder if tenure at Wesleyan University has just become a pipe dream. (I should note that on the following Monday, a check arrived at my office for $25, signed by the president's wife!) We move on and I change the song to "Rara Blan Fou Yo Nou Antyoutyout, n' ap met banda' n sou wout" (The Rara of the Crazy Foreigners is all worked up, we'll be getting our asses out of here).*

Of the many performances that night, this one stuck with me most of all. Our largely improvisational attempt to sacralize the space of the concert hall and to find a parallel in patronage relations toyed or messed with notions of the safely distanced performance-concert setting. Into this peculiarly carnivalesque stew, we mixed in—and not always with forethought—pinches of obscenity, authority, religion, and fun. About half the *rara* group was Haitian, a combination of Haitian students at Wesleyan and members of an invited Haitian dance troupe, and one of the delights for me was their frank amazement at finding this performance at Wesleyan and at seeing how the genre was stretched in novel ways to match the intercultural context.

To end the night, my graduate steelband, Pandemonium, plays a set of carnival steelband calypsos, including a Panorama Trinidad National Steelband Competition arrangement of "Fire Down Below" by Boogsie Sharpe and shorter arrangements of "Trini Carnival," "Bacchanal Woman," and "Rant and Rave." Half the audience is in the aisles and on the stage dancing. We've created a Wesleyan bacchanal, although I have no idea if the audience has experienced the event in any of the ways I'd hoped. Has anyone read the program notes and the lyric translations? Has anyone confronted their essentially touristic relationship to Carnival or their stereotypes of carnivalesque abandon? Has it all been a chance for bored students to shake some booty to some exotic beats? And if so, is that so bad? After all, right now on stage, I am really enjoying my own booty shaking.

THE HOOD LEGACY

One of the organizing ideas of this volume is that performance ensembles are central to the mission of many—or even most—ethnomusicology programs. In many institutions, the arrival of a gamelan or a set of Ewe drums or steel pans consolidates an ethnomusicology program. This collection of essays proceeds from the shared sense that now, more than forty years after the founding of the UCLA program, we find ourselves able to look broadly and self-critically at this phenomenon. My own chapter focuses on the epistemology of such ensembles and their pedagogical value. How do they serve as a means to a particular kind of knowledge about music, and what do they teach those who encounter them as participants or audience members?

It is important to consider the differences among: 1) music apprenticeship during fieldwork as a part of participant-observation ethnology, 2) the role of world music ensembles as a training ground or preparation for ethnomusicological research, 3) the role of world music ensembles in general liberal arts education, and 4) ensemble performance as public education. Early articulation of the goal of bimusicality by Mantle Hood (the term was originally suggested by David McAllester of Wesleyan) was focused largely on the epistemological requirements of fieldwork in cross-cultural music studies.[2] With a nod to social linguistics, Hood envisioned that long-term study in the field with master artists would result in a mastery of the musical idiom akin to a second language. He also argued that this mastery was a critical element in building the analytical armature of the ethnomusicologist, who could only acquire the insight necessary to produce musically and culturally significant studies if she or he learned to play the music as would a native of the culture in question.

I consider the role of "apprentice" as only one among many possible roles for participant-observer field researchers, but I do hold a stubborn attachment to the importance of performing (or studying how to perform) in the field. Why? In combing through materials for this article, I came across an interview I gave to a student working on a Wesleyan music department history project in 1996, in which I said:

> I don't think it's absolutely necessary to play music in order to produce music scholarship. However, I think music performance sensitizes a scholar to aspects of musical performance. I think one has better access to the terminology the musicians use, a better window into the experience of the musicians, perhaps an advantage in understanding musical sound and in being able to translate that sound somehow or other for an audience. . . . So I think it's a good idea—not absolutely necessary (especially if one is doing reception studies)—but a very good idea. And I like the idea that this institution [Wesleyan] has produced people who do both.[3]

I would only add now that performance studies in the field also acquaint the student with the microinteractional details of performance practice— including gestures and visual cues—that would be lost on most observers.

Hood's apprenticeship model can lead to a deep understanding of the terminology, cognitive structure, rules, and aesthetics of a second musical language. Performance in the field also allows the researcher to make mistakes and to improvise new compositions so as to help define the boundaries of acceptable performance.[4] Hood-style studies that employ the bimusicality paradigm also carry the potential to train exceptional performers in a nonnative musical tongue. The legendary case here would be the Wesleyan graduate Jon Higgins, whose popularity and renown in South India as a concert and even film artist provided striking confirmation of his bimusical proficiency. As some noted at the time, Hood's focus on the mastery by students of a second musical language reinforced the move away from comparative studies and toward in-depth explorations of single musical cultures.

Mantle Hood's approach embraced not only fieldwork methodology but also institutional pedagogy. Hood believed that master artists from around the world could, by teaching at Western institutions, prepare ethnomusicology students for fieldwork in musical traditions by giving them a head start at bimusicality, and so he inculcated a "world music conservatory" (my term, not theirs) approach at UCLA. His ensembles took on a life and power of their own, helping to shape the discipline of ethnomusicology, Western understandings of global music traditions, and indeed the practice of a wide range of ensemble traditions in their home locales. It is critical to assess the impact of these ensembles more broadly on research, educational institutions, the discipline, and the strength of regional or local music traditions around the globe.

It is important to point out that the great bulk of ensemble activity in ethnomusicology programs was devoted to court musics (Javanese gamelan, Imperial Japanese *gagaku,* Hindustani and Karnatic chamber music, Ewe and Ashanti drumming), which emerged as an ethnomusicological canon of sorts. This elitism inexorably shifted ethnomusicological attention toward structurally complex, high-status, theorized, ensemble traditions, and away from the alternatives (so-called "folk" and "primitive" musics that had occupied many early-century researchers, solo or nonensemble traditions, and musics lacking explicit theory), thus reproducing or reinscribing along the way a Euro-American fetish for sophistication even while purporting to stand for its negation. Hood's institutionalization of the ensemble approach and its dissemination throughout North America by his disciples has had real implications for scholarship. Ensembles have provided formative experiences for young scholars, many of whom have taken up research in areas linked to their ensemble interests.

"CURRY CONCERTS" AND "MASS BELLY DANCING" AT THE BARN

The ensemble programs, by virtue of their intercultural mission, became touchstones for political conflicts over issues of power, representation, voice, migration, diversity, and transnational labor in university life of the postcolonial era. Over the decades, a significant sample of the globe's traditional artists were attracted away from communities that had nurtured their art to the universities at the heart of the former colonial system, where they could teach their art to eager foreigners. This was taking place while leaders of the third world were complaining of a "brain drain" that was depleting the developing world of just the sort intellectual capital and resources it needed to survive, develop, and compete ("brain drain" paralleled forms of asymmetrical resource depletion in subaltern spheres under colonialism, neo-colonialism, and imperialism). Having appropriated much of the world's natural resources, labor, and intellectual capital, was the West now pillaging subaltern cultural capital, a last stubborn vestige of cultural and aesthetic difference (or even resistance)?

For many reasons the musical-talent drain wasn't subjected to this type of postcolonial critique. For one, musicians and dancers are seldom taken as seriously as engineers and doctors. For another, the talent drain was often rationalized as a form of salvage: expressive traditions were considered "endangered" in many regions of the world as modernizing and Westernizing youth showed little interest in devoting the time necessary to master them. Westerners, or so this narrative goes, would rescue these traditions through their newfound passion for world music performance. One other reason that talent drain was never subjected to such negative scrutiny is that the success of subaltern musicians in the metropolis was often viewed as a *collective* success (to be shared with proud compatriots at home), or it was considered as a cultural ambassadorship or even as countercolonization (the "peripheralization of the core").[5]

Hood and the other exponents of ensemble programs, such as Robert Garfias, Robert Brown, and David McAllester, reduced the impact of musical-talent drain (whether or not this was their intention) by offering only short-term work contracts for visiting artists. They did speak in terms such as keeping artists from becoming "polluted" by long-term contact with Western institutions. Critics claimed that the Hood-style ensemble system discriminated against foreign artists by refusing them long-term teaching contracts, reasonable pay, and institutionally respected titles. As pianist and medieval music scholar Jon Barlow said of his early years at Wesleyan, "That I was a member of the faculty, and that Palghat Raghu [*mridangam* teacher] was not a member of the faculty, was a transparent example of colonialism playing its old games again. Because, of course, I was getting paid a lot more than Palghat Raghu."[6]

Robert Brown's large, barnlike home, miles from the Wesleyan campus and downtown, served as the communal dorm for Wesleyan's visiting artists and the venue in the early 1970s for Friday night "curry concerts" and "mass belly dancing" (as they were called), featuring the resident artists as performers. This particular vision of radical communitarianism ran headlong into a postcolonial critique that viewed "The Barn" as a neo-Mughal court full of isolated and exploited musicians (often with the musicians' wives cleaning, cooking, or teaching for no additional compensation). Indeed, struggles of this type were endemic to the early ensemble programs, and most of the institutions with ensembles were forced to confront at least the appearance of discrimination in the contracts of visiting artists. I dredge up some of the more unpleasant aspects of the ensemble past to suggest the many thorny political and cultural issues program administrators, faculty, and students were forced to confront, such as when one person's communal, intercultural ideal becomes another's exploitation.

My own formative experiences with world music performance in university settings were at the University of Washington in the mid-1980s in the context of a system instituted by Robert Garfias. I say "in university settings" because I had been playing in ensembles that might be dubbed "world music" (Irish traditional dance, Cuban *rumba* and *comparsa*, Brazilian *samba batucada*) for more than ten years before returning to school, and these were certainly influential in my own development. True to his generalist and polyglot background, Garfias championed an approach at the University of Washington whereby the faculty contracted with a set of master artists each year, most of whom didn't remain in the employ of the university for more than a year or two. More often than not they taught private lessons rather than ensembles, although a number of instructors combined the individual lessons with ensemble practice sessions. This approach was intended to fit seamlessly into the existing private lesson program for Western instrumental and voice studies in the School of Music, and it allowed for great flexibility in incorporating solo and nonensemble traditions.

The turnover of artists and the diversity of their musical and cultural backgrounds tended to avoid the production of narrowly specialized student researcher-performers of non-native traditions, and it permitted exposure to a greater diversity of musical traditions on a smaller budget (there was no effort to create a world music conservatory of the scope envisioned at UCLA or Wesleyan). The lessons were intended to serve as "proto-fieldwork" experiences. Here, students would experience musical encounters that could involve linguistic incompatibilities on the one hand and pedagogical discord on the other (especially between the traditional and the institutional).

I found myself welcoming the diversity and turnover in the program, even though I recognized that it perpetuated many of the power imbalances that I've discussed previously in this chapter (low pay by American institutional standards, no chance to extend contracts, essentially no bargaining position from which to negotiate better packages). Students, teachers, and instructors were forced to confront communication problems, lingering resentments about status differentials, drug and alcohol abuse issues, and inevitable questions about sexual and romantic relationships in a North American institutional culture anxious about sexual harassment.

Finally, the personal relations that developed between master artists and students during the artists' difficult transitions to North American teaching had a lasting impact on me, whatever their global cultural and political implications. Serving as a pall bearer for a great Irish singer, functioning as translator for a *son jarocho* harpist, helping an aging Gambia *griot* adjust to Seattle apartment living, and running errands for my tabla guru were intercultural real-life challenges of the first order for this naive ethnomusicology student. One of the object lessons of this program was that no amount of institutionalization could bleed the artist-apprentice relationship of its complex human dimensions or its cross-cultural pitfalls.

FROM "MUSICAL TRANSVESTISM"
TO DIALOGIC PERFORMANCE PRAXIS

The meticulously imitative nature of most world music ensembles—at least in terms of the sound of the music produced, but also often of dress, demeanor, performance practice, and even pedagogy and transmission—reminds us that the aesthetic ideal to which they aspire (and never reach) is the "authenticity" of the model ensembles in their regions of origin. I wonder out loud here in this following section if mimesis can constitute an adequate rationale for ensemble praxis.

While teaching at Wesleyan University, I used a number of terms to describe this mainstay of ethnomusicology programs, including "musical transvestism" and the related "ethno-drag." It turns out that the former term was used many years ago by a doctoral student at Wesleyan, and according to some who were there at the time, it had an ugly, antigay bias built into it. My more recent use of this phrase was intended simply to critique an approach akin to donning the musical skin of the "Other." I used the term to caricature the "transcendentally homeless" Westerner who finds a spiritual home and belongingness—even a new personality—in a musical tradition not his or her own. This could also be described as "going native" at home.[7] Extreme versions of musical mimesis are common among those who view Western modernity as a sickness that can be cured by identifying with another culture through the mediumship of music and dance. It is the identity of the performer that is at stake and at issue here. Musical transvestism—performance within another cultural configuration—temporarily displaces aspects of the cultural identity of the performer as though she or he were engaged in a light version of a possession trance.

What kind of education does the world music ensemble provide to its concert audiences? For audiences largely unschooled in the genres being performed, the student ensemble becomes a principle vehicle for transmission of cultural diversity, performing "ethnicity by proxy," however attenuated and/or mediated. Many world music ensembles take great pains to "get it right," but they, or at least their instructors, are only too aware that the performances typically lack many of the characteristics that may be most important in a culture of origin: spontaneity, subtlety, virtuosic flourishes, originality, or timbral nuances. Although these world music ensembles provide at best a pale simulacrum of "the real thing," the implicit goal is still to maximize "authenticity" by performing near exact replicas of musical models from other cultures, enhanced by appropriate dress, demeanor, or—ideally—musical and choreographic direction from culture bearers.

In searching for an alternative role for intercultural music performance, and especially world music ensembles, I fall back on a dialogic perspective that has guided my ethnographic research. Russian literary critic Mikhail Bakhtin provided a philosophical foundation for dialogism in the social sciences and humanities by querying the epistemological sufficiency of "identification," "empathy," and "unity" in the process of understanding:

> There is an enduring image . . . according to which, to better understand a foreign culture one should live in it, and forgetting one's own, look at the world through the eyes of this culture. . . . To be sure, to enter in some measure into an alien culture and look at the world through its eyes, is a necessary moment in the process of understanding; but if understanding were exhausted in this moment, it would have been no more than a single duplication, and would have brought nothing new or enriching. *Creative understanding* does not renounce its self, its place in time, its culture; it does not forget anything.[8]

The dialogical approach to intercultural studies that I advocate privileges the space of the encounter rather than the mastery of the codes. For the world music ensemble to become such a space of encounter, performers are not expected to renounce their musical selves but to bring a set of cultural and individual experiences to the ensemble as a precursor to the production of genuine understanding of both cultural difference and commonality. The world music ensemble can thus be reconceived as a context in which students engage in dialogue and collision with musical and cultural codes other than their "first-language" codes. When this is the goal, students and faculty alike should find it less threatening to "interrogate" the representational politics of world music ensembles even while performing in them.

MUSIC/POLITICS/THEATER

Another influence on my approach came from the cultural politics of the North American New Left. The perceived failure of "politics as usual" (that is, the old left tactics of strikes, pickets, marches, and agitprop), and a conviction that the American people had had its critical faculties dulled by its immersion in a fully mediated commercial environment, led activists to embrace a form of public theater meant to grab media and popular attention, shock, and mock conventions even as it entertained. A seminal influence on political theater was a group of experimental artists in North America in the early 1960s dubbed the Fluxus group, whose radical artistic praxis (influenced by Dadaism, Futurism, John Cage, and others) was expressed in dramatic conceptual events, which the media often characterized as "happenings." Indeed, certain elements of the New Left, notably the

Youth International Party (Yippies), employed the ambiguous term *happening* for events like the exorcism and levitation of the Pentagon.

My own inauguration in political theater occurred in high school in 1968 when a group of us from the drama club decided to stage an antiwar guerrilla theater "action" in the school cafeteria during lunch. Our nascent happening was doused, literally, when one of the cafeteria workers threw a pot of potato water over our heads. In retrospect, the guerrilla theater had provoked an even more interesting countertheater of hydrocensorship; the cafeteria worker was no longer a spectator but a participant, and she had literally bridged the walls of the performance event by standing on a step ladder to pour the bucket over a dividing wall onto us. Thus, my first taste of political theater convinced me of its potential to provoke powerful emotional responses.

My own first stirrings of interest in things ethnomusicological during the 1970s (my Irish music group, a world music radio show, my studies in Cuban drumming) all had a direct connection to my commitment to anticolonial and anti-imperialist organizing.[9] As a result, the essentially conservative function and orientation of world music ensembles in ethnomusicology programs came as a shock to me. Did promoting the notion of aesthetic density and complexity of world music traditions require that they be staged with Vatican-like solemnity? I discovered that end-of-semester concerts of ethnomusicology ensembles resurrected all of the stale conventions of Western European decontextualized, entertainment-oriented, concert music, with rigidly enforced distinctions between performers and audiences, printed programs, applause after individual numbers, and so forth. It wasn't until the formation of a department-based Afro-pop ensemble, Je Ka Jo, at the University of Washington that I was able to reconnect my musical ensemble activities to the irreverent, rebellious spirit that had inspired my Irish band of a decade earlier.[10] Je Ka Jo played anti-apartheid concerts with Zimbabwean musicians and throughout its life span retained a focus on dance grooves, politics, and fun, much of which I found lacking in the otherwise extraordinary lesson program ensembles in the department itself.

Although my linking of world music ensembles to the avant-garde and New Left currents of the 1960s and 1970s might seem personally indulgent on my part, I believe that the real links among ethnomusicology, world music markets, the artistic avant-garde in the United States, and the New Left have been written out of ethnomusicological history. Instead, the history of ethnomusicology has hewn to a hermetic, discipline-specific narrative, stretching from the German *Kulturkreislehre* "school," through the founding of the Society for Ethnomusicology, and to contemporary studies on musical globalization.

Barbara Kirshenblatt-Gimblett addresses the role that the avant-garde played in creating an audience for world music, writing "Audiences who have learned the pleasures of confusion from their experience with avant-garde performance are prepared to receive performance forms from other social and cultural worlds as if they [the performances] had emanated from the avant-garde itself."[11] I'll have cause to mention the role that John Cage played in the evolution of the world music program at Wesleyan (below), but the involvement of avant-garde and minimalist composers and Fluxus group artists and others in the sponsorship of early Indian, African, and Japanese music concerts in the United States is largely unexamined in most ethnomusicological histories.[12]

"DILETTANTE EGGHEADS WITH OIL BARRELS"

I was hired at Wesleyan University in 1990 after a year teaching at Columbia University (which had no performance program). I was told during the hiring process that the current faculty viewed my appointment as a possible bridge to the graduate students and that they hoped I would direct an ensemble. This arrangement would be unique at Wesleyan, where all other ensembles were directed by "culture bearers" (master artists) rather than by North American academicians.

One day I encountered an old set of steel pans under a stairwell at Wesleyan. They had been donated to the school a decade earlier and had been briefly used by a student-led ensemble in the mid-1980s. By 1990 they had degenerated into a mismatched, out-of-date, and terribly rusted set, and a few of the barrels had been used by the custodians for storing mops.[13] I held a pan-refurbishing party and contracted with a local tuner to get them playable and to hold a workshop on pan. I had only minimal pan experience (sitting in with a Seattle band), but I had listened to steelbands since I was five years old,[14] and it dawned on me that such an ensemble could function as a centerpiece in a broad program of Caribbean music studies, forming a link to my own curricular offerings ("Caribbean Music" and "Carnival and the Carnivalesque," among other courses). However, I was completely unprepared to lead an ensemble, never having prepared ensemble lesson plans nor having conducted group or ensemble rehearsals.

I had little interest in making this band an "authentic" exponent of Trinidadian culture, particularly because it wasn't to be directed by a "culture bearer." I *did* want to use it as a vehicle for exploring the aesthetics of contemporary Trinidadian music making, and I did hope we could fashion the ensemble into something that reflected our unique circumstances, especially the experimentalist history of the Wesleyan music department. In short, I wanted it to be fun and celebratory, respectful toward its source culture, provocative and productive of intercultural dialogue but not derivative.

Over time it developed in a number of sometimes complementary and sometimes competing directions: I formed the Pandemonium Steelband[15] as a primarily graduate, gigging ensemble that played around the Northeast on a near-weekly basis. I also began to offer an undergraduate steelband course, originally using teaching assistants and then taking it on myself. For two years I instructed the ensembles as "overload" credits, but I eventually wrangled course relief for the undergraduate group.

The physical education department generously granted me use of an old second-story gymnasium, which became my panyard . . . and it was exquisitely panyard-like! Pigeons flew freely in the room, and they—along with the squirrels that ran along the beams—defecated profusely on the pans. The rain poured through the glass skylights with abandon. Wrestling mats peeled off the walls, leaving bare plywood sheets to hide the piles of pigeon guano. The temperature plummeted in winter and soared to metal-warping and sweat-inducing levels in summer (it could reach 120 degrees during midday). The parabolic shape of the pans concentrated the sun's rays and forced the pans to veer wildly out of tune, while drips of sweat ate their way through the chrome plating to rust the pans. We often had to rehearse while the crew teams lifted weights in the other half of the room. In the end, however, it was gloriously chaotic space for rehearsals, meetings, dances, and performances, and after all, it was (almost) all our own.

Ranging from nine to sixteen players, Pandemonium developed a varied repertory. Its Trinidadian repertory was anchored by the complex, long, and mind-numbingly fast Panorama arrangements for Carnival and by shorter calypso and soca arrangements that we emphasized when playing parties. However, I wanted each of us to bring something distinctive to the ensemble, and so we began to experiment with classical music, jazz, dodecaphonic pieces, pop, and a range of global musics, including Jewish klezmer, Bulgarian vocal music, Balinese gamelan, and South African choral pieces. For a time, at least, I believe we may have been the only steelband in the world playing klezmer and gamelan tunes!

To our credit, I think, we always tried to keep the band's modest abilities in mind and tried to avoid taking ourselves very seriously. One widely circulated poster for the band featured a number of fictional excerpts from reviews:

> "This is a must-see group. However, one should avoid listening
> to them at all costs."   —Will Santini, *Option*

> "Dilettante academics with oil barrels . . . need I say more?"
>   —Samantha Carver, *Hartford Advocate*

> "On the other hand, they did wear matching t-shirts."
>   —Jon Pareles, *New York Times*

In a couple of performances, Pandemonium put forth the conceit that we were a washed-up heavy metal steelband that had gone acoustic-alternative to capture a gen-X audience. Our "theme song" for this avatar of the band was a contrafacta version of Suzanne Vega's "Tom's Diner," with lyrics that included the following (the rhythmic accompaniment consisted only of an "egg" shaker):

> We were practicing our pans up in the Fayerweather panyard
> When our neighbor Phyllis Rose called Public Safety to protest
> Saying "What is all this racket? Please make sure they don't disturb me,
> It's already past 10:30 and I've got to get my rest."

> So we unplugged our electrical supply and went acoustic
> We devised a hipper logo and applied it with a glue stick
> We're alternative and gen-X; we grew radical goatees
> We put pedal to the metal, so get ready for our new shtick

> We got New York City agents who supply us with our drugs
> And they're trying to get a try-out soon for MTV's "Unplugged"
> Backstage passes for our groupies, detailed in our contract rider
> Got a crew of brawny roadies, 'cause there're lots of pans to lug.

INVADERS

Pandemonium had an active presence on campus, playing at everything from Martin Luther King Day celebrations to convocations and the graduation interfaith services, and we performed at a standard variety of frat parties, weddings, pool parties, school assembly presentations, summer festivals, park concerts, benefits, and gigs in malls. Our willingness to play just about anywhere led us to be the opening act for Queen Latifah, to perform at Sunday morning Unitarian church services, to set up under rain tarps at New Haven street parties, and to play in the dark in front of a giant fish tank at a museum opening.

One of my favorite activities for the Wesleyan steelbands was to premiere new works for pan ensembles, and this also resonated with a certain institutional and historical logic. The graduate program in world music at Wesleyan had been launched in the mid-1960s by the combined efforts of anthropologist David McAllester, Hood student Robert Brown, and choral professor Dick Winslow, with input and inspiration from composer John Cage, who was resident for a period at the Wesleyan Humanities Institute. They envisioned a healthy interchange between the experimental composers on the one hand and the artists and ensembles from around the globe on the other: all were subsumed under their avant-garde notion of "world music." Therefore our own participation in experimentalist projects seemed to respond to this early vision of the program.

Composer Neely Bruce composed for us and coordinated two megaproductions of world premieres of site-specific compositions by Henry Brant for steelband and other orchestral resources, both of which took place as part of the Lincoln Center Out-of-Doors summer concert series. For Brant's composition, "500" (commemorating the five-hundredth anniversary of Columbus's invasion of North America), we were arrayed at one end of the reflecting pool playing against three military brass bands, including the West Point Band and the Coast Guard Band. The sinuous and harmonically slow-moving parts that Brant had written for the pan ensemble suggested a timelessness and naturalness/innocence associated with preconquest cultures, and contrasted markedly with the strident and militaristic fanfares of the military brass bands. Through a slightly jarring chain of association, Brant had seemingly located the preconquest cultures in the voices of the steel pans, and this symbolism was apparent to the other bands as well; at one point in the rehearsal, the conductor of the West Point Band walked over to me and said, "Aren't you guys getting tired of being run over by us imperialists?" The fact that we were wearing T-shirts that read "Columbus didn't discover America, he invaded it" may have reinforced the impression that we were subbing as the voice of the subaltern.

One year I took Pandemonium to compete against Trinidadian community bands at Lincoln Center. With no expectation of doing well in competition, I still hoped to 1) see how the largely Caribbean audience would react to this band of college kids from Connecticut, 2) interact with the Brooklyn bands, and 3) impress my own students with how far they had to go. The experiment bore strange fruit, however, when we took second prize in what was evidently a rigged contest and were booed during the award ceremony. My best guess is that the organizer, interested in promoting pan in North America and concerned with "uplifting the art form" (read: make a more elite and literate tradition), was impressed by our reading of a Panorama tune from scores (which to us was an embarrassment) and our jazzy rendition of the test tune. In any case, the Trinidadian judges awarded us second place despite the fact that our playing was clearly of lesser quality than at least two of the other bands. But this is exactly the kind of intercultural interaction that provides windows into local cultural politics, insider-outsider polemics, and aesthetic negotiations. Our prize for coming in second was to be the opening act in a concert the following fall, also to be held at a Lincoln Center concert, for the most historic of all Trinidadian steelbands, The Invaders. At both events, however, I had the sneaking suspicion that *we* were the invaders. Perhaps, to paraphrase our T-shirts, we didn't discover pan, we invaded it.

INTERLUDE: URBAN GUERRILLA MUSICFARE

At New York University for the last three years, I find myself increasingly reliant on a version of the Garfias model, but in a unique configuration adapted to the city. As perhaps the most culturally diverse city in the world, New York offers an unparalleled range of musical talent and expertise to draw on, and the university has a century of commitment to an ideal—however imperfectly realized—of "a university in service to the community."

As a result, I began to conceive of a rotating ensemble offering that draws on local artists, resident faculty, and visiting adjunct faculty. Thus, there are three basic models that we use for ensemble instruction: 1) faculty-led ensembles with community "ringers" and workshop leaders (for example, I have offered an Afro-Cuban ensemble and Mercedes Dujunco has taught a Chinese instrumental ensemble, both of which link up with courses we offer at the graduate level), 2) community artist–led ensembles (music of Santería led by Felix Sanábria, for example), and 3) ensembles directed by adjunct visiting professors—these may coincide with graduate courses on similar topics offered by the same faculty (our Irish music ensemble offered by Mick Moloney or a recent klezmer ensemble led by Walter "Zev" Feldman, for example); and 4) existing community ensembles (such as the Indonesian consulate Balinese gamelan) in which our students play. All of the ensembles have been drawn into musical participation in the community, from attending Irish sessions with Mick Moloney or Santería ceremonies with Felix Sanábria. We play down active concertizing for these ensembles due to the limitations of the single-year courses (and due to the various reservations I've raised on this point), but the groups occasionally perform for the department and for university and community audiences as well. In addition, we've used the ensembles to make strong links to area studies programs at NYU (Irish House and the Bronfman Center for Jewish Life, both of which have cross-listed and cosponsored ensembles).

Our ensembles are tailored to their location in a small ethnomusicology program, in a department without a conservatory tradition (the only other ensemble in the music department is the Collegium Musicum, with whom we share space and an instrument-purchase budget), and in a large urban area. As a result, I've likened the NYU ensemble idea to urban guerrilla warfare: the ensembles are small, flexible, constantly changing, and base themselves in the community. We use these ensembles to attempt to

- pry open students' cross-cultural learning skills
- encourage students to ask the right ethnographic questions
- expose students to a variety of pedagogical methods
- expose students to the terminology, theory, technique, and ethos of a musical culture
- create a bridge between the university and the community
- introduce students to artists with whom they may want to continue to work

- make clear ties to the graduate curriculum for a richer experience of music
- train graduate students to offer ensembles in their own academic praxis
- bring students together to make music and develop camaraderie
- create productive confusion and dislocation
- challenge assumptions of cross-cultural music performance.

The limitations are that these ensembles need to make little demand on university space (almost nonexistent) and budgets (small). As for the impact on the community artists, the "gig" allows them to make additional contacts and add to their income, but it doesn't displace them from their communities or interfere with their existing forms of patronage. Do either of the ensemble models I've championed do away with the ethical or representational challenges I've raised? Decidedly not. However, I am reasonably confident that they've allowed me to raise and confront these issues and even to enact or perform them, not cover them over.

THE ETHNOMUSICOLOGIST
AS ENSEMBLE AGENT PROVOCATEUR

One of my goals in this chapter has been to begin to subject ensemble formations—in which so many ethnomusicologists participate—to the critique of representation that has been applied fruitfully to museums, festivals, literature, and a variety of performances of cultural otherness. That no form of representation stands outside relations of power has become an axiom of contemporary cultural studies, and ethnomusicologists can no longer avoid confronting the political implications of their own performance of cultural difference.

I have argued, perhaps uncharitably, that the current praxis of many world music ensembles is based on the aesthetics of imitation (mimesis) or, in its most extreme form, musical transvestism. At worst, we (ethnomusicologists involved in world music ensembles) threaten to trivialize and exoticize cultural traditions even as we purport to advocate for them. We may unwittingly indulge our student participants and our audiences in a form of concert tourism that superficially nods to multicultural diversity without challenging preconceived notions or acknowledging the noisy clash of cultures, politics, and musics in the contemporary world. In short, we may be in danger of erecting our own performative museums for the display of quaint, timeless, well-preserved, and exotic sounds for passive and complacent consumption.

I do not advocate that ethnomusicologists abandon performance or the idea of university world music ensembles, but I don't believe that we can hide from the serious epistemological, pedagogical, and representational issues raised by this praxis. My solution—which is temporary and partial at best—is to replace mimesis with a self-conscious distantiation; to involve student ensembles in the discourse about cultural representation; to use our rehearsals and performances as platforms for raising questions; to reimagine our musical performances as spaces of dialogic encounter; to problematize the very nature and existence of these ensembles; and to use ensembles to provoke, disrupt, and challenge complacency. In this way, we can make the ensemble encounters a part of a student's intellectual, personal, aesthetic, *and ethical* transformation. Such a transformation in the grounding of world music ensembles would require an embrace of the problematics of performance studies, performance/conceptual art, and cultural studies more broadly. It would mean fighting against Western stage conventions and above all the use of expressive culture as passive entertainment. It would also require that ethnomusicologists place their ensemble praxis in a much wider historical (as agents of musical globalization) and intellectual framework. It should not require, I hasten to add, that we make playing music any less fun or less thrilling.

NOTES

Because this essay grows from my experiences in ensembles over many years, it is impossible to properly acknowledge the many influences on its genesis. I would like, however, to list some of the student members of these ensembles whose special contributions bleed through: Julie Searles, John Rapson, Erin Ryan, Michael Veal, Mirjana Lausevic, Paul Austerlitz, Karen and Ted Canning, Robert Rumbolz, Peter Hadley, Zoe Sherinian, Brandon Patton, Philip Galinsky, Kera Washington, Ingi Loorand, Melinda Alcosser, Chip Boaz, Jay Pillay, Mark Braun, Susan Tveekrem, and Debby Teason—with apologies to many others unacknowledged.

1. To query the divide between passive and active modes of cultural consumption is, clearly, not a very new activity, and it may not even be especially radical any more. Bertolt Brecht confronted the issue squarely in his quest for a theater without walls and for the aesthetics of "defamiliarization," as did a large segment of conceptual and performance artists from the late 1960s onward. Many years after this event, I read about the work of New York artist Dan Graham, who, in the early 1970s, used video in a similar fashion to "impose an uncomfortable and self-conscious state on the audience in an attempt to reduce the gap between the two [audience and performer]" (Goldberg 1988: 162).

2. The much-discussed "Hood-Merriam polemic" raged in ethnomusicological publications in the early 1960s and concerned the pros and cons of bimusicality. See, in particular, the proceedings of a panel of leading scholars in 1959, "Whither Ethnomusicology?" (1959: 99–105). Mantle Hood, Bruno Nettl, Mieczyslaw Kolinski, and others are featured; notably absent was Alan P. Merriam. Merriam sometimes praised Hood's approach and included apprenticeship in performance as a part of his own fieldwork methodology. He did, however, believe that Hood's empha-

sis on ensembles in universities had the potential to steer researchers away from the study of music as culture and into a narrow preoccupation with musical sound.

3. Interviewed by Junko Oba, 1996.

4. The issue of performance apprenticeship in fieldwork has been relatively neglected in recent decades. Exceptions include Koning (1980) and Seeger (1994). For diverse instantiations of learning music in the field, see Feld (1990), Seeger (1987), and Chernoff (1979).

5. This phrase is borrowed from King (1990: 46).

6. Interview with Harriotte Hurie, 1996.

7. I am referencing an argument developed by Torgovnik (1990: 227–29) in which she borrows Georg Lukács's term "transcendentally homeless" and its sense of social alienation and links it to the modernist project of seeking "immanent totality," freedom from repression, and physical and metaphysical vitality through primitivism.

8. Todorov 1984: 109. The rejection of identification pertains to a larger argument of Bakhtin's concerning the interaction of texts over time (intertextuality) and the role of the critic vis-à-vis text and author. The literariness of this argument shouldn't detract from its broad implication for interpretation and understanding in the social sciences, especially in the negotiation of cultural difference.

9. This is the subject of my book in progress about playing Irish music on the American left, tentatively titled *The Frost Is All Over.*

10. Je Ka Jo comprised a number of rock, jazz, and traditional African musicians around a core of ethnomusicology students (Jon Kertzer, Stuart Goosman, Peter Davenport, Andy Frankel, and myself) and one of our ethnomusicology professors (Chris Waterman).

11. Kirshenblatt-Gimblett 1998a: 205. Although Kirshenblatt-Gimblett's discussion centers on the reception of world music and dance at the Los Angeles Festival, her comments about the avant-garde are more generally applicable. She argues that the festival directors were confident in the transformative power of "brief encounters with work not necessarily understood" (ibid: 204).

12. The best source for this history of musical interchange can be found in two books by music critic David Toop (1995, 1999).

13. This story, which made its way into an early interview about the ensemble, was thereafter reprinted in nearly every journalistic reference to the band. Without realizing it, I had fashioned a very persuasive "legend." In this story, the pans begin their lifecycle as industrial refuse; they are claimed by pannists as musical instruments and transformed. The Wesleyan legend picks up as the pans have been converted *back* to refuse, only to be *reclaimed* as musical instruments. Articles about the band reported this development with an exaggerated narrative of discovery and salvage, with me as the heroic interloper.

14. I traveled fairly often as a child with one or another of my parents to the Caribbean, where my father had business ties and where both parents had friends. Some of my early musical encounters were with a steelband in Puerto Rico and with *ska* and *mento* bands in Jamaica.

15. The name of the band, Pandemonium (Wesleyan Steelband), was both an asset and a drawback. A pan neophyte when I formed the band, I came up with the name, which I thought was rather clever at the time. It allowed us to use the term *pan demons* for the players, suggested the chaotic praxis of the group, had a carni-

valesque ring, punned on the name of the instrument, and allowed us to use a travestied etching of the god Pan (playing not a panpipe but a steel drum) as our logo. However, I soon discovered that there was a venerable orchestra in Trinidad by the same name, and I also realized that punning on the word *pan* was the most common—and therefore trite—generative strategy for devising names of steel bands in North America. Indeed, there were soon at least two other groups in North America using the same name. Although the name always worked well on a local level, I came to regret the baggage attached to it.

PART TWO

Square Pegs and Spokesfolk

Serving and Adapting to the Academy

Chapter 5

A Square Peg in a Round Hole

Teaching Javanese Gamelan in the Ensemble Paradigm of the Academy

ROGER VETTER

I have had the good fortune over the past twenty-nine years to integrate into my studies, research, and teaching an involvement with the performance of central Javanese gamelan music. For nearly that entire time span I have been aware of the significant impact my gamelan-centered activity has had on my personal and intellectual development. Through my studies, performance activities, and collaborations with Javanese artists I have forged friendships with individuals from a distant culture. My studies of relevant foreign languages have allowed me to live for extended periods among my Javanese friends and teachers in their homeland. I have experienced the gratification of sustained self-motivated study of a topic that I find challenging, at times tantalizingly elusive, but endlessly fascinating and rewarding. My studies and encounters have provided me with a perspective on and attitude about the world and its diversity that I may well not have developed had I not enrolled in a Javanese gamelan ensemble during my undergraduate days.

This acknowledgment of the impact that my gamelan studies have had on who I am is personal reason enough to justify my commitment to teaching such music in the academy. Although probably not a single student to whom I teach Javanese music will pursue its study to the degree that I have,[1] I believe that even a brief encounter with this or any other "Other" music tradition has the potential to shape my students for the better. Until the opportunity arose to participate in this project, I never challenged myself to clearly articulate why I believe experiential cross-cultural performance study to be a valuable enterprise in the context of the academy. As I delved deeper into my thinking about all aspects of my ensemble teaching of Javanese gamelan at a rural liberal arts college (Grinnell College, in Iowa) over the past fifteen years, I found the going a good deal more difficult than I ever imagined it would be. The traces of these musings constitute this chapter. It documents the process I went through to elucidate for myself why I teach a Javanese music ensemble and how the institutional context in which I teach makes this endeavor such a daunting and at times problematic undertaking.

Three aspects of the ensemble enterprise that came to occupy my thoughts most centrally while producing this chapter and that will be addressed in its course are: the objectives of my ensemble offering, the transmission of performance knowledge, and the public display of the music studied. I will then present an idealized instructional model for teaching Javanese gamelan in my institutional context that I sense would enhance the educational outcomes for my students. Although I am not suggesting that these highly personal perspectives be taken as universally applicable to the teaching of world music ensembles (that is, ensembles other than the standard orchestra, concert band, jazz band, and choral groups one expects to find in collegiate music departments; I will refer to these as "canonical ensembles"), it would surprise me if colleagues likewise engaged in directing such ensembles do not find that the ideas and concerns explored herein resonate with their own experiences.

THE QUESTION OF GOALS

When in the late 1970s at the University of Hawai'i I first took on the directorship role of an ensemble, it was as a stopgap measure to cover for the one-year sabbatical absence of my own mentor, Hardja Susilo. I was an M.A. student at the time and very much smitten with Javanese arts in general and gamelan in particular. I had by then already visited Java twice as a participant in summer study abroad programs, studied the Indonesian language for several semesters, started building a collection of commercial recordings of Javanese gamelan music, released a record of field recordings of Javanese street musicians, and developed enough proficiency as a dance drummer to occasionally free Pak Susilo from his musical directorship role and allow him to perform a few dances. Although at the time I was majoring in music theory, I was also taking a few ethnomusicology courses. Through those courses I was developing notions of what ethnomusicology was, and was especially influenced by Mantle Hood's conceptualization of the discipline, since two of my mentors, Hardja Susilo and Ricardo Trimillos, were themselves UCLA graduates. I was becoming aware of Hood's concept of bimusicality, which was beginning to shape how I interpreted my gamelan studies. In a nutshell, I saw myself as a budding performer of Javanese music who was familiar with the cultural context of that tradition. The high points in my life at that time were the University of Hawai'i gamelan ensemble's public performances, for which I and my peers dressed in traditional Javanese attire and performed with little or no notation in front of large and appreciative audiences. I had found my musical and social (in the sense of belonging to a community) nirvana.

I have described my early gamelan life because it places in context my attitudes concerning the enterprise of teaching gamelan ensemble that I have held uncritically throughout much of my career. If I were to reconstruct the goals I had for my students when I first started directing gamelan ensembles in the late 1970s, they would go something like this:

1. My students will understand the workings of central Javanese gamelan music through becoming competent performers of that music

2. They will learn to play the music primarily by ear, in a way that replicates the learning process of Javanese musicians

3. They will emerge from the ensemble experience with some general sense of the place of gamelan music in Javanese society.

These objectives are rooted in how I viewed my own learning encounter with Javanese gamelan music and in my (rather naive, at the time) self-assessment of my understanding of the music and its cultural context.

Over the years I have never attempted seriously to measure my success at meeting the goals stated above. Achieving them constitutes a tall order, especially considering the institutional paradigm for canonical ensemble offerings that most of us inherit with our positions and are expected to work within. The paradigm to which I refer consists of a bounded period of time, usually a quarter or a semester, during which student performers already trained in vocal production or instrumental technique rehearse and polish a selection of composed, notated works conceived in a general musical system familiar to the performers since childhood. The product of the ensemble's efforts is then displayed in a public performance within a format familiar to both performers and audience. Audience members and performers are also familiar with the general musical system in which the selected repertoire for a concert is cast, even if they happen to be unfamiliar with the repertoire items themselves. In general, ensemble rehearsal time is dedicated to musical matters; any cultural contextualization of the works is typically relegated to printed program notes. A high standard of musical presentation in public performance and the honing of the performers' technical skills and expressive potential are the primary goals of most canonical ensemble organizations in the academy.

This ensemble paradigm, with one or more public performances at the center of the enterprise, works fairly well for ensembles the members of which are already "of the tradition." But how appropriate is this paradigm to the teaching of a repertoire such as that of the Javanese gamelan to undergraduate students at an American liberal arts institution? Students who enroll in my ensemble are not at all familiar with the Javanese gamelan repertoire, nor have they had any previous encounter with the Javanese musical system and its non-equal-tempered tunings, stratified textures, heterophonic relationships between parts, phrase-marking principles, and so forth. How am I to simulate in a few weekly hours of rehearsal supplemented by some individual lessons the lifelong absorption of contextual musical experience that produces competent native musicians and listeners in Java? Since very few of my students have ever been to Java, how can I in words alone convey to them the cultural context of this music while at the same time transmit to them the necessary musical knowledge to function as beginning performers of this music? Now that I have taken the time to reflect on where I start, who I instruct, and the structure of the institution in which I teach, it becomes clear to me, first, that my original teaching goals are unrealistic and, second, that the operative ensemble paradigm in the academy is not easily applicable to the gamelan ensemble enterprise.

Given these revelations I have scrambled to articulate a new set of goals for my ensemble teaching that justify for me all the energy I pour into this activity and justify for my students the time they invest in the study of Javanese music in their otherwise full academic schedules. These new goals are:

1. Provide my students with an experiential introduction to a form of musical expression significantly different from that of their own culture, allowing them some small degree of insight into the varied ways that humans can craft sound for artistic ends

2. Provide students with a face-to-face, long-term interactive exercise in which they can experience a sense of collective accomplishment achieved through cooperative effort

3. Provide students with the opportunity to challenge themselves by choosing to study progressively more challenging instrumental or vocal roles within the performance practice of the tradition[2]

4. Share my enthusiasm for and perspective on Javanese culture during rehearsals and lessons through anecdotal references to my experiences in Java and my encounters with Javanese

5. Provide students with guidance in finding resources for self-motivated exploration of gamelan music and its cultural context.[3]

These goals have emerged from what I believe to be a more thoughtful reflection over my own learning and teaching experiences than was possible earlier in my career. They are not as focused specifically on the transmission of knowledge about Javanese performance practice and culture as my first set of objectives. These new goals instead characterize the ensemble experience as something that will contribute to my students' preparation for lifelong musical and social encounters of sorts that I cannot predict. They hold the potential for artistic and intellectual reward for the student who is a self-motivated learner and who is willing to invest time and energy beyond minimal levels of engagement to take a proactive role in learning. They recognize the educational merit of going through the process of learning a second musical language, even if fluency in that second language cannot realistically be achieved. Insights gained in this process will probably have greater application in my students' lives after college than will the specific performance skills they hone while in the ensemble.[4]

By viewing the ensemble experience as something that will contribute to the equipment of my students for lifelong musical encounters, I find new meaning in what I do beyond the immediate rewards of introducing gamelan music to and performing it with them. But I feel that the ensemble model within which I operate seriously constrains both what I do as an instructor and what my students get out of the ensemble experience. I will examine in a later section the problems I have with the centerpiece of the canonical ensemble paradigm, the public performance. But before that I wish to explore in some detail how I have come to view myself and my teaching of Javanese gamelan music as parallel to teachers and teaching in another area of the academy, foreign language acquisition.

THE TRIALS OF TRANSMISSION

Few would disagree with the ideas that the most effective means of acquiring fluency in a language system, whether spoken or musical, is to grow up with it as your first language, and that the ideal method by which to achieve foreign language fluency is through prolonged and preferably total immersion. The more completely one is forced to operate and interact exclusively in a foreign spoken or musical language environment (that is, live that language rather than study it), the more quickly one will achieve fluency in it. Unfortunately, the structure of the academy does not allow this sort of approach to foreign language and music acquisition.

College foreign language instructors and ensemble directors of traditions totally outside their students' experience are faced with the daunting challenge of teaching language or performance proficiency in an institutional environment that is simply not ideal for the acquisition "from scratch" of such complex systems as language and music. It is not possible to create on a college campus the condition of total immersion in a language or music that would make the acquisition of that foreign system of communication most efficient. Perhaps we can come close to orchestrating an immersion approach to language or music acquisition during the bounded period of the language class or ensemble rehearsal itself, but as soon as that period is over our students revert to speaking their first language and listening to their first music. In the artificial learning environment of the academy other learning methodologies have had to be devised in order to provide our students with a functional command of the foreign language or music they study.

I have come to realize only recently that I must have long ago subconsciously applied a generalized version of the classroom instructional strategy used for college foreign language study to my own teaching of Javanese gamelan music. In my teaching of gamelan I do such things as articulate underlying structures, present melodic and rhythmic vocabularies as building blocks of more complex musical utterances, and impart abstracted principles of musical syntax. I make explicit for my students many languagelike features of the music system of which native performers might not be consciously aware unless they have been exposed to the conceptualizations of someone who has studied their tradition. I utilize these teaching strategies because they seem to provide for my students some cognitive bearings as I attempt to introduce to them simultaneously the Javanese music system, its repertoire, and its requisite instrumental and vocal skills and vocabularies. And it is with this point that the difference between teaching a gamelan ensemble and a canonical ensemble in the context of the academy comes to the fore. The formidable challenges I face in preparing my students to perform a foreign music are made even more burdensome because, in addition to preparing repertoire, I also need to introduce to them the musical system in which that repertoire itself was conceived and the instrumental and vocal skills requisite for its realization. How many college orchestra conductors arrive at their first rehearsal of the semester to face a group of students who have never before heard any Western music, much less any orchestral repertoire, and who do not even know the names of the instruments they are holding, much less how to play them in a culturally acceptable manner? Ridiculous as this scenario might sound, it is fairly close to what I face semester after semester.

By now it should be evident that the enterprise of teaching a gamelan ensemble has as much if not more in common with the teaching of a foreign language than it does with the directing of a canonical ensemble. It is truly unfortunate that ensembles such as gamelan in institutions of higher education are thought of as parallel to canonical ensembles when the two types of ensemble are really so dissimilar. A clear mandate or strong expectation from a department that all ensembles should present a public performance every semester forces instructors such as myself to compromise in how we go about introducing our students to a new music tradition and frantically train them to perform for the sake of conformity to the canonical ensemble paradigm. This is the central pedagogical dilemma in and the greatest frustration of my ensemble teaching activity.

THE PROBLEM WITH (RE)PRESENTATION:
WHY THE PUBLIC PERFORMANCE?

The final facet of the ensemble enterprise I will touch upon is the public performance, that central event in the canonical ensemble paradigm that all directors inherit. Whereas I feel comfortable teaching Javanese gamelan and consider that the study of this music is of educational value to my students, I have yet to come to grips with the public display of it in the Western concert hall setting. I have no problem with an informal culminating performance event, such as in the rehearsal room, that allows my students and me to put closure on the educational process of the preceding semester. I am less sure of what an audience unfamiliar with the gamelan tradition gets out of passively witnessing us perform in a concert hall setting, and it is a concern to me that our performances constitute for most of our audience members their entire exposure to Javanese music. Even if this does not bother our audience members, I cannot help but feel disconcerted with the thought that I and my students function as de facto representatives of Javanese culture to American audiences. More than anyone else at a performance, I recognize the discrepancy between our music and that which is performed by competent Javanese musicians in a traditional setting, as the music has been distilled through my own learning experience, and then further compromised as I pass my understanding of it on to my students. I cannot help but feel as though I am playing the role of some sort of illusionist, creating for the audience a false impression that the performers in front of them are competent and fluent in the musical tradition they are presenting. It concerns me that my students feel elated following a performance because we did not experience any musical derailments that would signal to even our uninformed audiences the precariousness of our command of the material. I am not at ease with these little charades I am forced to engage in because directing an ensemble in a music department carries the burden of conformity with other ensembles that operate under a different set of conditions. This dilemma is compounded for me by the reality that, beyond the operative departmental expectations for public performance, my students by and large express a strong desire to perform publicly every semester.

IMAGINING A BETTER MODEL

For the past fifteen years twenty to thirty students have enrolled each semester in Grinnell's Javanese music and dance ensemble.[5] In any given semester typically about half of the ensemble members are returning students, and half are newcomers with no previous exposure to Javanese gamelan music. Since the ensemble presents a public performance on campus every semester, this means that approximately half of the performers on stage have less than four months of not very intensive instruction in Javanese music behind them. I am not at all comfortable with this situation.

In the following paragraphs I allow myself to imagine an ideal way of structuring a gamelan program in the context of a four-year liberal arts college. The details of this scenario are intended to increase the likelihood of two desirable outcomes that in part address concerns I harbor while operating in the canonical ensemble paradigm. First, I want my students to be more deeply indoctrinated into the Javanese music system before they start performing gamelan repertoire in public. This could only be accomplished through a longer period of formative study unencumbered by the exigencies of frantic concert preparation. If *learning* rather than *preparation* were the primary activity for the first few semesters of my students' introduction to Javanese music, I am confident that their comprehension of the uniqueness of this music would be deeper and serve to inform them better in future encounters with unfamiliar musics. Second, I want my students, once they do take the stage, to have had ample preparation time to feel confident in what they are doing rather than simply hope that they will not "screw up" in performance. Only when my students have achieved a modest command of both gamelan performance practice interaction (for example, responding effortlessly to musical cues and hearing their part in relationship to others) and their assigned parts for a program will I feel less self-conscious about presenting our product in public. Although this will not redress the most difficult issues of representing the cultural Other, it will at least result in a better musical representation of Javanese music and a richer educational experience for my students. With these outcomes in mind, the ideal structuring of gamelan instruction in my institutional setting would be as follows.

My students would be required to commit themselves at the beginning of the fall semester to an entire year of involvement in order to earn credit. The new students in the ensemble would comprise a one-year study group with no performance expectation beyond participation in an open rehearsal at the end of each semester. An open rehearsal is more conducive to presenting the ensemble's work as ongoing educational process rather than a finished product, which a formal performance suggests it is. I could select as many or as few pieces to work on as I felt was appropriate for a particular mix of students, and I could introduce new repertoire or new treatments of already studied pieces whenever I felt it was most advantageous from a learning standpoint to do so. I would not have to be concerned with whether or not a piece selected for its pedagogical value is appropriate for a concert program since we would never present it in that setting. My primary teaching objectives for this group would be to introduce the Javanese music system and the rudiments of its performance practice to my students, train them in and give them ample time to internalize basic instrumental techniques, and provide for them ample opportunity to learn how to fit their parts in with the others and to respond to musical cues—all without the pressure of preparing a public performance.

A second group within the ensemble would consist only of students who had successfully finished the study-group year of instruction. This group would be expected to present an open rehearsal at the end of the fall semester and a public performance at the end of the spring semester, and would focus on the same repertoire both semesters. The pieces and the way in which they would be treated musically would be selected with two primary goals in mind: 1) to reinforce and expand upon the students' understanding of how Javanese music works, and 2) to put together a varied and musically interesting program for public presentation that would honestly display the modest level of musical fluency this group had attained in their studies of Javanese music. Students in this group who have demonstrated a good command of the instruments introduced in the study group would have the opportunity to study privately with me on one of the more technically and musically challenging elaborating instruments. Typically it takes more than a semester of study to gain a functional command of the technique for these instruments and to internalize the vocabulary of motivic modules that are used to generate the parts performed on them. Students who remain with the ensemble for more than two years can continue to be challenged to expand upon their understanding of this music through studying further elaborating instruments.

Unfortunately, a number of factors discourage the full implementation of this model in the particular context in which I teach: 1) a small student body, the members of which have a plethora of activities from which to choose, limits the number of students enrolled in my ensemble and makes it difficult to populate two distinct groups; 2) well over half of my students are not on campus for at least one semester of the typical four-year academic program and, according to this model, they would not be able to participate during any year in which they could not commit themselves to both semesters; 3) many of my students do not come to the ensemble until their final year at the college; 4) students do not remain in town following graduation and therefore do not have the option of continuing their involvement in my ensemble beyond the bounded period of their undergraduate years (although many of them do find outlets for continued gamelan study elsewhere); and 5) I periodically take sabbatical leaves during which I cannot find a qualified replacement to keep the ensemble operating in my absence. For these reasons, the full implementation of the model outlined above will likely never be a reality for me. If and when I do have sufficient enrollment—at least twenty or so students—with some previous experience (at least one semester of participation in the ensemble), I will experiment with separating the new members from the returning ones and work toward only one public performance per year with the latter group. Even implementation of this compromised version of the model would allow me to feel better about the educational experience I would be offering my students and about the level of proficiency my performers would display as public presenters of Javanese music.

CLOSING THOUGHTS

Any educational advantages brought about by the partial or full implementation of the above idealized paradigm will not, unfortunately, address the deeper issues of cultural representation (how individual audience members view, interpret, and understand our performances, for example) and exploitation (such as a non-Javanese individual making a living by teaching Javanese cultural property) that come so sharply into focus in the public performance event. I attempt to address cultural representation issues in part by including text in the concert program notes that is intended to provide some cultural contextualization of the Javanese gamelan tradition for the audience. But, in the end, I remain humbled as to how to cope with these issues shaped by Western colonialism and the economic and power imbalances left in its wake. I currently seek refuge in accentuating the educational value of the ensemble enterprise for my students independent of its problematic ethical issues, the burden of which ethnomusicologists such as myself must carry.

The experience of studying a music such as that of the Javanese gamelan can approach its full educational potential only when it is not unnaturally forced to conform to an instructional model that presupposes participants who are already "of the tradition" being studied. Music departments offering world music ensembles such as Javanese gamelan need to be cognizant of the distinctive challenges of such enterprises; such ensembles are *not* just another performance ensemble and thus should *not* be treated like canonical ensembles. Alternative performance expectations and longer-term registration commitments might have to be articulated and instituted to accommodate the differences in the natures of these ensembles; these are small inconveniences to pay for the potential educational benefits such deviations from policy might engender. But as long as music departments remain oblivious to the essentially different instructional challenges that exist for their world music and canonical ensembles, they will be unwittingly engaged in the futile act of forcing a square peg into a round hole.

NOTES

1. Two of my students did choose a program in Java for their off-campus study experience as a result of their participation in my ensemble. However, neither of them selected Javanese gamelan in particular or ethnomusicology in general as the focus of their graduate studies.

2. In addition to running full-group rehearsals, I, like most gamelan directors, teach about ten hours per week of one-on-one or -two lessons on the more challenging musical roles. In order to achieve satisfying musical results this sort of investment of my time and energy is essential. Many of my students are eager to take on the study of these more challenging instruments and express to me directly and through end-of-course evaluations how much they value the learning process over the course of a semester's lessons.

3. Since I began providing my students with a suggested listening and suggested reading handout about ten years ago, a few students each year have made passing comments or asked questions about recordings they had listened to on the list. So it would appear that at least some of my students take the "self-motivated exploration" bait.

4. I do occasionally receive e-mails from former students informing me of their recent encounters with "new" musics. I can only deduce from such occurrences that their enthusiasm for the new music in their lives, and the fact they chose to share the experience with me, is at least subconsciously linked to their "ear-opening" gamelan encounter.

5. I collaborate with my wife, Valerie Mau Vetter, a Javanese dance specialist. Typically fifteen to twenty students choose to study music, and another five to ten choose to study dance. Valerie and I create a dance drama from traditional resources each spring semester, designed to accommodate the skill levels of the group at hand.

Chapter 6

"No, Not 'Bali Hai'!"

Challenges of Adaptation and Orientalism in Performing and Teaching Balinese Gamelan

DAVID HARNISH

Four interdependent questions seem fundamental when considering the teaching and directing of non-Western music ensembles at institutions: 1) How does one become a director? 2) How does one teach the music? 3) In what context does one present the music? 4) How does one adapt to the institutional environment in which one finds oneself? All four questions are deeply intertwined, and both the first and last inform ways we approach the second and third. To succeed, we must adapt to our teaching and performing environment, just as we might adjust to situations during fieldwork. In doing so, we adjust our transmission strategies by both embracing and reacting to our own pedagogical histories. My own history, in ways both obvious and intangible, led to my career as a scholar and director of Balinese gamelan.

I have now taught Balinese *gamelan gong kebyar* (large modern concert gamelan) at Bowling Green State University (BGSU) in northwest Ohio for ten years.[1] Coming from urban academies and community teaching on the West Coast, I had to adapt to new surroundings and develop new teaching strategies because the nineteen thousand BGSU students are nearly 90 percent white and provincial Ohio residents living in a small college town. I also had to deal with the college administration. Ethnomusicology and non-Western ensembles (the gamelan plus an Afro-Caribbean ensemble taught by my colleague, Steven Cornelius) are firmly established at BGSU, yet we find little internal acknowledgment of our existence. Most members of the administration and faculty beyond my immediate department neither expect nor encourage students to study in these ensembles. Consequently, the ensembles are marginalized and attract mostly marginalized students. Many of my students dress, look, and behave differently from "mainstream" students. A music student who appears different is often informed about the gamelan by advisors. By wearing *batik* and *ikat* shirts to work (among other behaviors), I either inadvertently or perhaps subconsciously nourish this notion of difference.

Teachers negotiate the experience of field study and transmission. Balinese musical culture certainly must pass through a number of learning, processing, contextualizing, and teaching stages between my Balinese and Javanese teachers (in Indonesia and the United States) and my students at BGSU. Regardless of the number of steps away from the original source, at most institutions the ensembles represent the non-Western and (generally) distant worlds of their origins. Those of us in areas of little diversity are charged with—or charge ourselves with—the task of representing the music and cultures of the ensemble. We may confront an attitude that treats non-Western music as the exotic, romantic, yet insignificant Other. The distance created with such a construct can be partially adjusted with education, but I feel that it can only be transcended through an active performance that collapses distance, initiates community, and alters perspective.

We are the sum of the collection of disparate selves of our lives. We have all studied different styles of music at different points in our lives, and these experiences—what we know, how we learned—directly influence our teaching and notions of who we are and what we want. I believe we owe a lot of what we are to our teachers, who help us see the music in ways we initially cannot and guide us through the winding roads of learning. Gradually we absorb the music, it becomes part of us, and if we can remember processes of learning we can effectively empathize with and guide our own students. Though I greatly honor my teachers, I do not feel constrained by their pedagogical strategies. I feel that as a teacher I must adapt to given situations, and I often seek compromises that produce greater results. I am also still a student. New insights and possibilities often appear when I study in Bali (for example, with musicians Wayan Suweca and Dewa Berata), and these continuously affect my teaching methodologies as I revisit the old ways, and discover some new ways, in which I learn.

I believe that students also bring the sum of their selves to the ensemble, and that teachers can be much more effective if we understand students' orientations; thus some flexibility is necessary to reach each individual. Meaningful goals now include revealing principles of gamelan music and its contextualization to my students, and removing mental and conceptual blocks from their paths toward increasing competence and self-discovery within the music. In the sections below I discuss means for achieving those goals.

My own self-discovery, ultimately coalescing into the transmission strategies I've adapted to my teaching environment, are traceable to the early 1970s, when I was a blues and rock guitarist somehow attracted to Asian culture and religion. I never felt like mainstream American material, and Asia appeared as a suitable alternative. After spending a year abroad in Japan in 1974–75, much of it in a Zen temple, through the University of the Pacific, I wanted to see more of Asia. I completed my undergraduate degree in international studies, worked briefly as a guitarist in Houston, then traveled throughout South Asia and sought teachers to learn music. I found the learning experience, however, stiff and formal, and had a much easier time later studying Indian music with Santa Cruz–based sitarist Ashwin Batish. Though a Brahmin, Ashwin took an informal approach to teaching that suited me, and he encouraged me to stick with guitar and to perform extensively with him. Our work led to several recordings and to his experiments fusing rock and jazz elements with *Hindustani sangeeta.*

Meanwhile, I continued traveling and wound up in Bali in 1979. In my imagination, Bali combined some of the fervent religiosity of India with a more relaxed attitude toward learning music. I discovered that the guy who sells you food in a *warung* might well be a music master. The music, with its ferocity, power, interlocking rhythms, and ritual contextualization, appeared complicated, fascinating, and mysterious, and I wanted to decipher and absorb its structure.

A few years later, I entered the graduate program in ethnomusicology at University of Hawai'i at Manoa and studied Javanese gamelan with Professor Hardja Susilo. I conducted my master's research in Bali and Lombok, concentrating on the development of Balinese music in Lombok. Since traditional Balinese music has a primary ritual function, I was able to combine my interests in music and religion. I also had opportunities to work with many new teachers, including Made Lebah, Wayan Loceng, and academy musicians. Years later, and after further research in Bali and Lombok and additional study in Los Angeles with K.R.T. Wasitodiningrat, Nyoman Wenten, Sue Carole DeVale, and others, I completed my doctorate at UCLA and had gradually become a gamelan teacher.

At some time during this transition, and perhaps as early as my work with Pak Susilo, gamelan music became familiar to me; being a gamelan musician became a part of my identity as my identity as a blues, rock, and jazz guitarist receded until it was nearly nonexistent. Perhaps this is testament to the sacrifices we make to become teachers, although deep in my mind I feel that this guitarist, whom I glimpse now and then, will reemerge someday. "He" undoubtedly has influenced the ways in which I learned gamelan, my orientation toward it, and my teaching methodologies. For example, my strength as a guitarist generally came from a quick grasp of rhythm and a good ear. These abilities allowed me to adapt to varied music styles; they also are of primary importance in gamelan playing, and so I naturally emphasize rhythm and listening in teaching. One aspect of Indonesian music that took a bit longer to absorb was gamelan as true ensemble. As a lead guitarist, I was used to occasionally dominating the sound of a group. When I began learning Javanese gamelan, I gravitated toward and quickly advanced on the *bonang* gong-chime, probably because this appeared as a lead instrument. I often played as if I were soloing, particularly during the "flowers" of *imbalan* interlocking parts. It was not until I heard other players on recordings that I realized the subtle beauty of *bonang* playing and that my part was merely one of many in the gamelan mosaic. This realization was reinforced by my Balinese gamelan study and is still fresh in my mind; thus, gamelan as ensemble community is a vital part of my teaching.

THE TEACHING ENVIRONMENT

Ethnomusicologists who teach non-Western ensembles are neither instructed by professors at academies nor by their master teachers in the field how to teach the music to students at universities. Instructors, I believe, endure a process of "translation" in which they must first recall—either through memory, notes, tapes, transcriptions, or a combination of these— the music, then situate this knowledge to fit the classroom. According to Clifford Geertz, translation of this sort is not simply a "recasting of others' ways of putting things into our own," but "displaying the logic of their ways of putting them in the locutions of ours" (1983: 10). Here, "translation" requires our own interpretive and expressive processes in taking the "isness" of the music as we know it and the "ways of putting things" of our teachers, and adapting these to our teaching environments. The process of becoming a director—learning, synthesizing, teaching, presenting, performing— often requires compromises in repertoire, performance practice, appearance, context, "authenticity" in representation, and so forth. The degree of compromise a director negotiates tells a great deal about his or her identity and overall plans and goals.

Complaints have rarely, if ever, been lodged against non-Indonesians teaching gamelan music on ethical grounds, partly because of the lack in this country of a substantial Indonesian-American community with a charged historical background. Teachers in Bali, moreover, are less concerned with issues of "authenticity" than with which style (for example, conservatory, region, or village) is taught to students by gamelan directors in America. In this sense, then, "gamelan" seems to be a noncontested area open to any ethnicity to become students, performers, and teachers. Perhaps because of the scant diversity at BGSU, my role as mediator for Indonesian music traditions (which carries a certain responsibility) is not disputed. On the other hand, there is no Asian cultural matrix in which the BGSU gamelan can function; I often wish that the gamelan, like some ensembles in Hawai'i and other parts of the country, had a role within the living local community. Very little of Bali exists in the Midwest; our gamelan may help create whatever there is.

Edward Said's definition of orientalism (1978: 1–2, 7) asserts that the West takes a superior position (culturally, politically, etc.) in dominating the discourse that defines and appropriates the East. This paints the Orient as a place of romance, remarkable experiences, and exotic beings, and as an icon for contrasting images, colors, and personalities. The gamelan represents a similar orientalism for BGSU. Excluded from the mainstream, it is an anomaly from the East that helps meet the needs of marginalized students seeking contrasting experiences. It perhaps is an icon of, and domesticates, "otherness" in this community. I believe that the main rationale of the gamelan for the administration is the alternative music experience and diversity that it represents and tames. At universities in larger, multicultural cities, diversity is more integral and performance is generally not meant to control but rather to celebrate otherness. Indeed, my studies in ensembles at University of Hawai'i and UCLA showed me that there can be a dialogue between Self and Other or Western institution and non-Western music, without one speaking for or attempting to dominate the Other. One of my goals at BGSU, albeit far from being realized, is creating such a dialogue.

New students and audiences alike often know nothing about gamelans (where they are from, how they sound, contexts of performance, etc.), very little about Indonesia (excepting information on economic or political problems or violence), and sometimes less of Bali ("Oh, do you mean 'Bali Hai' from *South Pacific?*"). I find myself in an environment in which many faculty and administrators, while supporting the gamelan, maintain an orientalist perspective.

Learning to Teach

In *Orientalism,* Said analyzes the dialectic between the individual writer and the collective discourse; here, let me substitute "teacher" for "writer" and "body of teaching strategies and methodologies" for "collective discourse" (1978: 24). Each teacher must deal with his or her own blinders and filters and ultimately evolve effective teaching methods that reach students. Methods vary, of course, from teacher to teacher, and perhaps certain strategies are more effective for certain kinds of music ensemble than others. We all practice trial and error, and gradually change our methods or develop a menu of methods for particular occasions or particular students. I may, for example, teach music theory graduates, undergraduate percussion majors, and ethnomusicology graduates differently, trying to relate to the different ways they are used to approaching music.

We also, whether consciously or not, speak to different students and audiences in different ways. On one recent occasion while teaching gamelan to urban high school students from Toledo, I suddenly realized that I was, not surprisingly, slipping frequently into the vernacular. I had used my imagination, whether correctly or not, in an attempt to appropriate a style of discourse to facilitate student learning and decrease student distance from both the music and the instructor. Although the music in each of these circumstances (presumably) remains the same, the methods of introduction and the positions—language, behavior, construction of hierarchy, perhaps even dress—of the instructor change.

The majority of my gamelan students have been music majors, and slightly more than half have been graduate students. They gravitate toward playing gamelan for various reasons. Some, often percussionists, seem enchanted by the vibrant rhythms; others, such as composers, seem more interested in structures; ethnomusicologists are captivated by the whole music culture suggested by the instruments and their sounds. As mentioned earlier, many students who consider themselves outside the norm somehow feel accommodated by the presence of the gamelan and the other students similarly attracted.[2] I even overheard one student saying, "All the cool people play gamelan."[3]

Transferring Knowledge

Balinese gamelan music emphasizes precision, not individual interpretation or improvisation. Without precision and a coordinated ensemble sound, the music, as Michael Tenzer states, is like a "boiling rock . . . going nowhere fast" (1998: 14). The gamelan at BGSU, Kusuma Sari (Inner Flower), performs at least twice a semester but meets for a total of only one hundred minutes per week. Though I often work individually with students outside class time, organizing extra rehearsals is nearly impossible due to busy student schedules. This creates the challenge of preparing three or four pieces of easy to medium difficulty by the semester's end. Students' absences and frequent turnover inhibit advancement beyond the intermediate level.

Since most students are not ethnomusicologists and may never play gamelan outside BGSU, I do not teach in a style calculated to develop Balinese music specialists. Some students study for only one semester, most stay on for two, and a few enroll for three, four, or more. My goals for non-ethnomusicology students include expanding their memories (weaning them off of relying on notation), increasing their rhythmic capabilities, developing a sense of true ensemble playing, learning something about Balinese culture, and experiencing some of the magic of Balinese music performance. A few have experienced other internal transformations and, as a result, changed their major or some aspect of their life. I expect ethnomusicology students to undergo many of these changes and to develop enough competency for gamelan leadership roles. Students also have opportunities to study in Bali in the alternating BGSU summer workshops. These month-long workshops, led by Steven Cornelius for Ghana and myself for Bali, provide experience and participation within a non-Western culture and an opportunity to study with local music masters. Those that study in Bali bring back an enhanced musical and cultural understanding that subtly contributes to the overall quality of the ensemble.

Teaching at BGSU is an ongoing dialectic with compromise. While I insist that students observe such customs as removing their shoes before playing and not stepping over instruments, and I expect them to remember the instruments' names, I often facilitate learning by limiting Balinese musical terminology or finding Western counterparts. I have also taken liberties with regard to conceptualization. Indonesian music theory generally holds that the last beat (where the gong falls), rather than the first one, receives an accent or emphasis. Years ago, I found that calling the gong stroke "beat one" was less confusing than calling it the last beat, particularly for the gong player. However, I include the caveat that students should hear the gong stroke as the last beat of a cycle.

I have also compromised in notational practice. Balinese gamelan transmission is traditionally an oral tradition, though the music/dance academies in Bali use a Balinese-script notation as a teaching device and some composers use it as a memory aid. I instead have adapted a Javanese cipher notation to indicate the core melody *(pokok)* and its punctuation. The ciphers are easier to write and read than Balinese syllables, and musicians playing the faster-moving parts must still rely entirely on memory.

I have modified the basic Balinese imitation-repetition style of teaching. I play a part over and over until a student finally can mimic it, then I turn to a different part and play it over and over again for another student while the first part is still sounding. After that, I may turn to the gong player and set the phrase structure, then turn to a more difficult part (for example, *reyong* gong chime) and play that part for the musicians sitting at that instrument. Eventually all the parts are more or less sounding, and I hope that students see connections between them. Unlike in Bali, I often stop and discuss ways to hear musical relationships between parts and explain how melodies fall within gong cycles. Sometimes I have students clap out interlocking parts; other times I ask them to sing melodies. These efforts expedite the process of learning for some. Others, however, have to discover for themselves the relationships and connections between the parts; this discovery comes only when they are ready to absorb it.

Two Balinese concepts of music form part of my teaching methodology: that when the music enters *(masuk)* you, you will not forget it; and that through kinetic response a striking mallet can become a teacher *(guru panggul,* literally, "teacher mallet"). To absorb both of these concepts requires extensive music repetition and a gradual, almost spiritual immersion in the music. When the music "enters you" and the "mallet is your teacher," you are a competent player. Benjamin Brinner describes musical competency as "individualized mastery of the array of interrelated skills and knowledge" required of musicians within a particular tradition or community, "acquired and developed in response to and in accordance with the demands and possibilities" of cultural and musical conditions (1995: 28). This is an internal process built upon experience; with only one hundred minutes of practice per week and two concerts per semester, however, it is difficult for my students to acquire any level of competency. Nonetheless, I have seen many wonderful moments of transition to greater competence, when students appropriate different fields of knowledge and are fully aware of the conditions of performance. At these moments, I know that I can rely on those musicians in performance and can concentrate on other students for whom the music has not yet "entered."

Many scholars have testified that gamelans themselves have a power to teach; that one who simply learns to listen to his or her part within the gamelan soundscape can learn not only the music but also musical values transferable to other musics (Cowan 1997; Doty 1983). The cycles of gamelan music can be repeated again and again, allowing for students to gradually grasp and master musical parts and to quickly develop proper playing technique. The music then "enters" and remains with students, and kinetic memory helps guide their playing. When students acquire this knowledge and experience, I no longer worry about their mistakes and instead concentrate, from my lead position as drummer, on shaping performance dynamics and expressions. Several students have acquired the competency to play the second drum with me; two have advanced to directing the group from the drum.

CREATING COMMUNITY

Cowan (1997: 29) reminds us that gamelan creates community because musicians do not play their parts alone but only in interaction with others. Gamelan playing teaches interdependence among players and my students learn to listen, at first perhaps only to their own part and mine, but gradually to all the musical parts sounding around them. They grow accustomed to this other world, which at first seems strange. Students have frequently stated that learning parts and structures and playing the music provide a much different perspective and experience from when they first heard gamelan music. Cowan calls this transformation a "powerful feeling of being a part of something bigger than oneself" (ibid.: 29). When the musicians attain this basic level of competency, the individual components (which often blaze along at a fast clip) come together in an entity greater than the sum of the separate parts (Tenzer and Cooper 1983: 12).

Traditional Balinese society is highly cooperative. Groups form for collective tasks, whether repairing roads, decorating a temple before a festival, flying kites, or playing music. The element of cooperation is reflected in the music, as musicians learn to hear all of the parts and to respond instantly when others signal changes. The Balinese term for any work group, including a gamelan club, is *sekaha*. These groups are fairly egalitarian; every member is responsible to the group and has a voice in decisions regarding rehearsals, the music, and logistics of performance. We cannot really follow the *sekaha* model; we have a more hierarchical structure (I make most decisions), meet infrequently, and do not apply all of the customary behavior associated with the instruments. Yet I try to preserve the aspect of social bonding, and hold biannual parties at my home for students to grow acquainted with each other outside class and concert contexts. These efforts seem to be paying off; I see a high level of cooperation when students move instruments together and help each other with the dress, and many like-minded students enjoy social camaraderie and musical solidarity. Those who have returned from a workshop in Bali are further bonded to each other through shared memories reenacted in performance. It is the gamelan that has made this unique sociomusical world possible.

PERFORMING A WORLD OF BALI

When I first arrived at BGSU, the dress for gamelan performance consisted of black pants and a yellow shirt. I tolerated this for a few years, not wanting the students (or perhaps myself, an untenured professor in a college with seemingly few ethnomusicological sympathies) to experience greater alienation or distance caused by "ethnodrag," the wearing and associations of ethnic musical dress. However, with some encouragement from colleagues, I acquired appropriate Balinese costumes for performances: *kain* (a long single Balinese *ikat*-style cloth), scarves (separate styles for men and women), headpieces *(udeng)* for men, and gold-leaf pieces for women to wear in their hair. Student, audience, and faculty reactions have been overwhelmingly positive, and now the music and dress are strongly linked. I think of the dress as an enhancement or extension of the music; it marks the students clearly as gamelan players and expands the overall process of performance, which now includes putting on and removing the clothing.

Turner's three-part paradigm of the ritual process (see especially 1969) is an apt metaphor for the performance experience. Donning the dress and readying the mind, body, and spirit are the preparation; the performance of music—in which behavior and boundaries are sometimes unclear and there exists an element of danger (mistakes) or the unknown—is the liminal state; and removing the ethnic dress and the performers' re-dressing as themselves are the reintegration back into society. The identities of the performers have been subject to a fluctuation and perhaps a three-part movement from Self to Other and back again. The "hermeneutical arc" theory tells us that the performers are not the same persons after such an experience.[4]

The physical context of performance is a challenge. We can do little to the stage to replicate Bali; a stage is certainly not a Balinese temple. Our fruit offering usually consists of more American than tropical fruits. We would also burn incense if it were not for one long-term member's strong allergy to the smoke, and the stage manager's fire marshal concerns.

The general BGSU concert etiquette contrasts entirely with that of Bali. Performers are met with applause, and the director receives further applause. In between pieces, the director leaves the stage to applause, then appears for the next piece to yet more applause. I try to subvert this norm by coming out with students and staying until we are finished. One compromise I have made is to briefly acknowledge applause after a piece and to speak to the audience on behalf of the group.

Gamelan Kusuma Sari performs on campus two to four times annually and off campus about twice a year. We sometimes do educational outreach programs at local schools or hold lecture demonstrations in music education formats, and now and again perform concerts at universities and festival events in Ohio and neighboring states. Each of these venues has a different audience, and reactions vary. Most audiences are uncritical, uninformed, and reserved, though children present may improvise dancing. At one performance at a school for the physically challenged, many of the students in the audience danced, clapped, and sang. They had little interest in my discussion about Bali and the pieces and only wanted to hear the music.

We frequently perform at institutions or events in areas of even less diversity than Bowling Green. On these occasions we are ambassadors for BGSU and Bali. Audience members often approach us and ask many questions ("Is Bali like this?" "Do all Balinese do this?"). The student answers I overhear show that they have synthesized information in unique ways and are expressing themselves in their responses. I try to avoid saying "The Balinese do this" or "They believe that," because these objectify a group and make them abstract, romantic, and monolithic; instead I say "I saw this" or "My teacher said this" to explain music and culture, conveying personal experiences whenever possible. I want us to bond with and be accessible to the audience. We are their conduit to Bali and everything it might happen to represent. The performances, dialogues, and gamelan itself may help to demythologize some lingering orientalist notions.

Our gamelan's claim to the role of cultural interpreter is sometimes a contested one. In the spring of 1995, we held two successful performances for the Asian Festival in Columbus. This newly formed annual festival brought together Asian performing groups from Ohio and neighboring states. We enjoyed the experience immensely, and I looked forward to an invitation the following year. The invitation never came. The booking agent explained that the Asian Chamber of Commerce, which sponsors the festival, did not think that a gamelan consisting almost exclusively of Caucasians and directed by one could properly represent an Asian culture. We did not appear "authentic," and therefore could not truly speak for Bali or Indonesia or Asia.

ADDRESSING AUTHENTICITY AND ORIENTALISM

I was fortunate to study with Balinese and Javanese music masters at several universities and in the field. Any students, including my own, desiring to specialize in Balinese music must eventually study with a Balinese master. However, I believe there are some benefits of studying with "outsiders" such as myself, who are often in a better position to mediate and optimally shape classroom experience. Students may also see me as a role model—an American dedicated to Balinese music and ethnomusicology—and wish to follow a similar path.

Through the decor, the dress, the music, and particularly the instruments, we stage concerts of Balinese music and reinvent a version of Balinese culture. Though we may feel very close to this experience, we are not and never will be Balinese, and our experiences are our own. We may gain a sense of an idealized Bali constructed from our imaginations, one full of magic, mystery, and shimmering sounds. This raises the possible problem of interpreting experience through a romantic orientalism.

Michelle Kisliuk (1997: 33–37), discussing her experiences performing Central African BaAka music and dance with BaAka people, submits that performance can break down the distinction between Self and Other, thus deconstructing distance and romanticism. I see this transformation within my gamelan students during performance, particularly with those who have played for several semesters or have gone to a workshop in Bali. For these students, the music has entered and the mallet is their teacher; I believe that they have learned to shape their subjectivity to interact with the music and with their fellow musicians. The music is no longer foreign and has essentially become part of who they are; thus, any orientalist notion is effectively dismantled. For most, this period of life with the gamelan is temporary. However, their experiences will inform future encounters between music and Self.

Just as it is necessary for ethnomusicologists to create reflexive images of themselves as ethnographers (Cooley 1997: 4), it is important that we consider our "shadows" as music directors. We affect our students directly, bring them into a foreign community, and introduce them to a new world of music. We offer an experience—not merely representation through words and images—that requires mental, physical, and sometimes spiritual participation. We are ultimately responsible for the development of our students and ensembles, and should reflect upon our training, strategies, and goals as part of a regular reassessment of ourselves as directors. A large part of this entire process includes adapting to the teaching environment and living with whatever compromises we feel we must make.

I see two kinds of orientalism at BGSU (and elsewhere), both grounded in "us and them" or "Self and Other" dichotomies. In the first, the gamelan sparks the imagination and represents exoticism; in the potentially more harmful second, an administration or faculty constructs a power relationship in which the duality of Self and Other is not complementary, where the Self defines the Other as inferior and even irrelevant.[5] We may always be the Other that some seek and others repel. However, *my* students may transcend that distance, enhance their musicality, and understand more about Bali, the world, and themselves through performance and immersion in the music. We can only hope that audiences sense these transformations and that administrations realize their importance.

NOTES

1. The late JaFran Jones established the BGSU ethnomusicology program by 1980. She was instrumental in purchasing two gamelans, one of which, a *gamelan angklung*, was sold to the Eastman School of Music in the early 1990s; the *gamelan gong kebyar* was acquired in 1991. She directed the ensemble for a few years, resigned, and was succeeded for a year by Michael Bakan (currently at Florida State University) before I arrived in the fall of 1994.

2. Brett (1994) has suggested that gamelan is a "gay marker": that homosexuals are perhaps attracted to gamelan as a voice of marginalized peoples. I have, however, not found this any more true of gamelan than of other ensembles.

3. Many of my students dress more casually or colorfully, have more body piercings or dyed hair, and frequently participate in drama and other arts. They are also more apt to smoke than the average student. Composers involved with contemporary or electronic music often enroll as well. All typically express alternative and sometimes subversive "takes" on food and popular culture. Unfortunately, this "alternativeness" seems to have led some students to think that they can be tardy to class or occasionally absent, an attitude that infuriates me.

4. The "arc" concept holds that as one rereads a text after an interval, its meanings seem to have changed. However, it is the individual who has changed between readings through experiences and adjusted foreknowledge. Music performance, like a text, provides an experience that reshuffles or reevaluates the self. See further Ricoeur (1981, esp. p. 164), Gadamer (1975), and Wallulis (1990) for more on concepts of hermeneutical arcs and circles, and Rice (1994) and Harnish (2001) for applications in ethnomusicology.

5. Note the application by some feminist scholars of this orientalist metaphor to gender (see, for example, Austern 1998).

Chapter 7

Cultural Interactions in an Asian Context

Chinese and Javanese Ensembles in Hong Kong

J. LAWRENCE WITZLEBEN

Most discussions of the study of performance in ethnomusicology have concentrated on Western students learning non-Western traditions. We have Mantle Hood (1982) to thank for emphasizing the value of performance study as an important component in the training of ethnomusicologists, but the term *bimusicality* itself presumes that one is already literate in a Western musical language.

The increasing prominence of intra-Asian cross-cultural study of musical performance—including the study of traditions from other regions or social settings within one's own country—is a phenomenon that also deserves our attention. However, the phenomenon has so far generally been ignored, despite the increasing attention given in ethnomusicology and anthropology to the nuances of intracultural or intraregional "border crossing" and "insider-outsider" issues. These very different encounters raise interesting issues of transmission, authenticity, and representation, as well as practical problems related to teaching and learning methods. What happens when Asian students learn to perform the musics of other countries in the region or of other regional subcultures within their own country? Are the problems, challenges, and successes in teaching and learning similar to those faced by students in North America? In this chapter, I will address these and related questions through a case study of the Chinese and Javanese ensemble classes in the Chinese University of Hong Kong's music department.

PRELUDE

Like many ethnomusicologists, I became involved with Asian music gradually. Although I was exposed to a fair amount of Japanese music when my father's work took my family to Tokyo for three years beginning in 1964, as an American teenager I was far more interested in the British invasion and surf music. As an undergraduate, I studied literature at the University of California at Santa Cruz, and I later became a music theory and history major at U.C. Santa Barbara. Although my interests were reasonably eclectic, my classes in literature and music were essentially the study of Western literature and Western music. During this same period, my parents and siblings were living in Taipei, and I was able to spend a few months there teaching English and taking a few lessons on the *zheng* (zither with moveable bridges). This experience, combined with a seminar in ethnomusicology taught by Dolores Hsu, led me to write a senior thesis on Chinese music under her supervision. Graduate study in ethnomusicology seemed to be a reasonable next step.

Learning to play Chinese and Indonesian music was a natural part of my studies and life as a graduate student. The typical scope of my vision was from lesson to lesson, performance to performance: even if a course in "world music ensemble pedagogy" existed, it would have held little interest for me, since the idea of teaching such ensembles myself was not even on the horizon. The largest picture I saw at the time related this learning and music making to things such as research papers, thesis topics, and chances to study performance abroad, either as an end in itself or as a component of research-oriented fieldwork.

The training we receive in ethnomusicology programs is a nexus linking the people and themes involved in this volume. Timothy Rice suggests that musical traditions are "historically constructed, socially maintained and individually applied" (1987: 473), and the same tripartite model can be used to understand the culture of teaching and learning ethnomusicology in Western universities. A certain degree of commonality exists in the way the performance components of these programs have been "historically constructed" and "socially maintained"; however, they have been "individually experienced" even by participants in the same program, and during fieldwork and other further studies, the individual nature of musical and cultural knowledge and skills becomes increasingly apparent. Moreover, whatever common ground may exist in the training we go through as graduate students, each of us begins this period of study bringing along a network of previous musical training, encounters, and values, in short, a music world view, however hazily formed or inarticulate. In this field without pedagogical models, how we teach and what we teach are highly individualized, shaped by our accumulated musical experiences and adapted to particular locales, institutions, and human resources in the form of student performers.

Before I studied ethnomusicology, my ensemble encounters included many years of singing in choirs, university choruses, and chamber groups, along with the more directly relevant experiences of playing acoustic and electric guitar on countless occasions in jam sessions, rehearsals, and occasional performances. Playing rock, folk, blues, and jazz music with friends and even total strangers helped me to develop skills in aural and oral learning, improvisation, interaction, and communication. At times, my playing also required that I take on leadership and teaching roles. I also practiced the useful skills of "faking it" when playing a new tune or getting lost in a chord progression, and dealing with musicians' egos. Although I rarely performed as a professional, except for a few months each as a busker (street musician) in Europe and in a rock band in Taipei, playing guitar in various contexts, with different combinations of instruments and in diverse musical styles, was a formative musical experience that provided both useful preparation and potentially hindering preconceptions for playing Asian music.

During a break from my undergraduate studies in Western music, I took several months of lessons on *zheng* with the late Liang Tsai-ping in Taipei. This began my long encounter with Chinese music, but when I chose the University of Hawai'i for graduate study, the attraction for me was the program's cultural diversity and emphasis on ethnomusicology as a cross-culturally applicable discipline rather than its suitability for becoming an area specialist. In fact, I was also quite interested in Indonesian and Japanese music, and my future research could have easily gone in either of these directions. However, although there was no Chinese music specialist on the University of Hawai'i faculty, I discovered that my professors, especially Barbara Smith and Lee Byong-won, had a keen interest in Chinese music, and they encouraged me to continue to explore research possibilities in that area. After hearing a performance in Honolulu by the Wo Lok music club, I tracked down the group and began to study the *erhu* (two-stringed bowed lute) with the ensemble's leader, Harry Lee. The music he taught me was from the ensemble tradition of Cantonese music, and during my lessons he would often pick up a bamboo flute or plucked lute and play along. After a while, I was encouraged to sit in with the group when they played tunes I knew during their weekly informal sessions of Cantonese music and opera. Although the musical language and media were unfamiliar, the informal context, flexible instrumentation, and overall ambience seemed comfortable and familiar, and I went on to do research on Cantonese music in Hong Kong for my master's degree thesis (1983) at the University of Hawai'i.

In 1981, I had an opportunity to enter the Shanghai Conservatory as a research student and spent a year attending classes, taking lessons, and beginning fieldwork on *Jiangnan sizhu*, the regional musical kin of the Cantonese ensemble music I had previously studied. In a subsequent, longer stay in 1984–85, I had extensive involvement with the amateur music clubs, typically playing *erhu* with them for a couple of pieces. As it turned out, my experiences playing popular music and jazz were useful preparation for these encounters, since my readiness to play without notation, to improvise, or to make my way through difficult or unfamiliar repertory set me apart from my conservatory-trained classmates and sometimes delighted the participants in the music clubs. However, my teachers were not always equally pleased, since they expected me to thoroughly master their own versions of the pieces they taught me (which I actually was usually trying to do, although not always successfully) before I went on to develop a voice of my own.

In 1987–88, while I was a postdoctoral fellow at the University of Michigan Center for Chinese Studies, ethnomusicologist William Malm encouraged me to use some of the fine instruments from the Stearns Collection to put together a Chinese music ensemble, and I found myself giving lessons on beginning *erhu* (two-stringed fiddle) and *yangqin* (struck zither) and, somewhat by default, playing *dizi* and *xiao* (transverse and vertical bamboo flutes) in the ensemble. Fortunately, several of the participants were skilled on related instruments (the *yangqin* player, Deborah Wong, played its Thai equivalent) or other Chinese instruments (Tsai Hsiu-huei was an excellent *zheng* player who started learning *erhu*). With the help of some fortuitous guest performers (Terry Liu on *erhu* and John Myers on *pipa*, a four-stringed plucked lute, both of who had written ethnomusicology dissertations about their respective instruments), the group was able to give a reasonably successful performance in conjunction with the Japanese ensemble.

My studies in Javanese gamelan were somewhat more circuitous. I had been attracted to the music via the Nonesuch Explorer Series of recordings, and in my first semester at the University of Hawai'i, I enrolled in the beginning gamelan class taught by Roger Vetter (at the time a graduate assistant filling in for Hardja Susilo, who was on sabbatical). After the first semester, I immediately jumped into strenuous rehearsals for a two-evening dance drama. Although my parts were not technically complex (gong, *siyem*, and *kenong*, all slow-moving "colotomic" or punctuating instruments), the correct placement of their notes was crucial for the other musicians and dancers, and I quickly developed a new appreciation of the complexity of ensemble interaction in the music. In the following year, I began to learn *bonang* (gong chime) and *gambang* (wooden-keyed xylophone) with Pak Susilo, and I joined a six-person study group to Yogyakarta the following summer. When I returned, I participated in several performances, including playing the *gambang* for a four-hour *wayang kulit* shadow play.

As my plans for a thesis on Chinese music came to take precedence over all else, my involvement with *gamelan* music promptly ceased. During the year in Michigan, I returned to Javanese *gamelan*, but in 1988 I accepted a teaching position at the Chinese University of Hong Kong, and Indonesia seemed to be destined to have no significant role in my musical life for the foreseeable future.[1] However, this would change dramatically in 1994.

"WHY IS CHINESE MUSIC SO BACKWARD?"
MUSIC EDUCATION, MUSICAL VALUES,
AND PRE-POSTCOLONIAL CONFUSION IN HONG KONG

In Hong Kong, the vast majority of undergraduate music students are trained in Western classical music. Most have considerable passive familiarity with Chinese music, but very little in-depth knowledge or training. Their experience with musics of other parts of Asia is usually minimal, acquired through stereotypes learned from movies and television, or perhaps through tourist performances encountered in travel with their family or student groups.

Under the British colonial administration, music in Hong Kong tertiary institutions was primarily Western art music. As in many parts of the world, upwardly mobile families had their children—especially their daughters—study piano or other Western instruments, and teachers would diligently put them through the paces of the Royal School of Music system of graded levels of achievement. In the university, they would continue the study of their chosen instrument, along with choral singing, ear training, harmony, theory, and history.

Within this Western-dominated system, Chinese music occupied a visible but ambiguous position. Since the 1970s, the Chinese University music department offered courses in Chinese music history (divided chronologically into three or four semesters) and "music literature" (genre-based studies of instrumental music, opera, narrative song, and folk song), and employed three or four full-time faculty members specializing in Chinese music (along with around eight others teaching Western music theory, composition, and musicology).[2] All students were required to take a few of these courses and to study a Chinese instrument for at least one year. Despite this, many students saw these courses as a distraction from their "serious" music studies, or even as a thoroughly unpleasant experience. One could often hear otherwise intelligent Hong Kong students saying things like "Chinese music is backward," or "I want to do my paper on Cantonese music to find out why it sounds so horrible" with a straight face. It is easy to blame such attitudes on the colonial legacy. Too easy, in fact, when we realize that students of Western music in Shanghai or Beijing often hold similar condescending attitudes toward their own country's music.

Within this environment, the few students majoring in Chinese music naturally felt marginalized, and the establishment of a Chinese ensemble as a course for which credit was offered in the early 1990s was a major step toward improving their prestige within the department and the university community. Their annual concerts drew appreciative audiences, performances in class were far more effective than recordings, and the group began to be in demand for receptions, banquets, and other engagements. These developments coincided with widespread changes in Hong Kong society, as the territory's return to Chinese sovereignty in 1997 approached. During this "pre-postcolonial" period, engagement with Chinese cultural values became increasingly widespread, and even students of Western music were affected by these changes. Coupled with an increasingly large and distinguished graduate program in ethnomusicology, the Chinese ensemble, along with Cantonese opera performing workshops, accompanied a major shift in student attitudes toward Chinese music, seen most obviously in a steady increase in enrollments in lecture courses.[3]

The teaching of non-Western, non-Chinese music at the university had a later start, and it was not until the 1990s that the survey "Music in World Cultures" was offered. The course soon became a popular one, and music students began to look for opportunities to learn to perform these other traditions. Some joined the Sun Drum Village African drum ensemble (organized by percussionists from the Hong Kong Philharmonic) in their spare time, and in 2000 this course finally became available for academic credit. The acquisition of a Javanese gamelan in 1994 gave non-Chinese Asian music an immediate prominence, and despite the absence of an expert teacher or a core of experienced musicians, gamelan classes have remained popular.

My own involvement in these ensembles has been rather different for the two types of music. As the coordinator of a Chinese string and wind ensemble, my aim has been not only to increase the visibility of Chinese music in a Western-dominated department, but also to pass on my concepts of "traditional" values learned from amateur "folk" performers in a largely aurally transmitted setting to these technically advanced students trained in a highly arranged, notated concert tradition. As a teacher of Javanese gamelan, I introduce the music to absolute beginners with no knowledge of gamelan music and no direct aural experience of the tradition other than hearing themselves.

CHINESE ENSEMBLE

While living and studying at the Shanghai Conservatory, I took lessons at various times on the *zheng, erhu, dizi, xiao,* and *pipa,* learning from highly detailed prescriptive notation that was intended to be learned and repeated precisely, supplemented by intensive oral instruction and aural imitation. In the world of the amateur music clubs, playing from scores was acceptable only for rank beginners; my formal and informal *Jiangnan sizhu* teachers all stressed the importance of *jixing jiahua* (improvised "flowers," meaning ornamentation), and an accomplished musician was expected both to develop a recognizable playing style within the stylistic parameters of the tradition and to vary his or her renditions of the familiar pieces with each performance.

Not surprisingly, this type of aural tradition was rather alien to Hong

Kong students learning Chinese instruments. When the CUHK Chinese ensemble first began in the early 1990s, most of the students had performed extensively in the Chinese Youth Orchestra. This large ensemble of Chinese instruments is a "Modern Chinese Orchestra" (see Han 1979 and Tsui 2002) modeled on the Western symphony orchestra, using part scores and led by a conductor with a baton—not with a *pipa, dizi,* or drumsticks, as in traditional instrumental or operatic ensembles. Their approach to learning and performing music was virtually indistinguishable from their classmates who studied Western instruments.

Most of the students who have joined the Chinese ensemble have already studied their instrument for many years, and some perform at the level of giving solo recitals at the university or in formal concerts with paid attendance. My role has been that of a curator or advisor, helping them to choose repertory and to coordinate and fine-tune their playing. Although we have performed many of the Cantonese and Jiangnan pieces with which I am most familiar, their preference is to work from part scores with precise instructions for fingerings, ornaments, and so on.[4] However, at times we have played pieces for which no separate parts are available, and in these cases the students have been forced to either play in stolid unison or to develop some "flower-adding" skills.

One of my colleagues, Yu Siu-Wah, is an outstanding *erhu* player with extensive performance experience in both the written and aural traditions of Chinese music. On several occasions he and I have joined a small group of graduate students or research assistants to perform small group pieces in a more traditional manner, working from commonly shared skeleton melodies and developing our own ornamentation for each instrument. Several years ago, we gave a concert with Yu playing *erhu* and other bowed lutes, a former student playing bamboo flutes, and me playing *zheng.* More recently, we performed one of the older pieces of *Jiangnan sizhu* in a quartet of *xiao, erhu, pipa,* and *sheng* (mouth organ). These performances serve a didactic purpose in presenting a model for realizing music in ways that go beyond the notes written in the score.

Since relatively few Chinese University music students specialize in Chinese instruments, the activity and quality of the ensemble has fluctuated widely, and from 1997 to 1999 there was no regular ensemble at all, since the combination of instruments available was not workable. In 2000 the ensemble sprang back to life, helped greatly by a new student, Yeung Wai-Kit, who had already obtained a diploma in *dizi* performance from the Hong Kong Academy for Performing Arts. He is quite confident in playing from memory and adding improvised ornamentation, and his contribution may lead to further developments in directions that are closer to my own aesthetic ideals of traditional Chinese music making.

The kind of ensemble "teaching" just described is rather different from the more typical ensemble in an ethnomusicology program, in that the performers are cultural insiders who are already skilled performers of Chinese music. Many of the repertory choices are made by the students, including what I would call aesthetically dubious arrangements of Vivaldi's *Four Seasons* and Mozart's "Turkish Dance." However, their music making includes a strong element of cultural advocacy, in this case promoting Chinese music in an environment that is dominated by Western music. In this aesthetic and cultural context, playing arrangements of Western music and using part scores and music stands allows Chinese music to claim the same right to attention and respect as its foreign rival.

Despite the discrepancies I have mentioned between my own aesthetic ideals and those of the student performers, the Chinese ensemble has reached a new level of public acceptance and enthusiasm. This was especially apparent in a performance at the Chinese University's Art Museum for the Friends of the Art Museum. The concert was attended by the head of the Chinese University, Vice Chancellor Arthur Li, and was warmly received by the Friends of the Museum. The performance led to requests for additional performances, and even the suggestion that the group record and sell a compact disc of their playing. In 2003 recordings of the group's most recent concert were being edited for a CD and DVD.

JAVANESE GAMELAN

In 1994, the Chinese University of Hong Kong purchased a *slendro-pelog* gamelan (with sets of instruments in both tuning systems) made in Yogyakarta by Suhirdjan, and I was asked to begin teaching the ensemble as a condition for buying the instruments. I had not touched any gamelan instrument for many years, and even when I was heavily involved in the music in Hawai'i and Michigan, I had never thought about teaching the music. I realized that an absolute minimal requirement for starting an ensemble was some knowledge of drumming, which I had never even begun to study, so I spent the summer of 1994 in Yogyakarta taking lessons on the *kendhang* (the drum that controls the gamelan tempo) with the late Ki Suhardi. I began teaching my first gamelan classes the following year. The students have been almost exclusively music majors, with most specializing in Western music.

Javanese gamelan has become perhaps the most widespread of all non-Western ensemble traditions in ethnomusicology programs, and there is great diversity in both the way it is taught and the kinds of skills the performers and teachers bring to the music. Still, every teacher and student faces a series of challenges in passing on or acquiring a reasonable degree of competence in the tradition. Some of these challenges are described below.

Technique and Cultural Background

Like most ethnomusicologists, I believe that musical understanding is closely tied to cultural understanding, and that the more one knows about where the music came from, how it is learned, and where, when, by whom, and for whom it is performed, the more effectively and convincingly one can play it. Students who have taken my courses in world music have heard and read about gamelan music and have seen videos of performances in the Yogyakarta palaces, in Suhardi's home, and on concert stages in Hong Kong, as well an introductory video with demonstrations of the individual instruments performed by University of Hawai'i students. Ideally, they have acquired some respect for the music and instruments and a feeling for its power and aesthetic complexity.

Students who have not taken the course may approach the ensemble class in much more practical terms. They want to learn to play music, to produce pleasant sounds, and to master some new techniques. Instructions on how to sit and admonishments to walk around the instruments rather than step over them may seem silly. Not sensing how important the gong and other punctuating instruments are to the music (and to conceptions of time, repetition, and harmoniousness), they view playing them as boring or even as a kind of punishment.

Of course, these two contrasting sets of attitudes cannot be matched directly with whether or not students have taken a course that includes talking about Javanese musical values, and every participant shares some elements of both orientations. Nevertheless, it is indisputable that, all other things being equal, students who have taken the lecture course are much more likely to approach the music with respect for these values, so much so that I have considered making the survey course a prerequisite for ensemble participation.

Stress, Beats, and End-Orientation

In my first semester as a gamelan student, I managed to learn the part for the *panerus bonang* (the set of horizontal gongs or "gong chime" on which a fast-moving elaborating melody is played) for a short piece ("Bubaran Udan Mas," as I recall). After practicing for many hours on my own, I performed it with the beginning group as part of the annual "Pau Hana" gathering of student ensembles, and felt quite pleased with myself. Pak Susilo kindly praised my performance, then went on to explain that "we don't play it that way in Java." I had learned the notes almost perfectly, but played them in the wrong place. Instead of:

656. 6565 323. 3232
6   5   3   2

with the last elaborating note of each unit of four corresponding with the *balungan* (skeletal melody) note, I had played something like the following.

656. 6565 323. 3232
6   5   3   2

Believers in musical universals may be pleased to know that students in Hong Kong have a similar difficulty internalizing a sense of feeling the stress at the end of a *bonang* pattern, *gatra* (group of four notes), *kenongan* (phrase ending with the stroke of a *kenong,* a large horizontal gong), or *gongan* (a melodic unit ending with a stroke of the large hanging gong).[5] In class, teaching one small segment at a time by rote generally produces good results, but even with a small group, teaching *bonang* patterns to each student in turn quickly uses up the class time. Practicing on their own, students tend to transfer the concurrences with the *balungan* to where they feel "right": on the first note of each group of four. In a recent final performance exam, all four students in a beginning group trying to play the *bonang* parts for simple pieces started off correctly, but they quickly shifted the placement of the notes to where they seemed correct according to Western/Chinese standards, and they stayed there for the remainder of the pieces.

Musical Notation

Throughout my gamelan studies, I approached the music primarily as an oral/aural tradition: the group in Hawai'i learned pieces by rote, and in both Hawai'i and Java, I also learned the elaborating instruments by rote during lessons, later practicing with audio tapes, and rarely writing down the parts. *Balungan* notation was written down, but anyone relying on it during a performance or even a rehearsal was considered to be a substandard player.

Many American music students have had considerable experience in playing rock, jazz, or other traditions that require extensive learning by ear and unwritten extemporizing, and most ethnomusicology graduate students are also eager to develop their aural skills. Undergraduate music students in Hong Kong are almost exclusively trained in Western classical music, and those who play Chinese music are also accustomed to playing and learning from scores.[6] Although I teach new pieces by rote and encourage students to play them from memory afterwards, the development of aural learning and playing skills among Hong Kong students has been an uphill struggle.

Successes and Failures

Despite the somewhat bleak picture just presented, student response to learning gamelan has been generally positive, and one group was able to achieve a standard of playing culminating in several successful public performances. This group had already been together for a year when we had an opportunity to work with a visiting artist, Poedijono, who was in residence at the neighboring University of Hong Kong. In a series of intensive sessions, he taught our students four new performance segments, including the accompaniment for two dances and a *wayang kulit* scene. Poedijono began by handing out notation for all the pieces, and although the students continued to use it, they had enough rapport from playing together that they were able to transcend the problems caused by reading one's notes at the expense of listening and watching. Playing for dance accompaniment is in itself an incentive to learn the music, so that the performers can raise their heads and enjoy watching the dance. The group played two concerts with the Hong Kong University Balinese gamelan, also directed by Poedijono with the help of ethnomusicologist Manolete Mora.

After this experience, the students were shocked to discover that my rudimentary drumming skills were not suitable for playing any of these new pieces. However, before they graduated a few months later, we were able to arrange a credible program, mainly of loud-style pieces, including the relatively long and difficult "Gendhing Bonangan Tukung."

This concert experience has led me to question my perhaps unreasonable prejudice against notation in performance. If a native expert like Poedijono (albeit one who has been teaching in Australia for many years) was able to achieve remarkable results in a month, why should a non-native such as myself stubbornly insist on processes that are undeniably slower and whose advantages are perhaps more philosophical than musical?

POSTLUDE

As discussed earlier, during the 2000–2001 academic year, the Chinese ensemble had two extremely successful performances that were enthusiastically attended and received. In this same year, more than twenty students enrolled in gamelan classes, forming three separate groups, including one group of continuing students who were already experienced players. As a result, in May 2001 the gamelan ensemble was able to give its first public concert since 1998, this time in conjunction with the CUHK African drum ensemble. The program included the Asian premier of American composer Jarrad Powell's "Ketawang Lagu Pangajabsih" for *erhu* and gamelan.

Learning or performing gamelan music without teachers, players, or singers for the more difficult instruments has obvious limitations in terms of both aesthetics and authenticity. Nevertheless, by offering the experience of learning gamelan and playing music that has different rules, values, and expectations from its Western and Chinese counterparts, "performing ethnomusicology" in Hong Kong continues to challenge players and listeners to develop new ways of hearing and experiencing music.

To return to the questions raised at the outset, it seems clear that the problems, challenges, and successes of Hong Kong students learning gamelan are not too dissimilar to those of their counterparts in Western countries: the temperament, structures, texture, accents, and senses of tempo and flow in Javanese music are rather distant from those of both Chinese and Western musical culture. Similarly, positive learning experiences and satisfying performances are closely linked to group dynamics and rapport, and are greatly enhanced by opportunities to work with indigenous experts and visiting artists, especially those who can bring in the additional dimensions of dance and puppet theater. However, it is clear from my involvement in gamelan performances at the Universities of Hawai'i and Michigan that American music students, when compared with their counterparts in Hong Kong, are far more willing and able to learn and perform the music as an oral/aural tradition. Although it is tempting to speculate on cultural values related to spontaneity and respect for written culture, I can suggest two more concrete reasons for this difference, First, American students, even those majoring in Western art music, tend to have had much more exposure to jazz, rock, and other forms of music that involve a certain degree of aural learning. Second, gamelan ensembles in the United States typically rely heavily on ethnomusicology graduate students, who are expected to develop aural skills as part of their training, while the ensemble in Hong Kong has been composed exclusively of undergraduate music students.[7]

The Chinese ensemble tells a rather different story. Rather than being a group of beginners learning the music of a relatively unfamiliar culture, the ensemble consists mostly of student performers who entered the university having already studied Chinese instruments for many years. The challenge of trying to bring in elements of folk styles and improvisation is one that has analogues in the West, but there is no exact counterpart to the systematized, conservatory-taught folk music that is the norm in all modern Chinese societies (including the Chinese mainland, Taiwan, and Hong Kong). For example, a classically trained violinist learning fiddle tunes encounters both new repertoire and different ways of playing the instrument, while in Chinese folk music such as *Jiangnan sizhu,* the instruments and ways of playing them are essentially the same as in modern concertized traditions,[8] and much of the repertoire is already familiar to the student performers. A student learning jazz in a university setting might have similar difficulties playing in a jam session, but it is hard to imagine anyone learning jazz who had never played an improvised solo, and in any case the scope of improvisation allowed in Chinese string and wind music is much narrower than in most small-group jazz. Unlike the participants in the Chinese ensemble at the

University of Michigan (some of whom had considerable skill on their instruments, but none of whom were familiar enough with the musical genres being performed to be expected to add improvised "flowers" idiomatically), the students in Hong Kong should be able do so, especially in their indigenous Cantonese music. In fact, their disinterest in developing aural and/or semi-improvisational skills is an attitude that was shared by virtually every Chinese music student I met at the Shanghai Conservatory.

Like other kinds of musicologists—as well as anthropologists—ethnomusicologists are trained primarily as scholars and awarded their degrees for their accomplishments in things academic, yet even a glance at job openings and teaching duties in the field of ethnomusicology shows that performance ensembles are an integral part of many programs. This phenomenon expands the visibility and prominence of ethnomusicology and non-Western music, yet it is not without its dangers. In departments or schools of music, most chairs, deans, and other administrators are specialists in Western music. Such specialists can easily distinguish between, on the one hand, an acceptable Western music student performance that is satisfying for the participants, friends, and family and, on the other hand, a performance of a very high artistic standard that represents the tradition as it should be heard. A similar level of artistic discernment can by no means be expected for evaluating and distinguishing performances of Chinese, Javanese, or other less familiar musical traditions. If an ethnomusicologist moonlighting as a performance teacher can already produce the first type of performance, which brings exotic sounds and publicity to a music program, why go to the expense and trouble necessary to bring truly outstanding performers as master teachers or artists-in-residence? It is an ongoing challenge to those of us involved in ensemble teaching not only to keep a sense of perspective on the nature and purpose of what is being taught and performed, but also to raise the level of multicultural aesthetic awareness of our administrators and colleagues as well as our students.

NOTES

1. Although a graduate program in ethnomusicology had been recently initiated in the Chinese University (CUHK) music department, my position was specifically that of a specialist in Chinese music. Fortunately, some of the faculty in Western music had gotten to know me during my research there in 1980–81, Tsao Pen-yeh of the Chinese music faculty knew me and my work from our studies together at the University of Pittsburgh, and my dissertation advisor, Bell Yung, was a former faculty member of the CUHK music department. All of these factors surely influenced the department's decision to take the somewhat controversial step of hiring a non-Chinese to teach Chinese music.

2. One faculty position is for a pianist, but, for the most part, "applied music" (that is, individual lessons in performance) is taught by part-time teachers, with the students traveling to the teachers' homes or studios for lessons. Some full-time faculty also supervise ensembles or conduct the choir and orchestra.

3. The first time I offered the lecture course in Chinese instrumental music, I had five students. Now, it normally attracts more than forty students, and several of my colleagues have noted similar enrollment increases in their Chinese music classes.

4. Some multipart scores are written or arranged by a composer, others arranged by a performer from the tradition being played. Sometimes, solo arrangements for individual instruments can be combined effectively.

5. In this respect, Western classical music and Chinese traditional music share similar principles of stress and beat placement.

6. Although a few graduate students have participated in the Chinese ensemble, not one has expressed interest in playing in the gamelan ensemble, a phenomenon worthy of some further scrutiny (see also note 7).

7. As of 2003, none of the ethnomusicology graduate students at the Chinese University of Hong Kong has joined the gamelan group, although several of the most recent arrivals have expressed interest. Although the reasons for this are complex, it can undoubtedly be linked to the separation of "performers" and "scholars" in contemporary Chinese societies: unlike in the United States, Europe, or other parts of Asia such as Japan, virtually none of the prominent Chinese music scholars in China are actively involved in performance or the teaching of performance.

8. I am speaking at the general level of being able to perform the music with a reasonable degree of idiomatic suitability. In fact, amateur *Jiangnan sizhu* music clubs in Shanghai use some instruments that are constructed, tuned, or fretted differently from their modern equivalents, and many folk performers use special techniques such as fingering the *erhu* with the pads of their fingers rather than with their fingertips.

PART THREE

Patchworkers, Actors, and Ambassadors

Representing Ourselves and Others

Chapter 8

"Can't Help but Speak, Can't Help but Play"

Dual Discourse in Arab Music Pedagogy

INTERVIEW WITH ALI JIHAD RACY
BY SCOTT MARCUS AND TED SOLÍS

This interview took place on June 14, 2000, at UCLA.

EARLY BACKGROUND AND CAREER TRAJECTORY

TED SOLÍS: Give us some general history of how you got into the field, progressed, and came to this country, how that all happened.

ALI JIHAD RACY: I was born in Lebanon on July 31, 1943, and grew up in a musical family. My mother played the violin. My maternal uncles played the *'ūd* [short-necked fretless lute] and violin. Although they studied Western music, they mostly played Arab music. Both sides of my family were musical, but also valued education. In fact, I have many highly established relatives at universities, scholars in Lebanon as well as in England, Brazil, and North America. So, there was emphasis on both the arts and scholarship. Going to school and getting a degree was imperative, but music was important enough to be recognized and encouraged.

Born in a small village, Ibl al-Saqī, I was exposed to the local folk music. I played folk instruments, including flutes that I made from reeds that grew in our own garden. I heard traditional Arab music on old 78 rpm's on the family's old phonograph, one of the remnants of the old days. Of course, also radio, and later on television. My early experience was eclectic, listening to the local folk music, listening to traditional Arab music, hearing my uncles and others in the village perform on various instruments. My village was famous for the *buzuq* [long-necked fretted lute]. Some made the instrument and many played it. Gypsies who came by the village also played the *buzuq*. I became obsessed with the instrument at a young age. By age thirteen, I expressed tremendous desire to have one. My father bought one for me and it became one of my main instruments. I began to play the *nāy* (end-blown flute) also around that time.

I also studied Western music. In high school, in the southern city of Saidon, I took violin lessons in the Western classical tradition. Moving with my parents to Beirut, I finished my high school degree and went to the American University of Beirut. I continued to study Western music at the Lebanese Conservatory, at the American University, and at one private academy. Also at the time, I was playing with local Arab groups, as well as meeting with and hearing well-established musicians. I was part of a trio that included my brother, Khaled, who played percussion. We all played periodically on TV. Being students of the American University of Beirut, we were known as the University Trio. I remember the time when we performed for Pete Seeger, who came to Lebanon and visited the university around 1967. I corresponded with him and later on visited him in his home in the United States. In Lebanon I developed a strong interest in world music, which became the topic of a program I presented at the Lebanese Radio Station during 1967–68.

I came to the United States through an interesting contact. I think it was in 1967, at the academy mentioned above. The director of the academy, the late Sami Salibi, said "We have an American professor who is visiting the country briefly and is interested in music of the Near East. Why don't you come play for him?" Certainly, I did not know who he was or what that could lead to. I did meet that person and played for him. It turns out he was an ethnomusicologist, namely William Malm of the University of Michigan. Bill, who was on his way to somewhere in Asia, was extremely encouraging. I said, "I am interested in pursuing graduate musicological study." He gave me several addresses and names, including Bruno Nettl, whose book *Theory and Method in Ethnomusicology* [1964] I had come upon at the American University of Beirut library. Through Bruno's enthusiastic support I ended up at the University of Illinois in the fall of 1968.

From Illinois I received my master's in 1971 and my doctorate in 1977. My thesis and dissertation were both under Bruno Nettl.

TS: What was your language proficiency or ability? What languages did you acquire at which periods of your life?

AJR: Obviously, my first language is Arabic, which is spoken in Lebanon. I am particularly proficient in classical Arabic. My father, Salam Racy, who has just passed away at the age of ninety-two, was a well-known author, folklorist, storyteller, and poet. People cherished his writings and his style of delivery. His verbal artistry inspired me in musical ways, particularly in terms of the intimate rapport with the audience. Besides Arabic, I studied French in elementary school, and I began to learn English when I was nine years old. At the American University of Beirut, the instruction was practically all in English. Later on in this country I took courses in German and Persian.

In the United States, I did quite a bit of playing. I performed in the Midwest, especially Chicago, and also traveled frequently to the East Coast, especially New York. I played in gigs and concerts with many well-known artists, including those who visited from the Arab world.

In the spring of 1977, I was a visiting faculty at the University of Hawai'i. There, I taught many courses, including performance of Arab music. Throughout the country, there seemed to be a growing interest in world music performance. Also, the influence of institutions such as UCLA was widely felt. There were professors who had studied with Mantle Hood and who had already been teaching performance, as well as doing research, at Hawai'i, Wesleyan, Washington, and other places.

There was also a significant Middle Eastern following. In the 1970s, the so-called "belly dance" movement was very popular in this country. Similarly, Middle Eastern music was very appealing to many Americans who were becoming musically connected with the Middle East. In Hawai'i there was a sort of subculture, a small pocket of devotees who played *saz* [Turkish long-necked fretted lute], *'ūd,* and the Arab drum or who took dance lessons or frequented Middle Eastern nightclubs there.

Then, after Hawai'i, in 1977, I went to the University of Washington in Seattle. Actually, I was brought there for a summer program, but the university extended my appointment for the following year. At Washington I taught performance, as well as regular classes and seminars. Seattle had its own world music circle. After that, I taught in two summer sessions on world music, organized by Bob Brown at San Francisco State. There, I came in contact with teachers, students, and musics from various backgrounds.

Then, coming to UCLA in 1978 introduced me to a stimulating world music scene both at the university and in the city of Los Angeles: musical ensembles, dance troupes, nightclubs, and the music business. There was also strong interest in the Middle East, the Balkans, and the Far East, among other areas. In this climate, I have been teaching, traveling, and concertizing. I have also recorded my own music and composed for such groups as the West Coast–based Kronos Quartet.

DUALITY OF ROLES

AJR: When I joined UCLA (at the time ethnomusicology being under the Department of Music), my versatility as a performer-researcher was found highly desirable. I remember when I gave my interview-lecture I both spoke and played. I came from Illinois as an ethnomusicologist with a minor in Western medieval music, as someone who has taken courses, for example, in early notation and research methods in historical musicology. I already had several publications. However, I was also a performer who had taught performance. At that time, the performance program at UCLA was quite alive, and since then it has continued to thrive. Among the UCLA performing scholars was Nazir Jairazbhoy, who gave me tremendous support and guidance over the years.

So, for the last twenty years or so, the UCLA Near East Ensemble has been a prime context for teaching performance of Arab music. Certainly, my dual role, as a university professor and as a performer, has posed certain challenges. There is always tension that pulls you in different directions, but at the same time the duality provides a sense of fulfillment.

TS: Before Nazir, few performers were involved with the academic stuff, it seems.

AJR: That is true. There was a time when our instructors were recognized mainly as artists. But there were professors—Mantle Hood, Bill Malm, and others—who also taught performance. I think such dual profiles have added a significant component to the academic makeup.

This leads to a basic question, namely, how do we reconcile the two roles, or how do we combine the thinking and the playing in our professional careers? I am reminded of Charles Seeger's philosophy, which underlay UCLA's approach, namely, that music cannot be fully represented through verbal discourse, but can be experienced in intrinsically musical ways. I met Charles Seeger once at an SEM [Society for Ethnomusicology] meeting. I think it was in Toronto. In one of the sessions, I remember him standing up and explaining his stance roughly as follows:

> If you bring a xylophone player from East Africa and he doesn't speak one word of English, can't you still learn something from him? If he has his instrument and is willing to teach you, can't you sit next to him and have him hold your hands to show you where they go on the keys? You could repeat after him. You could learn something from the experience, couldn't you?

In my own teaching, I thought that there was ample room for that sort of experience. The idea makes me think of an informal expression I have heard in this country, namely the musicians' friendly admonition "Shut up and play!" Obviously, as performing scholars we attempt to find the appropriate balance between academic discourse on the one hand and "shutting up and playing" on the other. We can't help but speak and we can't help but play. I think that is pretty much our predicament.

SCOTT MARCUS: That's brilliant.

AJR: You know, people say, "Why did you decide to become a researcher, and why did you decide to become a musician?" The answer on both accounts is always, "I had no choice; I simply wanted to do both." The two modes are complementary—and certainly we are not favoring one mode over the other. Obviously, when you teach performance, you may explain how things ought to be done. Certain students are particularly interested in verbalizing the experience. Some ask me, "How do you play that ornament?

Can you explain it?" And oftentimes I say, "I wish I knew how to." Certain aspects of the music I do not know how to explain, and I do not know if anybody can, or perhaps needs to. During a rote training segment at the beginning of my performance class early in the quarter, one student from the Far East said to me, "I am not used to playing anything by ear. So when you play phrases and we repeat after you, could you notate everything for me ahead of time so that I know exactly what to play?" I had to explain that teaching her to play by ear, to hear, was what I was trying to do, not to mention that I was also improvising my drilling phrases as we went along.

I find it somewhat liberating to go to my performance class to teach without bringing notebooks, lecture notes, and the like, but instead attend class with my violin or *nāy* and some recordings. I look forward to interacting musically with my students, with whom I may have been discussing various conceptual issues in lecture courses a few hours earlier. Performance classes, which complement what we learn in lecture courses, tend to create a different mindset and to connect people on a positive, nondiscursive level.

ISSUES OF REPRESENTATION

AJR: Another area that comes to mind concerns representation. In other words, to what extent are performance instructors to be seen as culture bearers, or some sort of messengers or ambassadors? We used to recognize our "native" teachers as embodiments of specific performance traditions: We brought this woman from Korea, we have Korean music here; we brought this gentleman from West Africa, we have West African music here; and so on. We may have done that at a time when we viewed our field informants as individuals who have somehow internalized the essence of their respective cultures. We also tended to see culture as a discrete entity, as something embedded in the minds of people, a notion then prevalent in our social scientific discourse. I think that now we are more likely to acknowledge our teachers' individuality or idiosyncrasies. Certainly, we have to create a balance between representation and individuality, in other words, seeing our world music teacher both as an artist in his or her own right and as someone who gives us access to another musical tradition. I suspect that as researchers-performers, when we teach the more abstract theoretical seminars, we are encouraged to break away from the conventional mold, but when we teach "our own" cultures, we are expected to uphold the paradigm of representation. However, both individuality and representation are manifested in the musical repertoires we choose to teach and in the methods of pedagogy that we prefer to follow. Basically, I am trying to bring the teacher directly into the equation.

SM: So, in that sense, it is the representation of both the individual and the culture. We have to understand both.

AJR: That is a good way to put it. In a way, we are studying the teacher's musical mind. As Clifford Geertz might have put it, we are interpreting an interpretation. We may view the teacher as a "text" to be studied and appreciated as such. I am connecting my students with a culture that I know. At the same time, I do not want them to lose sight of me as a mediator.

Obviously, in this country we are teaching students who largely did not grow up in the culture, although many are excellent musicians in their own right. Our students usually come with such ingrained conceptions as major and minor tonalities, diatonicism, harmony, chords, the notion of a musical measure or bar, and so on. How do we select our instructional material and tools? In my case, I am guided by at least three criteria. I think the first is: what do I know best, or what is my forte? The second, which is closely related, is how best can I convey to my students the basic musical knowledge I assimilated in my own culture? The third is, what excites me most? There has to be a passion. I enjoy teaching repertoires that are rooted in the Arab modal tradition and that convey the emotional effect of the modes. I am similarly interested in covering techniques that are associated with such instruments as the *'ūd*, the *nāy*, and the *qānūn* (plucked trapezoidal zither). I think knowledge, communication, and interest are direct manifestations of our representativeness and individuality.

As a teacher of Arab music, I must also offer the students a new experience, something that broadens their musical horizons. This has to be done through pedagogical approaches that suit the particular context of instruction. Part of that experience is learning the Arab system of intonation, which embraces microtonality. Incidentally, when we play the "neutral" intervals, beginning students almost always play them too flat. This seems fascinating, although at times it is also frustrating. I wonder, in the case of these "in-between" notes, why they do not err on the higher side instead.

TS: How do they react when you point these things out?

AJR: Usually, I do not verbalize but rather repeat until they correct themselves, at least momentarily. I try to demonstrate first, then, if they do not catch the problem and correct it, I say something. I may point to the mistake and explain roughly what needs to be done. However, I would ask them to pay attention to what I am doing and ask them to emulate it until they perform it correctly. During drilling sessions, when they hear me repeating the same phrase vocally or on the violin five or six times, they usually realize that I am repeating it because there was a mistake; perhaps an accidental note was missed or a microtonal readjustment was ignored.

One question is: Are they in fact hearing the neutral interval as a flat note, as being "minor-ish"? Or, do they hear it properly but cannot play it as such because some acquired control mechanism is holding them back? Are their minds "correcting" the intervals by fitting them to a familiar intonational paradigm? This might be like learning French or any foreign language and realizing that you are speaking with an accent. You know what the native speakers sound like and probably can imitate them if you really try. But somehow your self-consciousness is standing in the way of your loosening up. You need to get rid of the inhibition. I wonder if taking a course in acting might help students play the microtones better. This is largely speculation, but also very interesting for a teacher of world music.

Another area is rhythm. I am not talking only about meter, but also about the durational structures of the notes and the pauses. Ornaments are also challenging. They can be quite intricate and particularly difficult to express in words. You can sit down and try to transcribe them, but even then the notes may not fully capture their nuances. The *qafla*, namely the cadential pattern, is another component that is difficult to execute well. In order to play effective cadences you must have full command of the temporal subtleties, including the pauses and overall timing.

The musical idiosyncrasies that our students tend to exhibit remind me of a story I heard many years ago. After about two or three years of teaching what may have been a gamelan ensemble, the instructor said to the students something like, "I am happy to say that you are beginning to make traditional mistakes, the type of mistakes that the natives typically make."

You might ask, "To what extent do I resemble a teacher in the Middle East?" I think I combine the primarily oral ways in which I learned the music myself with the formal methods followed in the modern Arab conservatory, as well as with the way students here are taught when they take violin and piano lessons. Over the years, I have developed a multifaceted approach. At the beginning of each class, I conduct aural exercises as I sing or play certain phrases and have the students repeat after me. I also bring in specific pieces, including my own compositions, and have the students learn them idiomatically. In the process I go into ornaments, intonation, rhythmic nuances, etc. I also use notated works coupled with recordings. I believe that the notation itself does not convey the whole musical message, but can be helpful in combination with other modes of learning.

MUSIC AND FEELING

AJR: Another issue is teaching the music as an experience, or as feeling. Are we really speaking of the shell or of the emotional core? This is a very serious question. You could spend time teaching students the music as the sound, or for that matter make them learn a *taqsīm* [instrumental improvisation] note for note, from a score. Is that really teaching them the music? In the tradition that I bring in, the music is strongly connected with emotions. *Tarab*, which means "ecstasy," is an emotional state that is embedded in the music; similarly, the music itself is generically referred to as *tarab*. You learn *tarab*. You perform *tarab*. You feel *tarab*. So how do you communicate

the ecstatic message? How do we teach the repertoire as a musical-emo-
tional package? I often wonder if my students are feeling the tonic note or
the notes of emphasis or the cadential patterns in ecstatically meaningful
ways. In my seminar on Arab music I usually assign a recording of a live performance by the Egyptian singer Umm Kulthūm for each student to analyze
modally and eventually to develop a sense of the ecstatic trajectory of the
performance. One student who was newly exposed to the music said to me,
"I heard the audience on the recording howl and whistle, but I do not know
why. I cannot tell why such responses happen when they do. I just have not
made the connection between what is happening in the music and why the
audience all of a sudden is getting so excited." Such a reaction makes me
more aware of the importance and the challenge of teaching the music as
an experience rather than just as a surface structure.

VARIETY OR FOCUS?

AJR: That brings me to a further point, namely how deeply can our university students immerse themselves in a specific performance tradition? At
least two models have been followed in our institutions. Each has its own
validity. One is that you take a wide variety of classes and get exposed to
many different ways of making music. You take gamelan to learn how the
colotomic structure works. You take Indian music to know how *ragas*
[modes] unfold. You take West African music to understand how polymeter
works, and so on. But we also have room for the in-depth approach. I have
students who have learned the music so well that they have been teaching it
themselves. There is a kind of gratification in in-depth learning, as a means
of advancing far beyond the mere notes into the expressive realm.

THE CULTURE OF THE MUSIC

SM: When you taught, first in Hawai'i, then in Washington, and finally at
UCLA, were you basically presenting Arab music to people who had no idea
about the Arab world?
AJR: That was often the case. At that time there were several students who
already had some proficiency on the *'ūd*, the *nāy*, and percussion. They
knew the Middle East through the familiar information channels. Some
heard "belly dance" recordings made in this country. Others may have traveled to the Middle East. But, there were also many students who did not
know much about the music and its cultural background.
SM: So was that an issue, instructing people who didn't know much about
the culture? My guess is that in the late 1970s, perhaps the hippie world
understood India, but they probably had no sense of the "Arab."
AJR: Right. When I first came to this country, during the tail end of the

1960s, the cultural differences seemed rather blurred. I remember that when I introduced myself as a musician from Lebanon, often the response was "That's neat! Do you know Ravi Shankar?"

SM: Shankar represented everything east of Greece, maybe.

TS: Yes, actually, back in the 1960s, a lot of people were making that sort of hippie overland Asian circuit, going east, and they would travel through this musical continuum area: the Balkans . . . through Greece. Then they would get into Turkey, then through Afghanistan, and then they would show up in India. A lot of people were doing that. I never thought about that before, but that might be one of the ways that the connection was established.

AJR: This all leads us to an interesting issue, namely, that our musical instruction, by necessity or by design, seems to focus on the music itself without reconstructing the rituals and social practices connected with it. Our performance classes are usually complemented by the cultural knowledge that our lecture courses provide and, furthermore, students, especially in cosmopolitan centers such as Los Angeles, perform in actual live events, or at least they attend such events and observe the various music-related behaviors. But, I must also say, as ethnomusicologists we are becoming increasingly aware that the connection between music and what we call "context" is not all that simple or predictable. I think on a certain level the music I teach can be, and has been, mediated and recontextualized without necessarily losing its appeal or emotional potency. Such versatility, I suspect, is inherent in the nature of music.

TS: Do you find yourself frustrated in trying to convey things such as *ṭarab* to non-Arabs?

AJR: Those whom we teach to perform may not know how the music is supposed to be heard, at least by the trained or "native" ear. Yes, that creates certain frustration. I always ask myself how am I going to make my students fully understand why a certain singer is so great or why a certain *taqsīm* is so brilliant, beyond their taking my word for it. Since the way the music is heard and appreciated is intimately linked to how we perform it, I sometimes wonder how best to teach the performers how to listen and to think musically. Demonstrating through sound recordings or videos of live performances helps develop a sense of how listeners process the music ecstatically. Meanwhile, when I teach the modal material, the inculcation of basic performance sensibilities allows the learners to develop a feeling of the music's emotive substance, its *ṭarab* content. But I also realize that music can be heard in many ways. I am not always sure if my students are hearing the music the way I am hearing it. It is clear to me that they are getting something out of the music. Are they appreciating it in their own ways? When they hear a good *qānūn* solo, are they moved by the tone color, the texture, the technique, the motivic structures of the phrases, etc.? Are they deriving pleasure from the performative process as such or from piecing together the music as a coherent aesthetic system? Or are they responding to the overall ecstatic content of the performance? Speaking from direct experience, I think learning to feel the music can be achieved through patience, proper guidance, and extended musical exposure.

WHAT DO WE REPRESENT?

SM: Do you end up having to reify the tradition?

AJR: I think some of that happens whenever we attempt to represent a specific tradition, or for that matter whenever we write a monograph about a musical culture. Certainly, we cannot claim that musics are static, or, just as important, that musical cultures are pure or monolithic. Having said this, I must add that the *tarab*-based stuff is quite alive, especially as a pedagogical tool. Today, it provides an aesthetic grounding for numerous musical expressions, including the urbanized folk styles and the more recent Arab MTV songs, material that I cover in my seminars and lecture courses. The *tarab* musical repertoire also has a large following both in the Arab world and among Arab Americans. A good illustration is the annual Arab music retreat organized by Simon Shaheen at Mount Holyoke College in Massachusetts. As a teacher at the retreat, I notice tremendous growth in interest in the music marked by a steady increase in the number of students, some of whom come directly from Arab countries. I think there is a sort of renaissance of Arab music in this country.

SM: Does that mean you're preserving something here that's not being preserved at home?

AJR: It is hard to judge, although some see that happening. What is done here seems to acquire a life of its own in the sense that it is part of a larger world scene that goes beyond what we call "ethnic." It is one of many threads in the tapestry of today's world music. In some form or another, what we do musically might be returned to other areas of the world as part of a multifaceted globalization package.

TS: Since so much fusion is happening, and you, yourself, are involved in that, does that, on the other hand, lead you to maintain a kind of traditional base in the classroom so you can move in other directions in your own personal work?

AJR: That is probably true. I have been playing with jazz groups and flamenco musicians, and have composed in various experimental styles. However, I want to make the traditional sound a viable option. Although in my performance classes various experimentations and crossovers have been incorporated, I seem to focus my attention on an established musical style that becomes the base from which I leap into other musical realms.

TS: Maybe a lot of us will be driven or pushed in that direction for the same reason.

SM: So, does this impel you to keep a keyboard out of your ensemble?

AJR: In the Arab musical system, proper intonation is essential for bringing out the feeling. The mastery of Arab intonation certainly goes beyond learning to play the "neutral" steps that intervene between some of the diatonic steps, since affective performing requires raising or lowering notes by small increments, readjustments crucial for the creation of *ṭarab*.

SM: They occur within a piece?

AJR: Certainly; microtonal readjustments may have to be made even within a single phrase. Given the way most keyboardists play today, equal temperament clashes with correct Arab intonation and goes against the finesse that I am trying to teach my students. For that reason I favor the more flexible, typically fretless, instruments. I devote considerable attention to the music's subtle, largely subliminal intonational grammar, which I have assimilated through many years of practice.

SM: So, in that sense, the representative part is very strong.

AJR: I suppose so, at least from this perspective.

SM: I must say, obviously not being from the Middle East, I treat my ensemble very differently. I treat it more like a study group, and we're trying to learn different pockets of Middle Eastern culture. So it can't be that I'm teaching my past because it is not there. So, rather, I'm saying, "Let's do a little bit of religious music. Let's do a little bit of modern music. Let's do a little bit of traditional music." And so the governing aesthetic ends up being completely different.

AJR: That is perfectly all right. Naturally, our methods represent our own musical backgrounds and interests and, furthermore, we work out our own comfortable balance between representation and individuality. Ultimately, we choose to teach in ways that excite us and enable us to connect with our students in ways that are musically most meaningful.

GRATIFICATION

TS: In your work, do you still think about your teachers? Do you think of them as models? Do you think that you have an obligation of some sort to them? And, if so, how do you think the obligation of your students to you compares to that?

AJR: I do not consciously emulate somebody's personal style. I see myself connected to the general practice. I have a lot of respect for the many musicians I have heard or played with. Implicitly I pay allegiance to the overall heritage.

SM: There's no guru tradition, right?

AJR: Exactly, not so much of a guru tradition in Arab music. However, I am extremely happy when my students take the learning seriously or show genuine enjoyment throughout the process. Although our students are not necessarily expected to become world-class performers, especially at the expense of other things that need to be learned, I admit it is always exciting to see musical devotees immerse themselves in the music. I have learned a great deal from my students through their musical input and creative insights. I do not expect them to venerate me, although many express respect and gratefulness.

TS: Do you feel that you owe something to the Arab community . . . that you have some obligation or something that you need to do . . . ?

AJR: It has always given me pleasure to see individuals from the community take my performance class. If they are motivated, I am willing to teach them. If some wish to "discover" their musical roots, I take great satisfaction in helping them do that. I had a female student who was born in this country and knew nothing about the music. When she took a class listening tape and played it at home, her mother, a Lebanese-American who had not encouraged her children to learn the Arabic language, was deeply moved. She was very excited that her daughter, in her early twenties, was learning the music. I also allow accomplished Arab musicians to sit in whenever possible. Over the years, these "natives" have inspired the rest of the students, aroused their interests, challenged them to excel, and taught them a great deal as musical role models.

TS: But there are other people in our book who have said . . . they're really concerned about giving, for example, a performance in front of a college or a university audience, one that is not really expert or competent in the music. The listeners may enjoy the music and give it a great reception, but the directors feel a little guilty because they are a noncritical audience. Do you feel that it is important to play in front of a critical audience and gain that feedback?

AJR: Definitely. When my ensemble, usually with guest artists, performs publicly here in Los Angeles, members of the local Arab community attend. It is an amazing feeling when the audience responds in culturally appropriate ways. I look at that as part of the students' training. Indirectly, such interactive behavior gives the performers a sense of the music's ecstatic or evocative nature. As you know, Arab music tends to be highly participatory. The feedback can also teach the performers how to listen intelligently.

TS: Would you teach your nontraditional listeners to utter certain typical exclamations in order for them to get into the participatory mood?

AJR: I may do that in my lecture demonstrations, probably to educate the audience about the typical listening mannerisms and to help break the ice among the more inhibited listeners. But in regular concerts this can be problematic, since I do not wish to create an artificial situation.

SM: It's a subtle thing, right?

AJR: Yes, indeed. Such utterances, if genuine, discreet, and well syn-chronized with the music, can be deeply inspiring to the performer, as I have indicated in one of my articles on the feedback between the artists and the listeners [1991], and more recently in my book, *Making Music in the Arab World* [2003]. However, if voiced randomly or out of place, or if not genuinely felt, they can wipe out the performer's sense of inspiration, or *saltana*.

SM: So what would you say to an audience?

AJR: In my concerts I usually do not instruct the audience to respond in any specific manner. I would rather have the non-native listeners do it their own way. Throughout the years, I have learned to feel and appreciate their subtle ways of interacting with my music.

SM: Indian music is similar in needing this response.

TS: Whenever you run into your Arab music colleagues or friends, or when you go to an international conference and run into other Arab schol-ars, how do they react when you tell them about teaching Americans . . . ?

AJR: Their initial response is often a combination of skepticism and fas-cination. Typically, they ask such questions as: "Do they feel the music?" "Can they really play the quarter tones?" or "Are they able to evoke the *rūḥ* [soul] of the music?" Somehow, the assumption is that certain musical (or cultural) things are unteachable.

TS: Yes. Bruno [Nettl] has that little chapter in his *Twenty-Nine Issues* [*The Study of Ethnomusicology: Twenty-Nine Issues and Concepts,* 1983] titled "You Will Never Understand This Music."

AJR: However, the notion that Westerners or non-Arabs are learning "our" music is also met with admiration and pride. The students are praised for their musicianship and accomplishment and at times described as role mod-els for "our culture back there." Furthermore, nowadays, as Scott knows from working with his own group, our students are performing frequently at local community events. In fact, our ensembles are found particularly desirable, not only because the academic institution adds a stamp of credibility to what they do, but also because the students bring to the local community a sym-bolically meaningful image of universality and boundary crossing.

Our rapport with the outside world owes a great deal to our performance students. It is quite rewarding to observe the growing mutual relationship between the community and the university ensembles and to witness the continuity of one's own teaching legacy. I see this through my students and their own students.

Chapter 9

The African Ensemble in America

Contradictions and Possibilities

DAVID LOCKE

[Orientalism is a] distribution *of geopolitical awareness into . . . texts; it is*
an elaboration not only of a basic geographical distinction (the world is made
up of two unequal halves, Orient and Occident) but also of a whole series of
"interests" which . . . it not only creates but also maintains; it is, *rather than*
expresses, a certain will *or* intention *to understand, in some cases to control,*
manipulate, even to incorporate, what is a manifestly different (or alternative
and novel) world. . . . Indeed, my real argument is that Orientalism is—
and does not simply represent—a considerable dimension of modern political-
intellectual culture, and as such has less to do with the Orient than it does
with "our" world.

EDWARD SAID, *Orientalism*

The study and performance of African music in the United States might
seem to be an apolitical activity that is focused on making good music, learning about unfamiliar music-cultures, and fostering international good will.
But global relations of power and issues of social justice simmer beneath the
optimistic humanistic surface. Especially in the United States, the study of
African music tends to raise political issues because of the nation's history
of African slavery and its troubled race relations. At the same time, African
music is also remarkably popular. Composers seek creative ideas from its
musical structures; players find that their musicianship is enhanced through
studying ensemble performance; and general listeners appreciate popular
and traditional African music. Thus, in terms of political sensitivity and
musical significance, people making African music in the United States operate within an especially intense field. I have spent years learning African
music and establishing myself as a teacher of ensemble performance. The
process has obliged me to meet head on the volatile issues of race, globalization, and Orientalism.

TRAINING FOR AN AMERICAN LIFE DOING AFRICAN MUSIC

I began studying African performance in 1969, when, as an undergraduate at Wesleyan University, I became captivated by sound recordings from Africa. Many a night I put my turntable on continuous play and listened to a recording of the Marshall expedition to the "Bushmen" of the Kalahari over and over again. I was gripped by the clapping, singing, and sounds of healing. I sensed honesty within that complex soundscape. Believers in traditional African religion are likely to attribute causation to destiny or unseen, unknown entities (a vodunist would call them *lwa*). Could I, a secular suburbanite born of a Yankee Unitarian mother and New York Jewish father, be the medium for a spirit force that needed to hear that music? If we are to be truly changed by an encounter with another culture, then scholarly discourse should admit into its precincts the validity of alternative beliefs.

Drawn to African music,[1] I asked Professor David McAllester, Wesleyan's senior ethnomusicologist, how I could get involved in a performance group. Since Wesleyan did not yet have its own African ensemble, he sent me to Professor Nicholas England and Alfred Ladzekpo at Columbia University. Professor England played me a recording of their Ewe ensemble that sounded like a precise rhythmic engine—dense, propulsive, forceful, and very controlled. I registered for the course but was utterly baffled by Ewe drumming. Mr. Ladzekpo's method, as I recall, was to repeatedly demonstrate correct performance. I could reproduce a short rhythmic figure in isolation; playing in polyrhythmic synchrony with the other parts was beyond me. Years later, when I started teaching, memories of my own disorientation helped me sympathize with students who would break down in tears of frustration and self-doubt because they could not stay steady on a percussion part.

After taking a year off to travel the world instead of reading about it in ethnographic monographs, I returned to Wesleyan and joined the new African ensemble taught by Abraham Adzinyah, formerly a member of the Ghana Dance Ensemble. Mr. Adzinyah's conceptualization of the music had a profound influence on me. He talked about listening to other parts, especially the bell; he developed the concept of the "hidden beat" and suggested we manifest it in bodily movement as a steady reference point for offbeat timing. Mr. Adzinyah's charisma enabled non-Africans to enter the affecting world of African music (see Armstrong 1971: 25). He was an emblem of cultural difference, at once inspirational and intimidating. Unlike the rigorous traditionalist teacher who insists that the seeker must prove worthy, he was generously making it easy for us to understand the music.

In 1972 I entered Wesleyan's Ph.D. program and was awarded a graduate assistantship to help the late Freeman Donkor, artist-in-residence from Ghana, teach African music and dance courses at Woodrow Wilson High

School in Middletown, Connecticut. Mr. Donkor would compare the Ghana Dance Ensemble's theatrical choreographic arrangements of dances like *Gahu* (see Ladzekpo 1989) with the traditional versions favored by Ewe funeral benevolent societies. He enjoyed setting up a friendly competition between his group and Adzinyah's college ensemble. It was a close contest because the young working-class teens at Woodrow Wilson, bursting with adolescent energy, brought more zest to class than did the more affluent and sardonic college kids at Wesleyan. Competition, I was learning, is an important factor in the music-culture of drumming.

I remember my excitement when Mr. Donkor asked me to teach class. Would I be able to generate the rhythmic force needed to stabilize the student's erratic timing? If I heard them "go off," that is, lose proper alignment within the network of parts, would I be sufficiently well oriented to put them right? I suppose I also wondered whether my race would undermine my legitimacy as a teacher. The dance training I received from Mr. Donkor helped me to understand musical rhythm and remember the phrases in lead drumming parts. Being a competent dancer also greatly helped in my field research. African audiences who would politely listen to my drumming seemed to really enjoy seeing me in motion.

For two years, 1975–77, I studied at the University of Ghana. My wife and I lived on the Legon campus several miles from downtown Accra. During the days, I took private lessons with drummers including Midawo Gideon Foli Alorwoyie (now at University of North Texas), transcribed tapes of lessons and field recordings, attended lectures, used the campus libraries, and took language classes. I practiced drumming so zealously that university faculty would ask me kindly to desist; I was duly outraged that even in Africa people would complain about the noise. Literate people in Accra accepted the idea that musical knowledge can be transmitted in music lessons and the concept that persons such as the members of the Ghana Dance Ensemble, who had learned their material in rehearsals, could stage valid performances of repertoire traditionally learned through gradual enculturation.

While in Accra I connected with the late Godwin Agbeli, formerly a drummer with the Arts Council of Ghana Folkloric Company and coach of many amateur drumming and dancing groups. Every evening I would drive downtown to rehearse with one of these "cultural groups," as they are known in Ghanaian English. As the only non-African in the groups, I was moving toward a co-cultural understanding of musical feel. I would play ensemble parts, dance, sing, and simply soak up the subtle feel of the style, the hardest feature of a music-culture to learn and teach. Mr. Agbeli accepted my invitation to live with us on the university campus. We were establishing a friendship that might pay off someday in an authentic interdependency: his poverty, like that of most African musicians, must factor into our relationship. Mr. Agbeli, like other African teachers, must have thought twice before passing information to a student who might one day take his job. Awareness of the hardships that face third world musicians challenges the moral authority of first world ethnomusicologists.

In addition to studying performance, I was doing on-site research of repertory that I had previously known only in class, private lessons, and rehearsals. Supervised by Professor J.H.K. Nketia, then director of the Institute of African Studies at the University of Ghana, I focused on *Atsiagbekor,* a masterwork of Ewe performance art about which I would later write my Ph.D. dissertation (Locke 1978). Rather than doing long-term on-site ethnographic field research, I made brief periodic visits to villages and towns to conduct interviews, witness in-context events like funerals, festivals, and rituals, and document performances that I had specially commissioned. The time I spent studying performance limited the amount of time I had to conduct ethnographic research. Having only a beginner's skill in the Ewe language, I was dependent upon research colleagues to translate interviews and song texts (see Beaudry 1997: 71–73). I also had begun an apprenticeship in Dagbamba drumming with an expert friend of Mr. Agbeli, Abubakari Lunna, then employed by the Arts Council of Ghana. Mr. Lunna helped me attend performance events in southern Ghana and in Dagbon itself. It was becoming clear that there are multiple versions of repertory among Ghana's professional and amateur performing arts troupes, and striking differences between the ways that these dances were done on stage and in their natural setting among the people.

For example, branches of the Anya Agbekor Society existed in both Accra, a sprawling metropolis of several million people, and the rural Ewe town of Anyako, so I was able to see "first existence" events in both locations (performances by African cultural groups can be termed "second existence," and those by non-African ensembles might be termed "third existence"). Lively debate on accuracy and taste occurs over performances in each category. Mr. Lunna, for example, notes that what the Ghana Dance Ensemble calls *Damba/Takai* is actually a creative combination of two entirely distinct works. One village may say the next village has got it wrong; one artist may say another artist failed to learn the work thoroughly; a critic may complain about the costumes or choreography used by a cultural group; a collegiate world music ensemble may perform a hybrid of styles; a composer or jazz fusion group may take culturally insensitive liberties with an item of sacred repertory. There is nothing to guarantee that a first existence performance will be a more accurate source than a private lesson in the United States.

In 1977, I returned to Wesleyan. I completed the requirements for the doctoral degree in ethnomusicology, and our family, now three, moved to Boston in 1978. After six years of part-time teaching at various schools, I landed a full-time faculty position in the Department of Music at Tufts

University, eventually earning tenure and serving two three-year terms as chair of the department (1993–2000). I wrote three books, each devoted to one item of repertory (see Locke 1987, 1990, 1992). From 1979 to 1996, I led drumming and dancing classes every Sunday night. The Agbekor Drum and Dance Society grew from these classes.

In Ghana, many performing groups are also mutual aid societies, credit unions, trade associations, or clubs formed for neighborhood or ethnic advancement. Performance strengthens a group's communal spirit. The Agbekor Society is loosely modeled on this African concept. Like an Ewe group *(habobo)*, we emphasize one item of repertory, *Atsiagbekor*, or *Agbekor* for short. Our main reason for existence is enthusiasm for the art, but we also make a commitment to the group and enjoy our social bonds. Newcomers pay tuition for classes, but once members gain experience they simply pay dues into the group's treasury. These contributions facilitate the teaching visits to the United States of Godwin Agbeli and Abubakari Lunna. Over time, the Agbekor Society has become a set of friends and associates, as well as a study group devoted to African music and dance. At Tufts University, my courses in drumming and dancing also serve social as well as musical functions. Like an Ewe *habobo* (see Ladzekpo 1971), the group has a signature T-shirt that announces our performance name, Kiniwe, an Ewe rallying call.

Ethnomusicologists who seriously study performance in their fields have distinctive obligations to their native teachers. When I was ready to leave Ghana in 1977, Mr. Agbeli and I had talked about the future. He was hoping, even expecting, that I would arrange opportunities for him in the States. I explained that he would need patience; I could promise nothing. I needed to get a job, establish my own identity as musician, experiment with new settings for performance, and try alternative classroom techniques. If Mr. Agbeli had anticipated an eleven-year wait, he might not have been as generous with his time and knowledge during the previous two years of field research.

By the late 1980s, I was ready. Annually since 1988, I have arranged for either Mr. Agbeli or Mr. Lunna to teach in the States. Neither of these gentlemen ever wanted to immigrate to the United States. They were happy to do their work, live with me and my family, meet people, sell handicrafts, and then take their money and go home. The visits enabled them to cement our bonds of friendship and also to transform their lives in Africa. Mr. Agbeli realized a long-standing dream: building his own arts center. The Dagbe Center for Arts and Culture, located near Aflao in his home village of Kopeyia, is both a family-run cultural tourism business and an institution intended to nurture the continuity of traditional culture in a changing world. Mr. Lunna has become a successful farmer and the backbone of a large extended family. By virtue of his relative prosperity and his unusually cosmopolitan experience, he is regarded as a leader among Dagbamba drummers. Given the opportunity to travel abroad, these two teachers became known to persons interested in African culture, and many people have gone to Ghana to study with them. Travel to the United States has helped them to enter the African middle class, but their status is precarious. In order to maintain their prestige they are newly dependent upon the economic relation between Africa and its Other. Although I have given back, by no means are we even.

TEACHING AFRICAN MUSIC

At Tufts, students in my course Music 65/66, "African Music Ensemble," earn 0.5 units of credit toward the 34 credits required for graduation (regular academic courses are worth 1 unit of credit) and receive a letter grade that figures into their grade point average.[2] Course requirements typically include punctual attendance for the class that meets twice weekly for two hours, constructive participation, improvement appropriate to individual ability, and two performances per semester. Students come from all corners of the university, including its College of Engineering. Of the fifteen to twenty students who enroll in the course, some are music majors and others are extracurricular musicians in jazz or rock bands, but most are general liberal arts students. For its first several years, the African Music Ensemble was only a one-semester course, meaning that I faced a different crop of students each term. Now that the course has gained a positive reputation on campus, students must enroll for the entire academic year. An audition process allows me to select students with stronger mind-body coordination and better ability to maintain steady time. These days, with a reasonably capable group in place for two terms, students make substantial progress in the unfamiliar music and we can enjoy playing a more interesting repertory.

For many years, I also offered a course through the Tufts Dance Program. Compared with the music course, the dance class attracted larger numbers (from twenty-five to fifty), fewer males, and more black (African, African-American, British, and Caribbean) students. The drumming and dancing classes would rehearse several times before a show and then perform together. The better and more committed students in the music course often came to dance class to practice their parts and, in a few cases, play the lead drum. Although singing is enormously important in most African performance idioms, I have never offered a course devoted entirely to vocal music.

I usually start my courses with *Atsiagbekor* and *Gahu*. Not only am I relatively competent playing these pieces, but I find them to be excellent vehicles for teaching fundamental features of the Ewe music style. Their percussion parts clearly illustrate crucial Ewe musical concepts such as 1) listening to the bell, 2) being comfortable in a matrix of pulsation fields, beat feels, cross rhythms, and displacements, 3) learning percussion technique and characteristic rhythmic motifs, 4) combining one's own part with others, and 5) feeling the music and sharing that sensation through body movement and facial expression. Because of its slow tempo, newcomers can hear the polyrhythmic interplay in the processional section of *Atsiagbekor.* The large number of separate instrumental parts in *Agbekor* enables all members of the class to play simultaneously without excessive doubling up. Furthermore, the parts do not change throughout the performance, enabling students to concentrate only on the composite texture without the added pressure of listening for cues from the leading drum. Rather early in the semester I introduce the basic unit of Ewe dance vocabulary, a folding and unfolding of the back and chest. I also teach several songs during this first heavy onslaught of new information.

After the group has a grip on *Agbekor,* I begin *Gahu.* Everyone enjoys this up-tempo piece, whose meter is roughly equivalent to 4/4 and which sounds a bit like Afro-pop or salsa. The faster tempo of *Gahu* challenges the students' sticking technique and ability to distinguish the divergent parts in the polyrhythm. After students gain competence in the basic parts, I teach call-and-response dialogues with the leading drum. Although changing from one rhythm to another in response to signals from the leading drum is typical of Ewe drumming, students find it tough to listen to another part while maintaining the concentration needed to keep their own part together. As with *Agbekor,* early in the first phase of learning the piece I do a quick lesson in the dance and teach several songs. Students are too focused on drumming, in my view. I encourage them to integrate melody and movement with the percussion that is their main preoccupation.

I like to introduce material at a quick pace. Even if some students still are unsure of the relationship between the bell and a given part, I nevertheless continue adding new parts until the whole texture is introduced. Then we go back over each part, its fit with the bell, its relationship to the matrix of beats, and the various ways it combines with other parts, the dance, and the melodic rhythm. African teachers would prefer students to become competent on one part before moving on. Mr. Lunna will refuse to give new rhythms, saying, "You cannot do the one I showed you, so why do you want another?" Mr. Agbeli used to say that too much material confuses students. I force the students to play many parts because I think that the biggest challenge in this musical style is polyrhythmic hearing. After all, African children always hear the full musical texture. Keenly aware of how little exposure to African drumming the students have had, I favor filling class time with music making by the whole group. African teachers, on the other hand, often have students play one by one or in small groups. They use competition and pride as motivators and know that in performance situations students will need to execute under pressure.

I avoid the language of music theory at the early stages. African performance asks for group-oriented, mind-body intelligence rather than a self-
oriented, visual-analytical approach. New students should experience physical sensations as directly as possible, with minimal filtering through familiar
concepts of music theory. To be perplexed by the music's mystery is both
humbling and exciting. This is a different culture and should not be domes-
ticated too hastily. Once the music begins to enter their ears and bodies, we
indulge sparingly in analysis and notation. Later in the academic year, I use
various styles of notation, including staff notation, graph paper, and
mnemonic vocables, to clarify musical relationships and assist memory.
Even then, I talk about the importance of hearing more than one part at
once and maintaining a creative way of hearing. We never play from a score.

Only after students grasp the entire musical idea do they play a part on
drums. First, we chant mnemonic vocables; next, we play on our legs while
vocalizing at the same time; then, we play the part in duet with the time-
keeping parts. Because I want the students to construct meaning from their
immediate encounter, I give out little information about the African context. Interestingly, although many drum phrases have meaning in the vernacular (see Locke 1996: 95), African teachers often do not divulge this
information right away. Abubakari Lunna says that this is because a student
must earn the right to advanced knowledge. I also think it is because he
wants them to get practical skill from direct sensory phenomena.

African music is at once familiar and foreign. I try to avoid mystification
without underestimating difference. Students always ask, "How do they
think about it?" Metaphors from my teachers guide students toward African
beliefs about the music: Adzinyah's hidden beat, Donkor's image of musical
texture as a musical stew, Agbeli's advice to compose a melody inherent to
the polyrhythm, Alorwoyie's message that drumming is a language, and
Lunna's insistence that players look outward and communicate with other
people. These images not only impart African cultural concepts, establishing respect for African teachers, but they enable the students to enter the
interpersonal world of African music. I try to move them toward human
associations with Africans. My own feeling for the music draws upon powerful memories of Africa.

PERFORMANCE PHILOSOPHY

Nothing can match the power of a good performance that springs from an
authentic context. The pace at which events unfold is grand and elegant,
singing is prominent, the dancing is heartfelt, the mood passionate, the
whole setting rich with sensory experiences of many kinds. Natural performance events have deep meanings that a stage show, in Africa or elsewhere,
only approximates. Most performers in cultural groups do not have the

same timing feel as do village drummers; for example, village drummers usually "stretch" the common offbeat figure of the high-pitched *kagan* drum (sixteenth rest, dotted eighth note, eighth note), whereas learners who are not born into the traditional cultural milieu play it "straight" (eighth rest, eighth note, eighth note) (see Locke 1992: 108).

Two social frames for the African performing arts were most satisfyingly genuine to me during my training: village events and formal lessons or classes. Among the most wonderful things on this planet is traditional African music and dance performed in the settings from which it arose and for which it was first intended. The grace, the force, the melody, rhythm, and sonority, the color, the drama, the humor . . . the thrill of seeing such performances in Africa reminds me why I was attracted to these arts in the first place. Such events can never be exactly re-created in any other context. Participants will not know each other, performers will lack the feel and knowledge, and the purpose will be more artificial. But that does not mean that in new contexts these arts cannot again come to life.

In fact, the artificial setting of the research documentation or music lesson can be a genuine context for African music. When African experts play for my tape recorder, the session can resonate with admiration for the remarkable genius of the tradition; the teachers usually enjoy skillfully displaying their cultural heritage for an enthusiastic student who appreciates its subtle beauty and the nuances of their artistry. Advanced American students may be swept away by the power of an African teacher's playing and, in turn, the teachers may become entranced with their role as a medium for their people's music. Everyone is in a transcendent zone. Even classes on fundamentals sometimes achieve this special flow (see Csikszentmihalyi 1991: 49), when students break through the perceptual fog that characterizes the early stages of learning African polyrhythmic music and begin to hear the music's multidimensional potential.

Inevitably, the African ensemble class performs. Students are excited to show what they have been studying, and I know that preparing for a show surely ratchets up their concentration in class. However, performance brings out many contradictions inherent in world music ensembles. For example, at Tufts, my classes usually perform in a room without a stage. The audience sits on folding chairs arranged in gently curving concentric semicircles. I supplement the written program by saying that although the event may appear to be a concert, the audience should take it more like a happening or drumming in the park. I encourage them to get out of their seats, listen from different vantage points in the room, dance or clap if they feel so moved, and not to worry if their kids make noise. Most people nevertheless stay seated, listening attentively, cheering for their friends, and applauding when selections end. While maintaining an informal manner, I try to present myself as a professor who is serious about the music and who cares about creating a space where others can also get into it.

In planning performances, I try to imitate the African first existence groups. Rather than play concerts consisting of excerpts of many different dances, I favor events with extended performances of pieces that have been rehearsed for a long time. I find that rehearsing the same substantial item of repertory for many months allows for a deep savoring of its personality. Only with patience do non-African performers—"we, the un-enculturated," as I jokingly put it—become competent in an unfamiliar style. If the gradual unfolding of a two-hour form bores some audiences, or if their expectation of entertaining variety is not met, so be it. We need not be controlled by what we think the audience wants. Art should disturb. Honest art keeps a commitment to itself.

In concert, we present singing on its own, without drumming, so that it can be heard. The group stands facing the audience, while I play bell, dance a bit, and sing the leader's part. In class, we practice moving with appropriate body style. We often drum the same piece more than once so that students can switch around among the instruments; even though this may seem repetitious I think it helps the audience realize that the music has an intentional structure, that is, it is not improvised or merely spontaneous. If there are dancers, we then present the drumming and dancing together. For Ewe music, we arrange two long benches in a "V" shape with the lead drum at the apex so that the players have eye contact with each other but also can interact with the audience. Because the drums are different in Dagbamba music, we stand in a group with a chorus of answer *luna* drums massed in back, two *gun-gong* drums in front, and the leading *luna* out front.

At American performances of African music, audience participation, often introduced with a remark that in Africa there is no separation of performer and audience, has become ritualized. Although this cliché strikes me as a romantic simplification, it is true that in Africa those who watch others perform often do sing, dance, or clap hands. At Tufts, we usually invite the audience to dance at the end of the show. Sometimes, I invite the audience to dance right before intermission, but this seldom elicits the same degree of involvement because it seems that people need to witness a sustained output of focused energy by the performers before they are sufficiently charged up to jump in themselves. In Africa, when people participate in the performance they do so in a culturally appropriate style. Rather than simply have the Americans get up and do their own thing, I give a minilesson so that members of the audience can form a big circle and dance *Gahu.* This feels more like village Africa: many people are moving together in kinesthetic and rhythmic synchrony.

Why am I so ambivalent about costumes? They look great, audiences love them, and my African teachers insist that we wear them. But for me, costumes trigger a negative response. The audience, I fear, misses the power of the music because its attention is focused on how well the costumes are tied. I want the performance event to challenge the audience's comfortable preconceptions, but costumes allow the audience to have a superficial, even irrelevant, response. After a show I hear, "The costumes looked so authentic and colorful. Did you buy them in Africa?" We struggle in class to learn challenging features of music and dance, yet we are complimented for the mere appearance of costumes that we had no hand in creating! When we put on unfamiliar garb, my students and I risk alienation from our normal selves. Instead of being comfortable in collegiate roles, we feel conspicuous and awkward. Our long hair does not easily fit under caps made for Dagbamba men with close-cropped hair, our well-nourished thighs challenge the seams of short pants made for the trim legs of Ewe subsistence farmers, and the pinkish skin in which many of us are sheathed looks weakly pale against the ochre-colored cloth designed for a glowing Ashanti bluish brown. If any of us imagine that we have achieved significant authenticity, the costume provides a reality check.

African teachers object when I start to rant about costumes. "You are showing the audience the correct thing. People will talk against me if they see you performing in blue jeans. We must respect tradition." More persuasively, they point out that the dance's gestures are designed to show off the costume's movement. Ever the cynic, I also know that they gain a helpful profit by supplying us with costumes. Inevitably I yield. If the sight of Americans performing African music and dance in the proper costumes is jarring, at least it is better than appearing disrespectful, unprepared, or ignorant by wearing something else. Despite my inner discourse on the contradictions of costumes, I find myself yet again packing the suitcases with horsetails and monkey-skin hats, cowries and kente cloth, and heading off to the show.

Leaders of ensembles performing African music in new contexts need not be bound by traditional conventions of presentation. Directors may decide what type of performance their group will put on: concert, dance drama, illustrated lecture, nightclub floorshow, or drum circle. Over the years, I have developed strong preferences. Performances that consist of many short excerpts of pieces from a variety of cultural traditions remind me of the imperialist urge to "collect the world" (see Clifford 1988: 215 ff.). Neither am I fond of realistic dance dramas modeled upon village life. Whenever I have performed in such theatrical fictions I feel that I must pretend to be an African.

Three presentation paradigms have suited my sensibility. First is the straightforward concert, presented as an artistic event that creates its own validity in the moment. By hearing African traditions in a format similar to that used for "classical" performing arts (Western and non-Western), the audience receives the music and dance with respect and might even have the profound experience that arises from an encounter with any great art. Second is what might be called a "performed report." As an example, the Agbekor Society once presented a two-hour performance of *Adjogbo* that was modeled on the style of an Ewe mutual aid society from Togo (see Conant 1988). The audience was not required to suspend its disbelief and imagine that we were Africans, but was asked to witness our best efforts as we tackled the musical demands of this complex work. In contrast, one summer Godwin Agbeli lead the Agbekor Drum and Dance Society in an extended performance of *Yevevu*, music and dance of the traditional religion known as Yeve (see Avorgbedor 1987). Mr. Agbeli had us stage an African scene, which required role playing, props, and costuming. He divided us into two shrine groups; the home shrine first established its presence on stage and then was visited by the members of a shrine from a neighboring village. The striking beauty of the music and dance helped counterbalance the artificiality inherent in the premise. Nevertheless, I remember being considerably more ill at ease in this "as if" mode than in less mimetic performances.

Third, I am fond of student recitals whose explicit premise is, "We have been learning this material. Here is the best we can do with it right here and now. We enjoy doing it and invite you to share in our excitement." If we project slides and videos of Africa, events like this become like installations; if we invite audience participation, they are like happenings. All participants are their natural selves and the context is one that is well established within the campus culture. We try to accurately re-create African music and dance, but the premise and mood of the presentation is decidedly American. Although members of the audience who had expected a touristic experience of Africa may be nonplussed, events like this seem very honest and unpretentious, not nostalgic or sentimental about an imagined Africa.

Fidelity to the source is important. Abubakari Lunna wants his students to improvise, but only through clever invention upon the vernacular meaning of the drummed phrases. When we just imitate his phrases, he complains, "Put in sugar; make your drumming sweet," but if our attempts at improvisation stray beyond the limits of the drum language, he admonishes, "Don't play jazz!" Frequently, leaders of cultural groups in Ghana and African ensembles in the diaspora adapt original first existence repertory to its new, re-created, staged setting. Does the original material degrade with each copy, or are the new versions improvements? As Karl Heider (1976: 10) has written about ethnographic film, ethnographic authenticity is a function of ethnographic understanding. In other words, the integrity of an adaptation depends upon the leader's quality of knowledge of both the original music-culture and the culture into which the new work is being introduced.

"AFRICAN" MEANING IN THE ACADEMIC CONTEXT

The various world music ensembles we ethnomusicologists generate are founded, it seems to me, upon the idea that music can be transplanted into new settings. Music is assumed to be a medium sufficient unto itself, abstract, nonreferential, communal (see Rouget 1985: 262), transcendent of its immediate setting, not de-cultured but more regional than local and moving toward the panhuman (see Slobin 1993: 17–19). When powerfully performed, in other words, music creates sufficient conditions for listeners to construct their own context. Meaning and exhilaration of the senses should emerge from the immediate response to what is seen and heard. A nonrepresentational treatment of the African arts is not limited by local detail, and is therefore more universal in its reach.

Why are we humans attracted to bird songs (see Cruz 1999)? It is not, I would argue, simply because of their beauty. We imagine that the bird's song expresses its inner spirit. Why are people interested in music from other cultures? Because it enables them to encounter subjectivity quite different from their own. In today's global village, this can produce ironic consequences. Here in Boston, my white American wife, an accomplished koto player who teaches Japanese-born women, sometimes gets calls from producers who prefer to hire the student who "looks right," that is, is Japanese, rather than the *sensei* herself. For an audience comfortably expecting a performer who looks Japanese, a Caucasian koto player presents them with unexpected work. They have a postcolonial moment.

Is a show "African" if the song texts, dance movements, and drum parts are well researched and the instruments and costumes are imported from the motherland? Convention dictates publicizing our American event as African, but this is visibly false. We have reinvented the African ensemble as an art object. In my view, performances of African music by non-Africans are at least as much about the attitudes toward Africa of the performers and the audience as they are about African expressive culture itself. Through posture, gesture, composure, and interpersonal style, the teacher and the students conduct a nonverbal discourse with the audience about their relationship to the material.

When I began directing my own African ensemble, I thought that its raison d'être would be our ability to successfully play this compelling music. Audiences usually experienced an initial visual shock, but if we sounded good and acted committed, they settled into the performance. When the feeling of the music was good, the performance had a meaningful connection to its African source. Later, I came to realize that this perspective reflected a modernist aesthetic preference for spare texture and an intellectual's fondness for abstraction. In contrast, Godwin Agbeli most enjoyed creating elaborate dance dramas with long choreographic sequences that his dancers had to memorize. From corny boy-meets-girl skits to violent tales of regicide, African audiences (and perhaps most audiences everywhere) love humor and narrative, not austere performances of music for its own sake.

Directors of world music ensembles face distinctive issues of interpretation and reception. Verisimilitude in musical detail does not ensure that a performance works as an authentic representation of African music-culture. We are performing works that are honed over many generations by a community of taste rather than unique products of one sensibility. Style has authority. Should resemblance to the original be compromised so that the concert is entertaining? What do I want students to achieve? I want their musical personalities to become Africanized. An Africanized musician values repetition, hears polyrhythmically, and plays interactively. In performance, I want them to enact an emergent intercultural approach to music that is neither African nor American. Although we attempt to replicate the repertory as performed by Africans, it is our selves that are really on display. Style is the hardest part. Things—melodies, song texts, drum rhythms, and dance movements—can be learned by approximating their originals, but shaping the whole is much more difficult to learn and teach.

Even if one accepts a notion of homology between music and other domains of culture, what truths about Africa can music convey to non-Africans? I talk about the context for music in Africa, but I do not presume to understand what it means to Africans. I have learned to perform music played by Africans, but despite having cracked the code of African rhythmics, I hesitate when it comes to extramusical meaning. Where is the theory to explain the cultural meaning of African music for Africans (see Nketia 1962)?

World music ensembles inexorably are affected by the world's imperial, colonial past. This is the condition of all ethnomusicological action, but the very nature of performance calls it forcefully into debate. Some members of an audience probably attend a world music show to endorse the ensemble's effort to foster understanding among cultures, to promote world peace. Music studies, unlike less performative modes of cross-cultural inquiry, encourage nondominant relationships. But like anthropology, ethnomusicology came into being during the period of Euro-American colonialism, so we are complicit despite well-intended efforts to redress its aftermath of social injustice. Our work among students, audiences, and employers is affected by global power relationships.

FACTORING IN "RACE"

Leading an African ensemble at a university in the United States means working within a racialized discourse. Courses about the music-cultures of Africa often become a setting where young people work through their

views on race prejudice, ethnic and gender stereotypes, international economic equity, the legacy of the slavery, and right action in the present. Race,
conceived as a bipolar black/white condition, is an ever-present issue. The
African ensemble is a rare setting in which nonblack participants may seem
racially out of place; we experience the feeling of Otherness. Icons of
Otherness abound—costumes, props, sets, musical instruments, song texts,
sound colors, sonic structures, musical style, and presentation format—but
audiences probably most readily locate difference in the physical presence
of the musicians themselves.

Performances of world music by born-in-the-tradition musicians reinforce comfortable categories, but anomalous presentations of the Other by
non-Others confound expectations. Whites may resent the challenge to
their neat little world. Blacks regard African drumming as a black preroga-
tive and note another instance of appropriation. Sound may seem incon-
gruous to the body. Interpretation depends upon shared codes and conventions, but the African ensemble is an anomaly that partakes of none.
Lacking experience in the African musical tradition, members of an audience may be at a loss. Understanding and appreciation are limited by the
chasm that separates the original cultural milieu from the context of reception. The voice—drum language, song, and libation—is at the juncture of
body and discourse, but African language is where non-Africans are least
competent.

At work in America, I do not feel estranged from Africa because I am
comfortable in my role. Sometimes, I hear myself talk in class as if I were a
cultural insider. For example, since the metrics of African music are elusive
($12/8 = 6/4 = 3/2 = 24/16$), students always ask, "How do they hear it?" (see
Friedson 1996: 155–58). Assuming the native role, I simply say, "We hear it
like this." It is a different story in Africa. In the mid-1990s, I made several
short visits to the Legon campus to help Tufts establish a link with the
University of Ghana. Usually I carved out time for a tantalizing weekend in
the field, just enough time to make me feel decidedly like an outsider.

RESISTING THE "CULTURAL GRAY-OUT"
OF GLOBALIZATION

The current unprecedented efficiency and scope of globalization encourages us to think of humanity as one worldwide society. Musical styles of
planetary popularity emerge in tandem with the growth of transnational
businesses. Simultaneously, as oppositions intensify among nations, regions,
and communities, local musical traditions prove able to withstand the forces
of cultural homogenization. How does my engagement with African music
relate?

World music ensembles are sites of resistance to the cultural gray-out predicted in the 1960s by Alan Lomax (1968: 4–6). I hope my work strengthens local African traditions that are at risk from media-driven popular culture. I serve as a de facto business agent for my African teachers, helping them find opportunities to work abroad and supporting their efforts to make money in Ghana through farming, crafts, and cultural tourism. My mixed media publications contribute to the interest of non-Africans in African music. As a professor, I validate African music's place within the academy. But these presumably positive actions have their negative valence. By intervening in the local political economy of traditional music in Ghana, I have set forces in motion that affect people's lives for better and for worse. The cultural tourists I encourage to visit Africa increase the exposure of local people to the very global culture that threatens to undermine traditional heritage.

Harder to place in this dialectic is my effort to distill principles of rhythm and melody from performed music. Although cross-border theorizing on music structures may seem progressive, it strengthens the conditions for musical globalization. Just as the early anthropologists helped develop new markets for transnational corporations, ethnomusicologists present the music of Other cultures for consumption. After African music is demystified, music theorists have new repertories for analysis and composers have new ideas for their own works. My concepts about rhythmic structure shape my own drumming, but rather than ensuring authenticity, my ideas may explain the difference between local Ewe or Dagomba style and the way I play (Locke 1982). Since theory's primary context is the synchronic world of ideas, the contextualizing information about the music-culture of origin becomes secondary. Inexorably, theory moves away from the ethnographically particular toward the interculturally general.

Musical transcription offers a neatly circumscribed field of action. For the scholar, paper, pencil, ruler, and eraser filter out the stresses of the real world, creating a two-dimensional graphic field that we can control. At the click of a tape recorder switch, musical experts perform at our command. Notation is orderly and visually beautiful. We manipulate time so that the music, only dimly perceived at natural speed, appears as if seen through a magnifying glass. African performances employ many arts at once. Indigenous multisensory experience resists refinement into an alien code.

In my first years of learning African music, I did almost no transcription and analysis. Self-servingly, I could write that I wanted to learn holistically, but it is more honest to admit that I was unable to figure it out. Once I could hear the music, I enjoyed trying to write it out. During field research in Africa, some of my happiest times were spent in seclusion, quietly transcribing field recordings and lesson tapes. My scholarly writing features extensive notation and analysis because I enjoy it. Despite this penchant for notation, I minimize its use in African ensemble class and rehearsal.

Conscious analytic measurement must come after the ability to produce musical sound. "Stop counting. 'One' does not exist. Hear the melody of the interacting parts." Rather than visualizing notation in their mind's eye, American students, who are so prone to visual intelligence, should use other senses. "Listen to the other parts. Remember the movement of your hands. Feel the vibrating air in your gut. Smell and taste your sweat." That music making is social needs emphasis. Students, sitting so close together on benches that they can feel each other's bodies, should look at each other rather than a piece of paper. Abubakari Lunna explains to the inwardly directed American student that in his culture drummers play for their audience, never for themselves, and commands, "Show your smile!"

On the other hand, notation empowers literate musicians to quickly play a facsimile of the tradition. But this fast pace entails risk. In using a familiar format, students may be encouraged to overlook the profound differences between African music and music of their own tradition. For example, in African music time is both linear and circular, meter is both unitary and plural, and every musical phrase has multiple rhythmic interpretations. A beginner's experience of bafflement, when the music feels compelling but eludes rational comprehension, is precious. The struggle to bring the music into focus engenders respect for African culture. I recall an incident recounted by Sharda Sahai, a North Indian tabla teacher at Wesleyan in the 1970s. At the end of a student's very first lesson, Mr. Sahai inquired about a schedule for more lessons. With incredulous amusement he reported the student's reply, "What? There is more?"

Notation also creates the conditions for intercultural misunderstanding. What newcomers regard as a "piece" of music may be conceived in Africa not as music at all but as voices of the ancestors or the sound of chieftaincy. Notation commodifies music-culture; a score can be copyrighted and sold. When students enjoy notation-centric discussions in American classrooms, African artists become uneasy. Because schooled musicians have notation skills, this discourse disempowers indigenous artists, alienating them from their own heritage. To the traditional artists who remember very well their rigorous path to knowledge, technical analysis conveys the impression that neophyte students understand the music better than the experts themselves!

THE AFRICAN MUSIC ENSEMBLE AS A FORCE FOR CHANGE

For the global consumer the arts may be equated with entertainment and cultural difference with tourism, but I still hope that art can be a force for change. When art is sponsored by state or business institutions, however, its transformative potential is weakened. For example, during the mid-1970s, the dance dramas of Ghana's national dance companies featured love stories or stylized representations of *durbars,* which are festivals designed to reinforce the authority of traditional leadership. On the other hand, Godwin Agbeli, from a professional position on the margins of Ghana's arts and culture establishment, created for his amateur cultural groups a ferocious dance drama in which a white-hot spirit cauterizes the wounds of society, littering the stage with corpses of corrupt chiefs and politicians. The drama expressed an obliterating rage at the misery caused by mismanagement and selfish leadership.

As a space for political action, what work is done by performance courses in African music? If the African ensemble in the United States is seen as a form of discourse, what are its features? We might theorize the ensemble as an "information highway" from Africa to non-Africa, the music and its reception by the students as "content," and the ethnomusicologist as a "modem with an attitude." We are not just a neutral conduit for information but model affect, belief, and a way of action. I try to present an attitude of respect without reverence toward African musicians; I believe that traditional African expressive culture is a transregional heritage available for fair use by everyone; and I act in the world to challenge stereotypes and empower others. Performances present these highly charged issues in a powerful manner. An African ensemble makes Africa tangible; it gives sensory reality to discourse. Information is literally embodied within an arena that is suffused with affect.

Professors and students open themselves to support and criticism when they perform in public view. Although an overworked concept in recent academic writing, "liminal" seems to apply to performers in world music ensembles whose hybrid condition clearly is between cultures, races, statuses, and norms. Faculty musicians unable to wield their normal powers of the word (lecture) or reward (credits and grades) temporarily become the vulnerable and weak, like "humbled chiefs" during their rites of passage (see Turner 1969: 102). If the performance succeeds, the risk of liminality yields to the rush of communitas as persons demographically divided temporarily sense their common human bonds.

Often these high-minded values are compromised by the particular institutions that structure our work and by the unintended consequences of decisions for which we are responsible. Although I strive for authentic interdependence, I must negotiate the appropriation issue: a privileged, white American becomes a tenured professor by specializing in music of poor, black Africans. No amount of giving back to Africa changes those facts. My African ensemble demonstrates the capability of Occidentals to learn Oriental (in the broad sense used by Said) expressive culture. Despite the intention to express global goodwill we imply that Western culture is triumphant. The very act of teaching an African ensemble fulfills the basic condition of Orientalism: an empowered Occidental subject isolates an Oriental object from its context and then assumes control.

In this perspective, a world music ensemble is an arena where the politics of globalization are played. Not surprisingly, these ensembles proliferated during the period when the United States became the world's most powerful nation-state. Like the victors in African wars, we brought home the enemy's drummers. By domesticating the sacred symbols of foreign competitors, world music ensembles inscribe the United States as a global construct. Globalization, however, means neither the total control of the world system by the rich, nor the abject dependency of the poor. Rather than this Eurocentric vision, a center-periphery outlook accords significance to the actions of people in the world's once-colonized regions. History is not a simple tale of extraction of African cultural capital by outsiders. Negotiation, participation, cooperation, avoidance, apathy, melancholy, hesitation, resistance, and radical action characterize relationships among ethnomusicologists and indigenous experts. The relationship between African artists and outsiders is profoundly ambivalent. African artists recognize their need for resources (dependence), but they also realize the richness of their heritage (empowerment). A story will illustrate. In the spring of 2000, Abubakari Lunna and I were team teaching at Tufts. One day we divided the students into two groups: I taught the *Takai* dance to some while he trained the others in drumming. I issued a playful challenge, "Now we will see who is the better teacher." The students told me later that Mr. Lunna jokingly assured them that their group could never lose. "After all," he said, "I can always say that Professor is doing it wrong."

Why has Ewe music become so widely taught in the American academy? Some reasons are diachronic. Since Ghana was colonized by Great Britain, English is the language of the Ghanaian elite; higher education is well developed in Ghana, and by the late 1960s, when bimusicality was catching on in the United States, traditional music already had been institutionalized (detribalized) at the Institute of African Studies at the University of Ghana; scholarship and fieldwork on Ewe drumming in the 1950s had already brought it to the attention of non-Africans; and by the late 1960s Ewe teachers were ready. Synchronic factors can be posited as well. Ewe music yields to systematic analysis and transcription without significant degradation. Although instrumental music has meaning in the Ewe vernacular, its intercultural reception as absolute music has proved more viable and resilient than drumming systems, like Yoruba *dundun*, that are more interwoven with spoken language (see Euba 1990). Lacking natural resources, the Ewe economy has long relied on its human resources; cash-poor Ewe musicians proved eager to work with non-African researchers. Because Ewe society is decentralized and drumming is a voluntary activity, Ewe musicians were free to accept work overseas, unlike Akan court drummers or members of Dagbamba artisan lineages, whose professional obligations tie them more closely to their home scene. Once the ball got rolling, the Ewe musical juggernaut proved irresistible. A reculturized Ewe music now exists as an idiom of global culture.

FACING ORIENTALISM THROUGH
A WORLD MUSIC ENSEMBLE

There is no ivory tower. The prevailing culture, so conditioned by the media, sets the frame of action for academic work about Africa. Non-Africans feel civilized and superior in comparison with an Africa they know only for disease, poverty, brutality, and primitivism. I avoid unqualified use of Eurocentric totalizing terms like "the West" because dualistic comparisons fail to recognize that the world has multiple centers of authority. As Kofi Agawu has pointed out, staff notation ceases to be Western after it has been used to write African music (1995: 186–87). In scholarly writing, comparing African music with Western art music needs justification since they have little in common.

The African ensemble can reinforce systems that perpetuate unjust power relations, or it can counteract them. Said argues that the Orientalist writer is outside the culture, existentially and morally. In contrast to writing, performance, it seems to me, is a move toward the inside. My drumming does not speak for my teachers; it enacts my knowledge of the tradition and the affect generated by my relations with African teachers. Said says that in Orientalist texts the cogency of the representation matters more than fidelity to ethnographic truth. I am not protected by my text but am subordinate to my teachers and subject to the audience's immediate evaluation. I aspire to get it right. Transparent communication of accurate information is an anti-Orientalist act, it seems to me, because it enables the audience to form its own response. In a small way, this may help us to unlearn the dominant Orientalized outlook.

I try to counter Orientalism in my publications. My chapter in *Worlds of Music* begins by questioning the triangular relationship between the object of study (African music), the authorial subject (me), and the recipient of my presentation (reader/listener) (Locke 1996: 71–72). Pointedly, I opted not to pen a touristic description of an exotic locale. Although my full-length studies of repertory appear to be positivist, they always link musical analysis to audio and video recordings so that readers convert music from an inert object of study into an active subject. Whereas the Orientalist author speaks for the Other, the African voice speaks for itself and my interlocutor's role is transparent. For example, in *Drum Damba* (1990) the reader studies with Abubakari Lunna. Although I readily adopt the role of analyst and intercultural facilitator, readers can compare the book's text and graphics to what they hear on tape. In *Kpegisu: A War Drum of the Ewe* (1992), video and audio recordings enable the reader to see and hear Africans; they need not merely trust the verisimilitude of my reporting or the plausibility of my ideas. Dialogue describes the relationship between me and Africans, whose personae in the texts are teachers, cultural experts, and research colleagues. I interpret data that we have created together and make it available to the reader. I do not speak for them.

At a minimum, I hope to achieve an unrepressive engagement with Africa. But I imagine outcomes of greater moment. If, as Said says, the Occident is made by its Other, then good information about the non-West helps open a contact zone. We need not be trapped in an inevitable world of exploitation. Art works, in particular, are capable of creating the ironic distance necessary to gestate change. Empire, so to speak, can have its subversive effect on the home population.

NOTES

1. Despite the shortcomings of the comprehensive label "African music," it remains a handy way to refer to the different musics from Africa that are relevant here. My teachers know genres of music from many parts of Africa and various ethnicities. In addition to southern Ewe and Dagbamba music, I have studied Shona mbira music and many different ethnic traditions from West Africa. I resist the label "Ghanaian" applied to music because the nation-state is a recent and rather irrelevant factor in these music cultures.

2. Although I mostly teach performance of Ewe and Dagbamba music, I also introduce other African traditions. Hence, my use of the broad term "African music."

Chapter 10

Klez Goes to College

HANKUS NETSKY

In the last quarter of the twentieth century the Jewish wedding-music tradition known as klezmer reemerged in America (and, later, internationally) as a popular ethnic musical style and as a creative point of departure, especially for younger musicians. In this chapter, I will share some observations about my experience during the past twenty-four years as one of the perpetrators of the music's revitalization and as a leader of academic klezmer and Yiddish music ensembles at the New England Conservatory of Music and several other colleges.

A NEGLECTED TRADITION

An orphan of a culture that affords its dance musicians a status only a small notch above that of beggars, klezmer music would seem an unlikely choice as a subject for academic inquiry. Until its revival in the late 1970s it received little scholarly attention (some notable exceptions were Beregovski 1937 and Stutschewsky 1959), and, because of its secular non-Jewish roots (in Romanian, Greek, Ukrainian, Gypsy, and other eastern European dance musics), it was thought by some to be outside the realm of Jewish music altogether.

Klezmer, a Yiddish word derived from the biblical Hebrew roots *kle* (vessels) and *zemer* ([of] song), has been used since the early Middle Ages to identify musicians who performed dance music at Jewish celebrations. Because of stringent post–Temple era restrictions on instrumental music (a genre that was seen by many rabbis as a frivolous challenge to the perpetual state of mourning the Jewish leadership declared after the Romans' siege of Jerusalem) and a general societal apprehension concerning the power of music and dance to elicit uncontrollable states of non-religious ecstasy (a fear first articulated by the ancient Greek philosophers), musicians had always struggled for acceptance. In some areas of Europe, *klezmorim* (klezmer musicians) had to deal with three sets of restrictions: those imposed on all folk musicians, those imposed by the secular authorities on Jewish musicians, and those imposed on them by the Jews themselves.

The klezmer life was a life apart. Although the klezmer musicians' skills were often acknowledged and admired, their status within Jewish society was in many ways comparable to the position of Gypsies in greater European society: they were welcome only when their services were needed, and otherwise thought to be "outside the pale of regular community life" (Slobin 1982a: 16). Much of Jewish folklore painted them as sexually active itinerants who gambled and drank at every opportunity and were not particularly trustworthy. Their strongly male-dominated culture was keenly focused on preserving their turf and maximizing their earnings. Musicians were often known only by nicknames—usually entwined with the names of the instruments they played—or colorful stage names, and they spoke a secret argot that was carefully designed to conceal their true thoughts and feelings from their patrons (see Slobin 2002). Even the virtuosi among them had little of worth to show for all of their efforts, and, since they lived in a world where book knowledge and money were badges of success, their status was often compared with that of beggars.[1]

Twentieth-century American Jewish musicians went to great efforts to distance themselves from the word *klezmer*,[2] considering it a derogatory term to refer to those who could not adapt to the demands of the contemporary American music scene—an ironic turn of events, since many *klezmorim* in Europe had been considered extremely versatile. By the 1960s, the traditional dance music they played had fallen out of favor, replaced at most Jewish celebrations by American pop, Latin music, and contemporary Israeli and Hassidic dance tunes.

RECLAIMING A LEGACY

For all of these reasons, *klezmorim* and their repertoire have been largely ignored by scholars of Jewish music, whose field has traditionally been confined to the study of more overtly religious musical traditions. In 1975, when I started sharing what I knew of the genre, there was no visible klezmer scene, virtually no English-language literature on the subject, no perceivable interest from the Jewish or non-Jewish counterculture or establishment, and seemingly little in the way of an oral tradition to draw on. Nevertheless, I set out to learn everything I could about the music, with the hope of passing on something of the tradition to my students.

My connection to klezmer is deep and oblique at the same time. In her seminal article "Sounds of Sensibility," Barbara Kirshenblatt-Gimblett writes eloquently about the "rupture" that separated the early revitalization of klezmer from the culture that produced it (1998c: 49). Indeed, as I was growing up, klezmer music was a vague concept, visible to me only through a thick haze. It was one variety of music that my grandfather and four uncles played, and I had occasionally heard them perform it both at family functions and at a kosher hotel (Teplitsky's) in Atlantic City, New Jersey. Still, despite my pestering, none of them seemed interested in sharing it with me. My uncle Jerry, the last of the older-generation clarinetists on the Philadelphia Jewish wedding scene, made his position abundantly clear: the only way to become a klezmer was to be born into it. To him the style was indelibly intertwined with eccentric old-world characters who plied their trade in dimly lit catering halls while family members and their friends reveled and fought in a manner evocative of old Odessa. Klezmer music as he knew it could no longer be passed on; in his view, it was "dead and buried."

When I reached my late teens, my curiosity peaked. By this time I was studying classical oboe and composition and various forms of Jewish religious music; performing regularly as a jazz saxophonist, pianist, and oboist; and dabbling in the worlds of gospel, blues, and Greek ethnic music. Despite these diverse musical outlets, I felt that something was missing, and I longed to know more about the music of my own ancestors. In 1974, my uncle Sam (my grandfather's brother, a cornetist who had given up music in 1936 to become a dentist) finally agreed to teach me. He played me recordings of great klezmer performers, including Naftule Brandwein and Dave Tarras, and told me wild anecdotes that framed the music in its American immigrant–era cultural context. He also prepared a list of other musicians who could help me, but after many frustrating phone calls I came to the conclusion that the only actual klezmer music I would ever hear was the relatively small amount that had been captured on recordings. I learned a fair number of these selections and went forth to spread my scant knowledge as best I could.[3]

KLEZMER IN AN ECLECTIC AGE

At the time I had no background in ethnomusicology but much experience as a jazz bandleader. At the New England Conservatory of Music (NEC), where I became a teaching assistant in 1976 and a faculty member in 1978 (teaching ear training, improvisation, and composition in the "Third Stream"[4] department, now known as the Department of Contemporary Improvisation), there were no world music ensembles; the emphasis was on individual expression. Students were encouraged to develop their own musical personalities. In the process, their search often led them to consider world music, although at the time there was very little Jewish music in the world music canon. As far as our faculty was concerned, any musical style was available for anyone to learn, and if no living performers could be found, recordings would do. Membership in or attachment to a cultural group was not an issue, nor were concerns regarding insider versus outsider perspectives.[5] Frank London, a founding member of my NEC-based Jewish music group, recalls the prevalent attitude:

> I was part of a larger scene loosely centered around Ran Blake's Third Stream Music Department. We studied a mixture of classical and jazz, as well as lots of other stuff—pop, folk and ethnic musics—while developing a practical philosophy that still guides my own musical life and that of many of my peers. The idea is that one can study and assimilate the elements of any musical style, form, or tradition by ear. You listen over and over to a Charlie Parker solo or a Peruvian flute player, and learn to replicate what you hear. . . . Hankus Netsky invited me to join in an ensemble performing a few klezmer and Yiddish vocal tunes. I was already playing salsa, Balkan, Haitian, and other musics. Why not Jewish? (London 1998: 40)

The group's first performance, which took place on February 17, 1980, was sponsored by the NEC Student Association and the NEC Jewish Student Organization (the first Jewish student group ever organized in the school's 113-year history).[6] The concert seemed to be the logical culmination of the "Klezmer Conservatory"[7] jam sessions I had been leading for a few years.[8] There was very little pretense about reclaiming a lost legacy; indeed, many of the students were not Jewish and were interested only because the music on the recordings was emotionally engaging and technically challenging. After we gave our first concert, everything changed. Frank London recalled the audience's reaction:

> Our focus was on trying to play the music, trying to play it well, trying to get better on the nuances, and others were saying, "Oh, that's not why you were trying to do it at all; you're carrying on your ancestors' legacy, you're re-igniting this torch that went out"—they were getting very heavy about this. (London 1998: 41)

Truth be told, my purpose in organizing the group was twofold: to spread exciting music and to re-ignite a torch. I had already been sneaking cantorials and Sephardic songs into my Third Stream classes for years, and, since klezmer had caught my attention, I didn't see why I should keep it from my students. On the other hand, I knew that, for me, it wasn't just another musical style; it was a basic cultural building block that my family had denied me, and I wouldn't be content until I had mastered it and passed it on.

I was actually completely unaware of the political implications of introducing such music at the New England Conservatory; I instantly became a hero in the eyes of the local Jewish community for flaunting my ethnic identity in a traditional stronghold of Boston *brahminkayt* (how's that for a

Yiddish word?). I also became aware of a hunger that existed in the community for older and less homogenized forms of Jewish expression.

Encouraged by our initial concert's success, I immediately approached the conservatory's administrators for permission to teach an accredited Jewish music ensemble at the school. My idea was rejected on the spot, and the students who played in our first concert became the professional ensemble still known as the Klezmer Conservatory Band, now a standby on the international Jewish music scene for more than twenty-three years.

The initial snubbing of klezmer by the New England Conservatory turned out to be relatively short-lived. Within a year, the Third Stream department had sponsored a Jewish music concert at the school, and the style was included in a schoolwide festival as early as 1981. To this day, the KCB is always mentioned as one of the school's two or three most important alumni groups, and we were prominently showcased in NEC's 125th anniversary celebration. More recently, my student group, the NEC Jewish Music Ensemble, has been featured with actor-folksinger Theodore Bikel in two widely distributed PBS/PRI Jewish holiday specials, "A Taste of Passover" and "A Taste of Chanukah." Perhaps most importantly, quite a few NEC alumni, including Don Byron, Dave Harris, Frank London, Anthony Coleman, Marty Ehrlich, Abby Rabinowitz, Greg Wall, Greg Selker, Paul Brody, Jamie Saft, Glenn Dickson, and Mimi Rabson, have gone on to become innovators in their own right in the revitalized klezmer genre.[9]

INVENTING A KLEZMER CURRICULUM

Yiddish and klezmer music became part of the official New England Conservatory curriculum in 1983, with the launching of a one-semester course entitled "Yiddish Music Performance Styles."[10] In this elective course, which is now offered one in every four semesters, I present the historical context of eastern European Jewish music, using such texts as *Life Is with People* (Zborowski and Herzog 1952), *Voices of a People* (Rubin 1963), *Tenement Songs* (Slobin 1982a), and articles by Mark Slobin, Walter Zev Feldman, Henry Sapoznik, and myself (many now available in Slobin, ed., 2002). I divide the discipline into eight subheadings: Klezmer music, Yiddish folksong, Yiddish theater music, cantorial music, Hassidic music, Jewish art music, Holocaust music, and the klezmer and Yiddish music revival. I consider it a priority for students to understand the interconnections between all of these genres; they are then free to choose an emphasis for group and individual performance projects.[11]

Jewish music is an eclectic idiom, so much so that many scholars have written it off as being entirely derivative of other styles. In my teaching I emphasize sound and phrasing, the Jewish *interpretation* of a melody. This is consistent with the approach I have always used in teaching jazz and gospel:

a melody can be a pop tune or an Anglican church hymn, but a jazz or gospel setting brings an unmistakable African-American sensibility and context to it, the same way a klezmer brings a Jewish sensibility and context to a Greek or Romanian tune.

I always begin with singing, and, since the style is very different from the music that most of the students are familiar with, every aspect of it must be examined closely. Our role models are recordings or, when possible, live performances of undisputed masters. Students prepare vocal examples of Hassidic *nigunim* (melodies), listening carefully for the dynamics, the phrasing, the trills and the *krekhts* (groans). I point out various characteristics that seem to unite all of eastern Europe's Jewish music traditions, and after students have captured the feeling and the sound they put the music on their instruments, listening closely to accurately mirror the vocal nuances.

Each instrument presents its own challenges. Guitarists learn the difference between blues and klezmer inflections. Drummers need to learn several new patterns, playing them with a feel that has little or nothing to do with the African-American grooves that are second nature to them. Pianists learn to imitate the *tsimbl* (hammered dulcimer), and otherwise to be satisfied with spare and percussive accompaniment. String players, trombonists, and saxophonists learn that their instruments are powerful sources of harmonic and rhythmic accompaniment.

Vibrato is often a major issue: clarinetists need to learn it (preferably a slight, fast one, like that of Dave Tarras. Classical singers, string players, flautists, and vocalists often need to widen their vibrato and slow it down. Over the years I have taught klezmer interpretation to players of all manner of brass, wind, string, and percussion instruments, including players of such unlikely instruments as the melodica (one semester I had three of them in my Wesleyan group), five-string banjo, and koto (an ideal klezmer instrument because of its extraordinary capacity for pitch bending).

Soon we take on an ensemble project; I teach the group some dance steps and emphasize the rhythmic drive that goes with playing for dancers— and inebriated ones at that. I also point out the extremes of expression *klezmorim* use, which often contrast with the subtleties of classical European interpretation taught by other faculty. The class learns a Hebrew text using eastern European pronunciation, "Asher Nusan Lanu Toyres Emes" (God Who Gave Us the Torah of Truth) as sung by *baal' tfile* (lay cantor) Leon Schwartz, and, once they know it, they put it on their instruments, taking note of the rhythmic subtleties that come from the accents of the language. I slow down a section of a deceptively simple sounding Dave Tarras *khusidl* (Hassidic dance), making sure to pick out the precise trills, ornaments, and rhythmic nuances.

What relationship do these assignments have to the traditional world of the klezmer, where music was often learned in great haste on the bandstand? Very little, but, then again, I didn't learn klezmer on a bandstand; I learned it on my own, applying every aural and analytical technique and tool I had at my disposal.

Lately, as I have become more aware of the klezmer world of my grandfather's generation, I've begun to incorporate more of what I know about musical transmission among traditional klezmer musicians. Our earliest written record of the klezmer music transmission process comes from the memoirs of a semiprofessional Ukrainian klezmer musician named Bogrov, who published the following account in 1830, which bears out the commonly held belief that many *klezmorim* learned their music by rote:

> I took lessons diligently and would practice for several hours at a time. The master of the black fiddle [Reb Leivik] had no method of instruction. . . . Written music was Greek to the maestro and his associates; they taught me by demonstration, straight from the fingers. Nonetheless, I made quick progress, and Reb Leivik took pride in me as living testimony to the efficacy of his method. (Bogrov, quoted in Beregovski 2001: 30)

Although the oral tradition is usually cited as the most common transmission method used by musicians from klezmer families, it is also clear that written music has been part of the training process wherever there have been musicians who could read and write it. Although I originally rejected music reading altogether in my teaching because of my concern about nonidiomatic habits that might affect students' interpretation, I now occasionally use scores once I'm convinced that students understand the interpretative parameters. I also do a fair amount of "bandstand-style" teaching, in which I simply play random tunes and the ensemble follows me as best they can. This way, the performers become accustomed to typical chord progressions that can be used with eastern European melodies.

At the New England Conservatory, it has worked out especially well to offer both a class and an ensemble in Jewish music. In this performance-oriented school, participation in an extracurricular ensemble has a generally social function, whereas enrollment in a class indicates a more intensive commitment to the musical style. I try to expose those who only play in the ensemble to the richness and depth of Jewish culture by programming a wide-ranging repertoire. A typical concert program might include several traditional eastern European dance tunes, a *badkhones* (wedding poetry) excerpt, several Hassidic melodies (for which the ensemble also sings the text), a cross-cultural piece (illustrating how a klezmer tune may well have Greek, Turkish, Israeli, Armenian, or American cousins), several folksongs, something from the cantorial tradition, some original compositions by members of the group, something from my family's tradition, and at least one vehicle for improvisation. I also bring in guest artists who bring with them the richness of their own repertoires whenever possible.

BRINGING MOLDOVA TO AN AMERICAN CLASSROOM

Although teaching klezmer in an academic setting has given me tremendous satisfaction, the classes I have taught alone can hardly compare to the Bessarabian klezmer workshops that I have now hosted twice during the New England Conservatory's summer session. For these week-long workshops I have had the privilege of hosting Edward (Yosef) Kagansky and German Goldenshteyn, two musicians with wide-ranging first-hand experience playing weddings in the klezmer heartland, along with Michael Alpert and Jeffrey Wollock, who served as auxiliary instructors and translators.

Born in 1933 and originally hailing from Molov, Bessarabia, clarinetist Goldenshteyn learned his craft in the late 1940s, mainly from a Gypsy clarinetist who performed for the surviving Jewish families in his region. He relocated to Brooklyn in 1979, bringing with him a handwritten tune book with close to six hundred entries. The much younger Edward Kagansky, born 1952 in Kesheniev, Moldavia, picked up klezmer in the early 1970s, having been recruited by Yefim Nakhes, an octogenarian *badkhn* (folk poet and singer) who had been performing at Jewish celebrations since czarist days.

For these men, klezmer is not only a powerful musical heritage, but also an emblem of their own rich, colorful, and often tragic culture. For young American musicians, who often think of Jewish eastern Europe as a place in the distant past, it is as if these *klezmorim* stepped out of the history books, giving us the opportunity to go back in time and experience the music as it existed a hundred years ago. Through them, we learned about klezmer dances as a basic wedding staple at Jewish and non-Jewish parties, played on unamplified portable instruments and punctuated with the *poyk* (marching tenor drum with attached cymbal). We heard of wedding ceremonies held in hushed voices behind pulled shades, week-long journeys home from gigs in blizzard conditions, and outrageous pranks that made our hair stand on end. We gained new perspectives on simple things that we took for granted, such as what it could take to save enough money to buy an instrument, or even the basics of earning a living for a musician:

> When you were hired for a wedding, the family didn't pay the band. The band gave the family a deposit for the opportunity the wedding created to earn money. . . . No small weddings like here—there, three, four, five hundred people was a wedding. . . . When we played in some towns we'd arrive at two in the morning. We'd get a list of the wedding guests and their addresses and go play under their windows. The head of the family would come down, usually in his underwear, since it was the middle of the night, and give us something, and then we'd move on to the next house. (Goldenshteyn 1999)

Goldenshteyn goes on to point out that the sleepiness of the patrons could, in some cases, make for very large tips, and the wedding hasn't even begun yet:

> As for the actual wedding, they'd put up a big tent, and as the families came in we would play a march for each family and each family would pay as they came in. While people were getting seated, we'd play dance tunes, requests, and they'd pay us for each of these . . . and the tables were long—they would stretch from here [Boston] to Washington. We'd walk around and play a short piece for each group of guests. This is how we earned our sustenance. It would all go into one cash box. . . . Sometimes we would use the bass case, and we'd fill it up to the point where we wouldn't be able to close it. (Goldenshteyn 1999)

From Kagansky we learned a few practical skills involving the most prevalent symbol of Bessarabian klezmer sustenance, vodka:

> When someone bothered you, made requests without paying, repeatedly requested the same song, or told us we were playing the wrong music, we'd call that person a Dostoyevsky, because, as you know, Dostoyevsky was the author of *Crime and Punishment*. People like this could ruin the whole wedding, so we had specialists in getting rid of them. We would prepare a special drink; we'd fill a glass half full with vodka, and then cap it off with wine. The next time the fellow made a request, I'd ask his mother's name, and if he said "Rukhl," I'd say, "Let's drink to Rukhl." He'd drink from his glass and within ten minutes he was asleep. I would drink from a normal glass of vodka, and in those days I could drink many of those. A similar technique could also be used for animal control. One time I was playing a wedding for about eight hundred people. As soon as we started in with the sad music, a dog started howling. I took some bread, soaked it in vodka, and threw it to the dog. No one heard from him for the rest of the wedding. (Kagansky 1999).

A tune learned from Goldenshteyn or Kagansky was a tune with a story: it served a particular function (like a special *bulgar*—a popular Romanian Jewish figure dance—that waiters danced while carrying towels), or it provided a window into another musician's personality. Their experiences and anecdotes brought the music alive and showed the students the rich potential of music when it interacts with a living culture, something too often missing when music is taught within the sterile walls of a classroom.

WHO WANTS TO BE A KLEZMER?

Students take part in my Jewish music classes and ensembles for various reasons, and what they do with the skills they acquire is entirely up to them. Many of my vocal protégés have gone on to become cantorial soloists, and a number of instrumentalists have found their way into wedding band work.

An equal number play in fusion bands or have become innovators in New York's downtown klezmer scene or participants in the European avant-garde. The neo-klezmer's home, within or outside the Jewish community, is entirely a matter of choice.

Now that there is a diverse and vibrant klezmer scene encompassing both functional and concert music, it is interesting to notice where students are coming from and what attracts them to the music. For many, their first exposure to klezmer came via two well-marketed recordings of the 1990s, Itzhak Perlman's *In the Fiddler's House* series, a virtuosic foray into traditional repertoire, and Don Byron's *Music of Mickey Katz,* an homage to the great clarinetist-comedian who revived klezmer in sophisticated Hollywood-style arrangements in the 1950s. Others are inspired by John Zorn's Masada, an improvisational ensemble that works with "Jewish" modes and Balkan-like rhythms, or more experimental Tzadik or Knitting Factory[12] artists who combine Jewish music with free jazz. A small minority has heard reissues and classic klezmer revival recordings, and an even smaller number of students have roots in traditional Jewish music. Over the years, I have become acutely aware that klezmer has become an alternative point of access to Jewish culture for music students of Jewish or mixed heritage. Mark Slobin summarizes some of the reasons for this:

> Secularized Jews looking for a diasporic tie-in to their music making . . . [parallel] the general drive for re-affiliation to varieties of Jewishness that has snowballed since the 1960s to become the most important trend in American Jewish life. The klezmer repertoire is one of the handiest points of connection, since it does not require losing yourself in the thickets of sacred text, and you can dance to it. But, most strongly, this body of tunes is always already Americanized, deeply and doubly diasporic. (Slobin 2000: 25)

On the other hand, many students of klezmer are not Jewish, and once they become professional, they still find themselves subject to the suspicions of the Jewish community, which remains strongly proprietary concerning their casually discarded ethnic culture. I always tell my students that anyone who aspires to play another community's ethnic music will eventually have to prove themselves to the *"mavens"* (experts) of that community, and that I hope they will pass the test. If they really grasp the essence of the style, they always will. In the early days of the KCB it was Don Byron, a clarinetist of Jamaican-American descent, who received the toughest scrutiny. As he has pointed out, his outsider status made him both a major symbol of the revival and a catalyst for its wider acceptance. More recently, I was amused when, after a radio appearance by one of my current singers, Aoife O'Donovan, I fielded a call from the owner of a local Jewish record store, who told me that that he had received several requests for recordings by the Yiddish singer Aoife Donovitsch.

One thing is for certain: these days, klezmer musicians come in all varieties. There are so many motivations for contemporary students of klezmer, who might be Germans or Poles looking to distance themselves from the thoughtlessness of their ancestors or American musicians hoping to diversify their professional portfolios or simply have some musical fun. Klezmer music, while still struggling to carve out its place in relation to the field of Jewish studies,[13] has found its way onto many college campuses, usually via student-led groups.[14] In recent years, several of the most popular East Coast groups have banded together to present an annual collegiate klezmer festival.[15] Older practitioners, lured by the enthusiasm of students and large audiences, have come out of retirement to lend a hand as artists-in-residence in special klezmer institutes such as Klezkamp and Klezkanada, bringing their much-needed expertise and contextual perspective. Klezmer has finally arrived on the world stage, poised to stake its claim in the academy.

NOTES

1. I was personally privileged to experience old world Hassidic hospitality toward *klezmorim* at a wedding held in the Borough Park section of Brooklyn in 1983. Because the wedding was held during the Jewish month of Adar, the coldest time of the year and a traditional time to show extra hospitality toward the needy, many beggars were present. The band, which included Frank London, Michael Alpert, Andy Statman, and me, was seated with the beggars and served food scraps from a large trough.

2. It is well known in classical music circles that Serge Koussevitsky tried to pay his biographer, Moses Smith, large sums of money to hide his klezmer roots.

3. It might seem audacious that someone who had just picked up a new musical style would be passing it on so quickly, but it's not really uncommon at all (for more on this subject see Kirshenblatt-Gimblett 1995 and Feld 1995). My early goal was simply to share what I had learned with my musician friends, filling in the background I'd gotten from my uncle Sam with information from printed sources that were available (Idelsohn, Sendrey). As a multi-instrumentalist and composer who went back to school to study ethnomusicology, I am still a bit confused by my insider-outsider role in the genre. It is clear to me that my position as an outsider twenty-five years ago was an obvious detriment in the minds of the musicians I approached, many of whom are now extraordinarily forthcoming as interview subjects in light of my success as a performer (alas, it would have been nice if they had been willing to talk to me back when they were still playing!). It is not as clear when or how I made the transition to insider, or whether I actually ever did; perhaps the boundaries are so blurry because the genre has been so thoroughly redefined.

4. The term *Third Stream* was coined by composer, conductor, performer, and author Gunther Schuller in the mid-1950s to describe the new musical amalgam that he felt was emerging as the result of the juncture of various "primary" musical streams, particularly jazz and contemporary European music. Schuller expanded his definition to include world and ethnic music syntheses when a Third Stream depart-

ment was initiated at New England Conservatory in 1973, during his tenure as president of the institution.

5. In *The Study of Ethnomusicology,* Bruno Nettl articulates a traditional ethnomusicological view of such concerns, warning students against the belief that they can easily cross cultural boundaries, or that they should aspire to do so. He relates how he formed this view while studying *dastgah* with a Persian master who told him that no matter how hard he studied the tradition, he would never understand it the way an insider would (Nettl 1983: 259). This dictum was formative in his articulation of the equally valid but proscribed role of an ethnomusicologist.

6. The performance was actually made possible primarily through the work of three individuals: Merryl Goldberg, the head of the Jewish Student Organization, David Mladinov, an extremely enterprising and energetic Hillel Outreach director, and Peter Schoenbach, one of the school's vice presidents.

7. The title was meant to be ironic, in that I was fully aware that *klezmorim* didn't learn their craft at conservatories.

8. I had modeled my klezmer jam sessions on the popular Celtic music sessions I had attended at the Philadelphia home of performer-folklorist Mick Maloney.

9. By 1980, I was also aware of the emerging klezmer scene in New York and on the West Coast, and I was incorporating recordings by Andy Statman and Zev Feldman on my source tapes. I would be remiss not to mention also the moral support I got in the early days from klezmer revival pioneers Henry Sapoznik and Lev Liberman.

10. In recent years I've been calling the course "Eastern European Jewish Musical Traditions."

11. The question of the music's context within a larger Jewish historical framework is particularly acute at NEC, where no courses in Jewish history other than an occasional Holocaust literature review are offered. When I teach the same course at Hebrew College, I become aware of how much richer the material can be for students who have a general background in Jewish history and culture.

12. Tzadik, which uses the tag line "Radical Jewish Culture," is John Zorn's record label. The Knitting Factory is a popular New York–based new music venue founded in the early 1990s by impresario Michael Dorf.

13. The roots of Jewish studies can be traced back to the great religious and intellectual institutions of Poland, Germany, and especially Lithuania, institutions that unfortunately paid little attention to cultural phenomena. It is also significant that klezmer tended to be a southern phenomenon, with roots mostly in Bessarabia, Galicia, and the southern Ukraine. Historical works on these communities are only now being written.

14. In her D.M.A. thesis, "Klezmer in Academia," Christine Gangelhoff notes that most klezmer ensembles are still extracurricular, and argues that klezmer would be an ideal entry point for many Western-trained students to experience a new musical style: "For practical reasons, klezmer is an ideal music to offer—no special instruments are needed, and students of all levels, music major or not, will find wonderful challenges in trying to learn the style. If students are inspired with a unique musical experience, they may discover a desire to explore further. Klezmer can offer students the chance to learn a new musical culture, relate this new study to other forms of music, and gain a deeper appreciation of one of the many varieties of music that exist throughout the world" (Gangelhoff 2002: 43).

15. Klezmerpalooza was first held at Yale in 1999. The second Klezmerpalooza, held at Brown University in April of 2000, included ensembles from Harvard, Wesleyan, Princeton, Yale, NEC, Brown, and Mt. Holyoke. Three of these seven groups had "official" coaches who were either faculty members or teaching assistants. The other four were entirely student-led.

Chapter 11

Creating a Community, Negotiating Among Communities

Performing Middle Eastern Music for a Diverse Middle Eastern and American Public

SCOTT MARCUS

We teach that music is specific to its culture, so it should come as no surprise that ethno performance ensembles tend to be unique entities. Each individual ensemble is a dynamic world representing vibrant and infinitely complex music cultures. Although one would intuitively assume that most of the defining aspects of a given type of ensemble are dictated by the cultural and geographic focus, a variety of other forces help to shape each group. Many elements are determined by the ensemble's director, others are affected by the environment of the home university, and still others come about because of the nature of the surrounding community, and often because of the active participation by specific members of this community. Further, ensemble membership fluctuates as new people join in and other members leave. Thus, it is part of their nature that ensembles grow and change over time.

STRUCTURING MIDDLE EASTERN AND INDIAN ENSEMBLES

At the University of California at Santa Barbara, I teach two different ethno ensembles, one Middle Eastern and the other focusing on North Indian classical music. I founded the UCSB Middle East Ensemble in winter 1990 following the success of a performance component within a Middle Eastern music lecture class that I taught in fall 1989, my first quarter at UCSB (students were given the choice of learning instruments and performing in a concert in lieu of a final paper). The ensemble consists of an orchestra, a chorus, and a dance troupe. Members include graduate and undergraduate students, faculty, and community members. The composition of the ensemble's orchestra is loosely modeled after a type of ensemble that developed in the Arab world from about the 1940s. Called a *firqa* (ensemble), the new ensemble distinguished itself from the earlier *takht* or chamber ensemble by being orchestral in size. While a *takht* might include some five instruments (an *'ūd*, a *qānūn*, a *nāy*, a violin, and a *riqq*), a *firqa* would commonly include a number of additional instruments, for example, a dozen or more violins and some three cellos (see Racy 1988). Cairo's Firqat al-Mūsīqá al-'Arabiyya (The Arab Music Ensemble), founded in 1967, provides the model for the formal joining of a *firqa* with a large chorus (see El-Shawan 1979, 1981, and 1984). At UCSB, the forty-plus orchestra members play *'ūd* (Arab short-necked lute), *nāy* (end-blown reed flute), *qānūn* (plucked trapezoidal zither), *santūr* (struck trapezoidal zither), violin, cello, bass, accordion, a variety of Middle Eastern percussion instruments, and, on occasion, *mizmār* (double-reed oboe), *zurna* (shawm), *bağlama saz* (Turkish long-necked lute), saxophone, electric guitar, electric bass, and keyboard.[1] Performance venues range from local children's fairs, ethnic festivals, multicultural dance festivals, classes and assemblies at local schools, and a variety of university events, to more formal concerts for universities, academic conferences, and Middle Eastern communities throughout the state of California.[2] At UCSB, the ensemble presents formal end-of-the-quarter concerts three times a year, regularly selling out the music department's 468-seat hall. The ensemble as a whole is supported by an official university support group, the Friends of Middle Eastern Music Association (FOMEMA), discussed further below.

The UCSB Music of India Ensemble, which I founded in 1989 during my first quarter at the university, is essentially a *sitar* ensemble. The group, which uses a collection of twenty *sitars*, is divided into two: one group of beginning students (new students are accepted only at the beginning of each school year), and another of ongoing students. The ensemble presents formal end-of-the-quarter concerts, again three times a year, for the university and occasionally gives informal university and community concerts and lecture/demonstrations for area schools.[3] The India Ensemble is loosely modeled after university-based classes of Indian music that I attended in India (at Banaras Hindu University, in Varanasi, Uttar Pradesh) and the United States (at Wesleyan University).

There are few similarities between the two ensembles. The methods and manner of teaching are completely different. For example, following Middle Eastern practice, the Middle East Ensemble uses modified Western staff notation, chairs, and music stands, and focuses on great works by renowned composers. Following Indian tradition, the members of the India Ensemble all sit on the floor, with their shoes by the door. And, since we must not step over the *sitars* or our notebooks, it is necessary to discuss at least briefly aspects of Indian philosophy, such as an Indian sense of purity and acts that might be considered defiling. Thus, from the first or second meeting of the India Ensemble, we are already involved with religion and philosophy, subjects that do not necessarily come up quickly in the Middle East Ensemble.

The position of the ensemble director is also quite different in the two groups. In the India Ensemble, the concept of the guru inevitably comes into play, especially for students of Indian heritage. Such students must consider, for example, traditional modes of showing respect to the teacher, including touching his or her feet upon arrival and when leaving class. (Interestingly, some do so, while others do not.) In contrast, the director of a Middle Eastern ensemble is commonly treated in a manner similar to that of a Western band or orchestra conductor.

Teaching within the ensembles occurs in a variety of contexts, allowing for many levels of student-teacher interaction. Periodic discussions during rehearsals address aspects of specific performance practices or provide the opportunity for cultural anecdotes from ensemble members who are from or have lived in the music culture being studied. With the Middle East Ensemble, the drum section, chorus, and dancers each have separate rehearsals in addition to the weekly general rehearsals. There are also group and private lessons that focus on specific melody instruments and on the melodic modes of Middle Eastern music (primarily the Arab *maqāmāt*). Guest teachers offer their expertise and unique perspectives first in rehearsals, and then in concerts where they are featured as guest artists. Readings and lecture classes add additional components to our ongoing studies in both ensembles.[4]

And yet, for all the aspects of cultural determinism, no two Middle East ensembles are alike, and different universities' Indian ensembles commonly end up being quite different from one another.[5] This is, in large part, because each director has different goals. I learned Middle Eastern music as a graduate student at UCLA from Ali Jihad Racy, professor of ethnomusicology and founder and director of the UCLA Near East Ensemble. In many ways I have fashioned the UCSB ensemble after the UCLA group. There are significant differences between the two groups, however, partly because of my own interests, but especially because of an unusually large and talented group of people in Santa Barbara who were eager to work with the ensemble as teachers, performers, and supporters. Ultimately, we are trying for something quite different.

THE "FRESHMAN-PROFESSOR" CONTINUUM

I was introduced to world music and the field of ethnomusicology in 1970 as a freshman at Wesleyan University. "Performance in World Musics" was taught by more than a dozen visiting artists and graduate teaching assistants at the time, and included classes in American Indian voice and dance, Indonesian gamelan and dance, Japanese *koto, samisen,* and *shakuhachi,* North

Indian *sitar* and *tabla*, South Indian *vina* and *mrdangam*, West African drums, Korean *Ah Ahk* (court music), and the Middle Eastern *'ūd*. As a freshman I began studying and performing Javanese gamelan, and soon afterwards I turned to the North Indian *sitar*. The *sitar* was not an obvious choice for me at the time: I wanted to study a stringed instrument, but I also actively considered the Japanese *koto* (long zither) and sat in on Middle Eastern *'ūd* lessons. I ended up studying the *sitar* in part because of the outgoing and charismatic personality of the *sitar* teacher, Ram Chakravarty. Noticing me looking in on his class from the hallway one afternoon, he urged me to come in and take my first lesson, putting a *mizrāb* (plectrum) on my finger, instructing me how to sit, and handing me a *sitar*. As a teacher, I have regularly repeated this same enthusiastic invitation when I have found a student looking in on my Indian or Middle East ensemble classes.

Able to major in gamelan and *sitar*, I quickly absorbed an orientation that emphasized the active study of some aspect of a culture's performance practice. When I later had the chance to spend my senior year in India, it was a given that my fieldwork would center around music lessons, and I quickly set up a schedule of daily *sitar* lessons. My "senior year abroad" stretched out to three years. During subsequent periods of fieldwork, I have repeated this approach time and again, studying first the *'ūd*, then the *nāy*, and most recently the *mizmār* during periods in Egypt, the sitar and *dholak* in India, and the *tammattama* (Buddhist ritual drum) in Sri Lanka. The study of music performance offers a rich introduction to countless aspects of a music culture. In my Arab music studies, for example, I was able to develop a number of lines of performance-based scholarship focusing largely on differences between the traditional written theory and explicit and implicit aspects of performers' theory.

Upon returning to the United States, I completed my M.A. at Wesleyan and then entered the Ph.D. program at UCLA to further my Indian music studies under Nazir Ali Jairazbhoy. My studies took a turn when Ali Jihad Racy joined the UCLA faculty after my first year there. I began *'ūd* lessons with Jihad, thrilled to realize the extent to which my Indian training aided my studies of the Arab modal system: clearly the Indian system of *ragas* and the Arab system of *maqāms* have many points in common.

I had begun teaching *sitar* privately when I returned to Wesleyan, but at UCLA I had my first opportunity to lead an ethno ensemble: I was appointed the *sitar* teacher of the India Ensemble, a teaching assistant position. I began teaching *'ūd* privately after returning from my first period of fieldwork in Cairo; a major step occurred for me when one of my students received official credit for his *'ūd* lessons. When I was hired at UCSB, a *sitar*-based Indian music ensemble was a part of my course load during my first quarter. That quarter I also taught a lecture class on music of the Middle East and offered students the chance to take music lessons instead of writing a final paper, with the stipulation that they would have to learn to play five pieces of music. At the end of the quarter we performed our pieces in a concert that included four Santa Barbara–based musicians and two dancers. The concert was such a success—it attracted the highest attendance of any concert at the two-year-old UCSB MultiCultural Center to date, with people leaning into all the open windows after the center had filled up—that I was encouraged to make the ensemble an official part of the music department's performance program. I did so the following quarter.

A MIDDLE EAST ENSEMBLE REPERTOIRE MODEL

Jihad Racy shaped my sense of an ethnomusicology-based Middle East ensemble by embracing at least three largely distinct spheres of Arab performance: Arab art music, Arab folk music, and Arab cabaret dance music. To my knowledge, there is no ensemble in the Middle East with a comparable breadth of focus. Rather, there are separate ensembles for each of these three repertoires. In Cairo, for example, a number of government ensembles are dedicated specifically to the performance of Arab art music, for example, Firqat al-Mūsīqá al-'Arabiyya (The Arab Music Ensemble), founded in 1967, and al-Firqa al-Qawmiyya al-'Arabiyya li-l-Mūsīqá (The National Arab Ensemble for Music), founded in the mid- to late 1980s by the Lebanese conductor Salim Sahab. Cairo's Higher Institute for Arabic Music and its College of Music Education, a part of Helwan University, each also have an ensemble dedicated to Arab art music, called, respectively, Firqat Umm Kulthūm and Firqat Muḥammad 'Abd al-Wahhāb.[6] A number of other ensembles perform folk music, including government ensembles such as Firqat al-Nīl (The Nile Ensemble) and al-Firqa al-Qawmiyya li-l-Funūn al-Sha'biyya (The National Ensemble for Folk Arts). Many of these groups include folk dances in their repertoire. And, finally, separate troupes, usually fronted by individual dancers, present cabaret-style music and dance. Thus, in Cairo, and I believe in the Middle East in general, there is a clear separation of these three repertoires.

Middle Eastern ethno ensembles in the United States do not maintain this separation. It seems to go against a goal of our ensembles, that is, to broadly represent different segments of vibrant, multilayered Arab culture. I want to be able to present aspects of folk culture, art music culture, and dance culture, all in one concert.

At UCSB, we present an even more diverse repertoire than Jihad's ensemble. Most significantly, in addition to Arab and Turko-Arab repertoire, we also focus on Armenian, Greek, Persian, Sephardic and Oriental Jewish, and Turkish music and dance. The impetuses for such a wide repertoire were varied, but they often included requests from members of these very communities (see below). The repertoire of the UCSB Middle East Ensemble is also diverse in other ways. For example, we perform repertoire from Middle Eastern religious traditions (for example, Turkish Alevi Sufi songs, an Egyptian Muslim pilgrimage song, an Egyptian Muslim song that presents the ninety-nine names of God, and Yemenite Jewish Sabbath songs). In Cairo, these works would be performed by yet another distinct category of ensemble, represented, for example, by the government Firqat al-Inshād al-Dīnī (The Ensemble of Religious Songs). Second, we perform examples of the latest pop hits, 'Amr Diyab's "Habībī Yā Nūr al-'Ayn," for example, or Hishām 'Abbās's "Yā Laylá." Third, we also perform regional folk dances (such as Lebanese *dabkas*, Upper Egyptian dances, Turkish spoon dances, Greek *sirtos*, and Armenian line dances), an obvious opportunity provided by having a dance troupe as one of the ensemble's core components.[7] And recently we've made a very touching addition to our repertoire, performing a number of well-known Arabic children's songs, including "Māmā Zamānhā Gayya".[8] I should add that the responses of audience members— especially those of Middle Eastern heritage—to this varied repertoire have been phenomenal.

One of the reasons for this great variety, once again, is the desire to present a dense multilayered sense of Middle Eastern cultures. The diversity is also based on a philosophy that individual pieces of music, whether a song, a dance, or even a culture-specific rhythm, are major sites for generating, recalling, validating, and celebrating personal, community, and national identity. Appropriating Western musicological concepts of "the work" (the "isolated" work) and "monuments of music," I would say that we ethnomusicologists want to highlight the musical monuments of the cultures we study, not because they are necessarily worthy of study as isolated pieces of art, but rather because of how deeply these pieces are connected within the culture, in terms of contexts, values, and meanings.

Each of these additional repertoires raises a variety of issues. Regarding the incorporation of popular music, I remember a new UCLA graduate student some twelve years ago arguing against a repertoire limited to the historic art music (what is commonly termed the *turāth* in Arabic), with its inherent reification of the past and ignoring of present-day music, including the latest hits with their new instruments, new sounds, and new overall aesthetic. However, just last week I was sternly scolded by a renowned Persian classical artist for presenting current Persian pop songs and pop singers in concerts that also feature extended sets of Persian classical music. This Persian musician expressed complete dismay that a university ensemble, with all its inherent "prestige" (his word), would stoop so low as to perform pop music. He felt that I was bringing dishonor on myself and the university. With the Middle East Ensemble, however, I am more interested in showing Middle Eastern cultural diversity than favoring a single category of music, say, for example, Middle Eastern art music.

A SENSE OF COMMUNITY
INSIDE AND OUTSIDE THE ENSEMBLE

The focus of the UCSB Middle East Ensemble was greatly influenced by the presence of a diverse Middle Eastern community in Santa Barbara. When I first came to Santa Barbara in 1989, I was introduced to a large and vibrant Persian community, and soon thereafter to a similarly large and equally vital Armenian community. There is also a considerable Greek community and small Arab and Turkish populations in the area. With the encouragement of members from these various groups, the UCSB Middle East Ensemble has learned and performed music and dance from each of these cultures. Heritage community support has been so strong that we formed the official university-sanctioned support group FOMEMA, mentioned above. This support group has a board that includes representatives of the various communities. Thus, the board presently consists of three Arabs, two Armenians, one Greek, three Persians, and one Turk, in addition to European-Americans like myself. One of the board members' functions is to keep the ensemble in active contact with the various Middle Eastern–American communities in the greater Santa Barbara area.

The Middle East Ensemble's diverse repertoire serves a variety of functions and has markedly different meanings for specific populations involved with the ensemble. Among the different populations, I point out four here: people of the various heritage communities, nonheritage audience members, members of the ensemble itself, and, a subgroup of this last set, ethnomusicology graduate students, including those focusing specifically on Middle Eastern music.

One of the defining aspects of the UCSB Middle East Ensemble is a strong sense of community—an enthusiastic esprit de corps—that exists within the ensemble itself. The ensemble is an open one: anyone can join, whether they are absolute beginners or experienced players. (Beginners are usually directed to the percussion section, where they are taught the skeletal structures of the various rhythms.) New members are enthusiastically welcomed. Rehearsals, similarly, are all open. People can come in and watch if they are so inclined, but they might well be offered a drum or lyrics to a song. The ensemble meets throughout the year, even during summer break, when rehearsals take place off campus in people's houses and begin with potluck dinners. The sense of community extends beyond the ensemble members to a larger circle of people that includes the board and general members of our FOMEMA support group, and to a still larger circle of our loyal audience members. For formal concerts at UCSB, board members pitch in by donating food (some homemade) and drink and helping to sell and serve the food at intermission. With audience members of Middle Eastern heritage responding to the concerts in traditional manners (singing along and occasionally calling out standard phrases of appreciation), it is common for first-time attendees to comment that it seems as if they had attended a family gathering.

For the heritage communities, ensemble performances can be important celebrations that include many aspects of cultural and personal affirmation. This would be true, of course, for any immigrant community whose culture is little represented here in the United States. But issues of affirmation are especially vital for many Middle Eastern communities in the context of America's often-hostile environment. America's unreasoned sense of a monolithic Arab, including images of camels, deserts, and terrorism, is tiring, to say the least. The immediate but ultimately false conclusion that the 1995 Oklahoma bombing was the work of Arab terrorists is but one example. For heritage community members, concerts function beyond the realms of affirmation and confirmation. For example, one's sense of identity is enriched when specific pockets of music repertoire are actively recalled, be it a long forgotten song from the 1950s, a beloved singer from the 1960s, or memories of having one's mother sing a certain children's song many decades ago. As Kay Shelemay (1998) has richly pointed out in her recent study of Syrian Jews in Brooklyn, New York, music making can enhance a community's collective memory in a remarkably vital and celebratory way. When older heritage community members bring their American-born children to our concerts, additional dynamics such as education and validation are present.

For many nonheritage audience members, the ensemble's diverse repertoire serves as a first glimpse at the cultural diversity of Middle Eastern culture. There is no monolithic "Arab," for example. For this population, songs by the superstar Egyptian singers, perhaps Umm Kulthūm or 'Abd al-Ḥalīm Ḥāfiz, with brief introductory remarks about the career of the singer, open up a whole world: Yes, there is an Arab art music. Yes, there is also a whole world of renowned Arab singers, poets, and composers, long adored by a general Arab public. A film song from the 1930s introduces Americans to the Arab musical film genre. An upper Egyptian folk dance (from southern Egypt) and a section of the *Bani Hilal* epic from Egypt's delta region (northern Egypt) performed by Professor Dwight Reynolds teaches that there is no monolithic "Egyptian." A Lebanese folk dance (a *dabka*) with, perhaps, a uniquely Lebanese rhythm, a Sa'udi song with a distinctive Sa'udi rhythm, and a Turkish dance with a characteristic Turkish rhythm all serve to emphasize a densely multilayered and multicultural Middle East. A children's song poignantly adds to the picture, conveying a sense of family and investing a world that is often associated with an array of negative stereotypes with a sense of warmth and normalcy.

For our ethnomusicology students, and especially for the ethnomusicology graduate students in the ensemble, the varied repertoire offers an interactive relationship with many of the cultures, musicological principles, and renowned figures that we study in our lecture and seminar classes. Along the lines of a picture being worth a thousand words, learning and performing a variety of melodic and rhythmic modes gives added levels of understanding about these modes. Experiencing the non-Western notes of Middle Eastern music through performance, trying to come to terms with the Arab half-flats (quarter tones) and how they are uniquely tuned in a variety of Arab modes, is an invaluable experience. Performing suites of Arab, Turkish, and Persian art or classical musics helps to ready students for doctoral exams in which they will have to demonstrate an understanding of these suite forms and the various genres found in each. Understandings of the Turkish *peşrev* genre, the Persian *taṣnīf* genre, or the Arab *taḥmīla* genre are all deepened by the experience of learning and performing examples of each.

The very cultural variety that I have praised is not without its occasional pitfalls. I have already mentioned that classical musicians have objected, on more than one instance, to the inclusion of anything "less" than classical. Occasionally, the very communities that have helped the UCSB Middle East Ensemble develop its program of cultural diversity find that members of their own communities object to our cultural juxtapositions. A respected Armenian member of our board was instrumental in encouraging that each of our concerts be multicultural. We have had concerts in the past that featured Arab, Turkish, or Persian music and dance to the near exclusion of other cultures. But he felt that each concert should have something for each of Santa Barbara's many Middle Eastern communities. However, when we have included Turkish music in concerts that especially featured Armenian music, a few members of his Armenian community objected. The board discussed this issue at some length and recommended that, in the future, we separate the two cultures by putting them in at substantially different points of a given concert. The same issue surfaced when we wanted to include both Persian and Iraqi music in an upcoming concert. In this case, a Persian member of the ensemble announced that he would not—indeed, could not—participate in the concert, informing us that he had lost family members in the (then) recently concluded Iraq-Iran war. After lengthy discussions about the ensemble's larger goals, this Persian musician did play in the concert. Should we play Persian pieces in a concert for Los Angeles's Iraqi American Association? Along similar lines, a Los Angeles Lebanese American association made it clear that they did not want any Jewish pieces in our upcoming concert for their organization. But what about a song that has been an emblem of the Israeli peace movement, "Shir la Shalom." (This song's position was solidified when the Israeli prime minister, Yitzhak Rabin, sang it at a massive peace rally moments before he was assassinated in 1995. It was reported that he had the words written on a piece of paper in his pocket.) Often, there are no easy answers. A multicultural repertoire juxtaposes a variety of identities, at times revealing points of great tension.

The ethno ensemble director does not have to run away from such points of tension, although addressing each requires sensitivity and careful consideration. Directors and ensemble members—the latter broadly conceived to include both performers, key supporters, and others in the ensemble's larger community—then, have the often-delicate task of balancing communal sensibilities, entertainment, and education. With appropriate sensitivity and compassion, cultural or religious conflicts can be confronted and tolerance furthered. The UCSB Middle East Ensemble has had some successes with this. Following a Turkish Muslim song (of the *ilahi* genre) with a Yemenite Jewish Sabbath song in a Sacramento, California, concert, each introduced with brief comments that made the juxtaposition explicit, was one of the more powerful moments in the ensemble's fourteen-year history. Yet, as with most public endeavors, we cannot expect that all involved, whether performers or audience members, will be entirely comfortable or pleased with such moments.

The varied repertoire performed by the UCSB Middle East Ensemble is clearly one of the defining characteristics of the ensemble and of my approach to it. However, I would like to emphasize again that each ethno ensemble can be, and probably should be, unique. For example, I have chosen a completely different approach for my Indian music ensemble. The UCSB India Ensemble, with very few exceptions, performs only North Indian classical music. This is, in large part, a response to values I absorbed during years of classical music lessons in India and the United States, and also to the nature of North Indian classical music. Performance items in the *raga* tradition are commonly of considerable length. A serious *raga* that might fill the first hour of a concert is naturally followed by the performance of a lighter *raga*. With ensemble classes devoted to learning classical repertoire on the *sitar,* there is currently no opportunity to study and present a separate popular music repertoire, a separate folk music repertoire, etc. What has worked so well for one ensemble is not necessarily appropriate for another.

NOTES

1. I lead the orchestra and the ensemble as a whole. The percussion section is led by community member Sue Rudnicki. The twelve- to twenty-member chorus was led jointly by Dwight Reynolds, UCSB professor of Arabic language and literature, and me until 2001, after which I became the sole leader. Many of the chorus mem-

bers also perform in the ensemble's orchestra. Non-Arabic texts are taught to the chorus by specific chorus members or by special guests. For example, Voula Aldrich teaches the Greek song texts, Ihsan Saib and Mark and Dilek Soileau teach Turkish texts, and Koorosh Haghighat-Kish teaches Persian texts. UCSB Arabic lecturer Magda Campo teaches the Arabic texts in Dwight's absence. All of these people are long-time ensemble members. The ensemble's dance troupe is led by Alexandra King and consists of a core group of six to eight dancers and a large class of beginning dancers. With occasional guest artists, the Middle East Ensemble usually includes more than sixty performers in its largest concerts; for smaller events, the ensemble may consist of as few as five or six people.

2. For example, we have performed for Lebanese, Syrian, Egyptian, Palestinian, and Iraqi community groups. We have performed outside California on three occasions: seven members of the ensemble performed a series of concerts in August 1999 in Samarqand, Uzbekistan, representing the United States in the biannual multinational Sharq Taronalari (Songs of the East) festival; a forty-member group performed a series of concerts in January 2000 in Tucson, Arizona, sponsored by the University of Arizona's Center for Middle Eastern Studies; and a nineteen-member group performed a concert for the Arab-American community in McLean, Virginia, in April 2001.

3. This configuration of concerts, stable for ten years, has varied over the last four years with formal end-of-quarter concerts occurring only after the winter and spring quarters. For two years, from 1995 to 1997, UCSB doctoral student David Trasoff directed the India Ensemble.

4. UCSB ethnomusicology graduate students Jim Grippo and Amy Cyr contributed to this paragraph.

5. I am aware of three university music department–based Middle East ensembles: at UCSB, College of William and Mary (see chapter 12 in this volume), and UCLA (see chapter 8). In addition, Harvard University's Center for Middle Eastern Studies sponsors the Middle East Music Study Group. UCLA has at times had a Persian music ensemble in addition to its Near East Ensemble. The University of Washington–Seattle has had a Turkish music ensemble directed by Münir Nurettin Beken. A small number of schools also have ensembles or classes not specifically dedicated to the Middle East that occasionally study Middle Eastern repertoire, such as the Balkan music ensemble at the University of Illinois, directed by Donna Buchanan.

6. Firqat Muḥammad 'Abd al-Wahhāb was disbanded around 2000.

7. The contribution of Alexandra King, the director of our dance troupe, to the overall success of the ensemble cannot be overemphasized.

8. I owe my initial acquaintance with Arabic children's songs to my two children, who, when aged two and five, lived with my wife and me in Cairo for six months in 1998. I would listen in as one of their babysitters taught them the song "Māmā Zamānhā Gayya." Subsequently, Magda Campo has introduced other children's songs to both the ensemble and to four Santa Barbara Arab-American children, aged four to nine, who have joined us as guest singers for formal performances on a number of occasions.

PART FOUR

Take-Off Points

Creativity and Pedagogical Obligation

Chapter 12

Bilateral Negotiations in Bimusicality

Insiders, Outsiders, and the "Real Version" in Middle Eastern Music Performance

ANNE K. RASMUSSEN

In the summer of 1998, I wrote a statement for my tenure file entitled "A Philosophy of Teaching, Performance, Scholarship, and Service." The subsection "Performance in Academia" explained to senior colleagues how music performance can occupy a crucial position in the scholarship, teaching, and service of an ethnomusicologist. Following a brief introduction to "bimusicality," one of the cornerstones of my education at UCLA,[1] I explained how musical performance has been integral to my research methodology among both Middle Eastern and Indonesian musicians (see, for example, Rasmussen 1997b, and 2001b). Learning about music through lessons and informal apprenticeships as well as performing have been important components of my fieldwork experience. When I first introduced myself to the senior musicians of Arab heritage in the United States, my playing the *'ūd*, the Arab lute, did more to convince them of my good intentions than my explanations of either ethnomusicology or my progress toward the Ph.D. During 1999, when I was in Indonesia, my performance in the classroom setting of religious songs called *tawāshīḥ* and Quranic passages let people know I was seriously interested in Islamic musical arts in Indonesia. My frequent playing and singing of Arab music at a variety of events, from informal gatherings to programs broadcast on national Indonesian television, confirmed my involvement in Arab arts and culture as both musician and scholar. Performance—and here I mean music making in any context—always helps me to discover the technical workings of music, and my work as a performer has often elevated my status from observer to participant in the very contexts that I am trying to understand and document. At times, performance that is requested of me has been a distraction from other obligations, for example, making recordings or talking to key participants, but more often it is the commodity of exchange that both I and my consultants seem to be seeking. Furthermore, I believe that when scholarship becomes text, the analysis of musical style and aesthetics comes more easily if it is based on a sense of the experience of performance.

"Students, too, respond to learning through experience," my self-congratulatory tenure sermon asserted. Explaining African polyrhythms is fine. Reading about North Indian raga is essential and rewarding. But to perform, even on a basic level, incites enlightenment through several channels simultaneously. The William and Mary Middle Eastern Music Ensemble, established in 1994, "invites students to study a major art music tradition of the world!" I declared. Through learning new instruments, different techniques of performance, and a non-Western system of musical organization and performance aesthetics, playing in the ensemble challenges and stretches students' musicianship on a variety of levels.

Happily, senior colleagues bought my argument regarding my integrated approach to scholarship and performance and granted me tenure. There is no question that ethnomusicologists are at risk when they devote time to performance. At Oberlin College and the University of Texas, Austin, where I had previously held visiting positions (for one year and one and a half years, respectively), I directed ensembles as a part of my teaching load. However, like some of the other authors in this volume, I suspect, in my current position I direct my ensemble as an overload. The commitment includes a weekly rehearsal, as well as about four hours of weekly sectional rehearsals and six to ten performances per semester. The time and energy required are significant. Yet, if I didn't direct this ensemble, my "Middle Eastern musical self" might atrophy and die. I wonder if I would practice and perform at all. Through my work with the William and Mary Middle Eastern Music Ensemble I am able to study and perform music from the central Arab world (including Egypt, Lebanon, and Syria), as well as music from the Turkish, Greek, and Armenian repertoires. We generally have fifteen to twenty-five members, most of them undergraduates, who play 'ūd (pear-shaped fretless lute with a round back and eleven strings, ten of which are in double courses), violin, cello, qānūn (trapezoid-shaped zither with seventy-five strings in triple courses), nāy (reed flute), accordion, clarinet, bass, and various percussion instruments, including riqq (tambourine with fish-skin head and heavy brass cymbals), daff (frame drum in various sizes), darabukka (goblet-shaped, single-headed clay or metal drum), bandīr (frame drum with snares on the inside of the head), ṭabl baladī (large double-headed side drum; one head is struck with a thick beater, the other with a thin stick). We have also begun to work with choral groups for our more ambitious concerts. One key to the ensemble's success is that it has managed to attract a core of very capable, creative, and dedicated musicians who stay with the ensemble year after year, and have even kept it going in my absences (1995–96 and 1999).

Although our "service" ratings soar as ensemble directors, it is never clear until we cross the threshold of tenure how our activities as performers will be evaluated as "teaching" and "scholarship." In a meeting about my third-year review, one senior colleague from International Studies advised I write an article about my ensemble so that the hours spent in teaching through performance could be evaluated as "scholarship" through the more easily recognized and prestigious commodity of a publication. At the time I resented his inability to evaluate performance on its own terms, but now I suppose that this chapter *is* that publication. Furthermore, I hope that this volume, by problematizing our performance in the language of the academy, will provide models for our colleagues and their institutions that are trying to make a place for world music performance and its evaluation.

As leaders of university-based world music ensembles, our responsibilities as professional "outsiders" loom large. We have all undergone rights of passage that legitimate our ability to play the music, and we explain these qualifications to our deans, students, audiences, our collaborators "in the field," and guest artists. Some of the contributors to this volume allude to the conflicted feelings they might have about performing the "Other's" music.[2] My hang-up about playing the music of a people "whose blood doesn't flow in my veins" has pretty much dissipated after living in Indonesia researching Islamic musical arts for two years (1995–96 and 1999). In Jakarta I witnessed live performance of rock and roll, reggae, *nuevo flamenco*, jazz, oldies, Western art music, disco, pop-*musak*, Christian hymns, and Arab religious and pop music—to name just a few of the kinds of "foreign" music that Indonesians play professionally. Not only do Indonesians "cover" these musics, I believe they identify with them as their own. Their attitudes have done much to allay some of the insecurities I acquired through academic socialization about performing music of the "Other."

Still, in spite of any insecurities we may harbor concerning the "masquerading" or "ethno-drag" to which Gage Averill refers in his chapter, I think we believe that the kinds of work and play experiences that such music learning and making offer cannot be found elsewhere on campus.[3] Politically, the mere presence of such an ensemble is a powerful and affirmative statement for multiculturalism. The William and Mary Middle Eastern Music Ensemble, for example, plays ambassadorial roles on several levels. We represent the university and their respect for diversity, and we represent Middle Eastern, and especially Arab, culture and community in both the global and local sense to a huge number of people. We serve as ambassadors for both the college and the Middle Eastern community in contexts that range from the academic performance/demonstration, to the formal concert, to the Middle Eastern community event, to the ecumenical recreational festival. In a discussion of Middle Eastern music in America for the *Garland Encyclopedia of World Music: The United States and Canada* (Rasmussen

2001a), I mention the significance of university ensembles not because of the quality of their performances, but simply because of the sheer number of people from the Middle East and from Middle Eastern–American communities and music scenes that intersect with these groups. I was introduced to this phenomenon first at UCLA where Ali Jihad Racy's ensemble, also assistant directed for a time by Nabil Azzam, was an axis for musical and social interaction among students, community members, and guests passing though town.[4] Finally, as directors of university-based, non-Western ensembles we invite our students into new social and aesthetic worlds.

WHICH SPICES ARE KEY FOR THE SAUCE?

What are the landmarks of an aesthetic world? Much of our time as ethnomusicologists is spent identifying, sometimes embracing, and explaining these key concepts and practices of the music we study and play. Through my work with our Middle Eastern ensemble, I have come to realize that the aesthetic pillars of the music may be somewhat different for me than they are for other performers of the music. In addition to the scales, the special intonation, the great rhythms, the dynamic repertoire, and the central role of improvisation, one of the things that I find exciting about Arab music is the musical texture produced by the interaction between musicians. My aesthetic preferences are certainly the culmination of my ongoing study of the works of Ali Jihad Racy, whose research on traditional Arab musical aesthetics I embraced early on. Added to his elegant explanations of *ṭarab* (Racy 1991) and specific analysis of heterophonic playing (Racy 1988) are my own experiences of music making in Arab-American contexts. Although some of these experiences have been concerts, many others have been performances in nightclubs and at weddings and parties where the interaction between musicians and audience purposely culminates in the common goal of collective euphoria. So, after teaching people how to hold, tune, and play their instruments, how to find the notes and embody the rhythms, *this* is what we work on in our group: musical interaction. Sometimes I feel like what I am really teaching is a kind of musical maturity, one that is not experienced under the conductor's baton or in the garage band rehearsal. What I might be trying to create in rehearsal, performance, and informal music making at parties is *context*.

Once I can get my students to "noodle around" and create heterophony, to actually listen and let themselves be moved by a fellow musician's solo and then to respond to a phrase of that solo or *taqāsīm* (improvisation) with an echo of the same or complimentary notes, to play a *lāzima* (musical filler) spontaneously without waiting for my directions, to take a phrase that is repeated four times and to play it differently each time—then we're on a roll! Charlie, a veteran orchestra violist, confessed after one semester in our group that he could hardly stick to the score in orchestra rehearsal: his fingers itched to embellish. Lillie, whose honors thesis tackled the analysis of musical style and technique, reflected on her gradual perception and appreciation of ornamentation. Initially reveling in the freedom of it all, she embroidered every note she could. Throughout her four years in the group, she progressively sharpened her perception of just how much of this embroidery was idiomatic as she studied the music in other contexts.

> For someone like me who learned the music without having grown up in the tradition, this kind of freedom to expand on a melody at first seemed like a free-for-all to add as many notes as my ability would allow. In every phrase I played, I would add innumerable turns, trills and syncopations. I came to find, however, that playing Arabic music on the violin requires a certain amount of control. In other words, it takes more skill to be selective about adding ornaments and grace notes than to perform the ornaments themselves. In a coached ensemble I participated in, I was instructed to make sure to not fill in every rest with a *lazimah*. If you take all the space out of a piece, trying to be virtuosic, the piece loses energy and excitement. (Gordon 2002: 55–56)

The degree of "noodling" depends on the repertoire. Certain genres of music—strophic *muwashshaḥāt* (a repertoire of Syrian and Egyptian songs with texts in a mix of classical and colloquial Arabic and literary roots thought to date to the Andalusian period of the ninth to thirteenth centuries) and folk music, for example—may require a good deal of arrangement and ornamentation so that the music doesn't sound too repetitive. This stands in stark contrast to the compositions of Muḥammad 'Abd al-Wahhāb, in which changes of rhythmic pattern, tempo, and instrumental color are carefully choreographed in the composition itself. Some of these changes in rhythm and instrumentation are better gleaned from listening to original recordings since they may not be indicated on scores, most of which are either transcriptions handed down from other musicians or from published collections. But, whatever the repertoire, when our group can move from a perfect unison groove into an ensemble sound that is like the loose weave on an old, worn-out sweater, I feel we experience something essential in Arab music.

In my ongoing experience as a learner, however, I have found few "native" teachers who articulate pedagogically the spices I consider key to the sauce.[5] Perhaps, as insiders, my teachers of Arab and Middle Eastern music have been unaware of how remarkable the live aesthetic sounds to the outside ear. Perhaps heterophony, delayed heterophony, creating melodic variations on the fly, and echoing and responding to a fellow player's solo line—what amounts to the "messiness" of the music—are the result of practices so inherent in the music that they cannot be explained or taught. Or perhaps the same musical texture of interaction that excites me is actually something that some of my past teachers find undesirable.

Recordings of Arab music produced within the last ten years or so suggest that there is an audible move away from the spontaneous live quality of Arab music toward the "organized" sound of the West. Let me explain this shift in production values by going back to some of the earliest recordings of Arab music. Although the process of 78 rpm recording in the early twentieth century naturally curtailed long performances, it did not entirely squelch spontaneity and creativity (Racy 1977, 1978, 1988; Rasmussen 1991, 1997a, 1997b). Musicians who were recording Middle Eastern music on both sides of the Atlantic, that is, musicians in the homeland and in immigrant communities, continued to improvise *taqāsīm* and to produce records that were rich in heterophonic playing. Furthermore, 78 rpm recordings by Arab and Arab-American musicians commonly included exclamatory verbal remarks by the musicians themselves to one another. The aesthetic of the live performance came through loud and clear in spite of the hard, cold material culture of the recording industry.

This live aesthetic and the premium placed on musical spontaneity can be heard on recordings of Arab music throughout the century. Consider, for example, that the majority of Umm Kulthūm's recordings and broadcasts were of live performances. In these remnants of material culture we still hear the spontaneity of live performance. The recordings preserve the ambiguity of her improvisatory sections along with the surprising repeats and the unending variation that made the axiom "she never sang a line the same way twice" a trope in Egyptian discourse (Danielson 1997: 146–58). Umm Kulthūm's recordings are also remarkable for the level of audience participation in the mix.[6] In my experience with working Arab musicians— people who perform every weekend in restaurants and nightclubs, at festivals, and for weddings, community parties, and social rituals like baptisms, engagements, and retirements—I frequently witnessed musicians trying to inspire these levels of audience reaction themselves by egging each other on with kudos in Arabic, or by performing an exciting *zaghārīt* (ululation) into the microphone. Even more interesting is the *zaghārīt* produced by the synthesizer commonly heard on pop recordings and in live music performances, something perhaps analogous to the canned laughter or applause spliced into the sound track of a televised sitcom (see also Rasmussen 1996).

On the other side of this live aesthetic of spontaneous interaction bordering on rowdiness is a sophisticated concert hall sound. Recordings produced in the studio and that employ the magic of overdubbing (Shaheen 1992) and recordings taken from live concerts that exclude audience noise (Racy 1997) are part of this trend. Recording projects that reflect arranged rehearsal may be the productions of musicians who actually strive for the quiet, controlled ambience inherent in Western production (Rouhana 1997).

From my perspective, however, the clean, arranged, notated sounds of the West are at odds with the music of the Middle East, a monophonic music that begs elaboration. Furthermore, arranging and elaborating upon a monophonic melody provides a much more original experience for our ensemble than were I to write out all of the parts. I also have to map my personal preferences concerning the music of the Middle East onto my non–Middle Eastern musical life. I like music that is acoustic and unplugged, like bluegrass; I like concerts that are experiences and not completely programmed, like Grateful Dead shows; I like ensembles that feature the individual sound and creativity of all musicians and not just a star soloist, like jazz combos. I like music made at house parties as much or even more than music made on stage.

Because of my experience with a variety of teachers and performers, I have not been surprised that the coaching and commentary of our guest artists have not addressed or advanced the special qualities and processes of Middle Eastern musical interaction just described. What *has* come as a surprise are the situations of conflict and negotiation between our guest and me, moments where my principles of Arab musicality have been challenged and consequently reworked or reinforced.

Our performance seasons culminate with a grand concert starring a master musician, a "real" Middle Easterner whose style and repertoire we feature in our program. This performance model was originally inspired by Scott Marcus and the UCSB Middle East Ensemble. That our guests are of Middle Eastern heritage may constitute an act of reverse discrimination in which many of us engage. In my search every year for guest artists, I may well be considering more than issues of musicianship, for example, the almost sacred position of the musical insider/native musician as well as the attraction of such an "authentic" performer for students and audiences.

The brief time that our artist is in residence—long enough only for one or two full rehearsals, a few sectionals, a visit to a class or two, the sound check, performance, and the postconcert party—is a wonderful, supercharged experience of exchange. In most cases, the only "real" Middle Eastern musicians the students have ever met or heard up close are former guest artists, and, for the artist, our ensemble is a novelty. For me, because my work as an ethnomusicologist has dealt with Arab and Middle Eastern Americans, bringing guest artists to campus is a reimmersion in the "field." For several days I am thrown back into a world where midterms and faculty meetings are irrelevant. My interest in the activities of our guests, their fellow musicians, their patrons, and their families takes precedence, and I am keen to discuss our respective perspectives on the changing nature of the music culture of Middle Eastern Americans. I began my research among primarily Arab-American musicians and audiences in 1986, so these matters are now a part of my life, not just research topics.

Inviting a master musician from "the community" into my world is also a way of reciprocating the gracious hospitality that so many individuals have shown me on the many occasions that I have barged into their lives. It is the part of field research where, as Michelle Kisliuk articulates, I am making myself known to them (1997: 27). It is also the ultimate test of my Middle Eastern musicianship. Here I review a couple of incidents during the visits of Syrian-American singer Yusef Kassab of Brooklyn, New York, who performed with us in 1997, and Lebanese-American nāy player Nadim Dlaikan, of Detroit, Michigan, who was our featured artist in 1995.

TRADITION: FLEXIBLE OR FIXED?

In Arab music, you follow the singer or, alternatively, the strongest musician. Following the leader or the musician who has the most convincing idea at the moment is one of the aesthetic trademarks of the music. This is how I explain it to my orchestra-trained violinists who ask again and again, "So, how many times do we repeat the A section?"

Although singer Yusef Kassab and I had discussed the program for hours on the phone, and I had sent him all of the transcriptions we were using (he also sent me a number of scores), our rehearsal was chaotic. From my perspective Yusef didn't seem to understand that his tradition really wasn't their tradition. My students knew how to play a number of muwashshaḥāt, but they didn't have enough experience with this repertoire to catch a new verse on the fly, and certainly not to learn it just one rehearsal before the performance!

"Come on, Yusef, let's just do it this way," I encouraged. Yusef wasn't satisfied. He insisted and I buckled. He had come prepared with his own transcriptions and willingly worked with any available ensemble members one-on-one in the two days preceding the concert. Together we worked madly to rewrite a number of our pieces so that students could sight-read, during the concert, a new verse here or a twist on the old one there. For our one big set the music was color-coded: "first the pink one, then the yellow one," we instructed the musicians and singers just before curtain time.

For all that we did to perform the music his admittedly more authentic way, we were disappointed when he completely forgot about some of the things we considered central to our arrangements: a carefully choreographed introduction or ending, for example, copied from the best-known recordings. Of course, the carefully choreographed arrangements he forgot during the performance were more than compensated for by the energetic spontaneity of the evening. Yusef Kassab is a fabulous traditional Arab singer. The concert was a hit and the students, however bewildered by our unpredictable repeats, new verses, and skipped introductions, learned a lot about the difference between rehearsal and concert, about listening to and following a soloist, and about playing in the moment.

During Yusef's visit, as I gave up my arrangements for his, I was reminded of how the tradition requires flexibility. In postperformance commentary, however, Yusef offered some advice on a showy instrumental piece that the ensemble performed on our own. "I'll teach you the *real* version of that piece" he offered, "from a recording by . . ." I cut him off. He had crossed my line.

According to what I know to be a "truth" in Arab music, no real urtext version of much of the repertoire exists. In fact, the practice of establishing authoritative versions of pieces in the canon is one initiated and enforced by people and institutions that were, perhaps objectionably, influenced by Western ideas (see for example, Marcus 1989a, 1989b, 1992; El-Shawan 1984; Davis 1992). My experience with musicians and texts all tells me that there are *many versions* of Arab music works. Yet here was my guest artist telling me he would teach me "the" version of the piece "Layālī Asyūṭ." I objected.

I believed our version was faithful to the teacher who taught it to me (*'ūd* player Haig Manoogian), as well as to recordings I had heard. I have the romantic notion that a piece of music is somewhat more prestigious or valuable when it is passed on to you through oral tradition rather than just copied off a recording or score. Furthermore, I felt that the piece had our signature on it. We had worked out a great arrangement, and, given the tradition's emphasis on originality (another "truth" of the music), I never wanted it to sound exactly like anyone else's recording anyway. Although I am certain I could have learned something valuable from Yusef's version, I was not ready to be taught the "right" version by anyone. In this instance, my version of the tradition prevailed.

INTONATION: INVITATION OR PROHIBITION?

It was with great pride that I invited Nadim Dlaikan to perform with our group in 1995. Nadim has been a cornerstone of my research in Detroit and is a key resource for other researchers, producers, politicians, educators, and public sector ethnomusicologists and folklorists in Michigan, the state with the largest Arab-American community in the country. He has welcomed me into his home, made instruments for our group, and allowed me to film him as he demonstrated tone production and fingerings for a video that I brought home to my insistent beginners at Oberlin College in 1990. Nadim has let me tag along to numerous gigs—even to play at some of them—and he has introduced me to many other musicians. I was excited to repay his generosity. I wanted to show him and, by extension, all the musicians in Detroit what it is that we do as performing ethnomusicologists in universities.

I invited Nadim to a freshman seminar, and he was the guest in an Arabic language class. He rehearsed with the group and spent extra time with John, a student who, several years after graduation, is still an active *nāy* player, probably in part because of his original interaction with Nadim. Nadim appeared to love the group. He had never seen anything like it. We tried to treat him like a king. The musical exchange seemed great; he complimented me on my choice of repertoire for the program over and over. As a professional musician in Dearborn/Detroit—home of the largest community of Arabic speakers outside the Arab world—Nadim primarily plays urbanized folk and pop music driven by the "plugged-in" power of the Arabic org or synthesizer.[7] For our concert with Nadim, we performed suites of traditional music *(min al-turâth)* in *maqām*s *Rāst, Bayyāti,* and *Ṣabá* (the distinctively Arab-sounding musical modes with quarter tones). We played a full-length instrumental version of "Anā fī Intiẓārak," composed by the Egyptian Zakariyyā Aḥmad and made famous by the archetypal Arab singer Umm Kulthūm, that I had transcribed, complete with space for an improvisatory section in the third verse. Nadim performed a crucial role not only at the concert but at the party too, taking over on the back deck with the barbecue and cooking *shīsh ṭāwūq* that he had prepared himself. For a variety of reasons, students commented that they learned more from Nadim than they had imagined possible.

On the way to the airport I asked Nadim if he could recommend any pieces I should try with the group. No, he answered, he couldn't think of anything specific, but he recommended "anything in the major and the minor." What Nadim meant was to stick to the music in modes that are like Western major and minor scales, *maqām 'Ajam* and *maqām Nahawand.* I was momentarily crushed. "But Nadim," I pleaded, "we just played a concert in *maqām*s *Rāst, Ṣabá,* and *Bayyāti,* and the students played *taqāsim* [improvisation] and you yourself were glowing." "Well, that's true," he conceded.

I will never know whether Nadim actually suffered through our performances of Arab repertoire or whether he was just automatically firing off an axiom of the music culture: non-Arabs can't do justice to modes with quarter tones (see also Rice 1997: 109–10). Arabs are proud of their quarter tones, and even nonmusicians know that their music is distinctive because of them.[8] Approaches toward Arab intonation vary, and a teacher's attitude can either invite you into the music or can cast an irreversible shadow on your ability to play or sing. For example, one of my past teachers encourages students to sing and find the intervals with their voice by providing continuous and gentle guidance through his example. Another teacher favors taking the note out of the context of the *maqām* and focusing on its various incremental positions. To find the note E-half-flat, for example, we start singing the "real E-flat," and then go "a little sharper . . . sharper . . . sharper . . . oh no, that's too high. Let's start again." Frankly, I find this method both unhelpful and demoralizing. Another teacher analyzes intervals visually in terms of their physical distance from one another on the neck of the *'ūd,* thus emphasizing the scientific basis of intonation and its imminently possible imitability.

Attitudes toward intonation extend to the world of improvisation or *taqāsīm,* which, in some teachers' eyes, I have felt, is a land where Westerners should go only briefly, if at all! For me, playing the distinctive modes of Arab music and incorporating improvisation by myself and the more capable members of the group is key to the experience of music making. Our mission is educational, experiential, social, and musical. We are continuously working *at* the music, not just striving for flawless performance. I suppose my idea of Middle Eastern music performance is influenced by the exciting community-based events that I have experienced among Arab musicians and audiences. These performances, often full of imperfections, are somehow more exciting to me than Western-style concerts and perfectly mixed studio recordings of Arab music. Process over product!

Furthermore, any tuning problems our group may have are due to much more than our remarkable un-Arabness. Between, say, five *'ūd*s (that's fifty-five strings); a *qānān* (add another seventy-five strings); three to five violins, tuned here to GDgd instead of the Gdae standard in Western music; an accordion that, when we use it, is just a bit sharp; and our two to three *nāys* that are not perfectly matched, the ensemble is most certainly intonationally challenged. But we do not discriminate! We can just as easily play a minor scale (similar to the Arab *maqām Nahawand*) out of tune as we can *maqām Ṣabá* (D, E-half-flat, F, G-flat, A, B-flat, C, D-flat), a mode that has no analogy in Western music.

MUSICALITY

Whether or not one is born and bred in a musical tradition, one's musicality is the result of a patchwork of experience. A culturally specific sense of musicality may certainly be developed through the process of being native to that culture, but musicians' musicalities are also collections of encounters and choices: pastiches of performances they have experienced, the lessons they have taken, the people with whom they have played, the other musicians they admire, other musics that they play or enjoy, and the technical and cognitive limitations of their own musicianship.

By passing on what I know I have given life to new performances and I have become implicated in the transmission of a tradition (see also

Shelemay 1997). Although I have engaged in this transmission in the most respectful and informed way that I can, I am not always able to control the process. During two different years when I was on leave from the college, my ensemble continued on an ad hoc basis without me, proof that this group has become more than a class. And, although I worry about the quality of these performances, I am proud of their efforts. At this writing three former ensemble members are in various regions of the Arab world studying Middle Eastern music performance, and a handful have gone on to graduate school in ethnomusicology. Other former ensemble members have incorporated aspects of Middle Eastern studies, performance, or activism into their professional lives or graduate work.

Sowing seeds and opening doors can be both satisfying and bittersweet. A few years after leaving the University of Texas, I received a CD recorded by an Austin Middle Eastern ensemble that featured two former students, Kamran Hooshmand and Robert Riggio. Much of the music on their CD consisted of pieces they first learned in the University of Texas Middle Eastern Ensemble that I directed in 1992–93. Their recording taught me that once you give the music away, you cannot control what people do with it. The CD made me uneasy: here they were recording pieces that I myself did not feel qualified to record. What would my teachers think? I did not mean for this to happen. This line of thought then led me to question issues of ownership. That music wasn't really mine to give in the first place; I was merely passing it on in an act of transmission.

Like ethnomusicologist Paul Berliner, whose pivotal lesson with Bandembira was learned after months of perseverance (1993: "Introduction"), I have learned, corny as it sounds, that music is a gift; I give and accept it regularly. Although I am always ready to receive this gift from the native musician in whatever form it takes (demonstration, advice, observation, lesson), I have also grown confident of my own version of the tradition. However limited it may be, my Middle Eastern musicality is grounded in ongoing experience, beginning in 1985, of listening, learning, performing, and studying. I am an outsider, but I am also in a sense a culture bearer. This is a role I have also inadvertently stepped into in Indonesia, where, in 1999, in a relationship of field research reciprocity, I taught, performed, and coached singers in Arab music repertoire within a community of Quranic educators and students.

That I am a performing ethnomusicologist is thanks in great part to mentors and colleagues who have encouraged me to teach and research through performance. Such performance has allowed me to communicate in the university, the community, and the "field" in ways otherwise impossible. As teacher, performer, and patron I am now irreversibly implicated in the very process that concerns my ethnomusicological research and publication: the transmission of Arab and Middle Eastern music.

NOTES

1. My graduate education at the University of California at Los Angeles advocated a philosophy of "bimusicality" or "multimusicality" first articulated by Mantle Hood (see, for example, Hood 1960 and 1982). How can you really study, understand, or begin to get inside a musical culture by standing on the sidelines? Hood questioned. Serious study of the *performance* of that music, he argued, is really the only way to move to deeper and *other* levels of communication about music. It is, of course, important to interview and observe (both basic methods of anthropology), but to sing or play an instrument constitutes the most fundamental level of "participant observation" for the ethnomusicologist. Professor Ali Jihad Racy, world-recognized performer and composer of Arab music, was my principal advisor.

2. In the spirit established by the contributing authors to the volume *Shadows in the Field* (Barz and Cooley 1997), I am bringing terms from the ethnomusicological lexicon into question by putting them in quotation marks, e.g., "Other," "insider," "field."

3. I find it ironic that the event our ensemble plays in that exhibits the most blatant qualities of "masquerading" or "ethno-drag" is the annual "Arabian Nights" extravaganza put on entirely by the Middle Eastern Students Association. The event is an important statement about ethnicity and identity for some of the students involved, but it also, due in part to the costuming, decor, and dance, seems (to me) to exhibit a kind of neo-Orientalism.

4. Racy's UCLA-based Near East Ensemble was a catalyst and inspiration for the newer community-based ensemble Kān Zamān.

5. I have been a student at various times of Ali Jihad Racy, Scott Marcus, Simon Shaheen, Nabil Azzam, Haig Manoogian, Souren Baronian, George Sawa, and another score of musicians you may read more about in my dissertation (Rasmussen 1991). I have attended the Mendocino Middle Eastern Music and Dance Camp at least five times and Simon Shaheen's Arabic Music Retreat three times. I came to this music after years of training as a pianist and cellist at the New England Conservatory Preparatory School and Northwestern University School of Music and—following a crisis of faith in Western art music complemented by lack of inspiration in the practice room—several years of study and work in Chicago, Denver, Paris, and Los Angeles as a jazz singer and pianist.

6. Compare the premium placed on the live performances in Arab culture with that in American popular music. My rock and pop music colleagues (Theo Cateforis and John Dougan) both point to the album *James Brown: Live at the Apollo* as the one that caused a revolution in American recording production values. During the decades that followed, countless live albums followed suit.

7. Planning a program that includes traditional art music along with some folk and popular music in various rhythms and modes has been my modus operandi for programming, something I learned from Ali Jihad Racy and Scott Marcus. Of course, I am limited by the number of pieces I know and that we can tackle as a group. In contrast to our concerts, the Arab-American community musician plays mostly parties *(haflāt),* usually connected to various life cycle events, where loud and lively popular music for dancing are called for. Because our concerts are intended

to both educate and entertain, we do not have to answer the demands of popular audiences. Although the guest artists I have invited have all played for crossover and academic audiences, the idea that the musician has total control over the program is novel for the nonacademic musician, I think. One of our guest artists, a community musician, didn't realize until the day after our packed concert that attendance had been free. He was flabbergasted, and he lamented the loss of the money we could have made.

8. The term *quarter tone* is the one most commonly used for the "special" notes in Arab scales or *maqāmāt*. Racy has often referred to these notes as "neutral" tones. Quarter tones in Arab music generally fall between two tempered semitones or half steps. For example, the note E-half-flat is higher than E-flat but lower than E-natural. Their exact tuning can vary depending on the mode, geographical region, and performer, but today synthesizers have done much to standardize a "50 cent" quarter tone. For further discussion, see my article on theory and practice among Arab synthesizer players (Rasmussen 1996) and Scott Marcus's work (Marcus 1989a, esp. chapters 2, 3, and 4).

Chapter 13

Community of Comfort

Negotiating a World of "Latin Marimba"

TED SOLÍS

This ambiguous, multivocal world makes it increasingly hard to conceive of human diversity as inscribed in bounded, independent cultures. Difference is an effect of inventive syncretism.

JAMES CLIFFORD, *The Predicament of Culture*

My goal in writing this chapter is to help myself understand the reasons I have developed and teach a "Latin marimba ensemble." I articulate the ways in which my teaching is informed, not necessarily by a self-assumed ambassadorial role in conveying culture to my students, but by the desire for an aesthetically satisfying, collaborative, emotionally comforting performative world. I also discuss ways in which the ensemble provides a means of furthering my ideas on performance philosophy and performer/audience relationships that have evolved partly in reaction to the Western concert paradigm. It would appear, moreover, that while I am striving against myself to define my own parameters, to free myself from obligation to a tradition, I am also reluctant to fully escape those roots.

I initially modeled this ensemble and its performative world on the regional marimba ensemble of the southeastern Mexican states of Chiapas, Tabasco, and Oaxaca. As we shall see, I stand in relation to that tradition as an "approximate insider." Its "classical" instrumentation (*marimba pura:* "pure [unaccompanied] marimba") consists of two large Mexican marimbas, xylophones of African origin (the word *marimba* is of Bantu origin) that have been transformed through centuries of mestization and creolization in Central America and southeastern Mexico. The *grande* (large) instrument has about 5½ to 6 octaves, while the *chica* (small) is about an octave shorter in the bass range. By the nineteenth century the marimba was a chromatic instrument with a double keyboard (see Kaptain 1992). The most characteristic remaining African-derived sonic feature is the *charleo* or buzz created by an extremely thin piece of pig intestine pasted to the small hole at the bottom of each wooden resonator.

The marimba is arranged according to Euro-American conventions of range–function. From lowest to highest, these *puestos* (posts or positions) are: *bajo* (bass), typically played on the beat; *armonía* (harmony), the off beat in, for example, a waltz; *segundo* (second), the countermelody; and *tiple* (treble). In traditional Chiapan style, *marimbistas* (marimba musicians) play bass, countermelody, and treble with two sticks, and harmony with three. Because the sound dies away rapidly, musicians prolong tones with a tremolo technique (ideally playing even and rapidly repeated notes), which, along with the buzz, is a distinguishing characteristic of the Central American marimba.[1] This style, with traditional repertoire played on unaccompanied marimbas (now somewhat of an archaic, although cherished, folkloric format), is considered quintessentially *Sureño* (Southern).

I have directed some form of this ensemble for more than twenty years, and at Arizona State University since 1989. I've named ASU's group Marimba Maderas de Comitán ("Woods" or "keys" of the town of Comitán) in homage to the birthplace in Chiapas, Mexico, of my paternal grandfather, a marimba musician. The ensemble fits into a performance world built partly upon traditional elements with a rich admixture of components drawn from many sources.

Most of my colleagues in this volume concern themselves with honest and reflexive representations of the musical traditions with which they are emotionally and professionally intertwined. I, however, find myself in the seemingly contradictory and uncharacteristic position of approaching this ensemble in a somewhat deracinated way, with some elements of its presumably typical ethnic context consciously suppressed, and with a somewhat ambiguous attitude toward "authenticity" for its own sake. I have embraced the satisfaction and comforts of an emotional world arising from an eclectic set of influences made tangible through performance interactions. This self-revelation is rather remarkable to me in view of the fact that I was probably drawn to ethnomusicology by an attraction to ethnicity and cultural diversity even more than an attraction to music per se.

I have at times been deeply enmeshed in pedagogically and behaviorally rigid traditions, such as the notoriously process-oriented Japanese *gagaku,* which I taught for a while at the University of Hawai'i. In India, however, my teacher (the eminent *sarod* artist and "thoroughly modern" Buddhadev Dasgupta) steadfastly disclaimed the validity of strict and traditional *guru*-ness. His incorporation of innovative pedagogical methods into the venerable Hindustani tradition may have influenced my later interrogation of musical orthodoxies. In light of my minimal gamelan expertise, entirely the product of Colin McPhee (1966) transcriptions and two excellent lessons from Professor Kuo-Huang Han of Northern Illinois University, my one semester of teaching a Balinese *gamelan anklung* ensemble in the Semester at Sea program adds some comic perspective and even more poignancy to

One record my father brought home was a discount 10-inch LP consisting of anonymous cuts of diverse ensembles, all grouped together under one concocted name (no personnel, of course, were listed). When, many years later, I was able to recognize that the styles on this record ranged from Afro horn/percussion *conjuntos* to *guajiro* (white peasant farmers) string-based ensembles, I was able to pinpoint two of the recorded groups as the Sonora Matancera and Arsenio Rodriguez's orchestra, both from Cuba. The latter's tight, driving interlocking percussion and *fauxbourdon* trumpet and vocal harmonies (arguably Congolese-derived) in parallel sixths particularly moved me, and they have become a signature of many of our group's *montunos* (call and response–based improvisations over an interlocking rhythm section ostinato, found in the second part of many Cuban dance pieces). On this record and those of Puerto Rican bandleader-pianist Noro Morales and others I also heard ingenious highly chromatic and cross-rhythmic piano *montunos*.

Another very different recording that was influential for me was Les Baxter's iconic mid-1950s "jungle music" classic hi-fi LP *Le Sacre du Savage/Ritual of the Savage,* conceived as a unified programmatic suite. The diatonic and quartal tonal harmonies and melodies were grounded in strong, hypnotic ostinati. This, combined with "jungle/exotic" motifs of the vivid cover art (sort of Easter Island meets the Yoruba) and individual programmatic titles and brief descriptions, contributed to a world of sonic/mental imagery of the colorful, romantic exotic that has nourished me even until the present.[6]

Over the years I also became familiar with much of the traditional Chiapas marimba repertoire through Mexican recordings. The marimba, both physically and as sound (in its most characteristic and iconic Chiapan stylistic sense with rapid tremolo in tight tertiary harmony), continued to represent for me something both near and far, something familiar, iconic, and mythic.[7] Although I was linked with these sonic worlds through my father's very real history of having grown up in the bosom of a part Mexican family playing the Mexican marimba, the images were largely isolated from any "real" Mexican or Latin ethnic context. They represented, more than anything, what I might neologically call a "pathoscape," an emotional landscape. This duality—on the one hand captured by aspects of the music, on the other relatively free of strong ethnic grounding—has continually influenced my ongoing relationship with the marimba tradition and Latin music in general.

MARIMBA BAND COLLEAGUES: SEEKERS OF SOMETHING

Marimba Maderas de Comitán has a reputation for accepting all comers and providing a creative outlet for those attracted to some aspect of our

the angst expressed by a number of this book's co-contributors as to the representations of their revered adopted cultures to uncritical audiences. My representation of Bali on the S.S. *Universe* exemplified (with apologies to Oscar Wilde) "the minimally competent leading the incompetent before the uncritical."

In this chapter I explore ways I channel diverse experience into pedagogy. I have long been fascinated with examining why it is that we do what we do. As editor of this volume, I urged my collaborators to explore this subject; each of them can provide stories at least as interesting as my own.

ETHNO AND ENSEMBLE

Ethno and *ensemble* are loaded words for me, eliciting a rich and multilayered variety of associations stretching back into my childhood, and in many ways they encapsulate the general and specific directions of my life. Their confluence has created a career for me and for many others.

The "Other" has fascinated me for as long as I can remember,[2] and the connections between sound and ethnicity are strongly imprinted upon me. Language sounds, for example, have always excited me, whether or not I understand them.

The word *ensemble* unpacks the general, deep, and early immersion in music that I share with most music professionals. I have never been completely satisfied with solitary performance; the pleasures of performativity are exponentially compounded through collaboration. Jeff Todd Titon eloquently expresses a similar feeling in what he calls his "paradigm case of musical 'being-in-the-world'": "For me, making music is incomplete when I do it by myself; it is completed in a social group when I make music with others" (1997: 93). Any satisfaction in progressing in a given performing medium was always only potential until I played with others. I remember the excitement of playing the string bass in my high school dance band for the first time with others, after struggling, self-taught, through a bass instruction book. This was followed by years of smiling, nodding, musicianly mutual appreciations in dance band and jazz settings. My jam sessions with my father (he on piano, I on bass) and later with my children (various combinations of piano and singing) and my brother Rick (my piano, his French horn) were profound bonding experiences that shaped our relationships, in some ways more profoundly than any others.

"APPROXIMATELY INSIDE" THE MEXICAN MARIMBA

The idea that the Mexican marimba might be a serious research subject and performance activity came to me almost as a revelatory afterthought, in spite of my part Mexican, part *marimbista* family background. It was not until embarking on a Ph.D. as part of my "roots" quest in the early 1970s, after completing an M.A. thesis on the North Indian *sarod* (fretless short-necked lute), that I learned much about either the marimba or my family in Mexico. My paternal grandfather, Margarito E. Solis,[3] a native of the town of Comitán, in the southeast Mexican state of Chiapas, came to this country around the turn of the twentieth century. He and his brothers Guadalupe and Olivio and a first cousin Enrique were *marimbistas* who soon became marimba players in the groups Four Solis, Solis Marimba Band, Solis' Marimba Band, and perhaps others unknown to me. His groups, in assorted incarnations and personnel configurations, were novelty musical attractions in vaudeville and Chautauqua circuits from the early 1900s until the ascendance of talking pictures around 1929. They never recorded, much to my regret.

I have deduced from photos that the group maintained a more or less traditional marimba *puestos* format. Their repertoire, however, apparently consisted of aural transcriptions of European light classics: overtures, Liszt's Hungarian Rhapsodies, and Strauss waltzes, for example.[4] Thus, my earliest anecdotal and mythic, as opposed to aurally experienced, knowledge of the marimba involved repertoire and contexts profoundly removed from those of Mexico. The traditional southeast Mexican marimba repertoire consisted of folk *zapateados* ("shoe-tapped" instrumentals), *sones* (a broad term for traditional regional dances), and once-popular waltzes and *danzones* (rondo-like dances of Cuban origin) (see Kaptain 1992; Solís 1982).

This separation from more traditional genres was accentuated by my very idiosyncratic exposure to the instrument itself. My father Max had grown up as a vaudeville child, traveling with the band throughout the United States and Canada. During that time he learned the traditional collaborative hierarchical marimba technique. Long after the demise of the large touring Solis marimba band, however, he developed a very different and unique style suitable for the exigencies of performing in clubs (then called "club dates") in New York in the 1930s and 1940s. This style involved playing a small 2½-octave marimba, cut from the upper octaves of a previously 4½- or 5½-octave *chica* or *grande,* on which he, like a vibraphonist, played all the parts himself with two to four sticks.[5] Moreover, he invariably played with "mixed consorts" consisting of assorted Latin percussion, accordions, trumpet, bass, and other instruments. Before my Ph.D. field research in Chiapas and Mexico City, this was the only "Mexican marimba" I had ever seen in the flesh.

The repertoire my father played in this context was that associated with New York City, Catskills, and Miami "society" music. It was a seemingly eclectic (but nationwide rather consistent) mélange of Broadway and filmically derived standards and Latin dance music à la mode, including internationally popular boleros, tangos, and "rhumbas." This music was for me, in

truth, deracinated; other than the Spanish titles, I never especially associated it with the somewhat mythic Mexican part of my background. My family was not particularly in contact with the Latin community. I never heard the merengue, for example, which, although it had by the 1940s been established for decades in the Dominican Republic and was heard at Dominican expatriate gatherings, had not yet become a general dance fad among the New York downtown nightclub set. The same held true for the *danzón, guajira, son montuno,* and other examples of Cuban *música típica,* which might have been heard in specifically Cuban or Caribbean Hispanic environments not much frequented by my father or the groups that hired him. All these musical forms my father occasionally alluded to. From Latin musicians he became acquainted with such genres, but he did not ordinarily play them on jobs, or later in the little family jam sessions that were so important to my musical development

It is clear, then, that I felt little ethnic allegiance to any of this music; I associated it largely with class ("high society") and a professional musical milieu. This, along with my heterogenous contacts with marimba performance practice, has clearly left me open to innovation in my own performance.

"PATHOSCAPE": A MEDIATED EMOTIONAL WORLD

The importance of media is not so much as direct sources of new images and scenarios for life possibilities, but as semiotic diacritics of great power, which also inflect social contact with the metropolitan world facilitated by other channels.

ARJUN APPADURAI, "Global Ethnoscapes:
Notes and Queries for a Transnational Anthropology"

In spite of the somewhat mainstream and commercial quality of the Latin music to which I was exposed to at an early age, Afro-Cuban melody, harmony, and improvisational practices significantly inform much of the repertoire I have adapted and created for marimba ensembles. I attribute much of this predilection to a few records bought by my father, often in surplus markets, because in Las Vegas, to which we moved when I was a child, the one record store carried little Latin music. Most of it was performed by groups with ad hoc names ("Royale Latin Orchestra" or "Latin American Orchestra," with no leaders or personnel listed) clearly assumed for the cheap, probably pirated recordings. The pirates had good taste, however; despite the poor sound quality, the performances were impressive. They featured Latin nightclub orchestras with tight, precisely interlocking percussion patterns; crisp maraca playing; high-pitched, leathery, full-palm slaps on the old tack-secured conga drum heads; and delicate *bongó* filigrees (derived from the old Cuban *son* tradition, still the model for *bongoseros*).

image or activity. The group, mostly university students, typically consists of a combination of music and nonmusic majors. I require no musical literacy in the conventional sense, and no experience with the marimba, Latin music, or indeed any instrument. Some, lacking musical literacy or musical ability, have always wanted to but never expected to be able to participate in any sort of formal musical ensemble. We hold no auditions; anyone can register for the one credit, and about fifteen are in the group at any given time. At our first meeting of the semester, I move at full speed into group dancing,[8] demonstrate an old piece with the help of any ongoing members available, push unfamiliar instruments of all kinds into the hands of novices, teach them a simple *coro* ("chorus" of one of our dance tunes) in Spanish, and initiate the first stage of the sort of creative chaos that ultimately leads (in time) to full-blown and (relatively) polished performances. This, in effect, serves as a way for prospective recruits to audition *us*. If this apparent pedagogical maelstrom is not an affront to their sense of order and decorum (occasionally a newcomer will walk out in the middle of the first class, never to return), if something in all this resonates with them, and if they are capable of having at least a little faith in my professions that "I'm not worried, and neither should they be" and other mid-musical encouragements, they remain.

Music curricula are notorious for extensive requirements, offering very little credit for the amount of work and class time required. This tends to box many music majors into fairly standardized, inflexible courses of study with relatively few electives. Most music majors on performance tracks also participate in a major ensemble (concert band, symphony orchestra, or choir), which requires attending two or more evening or very late afternoon rehearsals per week plus frequent evening performances, which conflict with ours. Thus, most of the music majors in our ensemble are not on time-consuming performance scholarships, and many are working toward the bachelor of arts degree in music rather than the more narrowly vocational bachelor of music. Many others are music therapy, music education, guitar, piano, or composition majors and do not perform in conventional ensembles. Although guitarists and pianists typically practice alone, and composers compose alone, they might, for a change, seek out the collaborative company of others. Guitarists, moreover, because of their instrument's organological, performance, and compositional history, tend toward an affinity for things Iberian and Latin American. Pianists, temporarily tiring of their incessant passage repetitions in preparation for upcoming performances, wander the halls seeking mental and physical relief. Composers are noted pack rats for sources of sonic and intellectual stimulation. Relatively few composition students—often more creative than proficient in performance technique—belong to major ensembles, and they also therefore lack credit-offering collaborative performance opportunities. Certain music major tracks also include some limited requirements for ensemble participation credits, which the marimba can provide outside the boundaries of the specialist and audition-defined major ensembles.

Other students, attracted to our group by the Latin/tropical image, music, and dancing, are Hispanics and non-Hispanics with an interest in Latin America. Many are familiar with and enjoy salsa or *música tropical*, but, without special musical skills, have hitherto been precluded from playing in such ensembles. Here, to their amazement, they find themselves with a vehicle.

ASU offers two Latin-oriented world music ensembles: the mariachi and the marimba. In both community orientation and pedagogical logistics they could not be more dissimilar. Mariachi ensembles are in evidence at every sort of "Hispanic" (which at ASU and in Arizona in general strongly implies Chicano, or self-consciously Mexican-American) function, such as "Hispanic Convocations"; no procession of robed Hispanic graduates would be complete without the mariachi's crisp "Marcha Zacatecas." The mariachi performers and audience both consist mainly of students and community members of Mexican ancestry. Their repertoire consists primarily of mariachi-specific or mariachi-evolved genres. By comparison, the marimba ensemble, although a potent symbol of the Mexican southeast (far from the U.S. border and Arizona), is not typically perceived as a national iconic ensemble by either Mexicans or U.S. Hispanics (see Solís 1980).[9] It has not, therefore, proven a focal point of Chicano activity or ritual. Our repertoire includes few genres of specifically Mexican origin; we usually include one Chiapas-style *zapateado* and one or two *cumbias* (Afro-Colombian/Panamanian song and dance very popular in Mexico and the American Southwest), but we emphasize call and response and "Afro" percussive and cross-rhythmic features. The bulk of our remaining repertoire, including merengues, *guarachas, son montunos,* boleros, a waltz, a *polca,* a Peruvian or Bolivian *wayño,* and an Ecuadorean *San Juanito,* are Caribbean, creolized European, or South American, and not specifically Mexican.

I have gradually ceased to introduce the group, either in concerts or in publicity blurbs, as "Mexican," preferring instead to verbosely describe us as a "Latin Marimba band built around two Mexican marimbas plus appropriate Latin percussion." In spite of the ethnic affiliation(s) that might naturally be suggested by such strong visual and sonic imagery inherent in the ensemble and its music, I eschew national political self-identification, preferring more neutral ground.[10] I have for the most part resisted politically specific repertoire. On one occasion, we were asked to perform for an opening of an exhibition of Salvadoran art featuring the work of a Salvadoran artist under threat as a critic of right-wing terror. We were asked to play a stirring revolutionary nationalist song with text exhorting the oppressed Salvadorans to oppose their oppressors. We did so, but afterwards I felt uneasy; I feel more comfortable not representing myself or the ensemble as the cultural arm of an ethnic group or as supporters of the political aims of any group. This realization came as something of a surprise to me, in view of my strong political views and my political activism. I emphatically feel that I do not exemplify the trope of the musician detached from everyday life, playing a self-marginalizing role, of the sort posited by Merriam (1973). I do, however, consider political affiliation for the group a sort of inhibitive burden, and feel that the addition of overt political message to the impact of musical style (certainly *the* most potent form of ethnic and political statement) is a form of gilding the lily.

The "African-ness" of our instrumentation (virtually all the instruments are either of African origin or commonly, although incorrectly, perceived as such)[11] and our predominant repertoire and performance style also attract Africa buffs, and sometimes drumming aficionados. The latter often are quickly disappointed, as I've always discouraged in our ensemble any sort of theoretical or practical emphasis on the symbolism of drumming, including ideas of "release." My students joke that if I even look in the general direction of the conga drummers, they laugh and play more softly, claiming that I think the drums live in a state of "too loudness." As crucial as drums and other Latin percussion are to our ensemble, I've never conceived of them as anything but a tightly interknit component of the "Latin groove" that I consider so essential to our group. Feld's definition of "groove"—"to groove, to cycle, to draw you in and work on you, to repeat with variation" (Keil and Feld 1994: 23)—is a helpful point of departure for this hip, vague, yet useful term. I aspire to smoothly integrated composite "rhythm/sonority patterns" (Koetting 1970: 120) held together by what Koetting calls a "fastest pulse," that is, "a consistently regular pulse appearing across the ensemble" (ibid.: 122). We seek a confident cohesion that generates a sort of internal "gravity" with some durability, a resistance to disruption, as a person with good balance can resist falling after a push. A natural and unself-conscious driving rhythmic cohesion such as this is both immediately perceptible and exhilarating.

The greatest challenges occur in rhythmically difficult pieces or subsections such as *cierres* ("closings"—brief complex unison passages that link larger sections and end pieces) or the beginnings of *montuno* sections, in which we make structural rhythmic changes (bell patterns change, we move into the anticipated bass, etc.). I deal with these challenges by helping students establish the groove, beginning with percussion, and then bringing the other players into the mix one at a time. When the groove feels comfortable, I cue the marimba parts. I stop them, start them, challenge them with some added polyrhythms, and test their confidence and their cohesiveness. This sense of groove, once established and familiar, can be a safe place to which the musicians can retreat. While rehearsing a difficult *mon-*

tuno section, the group may become self-conscious and waver, the tightly knit rhythms diverging ever so slightly from their evenness, as a seam bulges. If they have achieved the groove in this piece but temporarily lost it, I do not stop, but rather allow them to experience their disorientation and urge them, working together, not to panic, to keep going, and to calmly pull together again.

CONSTRUCTING A PERFORMANCE PRACTICE:
RHYTHM, RISK, AND REWARD

Although the ensemble itself is built upon a traditional base, nothing is a "given"; virtually no aspect of the traditional performance practice as I researched and learned it has become part of our performance practice without examination and sometimes considerable adaptation. The characteristic *charleo* (resonator buzz), for example, can become rather overpowering, especially in the bass register. I've therefore experimented with various combinations of unbuzzed resonators in the interest of greater synergy with the other percussion instruments. Likewise, our accompanying instrumentation, numbers of sticks used at a given position, sticks format, roles musicians play at a given position, repertoire, pedagogy, interaction with both one another and our "audiences," and interartistic roles have all more or less been turned upside down and inside out, creating a sort of postmodern environment based entirely upon my desires for maximum participation and spontaneity, minimal artistic exclusivity, and enjoyable performative community. It is at the level of performance practice that we most directly and actively interrogate the performance philosophy of inhibition and perfectionism so basic to the Western concert paradigm.

"Smile and Move"

Our repertoire, like those of traditional Mexican and Central American marimba ensembles, consists primarily of folk and popular Latin American dances. My love of social dancing (enthusiasm often outstripping expertise) informs all the community building; dance is in various ways basic to everything in the ensemble. Most techniques I use in both rehearsal and public performance to eliminate inhibition, alleviate self-consciousness, and minimize the distance between the performers and the audience stem from dance movement. I expect our *marimbistas* to always be "dancing" (defined as moving in appropriate rhythm) while performing, both with each other and with our audience. At the beginning of the first class of each semester, and in most subsequent classes, I have us all dance, separately (or together, if they wish), to recorded Latin music. The students thus see immediately that the reason we are together and performing is to create the opportunity for ourselves and others to participate in pleasurable shared but individually interpreted dance. My incessant mantra is "smile and move": I push everyone to "move" (compatibly with the prevailing bodily rhythm of the particular dance at hand) at all times, and to project their feelings of having a good time with a "happy" demeanor. Neither of these behavioral modes is typical of traditional Mexican marimba musicians, who often stand quietly and somewhat impassively over their instruments. It is my experience that many Americans feel uncomfortable disporting themselves thus, and in comparison with our notoriously terpsichorean jitterbug-era hepcat antecedents, are especially uncomfortable with the act of dancing. This is somewhat truer of males than females; when coerced, however, as they inevitably are in early stages of many of my classes,[12] males good-humoredly go along with the "joke." Typically the greatest difference between the sexes is in their willingness to move their upper bodies. Males, with few exceptions, only reluctantly move their arms as part of dance motion, often limiting themselves to somewhat gorillalike arms, stiffly crooked at the elbow. I have reacted to this by beginning dance sessions with an exercise in loose, flowing arm movements—what I've come to refer to as "arm liberation." The feet soon follow. Our new recruits are as inhibited as any (even though many come to us because "it looks as though you guys are really enjoying yourselves," presumably including the moving).

Can one mandate enjoyment? One way I work toward this is by creating a humorous low-risk, high-action environment. I also embrace the idea that, in the words of Deidre Sklar, "different ways of moving generate different kinds of feeling experiences that are not only somatic [of the body], but affective" (1994: 11). By requiring "smiling and moving" I have found that, as silly as they feel, students are eventually able to transfer these symbolic physical actions into internalized and reasonably sincere feelings and a group ethos.

Aurality and Interdependence

All our arrangements are "head arrangements"; I dislike notation anywhere in our rehearsal or performing space. This typically creates initial score-withdrawal anxiety for some. My long experience with assorted aurally/orally transmitted musical traditions, great interest in multicultural ear training and musicianship, and dismay at the widespread total dependence of classically trained American musicians upon notation have propelled me to use the marimba ensemble as a sort of "fifth column" in which I try to eliminate that dependency. I demand that our groupness extend to aural and visual interaction at all times (dependence upon written cues hampers that goal), and that this interaction be mutual and multidirectional rather than centered on the director. I introduce repertoire aurally in every case, either through tapes assigned before class or during the rehearsal. I place high priority upon active participation from all present from the very start.

In the Western orchestra we do not actively promote the idea that one becomes a better trumpeter if she or he learns the clarinet or drums and so forth, but writers on gamelan pedagogy often espouse the idea that the more parts of which a player has practical knowledge, the more effective the player's command of his or her own part.[13] It is likely that this idea has influenced me, as well as my experience with the conventional wisdom that many of the best Indian melodic soloists are also competent in tabla, *mrdangam,* or other instruments. At any rate, I work toward a modest versatility, from the outset emphasizing practical knowledge of the essential components of genres we commonly play. This means that everyone should have some concept of both the physical techniques and interlocking composite rhythms of, for example, the *cumbia,* the merengue, and the *son montuno.*

The practice is useful and advances my aims—achieving ensemble exuberance and closeness—in at least two ways: 1) it helps eliminate the specialization that results from the tendency of individuals to gravitate toward the safety of the most familiar instrument for each piece; and 2) it provides insurance that we will not be left hanging with no one on maracas, *güiro,* bass, or so forth, for a given piece. Toward this end, I have developed a sort of occasional volleyball rotation–cum–musical chairs pedagogic exercise: during the course of a piece we stop many times, and everyone moves to another position (maracas moves to claves, claves to conga, *bajo* to *armonía, tiple* to *segundo,* etc.). This usually stimulates a great deal of chaotic bustle, humorous chagrin, self-deprecation, and muttered disclaimers about the technical and rhythmic challenges of changing parts so quickly. However, I use this frustration as a tool to further my aim of desensitizing students to performance anxiety by placing them in, to use counseling jargon, a safe environment in which they are not chastised for mistakes.

I hold very strong feelings about the formal Western classical concept of performance as an ordeal that is to be judged for its precision, and during which avoidance of mistakes is of paramount importance. I feel that the sort of exuberant ambience toward which I strive is impossible under such conditions. The goal of performing without mistakes is especially impractical under the condition of multitasking (simultaneously singing in Spanish, playing, and "dancing") that I create in both rehearsal and performance. As we have no written scores, students must commit to memory names and genres of pieces, and their roles in these pieces. Since they sometimes forget any or all of the above in the course of a performance, I find it beneficial at times to either create for them, or throw them into, situations to which they must adjust on the spot. A common verbal exchange in rehearsal or performance: "Hey, this is a *cumbia;* got to have a *güiro* in a *cumbia.*" (The part is, in fact, quite prominent in *cumbias.*) "Who's playing *güiro?*" Sheepish looks at one another are exchanged. "Sarah, you play *güiro!*" "Me?" "Yes, you!" Thus, Sarah learns (as do the others) once again that: 1) I'll accept whatever she can give under those circumstances; 2) however limited her playing, it will be enhanced by her "smiling and moving"; 3) the rest of us will pull together and support her; and 4) in spite of her insecurity, enough secure parts are in play, glued together by our sense of "groove" and mutual enjoyment, to present an effective performance.

So averse am I to set and self-satisfied presentations of a piece, in fact, that I nearly always in the course of a public performance make some ad hoc structural changes: concocting a *montuno,* sometimes with a group response text (in Spanish) that the students must try to catch; adding repeats; cutting sections; pointing at someone to take a solo during part of a long *montuno* (sometimes panic-strickenly and vehemently declined with vigorous head shaking, but more often undertaken, sometimes leading to a profound personal watershed of self-confident accomplishment); teaching the group a brand-new (usually relatively simple) piece on the spot. The ability to do these things depends, of course, upon their basic functional knowledge of genres, acquired through some of the methods discussed above.

Although I encourage students' confidence in "taking [solo] flight," and I never respond to their enforced improvisations with anything but praise, I insist in rehearsal on their working toward appropriate Caribbean Latin style. This means, more than anything, awareness of three domains: 1) proper durational rhythmic values (equal, rather than jazzlike dotted eighth and sixteenth notes); 2) what I consider an acceptable (not capricious and haphazard) relationship to the underlying chord structure; and 3) general submission to, and incorporation of, clave rhythmic phrase structure (a challenging concept indeed). The first can be learned and inculcated rather formulaically; the last two are much more elusive. I consider it my obligation to provide ongoing appropriate performance models for my students by soloing often. This, plus the recorded tapes of choice performances and repertoire that are required listening, provides the basis for their stylistic development.

Astride the Great (Aural/Literate) Divide

Except in cases of slow, lyrical waltzes and boleros, in which the lovely two-stick tremolo technique is fundamental, I have eschewed much of this technique, so effective in melodic counterpoint, in favor of richness in harmonic voicing and rhythmic interest. Although in traditional Chiapan marimba performance two or three players on the *grande* and *chica* will be engaged in melody and countermelody at any given time, I've expanded the three-stick *armonía* technique to frequent use in other marimba parts, and have emphasized empirical knowledge of simple harmonic formulas. Many of our dance pieces consist of four, three, or even two chords, although most waltzes, boleros, *chachachás, paso dobles,* and some others tend to be more harmonically complex. A common exercise to which I set new students is playing the I–IV–V–I chord progression in a few common keys, with spatially close, ergonomically convenient voicings.

Ramifications of this activity make it clear that, although I promulgate an egalitarian ethos in the group, some, to quote Orwell, are "more equal than others." This "tweaking the margins" between orality/aurality and literacy draws in some ways upon traditional hierarchies within the marimba ensemble.[14] Music skills within the group range from those of nonmusicians who don't know the names of notes to those of graduate students studying piano performance or composition. Regardless of background, all approach the keyboard and its concepts in ways we find mutually appropriate.

The nonmusician may only be able to relate to the visual/spatial/kinesthetic. In describing a tonic chord in first inversion I might go through the following steps:

> This note is G; it's also the name of an important key we play in (briefly explaining the concept of "key"). You need to know these chords in the key of G. Hold your hands like this, two of these keys between the two right sticks and one between the left and middle, move your left stick up three notes from that G; do you remember where G was?

and so forth, detailing further moves to IV in root position, a V chord with seventh in the bass, and its resolution to I. I provide very simple theory ideas, reduced to simple spatial formulas without much reference to theoretical terms other than, perhaps, I, IV, V, and I. I might sing or play a simple tune along with the student, who, still holding the sticks as instructed, now strikes the keys in appropriate accompaniment to some dance rhythm I have demonstrated. If the student can, through experience, hear some places for appropriate chord changes (the easiest typically being phrase-ending V7–I), so much the better.

Whereas a musically literate student with keyboard skills might be able to produce the cadential formula in assorted keys with little help from me, for the uninitiated I may have to replicate this process in each key. However, I gratefully and positively accept (for the moment) all abilities and offerings, while providing as many harmonic, melodic, and dynamic hints as possible, augmented by considerable body language as required, to gradually bring the student into a functioning relationship with the group. From the beginning, all perform at levels appropriate for them.

Students may not be ready for the challenges of melody or countermelody parts. Playing these parts involves both the ability to learn songs by ear and the ability to negotiate, with acceptable stick-stroke patterns and at the greater rhythmic density demanded by such parts, the new and strange space relationships of the Chiapas marimba chromatic double keyboard. In this system "black" keys are placed not *between* and *behind* the two white keys they link (as on a piano), but directly *behind* and slightly *above* the white keys they flat.[15] I do not hesitate to throw students with more background into melodic parts. Less advanced students, however, can also immediately contribute, playing simple chords in simple dance pieces. The doubling and tripling of the three-stick *armonía* chord format on various *puestos* around the marimba (with staggered different chord inversions for acoustic variety and richness) brings a relatively large group into play quickly, while providing the insurance of part duplication.

Having been a bassist, I bring a strong bass consciousness to the group. I reserve bass parts, unless extremely simple and repetitive (as in some *cumbias*), for those with ears sufficiently sophisticated to hear chord changes and those with dependable time sense. This is because: 1) the bass, with its unique timbre and impressive sound projection owing to its large resonators, is sonically exposed; 2) it is a key component of the interlocking rhythmic structure; and 3) the chordal roots and fifths that it most typically plays must be aurally abstracted from the melody and chordal structure, in a relatively sophisticated process of musicianship. In the interests of efficiency I tend to assign the bass part to students who can undertake this process without needing to be taught every note by rote. Because of the bass part's importance, I insist that it must always—quite untraditionally—be doubled on the *chica* bass (an octave higher, as the *chica* lacks the *grande*'s lowest octave).

PUBLIC PRESENTATION:
"YOU DON'T DANCE, YOU DON'T EAT"

A voice from the audience called out "Robert le Diable!" *At that time Liszt had composed a very brilliant fantasia on themes from [Meyerbeer's opera] . . . and played it always with brilliant success. The call was taken up by other voices. . . . Liszt rose, bowed, and said: "Je suis toujours l'humble serviteur du public, mais est-ce-qu'on désire la fantaisie avant ou après la sonate?" Renewed cries of "Robert! Robert!"*

HAROLD SCHONBERG, *The Great Pianists*

The second part of the Western concert paradigm that I resist is the physical and emotional separation of the audience from the performers. Note the highly formulaic concert rituals that one encounters several times a day in any music department: the deliberate elimination of musicians' facial expressions other than one of profound concentration; the lack of acknowledgment of the audience's presence other than when the performers enter the stage and carefully coordinate their bows at the ends of pieces; and the control and suppression of spontaneous audience interaction, including the arbitrary and unconvincingly rationalized (the "need to hear, assess, and react to the entire work") elimination of applause between movements. That these did not always obtain in the world of Western art music is well known (as well as evidenced by the anecdote about Liszt above).

When I first created the marimba ensemble at ASU we played on a formal stage. This format evolved into (still formal) programs in conjunction with the dance department's Mexican folkloric and salsa dance classes. We also played frequently for assorted multicultural festivals and celebrations, usually also on stages. Because of the physical distance between the performers and listeners, all of these performances, even during the most exuberant Mexican holidays, somewhat resembled academy concerts. In contrast, I derived much more pleasure from gigs in which we were close to the audience and the hubbub of human interaction, even if we performed as background music for parties or art openings during which people socialized rather than paying us meticulous attention.

Ultimately I decided that the stage presentation of a group eminently suited to the production of "happy" dance music in informal settings was absurd. I decided to change our semesterly formal concert into an evening dance party, the Latin Dance Pachanga, of which our group is the focal point. We moved to the music school lobby, and ultimately to an outdoor courtyard. We eliminated the performers' physical distance from the listeners by placing the group at floor level; encouraged the audience to stand near, around, and even behind us; and eliminated emotional distance by making our audience part of the performance. The marimba performers and members of my other classes, all of whom are prepped throughout the semester with dance lessons, are strongly encouraged to attend and provide snacks and soft drinks. The semesterly *pachanga* has become a much-anticipated occasion for many students and members of the community, who find few opportunities for exuberant dancing to live music without the fuel of alcohol or the danger of judgment. Our posters declare "all steps cheerfully taught" before each dance. I humorously announce to the assemblage eagerly lining up by our tables laden with high-fat, low-fiber munchies our (much-breached) rule that "you don't dance, you don't eat."

With the band providing the dance's basic rhythm, I point out the close relationship between the bass and step pattern rhythm, demonstrate the basic dance steps, and incite everyone to movement. We begin by playing dances with relatively easy bass-step rhythms, such as the merengue (straight quarter notes with a simple sidestep motion) or *cumbia* (nonsyncopated half note and two quarters). I demonstrate without a partner; leading and partnering can be daunting prospects. Many of those who attend are already proficient dancers attracted to the *pachanga* by e-mail messages and word of mouth within the broader campus ballroom dance communities. They often dance in pairs in flamboyant "ballroom dance studio" mode. I invite and welcome their attendance, but I am as unhappy with the perfectionist ballroom dance studio aesthetic as with the analogous classical music performance mindset. I thus find myself reassuring the attendees that they need not be intimidated by these specialists' expertise; on the contrary, I prefer that their participation should be idiosyncratic and uncritical, and that the rhythms and steps I teach them are only suggested frameworks that they are free to transcend. These dances, all traditionally performed as collaborative couple dances with specific steps, have become, for many in our safe environment, individually danced and interpreted vehicles for release and self-realization.

We have found that even neophytes are eager to participate in large group circle dances. Beginning with some dances, such as the *zapateado,* which are typically danced in "open" rather than "ballroom" position and which thus lend themselves to group treatment, we create further opportunities by adapting Latin couple dances to the group format. Holding hands in a circle provides physical proximity and reassurance and helps maintain relatively consistent spatial direction and step format, while, however, relieving dancers of the potentially traumatic responsibility of partnering. We frequently open with such a dance and intersperse others throughout the evening.

THE IDIOSYNCRATIC ETHNOSCAPE

While ethnographic writing cannot entirely escape the reductionist use of dichotomies and essences, it can at least struggle self-consciously to avoid portraying abstract, ahistorical "others."
JAMES CLIFFORD, *The Predicament of Culture*

Finding myself impaled on the prongs of Clifford's admonition, I am somewhat perplexed and conflicted. I have always been aware of my profound fascination with ethnic identity in its myriad sensual and behavioral manifestations, and that this fascination has helped provide some semblance of coherence to my life and career. In this regard I have often been quite guilty of the "reductionist use of dichotomies and essences," which have served as important symbolic landmarks for me. I have, moreover, rejected most world music fusions, which I consider ungrounded and, for the most part, infelicitous aesthetic and procedural "shotgun weddings."

Why, then, does it seem as though I have in many ways embraced the very "abstract, ahistorical 'other'" against which Clifford warns us? It would appear that I have chosen a "pathoscape," or psychic nest constructed from my sonic imagination, rather than ethnic grounding. I have rejected the representation of an external world, with its inconvenient cultural and political obligations, in favor of a constructed performative world. But is this, in fact, any less "authentic" than if I in Tempe, Arizona, meticulously imitated Chiapas marimba repertoire, performance practice, instrumentation, musicianly body language, and so forth?

In fact, the essential components of the Latin marimba tradition as I promulgate it are "neo-Latin": they are consistent with the established procedures and aesthetics of Hispanic pan-Caribbean Latin dance music. The means by which we achieve them are, of course, disparate and eclectic. For example, I found that the challenging compound duple Zimbabwean Shona *hosho* rattle technique I learned from Roger Vetter (newly and enthusiastically returned from Zimbabwe) worked perfectly for maracas accompaniment with Chiapas style 6/8 + 3/4 *zapateados*. My maracas model for fast rumbas, *guarachas*, and salsa, on the other hand, was the dry, crisp 1940s sound of the old Cuban Orquesta Casino de la Playa's Ernesto de la Vega. I sometimes teach on the marimba itself in ways drawn more from observations of Hardja Susilo's "face to face and backwards" technique of teaching the Javanese *gender* metallophone than from anything I observed in Mexico. The *güiro* scraper is probably far more prominent in my group than in most Cuban ensembles because of my research in Puerto Rican diasporic Jíbaro music, for which the *güiro* is an iconic instrument. It is also clear that I am playing fast and loose with the literate/nonliterate musical transmission continuum. Having been struck by the "literacy divide" between Mexican marimba directors and their dependent sidemen, I work in our group toward its elimination. I do so by introducing simple theoretical terminology as a lingua franca within which I hope that even those without a prior musical background will eventually be able to function. In this I may have been influenced once again by the gamelan, which provides such powerfully paradigmatic models in ethnomusicology.[16]

Hearing and performing music largely rooted in Afro-Cuban sonic images with deep associations still moves me. In order to actuate this evocative imagery I have developed the ensemble, and its eclectic neo-Latin performance practice, as a sort of community of comfort for myself, my students, and others. Involving students and "performance guests" (that is, the audience) enables me to communicate these feelings and thus to create an ongoing vehicle for pleasure that significantly increases through performative interaction.

It also provides a vehicle for the implementation of my strongly held ideas about performative roles and relationships. Apathy and passivity in any sphere—musical, political, or otherwise—are for me unacceptable and debilitating behavioral patterns. I also see the typical academic concert as pathologically perfectionist, pretentious, and an unnaturally constructed generator of performance anxiety.[17] I consider the marimba ensemble in its rehearsals and public presentations to be a locus of resistance to such behavior, and a forum for my own desire to make a difference. "Making a difference" through the marimba happens not necessarily through overt political or ethnic symbolism, but through support of joyous, uninhibited collaboration. Marimba performance provides, for the students, a site of serious personal challenge because of the "exotic" nature of this music world. They are, however, encouraged to risk; through my confidence in them, and the positive feedback that the group receives, this becomes more natural. They know that I am willing to accept their sincere attempts, whether they are capable of little more than "smiling and moving" or they are able to improvise a marimba solo, "in clave," over a complex *montuno* accompaniment. Statements such as "I never thought I could play this music," "I never danced before," "I never played an instrument before," and "I never thought I could do things like this in public" are important and validating ritual affirmations of the importance of this idiosyncratic but comforting performance world we have constructed together.

NOTES

My thanks to Julie F. Codell, Katherine Hagedorn, and R. Anderson Sutton for helpful commentary on this chapter.

1. For an examination of this technique in its context of regional identity see Solís 1980.

2. As a young child I listened, fascinated, to my granduncle Jack's stories of his World War I experiences in the U.S. army, particularly to his barbed and somewhat misanthropic assessments of the different national characteristics of assorted combatant groups (the Russians, the French, etc.). Having been involved in military intelligence, he sometimes took the German role and played "interrogation" with me (an early "performance" context for me?). Such awareness of national characteristics has clearly stimulated me for most of my life.

3. He Americanized his name from Margarito Solís Espinosa, the customary Hispanic matronymic (Espinosa) becoming a middle name and initial.

4. Their formal musical training and literacy were minimal. Although he was the group's leader and manager, my grandfather could barely read music. My uncle Joe remembered that sheets of music were spread out on the marimbas and then the music was taught oral/aurally to the individual musicians by the musical director (for a long time Lauro Lomeli, a musically literate former town band clarinetist from Tuxtla Gutierrez, the capital of Chiapas). This method is consistent with the hierarchy between musically literate and nonliterate musicians typical of marimba ensembles that I discuss later. I can attest that the versions of these pieces that my father knew from his childhood in the marimba band (we used to play some of them by ear in our jam sessions) were more or less identical to standard recorded versions. They were not the bowdlerized arrangements one might have expected in vaudeville.

5. This severely truncated instrument was easily taken apart, the keys (attached to cords) rolled up, and the frame detached, so that he could carry it on the subway to gigs, sometimes with my mother Hazel's assistance.

6. When many years later I first viewed the Amazon River at the bustling wharves

of Manaus, in Brazil, I found myself exuberantly humming "Busy Port," from the album.

7. I found this idea of a mediated mythic emotional life very applicable to my diasporic Puerto Rican research (Solís 1994, 1995, 1999).

8. Dancers and those interested in dancing also form a group of potential recruits, in view of the emphasis on dancing both within the group and in public presentation (see below).

9. By comparison, note the widespread popularity in the United States among Mexican Americans of some regional Mexican traditions such as military-style popular bands (originally associated with the state of Sinaloa), which morphed into U.S. *banda; Tejano*/Tex-Mex (originally *Norteño,* "Northerner") ensembles of Northern Mexico and the Rio Grande Valley in Texas, consisting of button accordion, guitar, and bass; *mariachi,* originally a regional ensemble of Jalisco; and the popular pan-Latin vocal/guitar *trio romántico.*

10. The statement (1999) by Joan Suyenaga, who heads a gamelan assembly and export business in Java, that the British government wanted gamelan for use in public schools precisely because they were *not* (due to the miniscule Indonesian population in Britain) "population-based," and thus invulnerable to charged ethnopolitical demands from any quarter, resonated strongly with me.

11. The *bongós* and *timbales* are Cuban creolized versions of the European timpani, and the *güiro* scraper and maracas are of Caribbean Amerindian origin.

12. I teach marches, waltzes, polkas, minuets, polonaises, and other dances in music history and music appreciation classes and Latin dances in world music classes both for physical relief and to demonstrate rhythmic/kinesthetic patterns.

13. See, for example, Mantle Hood on the UCLA gamelan (1963a: 243–44): "The student participating in the program is encouraged to acquire a basic skill in each of the four large instrumental families. . . . He is also expected to learn one or two vocal styles."

14. Many, although by no means all, successful marimba orchestra directors have some musical literacy. This has led to conditions approaching musico-economic serfdom for many marimba sidemen, who are dependent upon the director's demonstration, phrase by phrase, of written arrangements (Solís 1982).

15. Even advanced musicians—including in a few cases doctoral percussion students—may be briefly nonplussed by the very different and disorienting visual schema. On one painful occasion early in my field research in Mexico, while I still had only minimal marimba skills, I was called up to sit in with a professional group in a restaurant. I remember the unfamiliar Chiapas-style keyboard as a sort of Bermuda Triangle whiteout, with no reassuring or familiar landmarks. The brief performance was notable for its unconventional polytonality.

16. Note, for example, in this volume David Hughes's apparent appropriation of the gamelan "skeleton" *(balungan)* concept in describing a Shona *mbira* nuclear melody.

17. I'm aware that I have created for myself a sort of alternative performance anxiety, relating to my great concern that, in spite of our most spontaneous and enthusiastic efforts, the audience will remain passive and uninvolved. To work toward a serene confidence that we will have our usual beneficial and exhilarating effect on audiences is my own personal challenge.

Chapter 14

What's the "It"
That We Learn to Perform?

Teaching BaAka Music and Dance

MICHELLE KISLIUK AND KELLY GROSS

What social and musical negotiations take place among diverse students at
the University of Virginia who learn to perform BaAka ("pygmy") music and
dance? Can or should once-distant sensibilities (from Bagandou, Central
African Republic, and Charlottesville, Virginia) be melded, considering
their radically different social contexts? Or, when our performances feel like
they work, are the social contexts (and the sounds) so radically different
after all? Michelle Kisliuk conducted field research in the Central African
Republic between 1986 and 2001 (see Kisliuk 1998b). She initially modeled her teaching after that of American scholars of West African music (her
teacher David Locke, among others) and that of Ghanaian performers who
had adapted their instruction to an American context. Once Michelle
began teaching BaAka "pygmy" performance, she discovered that this "tradition" too had to be reinvented—polished up, in a sense, in order to make
it teachable in America.

At the University of Virginia (UVA), the African Drumming and Dance
Ensemble has become a community of performers. We have learned, and
continue to learn, that in order to perform we must take off with our BaAka
style and make it our own—claim it by creating a new branch of the tradition that in fact defines us musically and socially. This leads us to ask crucial
questions about how these processes are actually negotiated and what,
indeed, is the "it" of the "tradition" anyway? Because BaAka performance
requires a heightened emphasis on immediate socioaesthetic negotiation,
this university ensemble offers a propitious opportunity for embodied study
of aesthetics and the politics of representation. Kelly Gross, a classical
pianist, has studied BaAka music and dance with Michelle for three years,
first as an undergraduate at the University of Virginia, and then as a gradu-

ate student in ethnomusicology. In this article Michelle and Kelly offer a written dialogue exploring these issues and processes.

Our approach here parallels the processes we are discussing; the interactive musical discourse that takes place in BaAka singing also informs the discursive shape of the essay. And just as our group warms into an increasingly improvisatory song, our writing here becomes progressively more interactive. Please keep in mind that the subsections below do not imply a separation of ideas, but rather, like in a BaAka song, we are layering theme upon resurfacing theme.

Embodied Experience

First-hand, embodied experience that students have with music and dance can facilitate an understanding, or at least an awareness, of both macro- and micropolitics. In learning to dance and sing in new ways, one becomes vitally aware of issues of self and other, and of "here" and "there," challenging the distancing that takes place in much disembodied scholarship. Direct involvement in a process of musical creation engenders a kind of self-awareness that leads to activity instead of abstraction (see Sklar 1994; Lakoff and Johnson 1999). For example, Kelly describes an experience in class:

> Emphasizing the varying contours of vocal lines by singing different melodies from my neighbor feels so new to my body, as does singing in general. As a young pianist, I was urged to express myself musically with that instrument alone, and to leave the singing to others. Since learning to sing these beautiful and intricate BaAka songs of the Central African Republic, I have felt increasingly more comfortable in this newly acquired expressive mode.
>
> Now as my voice simultaneously blends and contrasts with my classmates, I smile as I sing. The polyphonic texture is so wonderfully lush and thick, that sometimes I can hardly differentiate the various parts we have learned. Many of us are creating new melodies and complementing the overall texture with improvised variations and yodels. The themes cycle again and again with some overlapping parts. After dropping down to a lower register (registers which tend to be neglected this semester due to our 21:3 ratio of women to men) I hear the lower melody immediately resonate in my ears. I figure that someone nearby has to be singing the same line. My eyes search the lips of others until I find Laura's (one of the ensemble's most long-standing members) and find that she's singing the same melody. Her smiling eyes lock with mine. (Gross 1999a: 2)

This description was written in the spring of 1999, during a semester in which membership in the ensemble was limited to students who had been in the class for at least one previous semester, and many had participated in the group for several years. It was the first time in Michelle's teaching career that her students had the depth of experience to learn to improvise.

A familiarity with the style, necessary for confident improvisation, was built within an environment of interpersonal trust and commitment—a social ease that comes only with time. By "improvisation" we mean not only varying our melodies, rhythms, and yodels in response to each other, but discovering a sense of play in creating performances of this central African genre in Virginia. When we reach a multilayered freedom in our sociomusical interaction, inviting singing and dancing among ensemble members and audiences alike, we become a dynamic community.

Sound and Community Aesthetics
But for various reasons we do not always attain the level of freedom we just described. For example, one evening we were invited to sing during an Amnesty International rally celebrating the anniversary of the Universal Declaration of Human Rights (December 1998). This event took place at the steps of Thomas Jefferson's Rotunda, where our ensemble was to sing a few songs between (very serious) speakers. On the steps we were immediately elevated and separated from our audience. Because we were standing up and facing the audience (instead of sitting and facing each other as we usually do), it was very difficult for us to hear, see, and therefore interact with each other. We remember singing and clapping, but the sound was sort of "dead"; we were not quite sure how far our sound or energy was projecting. This audience had already been involved in a very particular kind of event in which we were asked to play a small part, and we could not justifiably reshape the atmosphere or the physical space. As one member of our ensemble, Deva Woodly, observed, "no matter how prepared we are, without the energy of the audience, we falter. This is true of most [performances] but what we do is especially based on interaction, and if we feel drained by an unreceptive [or unprepared] audience or unfamiliar surroundings, there's no way we can be in top form" (quoted in Gross 1999a).

By contrast, on another occasion we organized one of our own performances in front of those very same Rotunda steps—this time on the eve of Halloween. We sang and danced within a circle of jack-o'-lanterns, while Michelle's video recording of BaAka women dancing projected abstractly across our moving bodies and across Jefferson's pillars. Many people in the ensemble and in the audience found this juxtaposition of worlds exciting and liberating. We moved from dancing on the grassy lawn in front of the Rotunda to singing under the pillared dome, where we could weave together our echoing voices and project them out into the night.

It is an amazing but simple discovery that we made: the music sounds how we as an ensemble are feeling! Environment, spatial connection, and energy flow of the group are crucial to the sound. In her experience as a pianist Kelly has been trained to "overcome," to "master" these variables so that she can play "well" under almost any circumstance. This aesthetic of disregard trains one to ignore variables that are about being in a particular moment, and the immediacy of the performance context thereby tends to be concealed. Yet in her own playing, Kelly finds that the circumstances of the performed moment indeed affect every note she plays.

An awareness of the moment, however, is not in itself enough to help us create successful and meaningful performances of a once-distant music such as that of BaAka "pygmies." To bring the performance "home," we must actually become hyper-aware of the radical recontextualizations involved in the presentation of any "world music," and perform with our particular awareness in mind. In fact, effective performers of music of any kind are always on some level aware of the essential theatricality and constant reframing that goes on within all performance. Be it a symphony concert in Tokyo, a bluegrass jam session in Massachusetts, or a jazz concert at Lincoln Center, musical performances reenact and renegotiate social identities, the politics of "place," and the relation of past, present, and future. But because of the aesthetic of disregard we've mentioned, especially in "classical" performance, these issues of recontextualization often conveniently "disappear" from aesthetic consciousness. And, unfortunately, many university world music ensembles in America have, to varying degrees, adopted this convention of erasure associated with "serious" music—probably out of a wish to "respect the tradition." (The "tradition" has, in this case, been objectified in terms of an idea of "the original," following the contemporary Urtext model in classical music.) The result is a stark disregard of who and where we are, and what we are actually doing aesthetically and politically—which is in fact wildly experimental. These performances suppose unproblematically to represent the "Other" in usually rigid, museumlike, and ill-at-ease kinds of displays that ironically impede the very respect for the tradition that performers were seeking. From a political standpoint this impediment is not only ironic, but also perhaps tragic in terms of lost opportunities for intercultural learning, creative self-understanding, and deep fun. Performers and audiences find themselves within a socioaesthetic context where they can be neither fully "themselves" nor "the Other."

We have not yet fully recognized that university world music ensembles can, by contrast, offer an especially vivid, detailed look at the aesthetic and political discourse that takes place during our creative recontextualizations. In our own group, questions like the one Kelly asks below help us to become aware of how our aesthetic practice is constituted. Kelly once e-mailed this message to Michelle:

> One day in class last year as we were preparing for a concert, I noted a huge discrepancy between my perception of our ensemble's singing and yours. It was very notable at the time, because I felt our singing beginning to really

groove. I was tuned in to not only what I was singing, but to the other ensemble members as well, and I even felt comfortable enough to begin improvising with melodies. I was pleased at the thought that we were finally clicking and coming together with the BaAka song "Bisengo Bwa Bolé," which we had been having particular difficulty with the entire semester. But just as I began to get even deeper into the singing, you stopped us. Quelle horreur! Something was off to your ear, and we ended up shifting to another song altogether. The question that immediately formed in my mind was: What does sound *good* to you? And how is that at times (crucial times, in fact) different from my own sense of our music making? Is "good" even the word to describe the sensation we are trying to capture? And what is that sensation—a sound or feeling or both? Is it the sensation by which, if you closed your eyes, you could imagine yourself back in the forest with your BaAka friends? Or is it a positive feeling that comes from our particular group doing the best with the materials we have learned and incorporated? (Gross 1999b)

Michelle picking up Kelly's thread:

Or, instead, what if the sound that feels "right" is neither exactly what I imagine BaAka sounding like, nor a free interpretation of a BaAka-like sound by my students in America? In fact, it is something other, not a sound of "here" or "there," but a third thing, the result of a melding of sounds (and experiences) of both "here" and "there"—a Baudelairean *correspondance*. When a particular song seems to work it incorporates the BaAka style that I've learned, with a difference that comes down to who we are here and now. These are the moments that seem excitingly "right" to me.

Redefining Authenticity

This experience makes us rethink what teaching, learning, and performing BaAka music really entails; it becomes clear that the goal is not *imitation* but *interpretation*. Like the trick candle that will not blow out, this approach provokes resurfacing questions about the nature of authenticity: What does it mean when the singing necessarily sounds different coming from students than on Michelle's recordings of BaAka singing the "same" song? Should we worry whether we are doing "justice" to BaAka music? Since BaAka never sing the "same" song the "same" way, how do we even know when we have learned what constitutes a particular song? Were we to become objectivist thinkers and be solely bent on imitating the sound of recorded examples, we would not learn to improvise in the style. How, then, could we judge if the sound is a BaAka sound without having come to an embodied understanding that sound is actually fused with social process? This performing and learning context allows us to ask fundamental questions about what it means to create expressive identities through performance. We wish to emphasize that this shift in perspective from sound object to sociomusical interaction does not mean that we aren't rigorous learners of BaAka music, but rather that we understand that the nature of cultural process is by necessity interpretive (see Schechner 1985).

Michelle remembers:

When I first began to teach BaAka singing in the United States, I was usually in situations where my time to teach was limited and the stakes of showing that I had something to teach were high (especially in terms of employment). To develop teaching strategies, I drew upon my experience as an undergraduate at Tufts University, where I had studied Ewe drumming, singing, and dance of Ghana and Togo with David Locke. His method was to isolate the somewhat fixed percussion parts and show how they fit together. Students learned to play all of the supporting parts, as well as to dance and sing, so that we could feel the texture of the whole and participate effectively. With experience, some of us developed a micro-improvisational sensibility. The nuances of rhythm became communication (see also Chernoff 1979). So, when I started teaching BaAka singing, I remembered how effective Locke's teaching had been and I too tried to isolate "parts," or at least to pick the most familiar phrases from the songs I knew best, and decide which parts could be thought of as themes. I would teach those melodies first, then introduce various kinds of elaborations and countermelodies. It's not that I was making it up, I heard these elements "in the music." I was, nevertheless, devising—even inventing—more tangible ways to make this music teachable in a new context. And it seemed to work, especially when the classroom time was limited to two-hour workshops or one-time introductory lectures. The more complex musical issues, however, would arise within longer-term teaching circumstances.

When I teach a group of Americans they almost always unconsciously adjust their singing to more familiar stylistic habits, which is perfectly understandable. They subtly transform what I teach by blending their voices, squaring "syncopated" rhythms, and, when encouraged to improvise, they usually add three-part hymn-style harmonies. Nevertheless, once they can sing together the basic parts I have taught, they clearly have learned something about polyphony. So even after only short sessions students seem to sound almost like BaAka. The snag, however, is that notwithstanding their experience, students who have heard many variations of the parts over a semester still tend to latch on to and repeat the first parts they have learned, as though they were fixed. So in reality, although they may have sounded initially "like BaAka," they in fact were unable to grasp musically the ongoing movement and variation that constitutes collective BaAka singing. The initial "parts" should only have been a temporary means, a first lesson; what they actually needed to learn was to expand their sociomusical aesthetic. But that often takes more time—and can also take courage.

This longer, more complex process becomes visible if we compare my most experienced ensemble, in Virginia, with another group. In 1995, I was invited to briefly train the combined choirs at CalPoly University in San Luis Obispo, California. They asked me to help them prepare part of a concert that would include some BaAka singing (joined by my ensemble from the University of

California at Santa Barbara). These CalPoly choirs were well trained; the students were quite skilled in listening and repeating almost exactly the lines or "parts" that I demonstrated, including difficult rhythmic nuances and unfamiliar pitch relationships. But, I found, we did not have nearly enough time for me to teach them to improvise. They were used to absorbing parts and singing them correctly, and that's just what they did. They also rehearsed and performed on concert hall risers, and I was unable under these circumstances to make them aware of the extent to which this was a radical transformation of the performance tradition in which I had participated in Africa. Yet these students were very eager to come down from the risers at the end of each "number," joining my Santa Barbara ensemble and the audience in dancing and celebrating their sense of community in a way not allowed by their usual performance conventions.

Kelly interjects:

In contrast to the CalPoly example, recently, in our more advanced ensemble at UVA, we have been able to discuss in detail how we want to present ourselves, and how we want to sound. Listening critically to ourselves and to each other, we've actively gained an awareness of our tendency to square rhythms and to momentarily be drawn into reproducing the harmonies of "Western" choral singing. We love the freedom to talk about different learning strategies and the various ways we might shape our sound.

Michelle:

And this frees me too. While I was looking for ways to teach students how to think about improvising, I allowed myself to experiment with the parts I was singing and became fully at ease improvising and yodeling in my BaAka style. I was trying to think of ways to get away from a fixed idea of any one song, whether that idea was based on my own recollection of parts, or on habits I had developed from teaching this music for nine years in America. I didn't want us to fixate on my field recordings, either, for fear that we would end up imitating those particular performances. But having had the time to develop our own, collective experience and sound, I could now ask students to go back and listen closely to the recordings. I encouraged them to compare our sound in terms of rhythmic nuance and harmonic relationships, watching out for unconscious infusions of musical habits that sneak in from the dominant aesthetic. These neither can nor should be entirely "removed," of course, any more than we could or should magically change who and where we are. But the more conscious we can become and the more we can hear what we are doing, the more developed and deliberate our musicality becomes. I also ask students to pick out new parts and improvisations they hear on the recordings—sometimes several different recordings of the same song—and then to share them with the group and to add them to our sound (or, better yet, add their own variations springing from what they've heard).

Kelly:

This exercise, I think, has been crucial to broadening our sound concept and giving us license to critique each other and the group's singing and dancing.

Michelle (playfully, as though in Kelly's voice):

It also expanded students' sense that they were free to contribute, to offer solutions to problems of creative practice, rather than just taking what a teacher might present as fixed doctrine.

Kelly (playing around with Michelle's voice):

This also blurs the line between performance training and academic study, demonstrating that theory is actually understood by way of practice. My ensemble-mates with various majors continually remark that they have learned more in this class about issues of representation, identity, ethics, and cultural politics (currently debated especially in the humanities and social sciences) than they have in purely academic courses.

Duet (back in our own voices):

Hold on! It feels like we're getting a bit self-congratulatory. In performance, when our singing loses its rhythmic groove, some of us try to compensate by infusing our musical texture with polymetric clapping—at times, even over-compensating and making our style seem more polymetric than many BaAka performances. Similarly, our enthusiastic writing at this point is also in need of counterbalancing. In fact, this is probably a symptom of our effort to write interactively while being limited to only two voices that come from similar perspectives. So, dear reader(s), please add your own healthy skepticism as you continue to read. Maybe that will help.

Come to think of it, only some combinations of students during certain semesters actually reach the ideal moments that we are selectively choosing to describe here. Often students who choose (or pass the audition for) this engaged and self-challenging kind of learning environment already have personalities and values that make them at least latently open to a spirit of musical collectivity. Those who succeed are also open to being changed by others, and are often looking for ways to actively change their world for the better (many are environmental science and anthropology majors—the "granola contingent," as their classmates call them). Of course other types of people are also in the class; some detract or even destroy the synergy of the group, while others, to their own and their classmates' surprise, add invaluably to the multifaceted collective spirit.

As a crossroads of intersecting personalities and ideas, our ensemble necessarily attracts a diverse group of people interested in music, dance, and Africa, and includes several students from Ghana, Nigeria, South Africa, and Uganda. (Michelle's husband, Justin Mongosso, from the Central African Republic, also joins the ensemble regularly.) At a university with a history of Southern white elitism, this racially mixed ensemble performing African music (taught by a Jewish woman) might be a glimpse of the shifting makeup and changing spirit of the University of Virginia, and perhaps of the larger world in this postcolonial era. Each semester the ensemble is comprised of a large number of African Americans (including Kelly), and an even greater number of blond-haired and blue-eyed European Americans (what UVA mostly looks like), with a sprinkling of students with Filipino, Turkish, Iranian, Chinese, Italian, and Indian backgrounds. Class discussions arise regularly surrounding sensitive issues of racial politics, identity, and ownership—particularly in terms of African-American students learning African repertoire, and of non-black students publicly performing African music and dance. We incorporate within our performance preparations questions and contradictions inherent in representing "pygmies." But by way of our undeniably non-pygmy visual impression ("race" and movement style), we prime our audiences to expect interpretation instead of representation. We also play with costume as a means of bridging this gap. If we were more ethnically homogeneous (as are most other classes in the music department), the risk of exoticizing a representation of BaAka would be greater. But with our diversity comes a multiplicity of perspectives on "here" and "there," place and identity, which curtails lurking essentialisms and helps relativize what we are doing.

Resistant Performance
Along with the challenges and advantages of our diversity, in the classroom we also negotiate musical details—such as those we've just dialogued about—battling the comfortable inertia of unquestioned musical habits and assumptions. Learning to resist musical habits allows us to work through the tensions that resistance engenders, thereby progressively liberating—while periodically challenging and renewing—our aesthetic.

During many of our public performances we have the opportunity to question broader conventions, such as the "aesthetic of disregard" already mentioned, that often dictate the behavior of audience members and performers. There is the expectation of decorum and silence that goes along with an idea of "serious" music in certain contexts such as concert halls and in the museum culture within which many world music performances have been categorized. But even museum exhibits of African arts are now addressing the disconnect between an objectivist display mentality and lived, ever-changing performance (see, for example, Kirshenblatt-Gimblett 1998b). In fact, we were recently invited to perform in a local museum as part of an exhibit that focused on African performance (especially masquerade); this gave us an opportunity to challenge those restrictive performance norms and their associated politics. Kelly describes one moment during this event:

> I arose from sitting on the floor where we had been singing and clapping and started to dance. A few members from the audience took their cue to participate and joined our circle of dancers that surrounded the remaining singers. At first I was so much into the singing that I didn't even notice the audience members. However, once I saw them join in smiling, I was proud that the space we'd created in our performance was comfortable and inclusive enough for audience members to feel free to join in and participate. That open and inviting space was unusual at the Bayly Art Museum where I'd expected stillness, silence, and distance from displayed objects to be dictated by invisible rules like "don't touch" and other such codes of decorum and control.
>
> I felt my own energy levels increase considerably as audience members joined us in dancing Mabo, a BaAka hunting dance. The intensity of that energy rose to such a pitch in the following dance, Dingboku (a women's line dance), that I felt one of these incredible moments of performance at its peak, where I was giving my all and was simultaneously feeding the immense accumulated and collective energy of the group. As we danced Dingboku, I was having the time of my life! As the sweaty energy and fun climaxed, it threatened to pull apart our four shifting and interacting lines of dancers. My arms were tightly interlocked over the shoulders of the dancers on either side of me, and we'd swoop forward while hopping or jumping toward another dancing line. Finally we dancers came so dangerously close to one another—and to knocking over museum displays—that we collided, collapsed, and exploded into laughter, which ended our performance with a disarray that maybe the audience wasn't expecting. It was an exhilarating, spontaneous and unchoreographed moment. (Gross 1999a: 4)

In the learning and performing context of our ensemble we are able to address many levels of boundary breaking. We loosen up the often-limiting roles of teacher and student, we reject the split between performance and scholarship, and we blur an idea of strictly formal or informal presentations. Breaking these boundaries helps us to reconstitute the frames of staged performances. The challenge, however, is finding contexts in which to fortify such efforts within institutions like universities. Institutions are, by their very nature, conservative, created in part to uphold the status quo whether in terms of local, regional, national, or worldwide power structures. So how do we make spaces within these establishments where "here" and "there," theory and practice, poetics and everyday life are not separated but intertwined?

The Fixed/Mixed Dialectic
In an effort to clarify her approach to teaching theory and practice holistically, Michelle has developed some strategies for helping students think critically about their aesthetic values and preferences. What she calls the

"fixed/mixed dialectic" helps explain the relational, ever-shifting under-
pinnings of aesthetic process. One aspect of this dialectic is the balance
between music as a marker of style (after Hebdige 1979, 1987, e.g., on punk
and hip-hop styles) and music in practice. In other words, performance style
is usually conceived of as a fixed marker that frames identity (ethnic,
regional, or age group, for example). Yet in practice, musical performance
is borrowable, plastic, and ever-changing (mixed), effectively subverting
essentializing frameworks. As another way of approaching this idea,
Michelle offers what she calls "the object(ive) subjectively conceived" (see
Kisliuk 2002). The "object(ive)" here might be the determining of particular rhythms and melodies, while the "subject(ive)" would be their transformation over time in performance. Grappling practically with these concepts
requires students to develop a level of critical awareness, and coming to
understand the dialectic is a step toward understanding the politics of culture both for individuals and for groups.

The dynamic force of this dialectic is *always* present in the transmission
of performed arts. But in BaAka practice it is redoubled because the fixed
"product" (or object) in sound and movement is so clearly fused with the
social moment that this "product" is undeniably always changing and different (mixed). Even if one moment may have been lifted into a sound or
visual document, in order to use that document appropriately we need to
remember that it is a radical reduction (fixing) of what is really multidimensional and unfixable. In other words, the "it" never really stops to have
its picture taken. BaAka performers have, it seems, mastered the fixed/
mixed dialectic. Each rendition of a song can sound quite different from all
other renditions, the differences unabashedly corresponding to the partic-
ularities of individuals and circumstances in each performance. Yet each
dance form and song keeps its distinct identity (based on specific rhythmic
relationships, dance steps, melody stylings, and paths of transmission),
while slowly evolving into new or "offspring" genres, including our own.

In our ensemble, the fixed/mixed dialectic comes vividly into play
whenever we need to begin with an ostensibly unchanging "it," that is,
when the goal is to learn a BaAka melody or a dance step that we are eventually to perform. This requires a temporary suspension of disbelief; we
need to begin with a (temporarily) fixed idea of "the song and the dance,"
then to forge a new performative pathway to get to "it." But in order for
our efforts to feel legitimate—"authentic"—we must balance the obvious
mixedness and contingency of the route by which these songs and dances
came (through Michelle to these students). Though BaAka in central
Africa are also constantly renegotiating through performance their changing cultural landscape (see Kisliuk 1998b), what distinguishes our process
in central Virginia is an even more visible shifting of contexts. This leads us

again to that ever-arising issue that becomes especially evident in the context of such clearly "transplanted" material: what is, in fact, the "it" that gets taught and performed?

One way that our developing microtradition can answer this question is by looking at our warm-up, a kind of sociomusical ritual (adapted from American choral and avant-garde ensemble practices) that helps us create the performative space we need. In fact, we've found that we cannot even start singing until we have "warmed" into a liminal sensibility. We cluster, seated in a tightly closed circle, and dim the lights. Making sure that our throats are completely open and relaxed, we begin by producing the lowest possible sound, letting the air pass over our vocal chords in a gravelly way. Then, with each relaxed breath, we gradually move our voices higher, responding to the collective ascent of the group, but at the same time maintaining a pitch that corresponds to the rhythm of our own breath. On our way up, there are unexpected harmonies and dissonances that form and dissolve. Depending on our mood the sound may be powerful or eerie; sometimes it is overwhelming in its volume and energy, as though our sound were communicating our collective personality, which evolves with every moment. When we reach the top of our range we break into yodels. We let our relaxed voices flip registers, playing within the high-low spectrum of pitches we have just been singing, and echoing off the classroom ceiling as if it were a forest canopy. We have discovered especially resonant spots all around the university (including the passageway under the Rotunda, and a dank stairwell in the back of the music building) where we periodically sing, surprising passersby.

Part of the dynamic that allows us to create our offspring genre is the humorous play that comes with the juxtaposition of social contexts, and the melding into a new idiom of once-distant sensibilities. During rehearsals of Dingboku—the women's dance Kelly described earlier—the few men who are in the class have the unique experience of standing back and supporting (or even joining) the female majority in singing bawdy, comic songs about male anatomy ("The penis is no competition, it died already. The vagina wins!"). These practice sessions often break into hilarity because they offer a liberating, safe space for egalitarian expression, within which individuals act collectively without conforming, and are independent without being egocentric. When the music and dance embodies this kind of social dynamic we finally understand what the "it" is we have learned to perform.

Chapter 15

"When Can We Improvise?"

The Place of Creativity in Academic World Music Performance

DAVID W. HUGHES

Let me begin by describing my experience when teaching the first session of a beginning Javanese gamelan class one recent September. For two hours we went through the basics: etiquette, instrument names and roles, basic technique, playing a simple *lancaran* (sixteen-beat structure), and so forth. Afterward, one student came up to me and asked, somewhat plaintively, "When can we improvise?" It turned out that he felt the time for improvisation was *now*.

His audacity at hoping to improvise within a tradition he had studied for a mere two hours was, if interpreted charitably, only a reasonable request for a chance to be creative. Thinking of it in that way, creativity—*appropriate* creativity—is certainly something we hope to encourage in our students in all their endeavors. At any rate, this experience got me to musing about the problem of creativity within performance courses. As the year wore on, the music faculty were also confronted with the first student in our program who wanted to be examined on a composition project involving elements of traditional music. Since she had become a talented performer of Shona *mbira* and associated vocals, her request was accepted, but at the end of the year we struggled to pin down criteria by which to evaluate her efforts. Let me contextualize our dilemma institutionally.

At SOAS (The School of Oriental and African Studies, University of London), the Music Department, in which I have taught since 1987, is comparatively small: seven lecturers typically teaching about fifty undergraduates, twenty students pursuing an M.Mus. in ethnomusicology, and fifteen Ph.D. students. As the school's name implies, our degrees and area course units must focus on Asia and Africa, with some extension into diasporic traditions. Our B.A. degrees are of two types: single-subject Music Studies, which normally requires some coursework in the Western classical tradition (currently taught via an exchange arrangement with King's College London), and two-subject degrees combining music with another SOAS subject, such as language or area studies, anthropology, religious studies, art history, and so forth. In addition to our own students, we also teach numerous students from other departments or from other schools of the University of London.

Although small, the music department has been able to offer a variety of performance classes, which, again, must relate to Asia and Africa. Traditions covered in recent years include Central Javanese gamelan, Balinese *gamelan angklung*, Thai *mahori*, Chinese silk-and-bamboo, Japanese folk song and *nagauta*, Korean percussion, North Indian *tabla*, Persian classical singing, and Shona *mbira*, all taught in group lessons, if not always as "ensembles" per se. Other, less official musical groups exist as well, including a student-run chorus. Many students also take private lessons (on the *kora, shakuhachi, shamisen, koto, pipa, guqin*, and other instruments), sometimes for credit, with one of the many skilled performers connected with SOAS and elsewhere in highly cosmopolitan London. (For students beyond their first year and for M.Mus. students, such private lessons are partially subsidized.)

Despite this wealth of offerings, several factors limit the time a student can officially devote to performance study. First, in England, bachelor's degree programs are only three years long (with some exceptions that involve overseas language study), and master's programs are one year. Second, more than half of our music undergraduates are pursuing two-subject degrees. Third, although the administration accepts that performance classes are essential in an academic music department, still, we are not a conservatory, and examination on performance can form only a small part of the curriculum (no more than one-sixth of course unit credits for undergrads, one-fourth for M.Mus. students). These three facts limit the time most students can reasonably devote to performance and thus to their progress. This also means that it will take relatively longer before they reach the stage where they can begin to feel that they have done something "creative."

It would of course be unrealistic to expect the learning experience at SOAS to closely parallel that in the home culture. Teaching staff recognize— even if students sometimes are reluctant to acknowledge—that what can be accomplished in a few hours of class time per week for a couple of years is going to be very limited compared with what is learned by, say, a Balinese who has been exposed to a particular music or dance style since early childhood and has possibly practiced almost daily. Teachers also recognize that different teaching methods are almost certainly needed in a classroom setting: mere absorption through repeated and intensive exposure over the years will generally need to be replaced (or at least supplemented) by more formal and explicit instruction, possibly accompanied by written or oral theorizing. In this respect it must be noted that for most of the traditions we teach, analytical works by scholars (usually non-native) are available. Although most of these aim to some degree to capture and convey the knowledge of a competent native performer, a student who reads them as an adjunct to lessons will still have a learning experience and resultant competence very different from that of the adult native.

MY EXPERIENCES WITH IMPROVISATION

Wrestling with issues of creativity at SOAS led me to think back over my own experiences on the receiving end of performance tuition (as did a request from our editor for each author to reflect on such experiences). These had brought me only slowly toward conscious consideration of creative possibilities: composition, improvisation, and so forth. During childhood lessons in classical piano and school-band trumpet, the constant presence of a detailed notation, staring me in the eyes, as it were, banished any thoughts that improvisation might be appropriate. But I knew that outside those lesson situations there were times when creativity was allowed. Jamming with friends and family, I improvised horrendous trumpet solos on tunes such as "Watermelon Man." Having taught myself guitar, I sought new riffs and accompaniments, but these would not be employed when slavishly duplicating recorded versions of folk and rock standards of the time: I saved them for possible use in my own compositions or for rearrangements of less standardized pieces. Thus Buddy Holly's "Peggy Sue" was too unique to change: everyone I knew who sang it imitated the original exactly, down to the finest vocal hiccup. But some other songs seemed less sacrosanct.

Still, I do not recall ever consciously thinking about the question of improvisation and its appropriateness: somehow one just *knew* when it was allowed. Of course, all the traditions I was tackling were somehow mine, of my culture. It was only when confronting the musics of other cultures for the first time that I had to ask. My first such encounter may have been a West African dance and percussion workshop led by Robert Farris Thompson in a basement room at Yale University (where I took a B.A. in linguistics and Japanese and an M.Phil. in linguistics) sometime around 1967. I can't recall why I went, but I am sure I would have found myself wondering whether the percussion patterns could be varied or not. Even with my limited experience of other cultures, I would have felt a certain humility in the face of a complex and unfamiliar music system—a humility totally lacking in the student quoted at the start of this paper. In a postmodern world where everything is available, where all cultures might be accessed via concerts, recordings, the Internet, and so forth, the powerful sense of ignorance and musical inadequacy that I experienced in that Yale basement is less likely to assail the conscience of a student of world music performance today. The "Other" is not as "other" as it once was, and yet it is distant enough that an outsider can still imagine—as have generations of Western classical musicians—that improvisation is a commonplace in "other" musics.

Arriving at the University of Michigan in 1972 to teach Japanese language and linguistics, I soon discovered the ethnomusicology program, entering it as a graduate student a year later. My formal experience of "ethno ensembles" began then, as a regular member and eventual instructor of the *nagauta* (Kabuki dance music) ensemble taught by Professor William Malm and a less regular participant in Professor Judith Becker's Javanese gamelan. I do not recall any specific justification being given for the existence of these ensembles, but I assumed that in that era of Hoodian bimusicality they were seen as crucial in creating card-carrying ethnomusicologists. Only later did I realize that they probably existed partly because a parallel was needed to the mandatory Western-music ensembles at Michigan (compare Nettl's discussion of such ensembles in *Heartland Excursions,* 1995).

In the *nagauta* ensemble, it was clear to all of us that there was no room for improvisation and little for interpretation. I noticed, though, some divergence between what we were being taught and the details of various recordings of the same pieces, which in turn differed from each other somewhat. Lectures and readings made it clear that such variation was due either to differences in "schools" or to minimally allowed on-the-spot variability in the timing of solo vocal passages. Japanese aesthetic preferences, I learned, were for the vocal line to diverge somewhat rhythmically from the much more metronomic instrumental parts. I recall repeated minor frissons of giddy achievement as I began boldly to play around with vocal timing a bit. But it took me a long time to become comfortable with even such minimal creativity: it seemed incredibly daring to tamper with another culture's music in that way, even after four years of playing. I was aware that my teacher was not Japanese and that I was not in Japan, and this certainly kept any creative instincts in check. The gamelan ensemble yielded a similar experience. When Judith Becker taught me a slightly syncopated alternative to a *bonang barung* part, which I was apparently free to use at any time, I again found great joy whenever I threw it in.

Friends would probably judge me as highly creative, although perhaps mainly in the verbal realm, where a constant stream of dubious puns betrays my past as a linguist. And I am not above tampering with musical instruments and styles, occasionally playing banjo pieces on the *shamisen* and so forth. I also have a great thirst for novelty. But somehow I have never felt the need to exercise major creativity in the musical language of other cultures. For me, the requisite novelty is obtained by learning new pieces or new musical languages rather than by creating new pieces myself (a view I also try to transmit to students).

Clearly the fact that I specialize in Japanese music has limited my improvisational urges, or at least made me fully aware of the restrictions placed on creativity in Japanese culture. Even Japanese folk songs, once full of spontaneity, have largely become ossified under the influence of the formal teaching structure and the weight of competitions. Students may even beg their teacher to teach them the "standard" version of a song so that they can succeed at a *concours*.

Only two traditional Japanese genres allow significant improvisation: the Tokyo-area Shinto festival music called *matsuri-bayashi* and the northern folk *shamisen* tradition called *Tsugaru-jamisen*. I studied performance in the former briefly around 1979, in preparation for serving as lecturer/stage manager for a tour to Hong Kong. During that period, I once attended a ritual performance by the senior members at a Shinto shrine. I remarked to the two young fellow students standing next to me that the flute and drum parts were quite divergent from the simple standardized versions we were being taught. "Yes", said one, "these old guys can't remember the music anymore." This was, of course, a totally false perception: the "old guys," unlike us neophytes, were not senile, but they were instead experienced and confident enough to vary their parts. Even though traditional Japanese genres rely only minimally on written notation, they tend to be perceived by young Japanese as fixed.

Tsugaru-jamisen is the exception. One of the few traditional styles to find favor with young folk today, *Tsugaru-jamisen* appeals with its powerful rhythms, romantic links with blind itinerants, and resemblance to blues guitar solos by B. B. King or Eric Clapton. But its major claim to popularity is its improvisatory nature, as seen in contests in which competitors take turns creating for a few minutes. Even here, though, there is quite a standard vocabulary of riffs and rhythms: too much deviation from the model will lose you points at the *concours*. (Moreover, as student numbers increase, teachers are increasingly forced to create fixed arrangements to be played in unison, thus eliminating spontaneity.) My own attempts at improvisation are constrained by an awareness of these limitations. I "invented" one riff that I quite fancied, my journey farthest from traditional motifs, but when I play it there is no response, no lighting up of the face that says, "Hey, nice going. Not only can you imitate the tradition, you can extend it." Quite demoralizing, really. One of my teachers, listening to another non-Japanese performing in a musical language rather too far from the core style, simply remarked, "It's not *Tsugaru-jamisen*."

A more equivocal experience befell me in Java in 1990, during my first long research visit. Under a respected artist named Paimin I had been studying the *siter* (plucked zither) and the ways in which it elaborates the basic melody in a gamelan. Prior to this trip I had learned a fairly coherent set of elaborating patterns from another teacher, Joko Purwanto; Paimin's vocabulary of patterns was often quite different. Both styles left some freedom to the performer to select from among variants or to minimally alter an existing variant. I could perform a handful of pieces almost exactly as my teachers had played or might play them.

Still, when Paimin dragged me along to play *siter* at a wedding, I was not yet confident in my ability to use patterns in new pieces. Nor did I yet know most of the tunes we played at the wedding, since they were not predetermined: the master of ceremonies would call out a request in the middle of a stream of speech, the gamelan would suddenly start playing, and I would start plucking while trying to figure out what the tune was. A *siter* player must match the main melody every sixteen or thirty-two plucks; it is usually possible to vamp with standard patterns until the last eight plucks, at which point you must prepare for a smooth landing on the main note. Since I often could not figure out what that main note might be until a few plucks in advance, most of my landings were, to put it mildly, rather unusual— indeed, presumably unprecedented! After this gig, Paimin said to me delightedly, "That's the best you've ever played!" He was apparently impressed with my creativity, a pleasant change from my usual slavish imitation, perhaps not realizing that it resulted from desperation born of ignorance. Alas, no recording exists of that event, so I have no idea what I played.

Presumably I had internalized enough of the grammar of *siter* parts to fake convincingly within the parameters. But when is this point reached? If we are to encourage creativity in our SOAS ensembles, the teachers must have a sense of the stage at which a student might reach this take-off point.

GENERAL COMMENTS ON IMPROVISATIONAL FREEDOM

Readers of this volume will be aware of the great differences in the degree of freedom traditionally allowed in the various genres mentioned above. Creativity may take many forms, whether variation, improvisation, composition, or "merely" interpretation (accepting that these four are difficult to separate; see Nettl and Russell 1998). Some traditions may allow significant creativity even in the first year (tabla and Persian classical singing, at least as taught by our native masters); others allow this only after considerable basic training (e.g., Javanese gamelan, Shona *mbira*, and Thai classical music); others by their nature are strong on interpretation but weak on improvisation (e.g., *shakuhachi* solos); still others allow little individual decision making for any player aside from the leader (e.g., Balinese gamelan *angklung*). Still, almost none of the genres taught will allow the kind of freedom that students generally mean when they refer to improvising. How, then, can students satisfy their more creative urges even from an early stage?

Our various performance teachers are as aware of the dilemma as students are. These teachers are a diverse lot, including native and non-native instructors, card-carrying academics and pure performers. Each of them, however, must come to terms with student attitudes toward improvisation that sometimes diverge from the instructor's preferred approach.[1]

Although the teachers' approaches and attitudes vary, most would agree that premature improvisation is not only impractical, it is also disrespectful of the tradition and its bearers. Independently, most of them have adopted a common pedagogical tactic: they say very little about improvisation, or even variation, in class at the beginning level, hoping that students will satisfy their thirst for novelty through slowly learning a new musical language. (Of course, at first students are expected merely to use this new language to memorize and repeat fixed texts, not to create new "sentences.") In our *mbira*, Javanese, and Thai classes, students do become aware very early that there are variant patterns on some instruments, but they seem generally to be left thinking that these variants preexist, that it is a matter of choosing rather than creating. (If they trouble to use the reading lists we give them, they easily learn the truth, of course.) Teachers are, more or less intentionally, slow to dispel this view, mainly as a strategy to keep improvisational urges in check until a musical grammar has been acquired that might allow successful creation. Some examples of teachers' approaches are given below.

About three-fourths of beginning performance students say they have thought, sometime during the first few months, about whether they can indulge in improvisation and variation. This is true even though in most classes the teacher has not referred to the matter at all. Students' comments on these matters are also found below.

In fall 1999 some of our students were forced to recognize the limits of improvisation. One third-year student who had been taking Cuban conga lessons with an external instructor was keen to start up some kind of intercultural percussion ensemble. His nickname is Jam, and that is basically what he originally envisioned: a mass jam session involving *djembe,* conga, Korean drums, tabla, Western drum kit, and, well, whatever. After the first session, however, he and the others came to the sobering conclusion that a sort of random jam was meaningless: one had to start with a structure, a framework of some sort. They needed what our colleagues working on improvisation have called a referent or a model (see the introduction to Nettl and Russell 1998). This experience may cause them to reflect more carefully on the need for such a referent in their formal performance classes as well.[2]

Jam had, in any case, begun to learn the limits of improvisation from his conga lessons. As he put it:

> There's an awful lot of groundwork to do before you get anywhere near improvisation. You can do a bit of variation, and then you learn certain patterns that are a sort of stepping stone to improvisation. But there are a lot of Cuban people who have been playing for three or four years who wouldn't think to have a crack at improvisation because it's not internalized. And also,

it's an important part of playing, but it's not the fundamental part, it's just sort of embellishment on top of it.

The last two sentences show him using a presumed emic—an insider's view as a guidepost for his own behavior—which is precisely the attitude we would hope our students would start with.

However, our incoming students are as diverse as their teachers. Some have plenty of formal Western music training but little experience of other musics, and others have precisely the reverse. Some are highly culturally sensitive, and others opine that music is a natural international language that all should be free to "speak" (or to sample) without cultural constraints. (Some of our ensemble classes are also open to non–music students, who may have no significant performance experience or musical training of any kind but are generally keen on the culture in question.) It is a challenge for performance teachers and academic lecturers alike to inculcate a measure of respect for the integrity of individual music cultures without taking the joy out of music performance and appreciation. Now let us see how different performance teachers approach this challenge.

EXAMPLES OF TEACHERS' APPROACHES IN SPECIFIC MUSICS

As noted above, among our performance teachers are both natives and non-natives, youngish and older, academics and civilians. The musics they teach are equally diverse. Finally, their classes also attract a diversity of students. Generalizations may elude us, but several ensembles will be discussed in varying degrees of detail as case studies.

Thai Classical Music

Dusadee Swangviboonpong (better known as "Gaew") came to SOAS as an English-language student in 1991, stayed on as planned to complete an M.Mus. in ethnomusicology and a Ph.D. on Thai classical vocal music, and has now moved on to a postdoctoral project comparing the gong-chime ensembles of Thailand, Cambodia, and Laos. He is highly reflective and analytical by nature. Even before beginning the academic study of Thai classical music, while still a "mere" performance student, he often asked probing questions of his Thai teachers—not something most Thai students would do. Moving from the study of mathematics and physics to Thai music while enrolled at a university in Bangkok, he eventually became a member of the personal orchestra of the Thai Crown Princess, HRH Princess Maha Chakri Sirindhorn, who is a leading patron of traditional music.[3] From 1991 to 1999, he taught a weekly Thai *mahori* class at SOAS and also ran the Thai

Music Circle based at the Thai Embassy; now he assists his successor when time permits. The latter group is made up mainly of London-based Thais plus a few alumni of the SOAS classes; the SOAS group, over the years, has included music students, Thai language or culture students, and occasionally others, among whom have been several Thai nationals.

How can one be creative in the Thai ensemble? And do the students seem eager to create? Dusadee says:

> It's quite a long way before you [are] able to improvise properly, traditionally. [Most students do] want to improvise, to change the melody. And I'm sure that's what an academic institution like SOAS wants them to be able to do. . . . So I normally let them change or make a mess or try to change the melody themselves. . . . Normally they ask me, "Is it OK to you?" and if it isn't, I say no. . . . Sometimes coincidentally they make a mistake [and] I have to point out to them, "What you've just done is not what I taught, but it was OK." And they learn that way too. When they've done that . . . it means that they understand a certain level already. . . . Sometimes it's right instinctively.

As Dusadee points out, this same description could apply to the learning process in Thailand as well, except that the average beginning student there would be more hesitant to experiment. At the beginning stage in Thailand, a student is not brave enough to "challenge the teacher," but in subtle ways it starts to happen. The teacher will push you, saying, "Don't just stick to what I taught you." From week to week, teachers will not normally remember what they taught you last time, "except in certain repertories, like solo pieces, where there will be a very definite composed melody." But in beginning songs and ensemble pieces, Thais will soon produce variations "naturally," and teachers will allow this. When a teacher says, "Don't do that," it's not because the student failed to play what the teacher had played, but just because the passage was wrong.

Dusadee himself learned this way, but given his relatively analytical bent, he also often intentionally tried new melodic phrases or patterns and clinically observed the teacher's reaction. His SOAS students sometimes do this as well, he says.

Dusadee confirms the findings of Silkstone (1993), who demonstrated in great detail that much learning of acceptable melodic patterns is almost by accident. A student has learned, say, a particular fiddle pattern that corresponds to a particular phrase of the gong circle (khawng wong yai) part in one composition. (The khawng part is considered the closest thing to a "basic melody," a referent for improvisation in other parts; all players should be familiar with it and may think back to it to guide their playing.) When a similar khawng phrase appears in the next piece to be learned, the student will likely—consciously or not—apply the same fiddle pattern. If the pattern is acceptable in the new piece as well, the teacher will generally say nothing; if the new context somehow excludes the use of that pattern, the student is corrected, possibly with some explanation.

However, as in most music traditions, detailed explication of the process of improvising is rarely encountered, mainly because even advanced performers tend to have difficulty accessing the mental processes that inform their creativity. With reference to Thai music, Anant Narkong, a skilled Thai drummer with analytical inclinations, struggled to document his own improvisatory thought processes, or even merely to describe his behavior, analyzing the range of variants he produced (Narkong 1992). Ultimately he felt he had not managed to understand his own behavior. Small wonder, then, that few performers would be able to explain how improvisation is actually done.

Teaching at SOAS, Dusadee as of 1999 would say nothing at all about improvisation until near the end of the first year. "Normally, the students wouldn't want me to change [my melodies]; more than 80 percent" of students feel like that: they are having enough trouble coping with the fixed bits without having to worry about how to create something new. In April 2001, in what I believe is a slight but unconscious evolution in the explicitness of his teaching method, he stated, "I will always tell them from the beginning that this is not the only melody. [But I tell them] to hold on until you are more confident, and you have a lot of melodies in your fingers, in your head, and then you can start exploring."

Dusadee now does articulate a few basic principles regarding melodic creativity to his students. First, he says, be sure that your new version does not alter the pitch played to coincide with the *chap* stroke of the *ching* cymbals, since that is a metrically important structural point. Second, stick to the basic anhemitonic pitch set: 1 2 3 5 6. Third, adhere to largely conjunct melodic movement. If you do all of these, "you've got a good chance" of creating an acceptable variant. He seems to have become conscious of the first and third principles only during his years pursuing an M.Mus. and Ph.D. at SOAS, which forced him to become even more analytical about his own tradition; his own teachers did not articulate these ideas.

Dusadee prepares fairly detailed notation for each instrument, and students may use this if they wish. Some students also record lessons. Given these facts, the students have potential reference points against which to measure variation. Students are therefore likely to say to him, "Hang on, you didn't do it that way last week." (In my experience, this is a question increasingly hurled at teachers in Japan, Indonesia, and elsewhere as oral tradition begins to give way to written and recorded transmission.) Dusadee uses this as one springboard for discussing variation: he tells them, "There are many versions. It's up to you, but you have to learn the grammar." Late in the first year, he may well demonstrate several versions of a passage to alert them to the possibilities, to the range of permissible variation. At first, though, the focus must be on technical matters, such as how to hold and play the instrument and so forth.

In April 2001 he further explained that beginning students need to be able to cope with the basic playing techniques "before they start changing the melody." For intermediate students, "variation, or improvisation, occurs when you *forget* the melody. . . . If you can find a melody to replace the one that you've forgotten, . . . that's the beginning of improvisation. I think the students are aware of that. . . . Sometimes the teachers don't notice because they forgot what they played [when teaching]."

So far, few students of Thai music at SOAS have felt comfortable experimenting with any significant amount of creativity, whether on their main instruments or when accompanying on drums. This is surely because our Thai teachers themselves consider such experimentation far less important at an early stage than do our teachers of tabla or Chinese silk-and-bamboo music (see below).

Zimbabwean Mbira

Chartwell Dutiro has been teaching the *mbira dza vadzimu* of the Shona people at SOAS since 1994 while simultaneously pursuing first an M.Mus. and then an M.Phil. degree in music. A former *mbira* player and arranger for Thomas Mapfumo and Blacks Unlimited, the renowned Zimbabwean pop music ensemble, Chartwell has also played in the traditional context of the *bira* or spirit possession ceremony. Thus his performance experiences are broad.

Chartwell says he always starts new students off with purely traditional material for a year. At the start, most students will try to imitate his every pluck (and similarly his singing, once they are ready for it). But there are generally one or two who are keen to explore new directions. Wendy, for example, always seemed to have another interpretation of pieces, even in her first year, and would often add nontraditional vocal harmonies in thirds. Chartwell would try to "guide her back" gently to the norm.[4] In her second year, Wendy made a harmonized arrangement of a Shona Christian church song for performance with two other *mbira* students; since this was not a standard piece from the *mbira* repertoire, Chartwell was happy for her to experiment with it.

Still, Chartwell's first goal is to have students absorb the tradition, not vary it. If there are five students, then he will have two play the lead part *(kushaura)* note for note as taught, while the other three perform perhaps two of the several variations *(kutsinhira)*. The *kushaura* is fixed, but *kutsinhira* can be varied once one has the confidence, or indeed new ones might be devised altogether. But one still has to stick close to the "skeleton" (he accepted this word from me and used it happily but noted that there was no single Shona term for this concept): there is a fixed set of basic notes that characterize a piece, and if you omit one note, it is no longer the same piece. This having been said, variation is still possible even for the skeleton, as Chartwell originally discovered by accident: "Sometimes you think you played a wrong note" while trying to repeat a passage exactly, but then you notice that it "sounds good," so you may retain that as an acceptable variant for the future.

In an ideal performance, the assembled musicians continually shift among different vocal and instrumental variants, creating a constantly changing kaleidoscope. Still, even given some scope for on-the-spot production of new variants, it is not common for a combination to arise that has not been heard before. Wendy, however, believes that "It's absolutely necessary to do some improvisation in order to embrace the subject, because it's such a fundamental aspect of the tradition that each individual within an ensemble will create their own voice through improvisation." Did Chartwell stress this point from the beginning? I asked her. "He *mentioned* it, he didn't *stress* it. It's just a fact." There is no single leader: "In *mbira* everybody has their moment." Debby, who has studied alongside Wendy for more than two years, suggests that Wendy's rather greater stress on freedom may be because she does much more singing than some students. Debby needed a full two years of just learning the preexisting materials for *mbira* before she felt ready to begin to go beyond fixed patterns and create variations; the vocals of this tradition may in fact be somewhat freer, which could have encouraged Wendy in her overall creativity. I think it is also a matter of individual personalities.

But how can students know whether a variant, accidental or otherwise, is acceptable in Shona terms? In the short term, they can do nothing but ask Chartwell. He described his experiences with three students. One day Ian, an advanced student, came in saying he had dreamed a variant and wanted an evaluation; Chartwell had never heard it before, but "it didn't sound wrong" to him, so he pronounced it acceptable. Katharina, after two years, "found" some new *mbira* patterns, which Chartwell felt "maybe someone had found before," since they struck him as well within the bounds of traditional style. Wendy too continued to come up with variants, but these, however pleasing, were generally well outside those bounds. These three students were not creating in response to prodding from Chartwell, who never suggests directly to students that they should experiment. They were responding to their own needs for novelty, albeit partly empowered by their awareness of the possibility of variation within the tradition as demonstrated by Chartwell.

Chartwell's own experiences in studying the Thai xylophone *ranat ek* were enlightening. He found it "a challenge" just to memorize the patterns demonstrated to him and to hit the right keys. When he encountered this new and difficult music tradition, thoughts of creativity were a long way off.

North Indian Tabla

Sanju "Vishnu" Sahai was born in Banares, a descendant of the founder of the Banares *gharana,* but he has long been a resident of England, where he teaches and performs extensively. At SOAS Sanju teaches a solo tabla tradition: students are not taught specifically to accompany other instruments, although some later move in that direction.

Until the end of the first year, learning is pure imitation and absorption, although students are free to reorder larger fixed units, that is, different variants in the realization of a rhythmic cycle *(tal).* In other words, in the first year students are taught the basic set of strokes for each of a few *tals,* plus certain fixed variants of these, as well as various special patterns such as *tihai* cadential formulas. Late in the first year or early in the second year, however, Sanju begins to encourage them to create new patterns: variants *(paltas)* of *qaida* patterns, new *tihais,* and so forth. He explains very precisely, as the students take notes, the principles and restrictions underlying such creativity. In performance exams, students are expected to be able to perform some of their creations, explain the process by which they arrived at these new patterns, and articulate the structural prerequisites of a *palta* or *tihai.* As one student, Natasha, said, "You know what you can change and what you can't change."

This sort of highly structured teaching with thorough elucidation is in line with the long tradition of detailed and precise music treatises in South Asia. A short essay is required in all SOAS performance courses, and second-year tabla students often choose improvisation as their topic; in effect, the students are writing minitreatises based on the oral instructions of their guru.

Not all tabla students cope equally well with the demands of creativity, of course, but all of them recognize its importance and willingly attack the challenges it offers.

Chinese Silk-and-Bamboo

One ensemble class in which creativity is stressed from the beginning is Shanghai silk-and-bamboo *(sizhu).* This is due in part to the nature of the music, but also in part to the personality, intellectual stance, and personal experiences of Stephen Jones, the current principal teacher (aided by Rachel Harris and Cheng Yu). Steve is infamous among China scholars for his antipathy to the "conservatoire style," whereby music is learned note for note from a score with little regard to traditional social contexts of performance and transmission. His own deep research and performance experience has focused on village and urban ensembles, in which flexibility of melodic realization is generally highly valued. His knowledge of *sizhu*, originally derived primarily from recordings and the works of scholars such as Witzleben, has recently been supplemented by an intensive period of playing and recording *sizhu* in the teahouses of Shanghai, all of which has confirmed him in his beliefs.

All group members are expected to delve into Witzleben, and they can be left in no doubt as to the importance of creativity after reading passages such as the following:

> The ability to play without notation is highly valued, and the musician must dispense with it before being able to interact with the other players and to vary his own interpretation of a piece. . . . a player eventually knows a piece so well that he does not even think about losing his place and naturally makes slight changes in each performance of it. (Witzleben 1995: 25)

Similarly, Witzleben writes, "Most *sizhu* musicians stress the importance of improvisation (at the relatively "micro" level of ornamentation and embellishment). A player should not stick to a fixed version of a piece but should vary it subtly with each rendition, eventually developing a unique style of playing" (ibid.: 34). Witzleben thus calls *sizhu* "semi-improvisatory" (ibid.: 29).

Steve Jones has struggled to devise a way to inculcate the process of melodic variation into students who begin with no experience and who can devote only a few hours a week to the cause. He tells students from the start that a major goal during their first year is to reach the point where they can think of (or read the notation for) only a skeletal "bone melody" *(guganyin)* while actually playing a more complex style based on "adding flowers" *(jiahua)*. The concept of a bone melody and adding flowers is widespread in Chinese music (see also Thrasher 1985 for early skeletal scores for *sizhu*), but the skeletal version that Steve has notated for them is his own abstraction from the more complex musical surface(s), not a version actually used by *sizhu* musicians: it was specifically a device to help novices grasp the process by which an undefined deep structure can yield a range of variants.

At SOAS, the fully realized, flowery melody, too, is actually learned note for note from a score (in cipher notation) rather than expanded from the model, but Steve and Rachel Harris have encouraged students to strive to understand the possibilities for elaborating the bone melody and then to experiment with new variants. This teaching method is not that of the Shanghai teahouses, but Steve and his coteachers hope that it can provide a shortcut to improvisation in the artificial context of a London classroom.

Students find this an extreme challenge, because the variational principles of *sizhu* are not spelled out by traditional musicians, nor have scholars yet found a way to explain pedagogically how to produce idiomatic variants. The SOAS teachers strive to find ways to articulate guidelines, but it is primarily up to the students to somehow discover relevant principles through listening to example recordings and to variants played by their teachers. The example recordings differ significantly from the notations used, which could provide a useful lesson in variation or simply confuse beginning students. A few students do seem to "get it" fairly quickly, but most find they have their hands full at first just mastering the technical aspects of a new instrument.

Since *pipa* (plucked lute) is technically far more difficult for a beginner than, for example, *erhu* (fiddle), it might be assumed that *pipa* players would be slower to begin to cope with questions of creativity. But our Ph.D. student San found that she was forced into being creative on *pipa* precisely because it was too difficult to play the fully realized melody of the detailed notation at the tempo the teachers demanded. She found herself devising an intermediate version by simplifying the full version a bit, substituting or omitting notes for ease of execution. Often such a change had to be made in real time as the group plowed ahead and she struggled to keep up with the tempo. This in itself was an important step toward variation, and surely not unlike the way that many traditional musicians learn. Although San was fully aware of the semi-improvisatory nature of *sizhu* (having written a review of Witzleben's book), her creativity in this case was not an intellectual attempt to imitate native practice but a desperation measure that nonetheless yielded unexpected fruit.

Steve has stressed that students should try to dispense with notation of all sorts as soon as possible. Playing from memory, as we have already seen in regard to some other traditions, is a surefire way to trigger unintended and often unconscious creativity, as the player copes with forgetfulness by playing whatever fits. Often such an act of desperation results in legal and indeed stimulating variants. Recently one *erhu* student, who had always relied on the full notation, was asked to try playing a bit of one piece with no notation at all. Overcoming her fears, she surprised herself by getting through a minute of music with little problem. Most interestingly, she did not realize that she had created several short variant passages that were so natural that even the teacher had not noticed until I, following the notation, pointed it out. As Steve's coteacher Cheng Yu puts it, when you have to struggle ahead with no notation, "a bit of creativity goes in"; notation may be "a frame that you can't jump out from." Cheng Yu, a Ph.D. student at SOAS, was already a master *pipa* performer before coming to the United Kingdom from China. While at the Xi'an Conservatoire (far from Shanghai), she did play in a *sizhu* ensemble for one term, and she had learned some *sizhu* melodies on *pipa* as a child in Beijing and Xi'an. But her lessons did not involve variation. Like Steve, she originally approached this tradition from outside; only when asked to help teach the ensemble at SOAS was she drawn to reflect on the questions of creativity that so occupied Steve. Cheng Yu now feels that the practice of teaching a skeletal version and encouraging students to be creative quite early is a good one, although she stresses that this is only feasible if students start with very easy pieces and are also given time to acquire adequate technique.

It is perhaps ironic that, far from begging for a chance to improvise, our *sizhu* students are often petrified when asked to do so. And yet some of them succeed. One student has suggested that they should be given only the skeletal notation at first, and then work toward a more ornamented version step by step as they meet the technical demands of their instruments.

Persian Classical Singing

Toraj Kiaras, a professional singer who became a political refugee from Khomeini's Iran, has been teaching Persian singing at SOAS since 1991, first only to other Persian speakers and then, as his language skills developed, also to SOAS students. His remarks quoted in this section (from 1999) were partly in English and partly in Persian with interpretation.

Even with his longstanding students, he says, he does not teach improvisation per se, but most will learn it naturally over time. (In the case of his Persian-speaking students, all of whom are familiar with various popular vocal styles of the region, his first task is to convert them to singing in a classical style, which means that technical matters of tone production and so forth take initial precedence.) Most students are aware that some creativity is expected, especially in the free-rhythm *avaz* vocal genre, but they do not at first consciously try to create variations. Instead, they aim to imitate the teacher closely, as he recommends. He teaches them scales and melodies from the *radif* (traditional modal repertoire), and in the process both he and they end up varying the melody "without trying." At first each student simply strives for exact imitation, but later each begins to improvise "naturally." Students find their individual style and timbre, which is precisely the desired result. This is one reason that it is ideal to study with several different masters: you will then inevitably become aware of possible variations of a single melody and gradually develop a personal style.

Our students tend to study with Toraj for at most two years (although some may continue after leaving SOAS). Having been encouraged to read about the characteristics of the style, including the improvisational element (as explicated in, e.g., Nooshin 1998), they are more than aware of what is expected in terms of eventual creativity, but they vary greatly in their individual reaction to this situation. Compare the following quotations from two student essays regarding their learning experiences:

> *Student A:* Generally it is expected that the *gushe*-s [melodic models] sung in free rhythm . . . are defined and shaped by extemporized melodic input. . . . It did not take me very long to understand the melodic characteristics of [the

mode] *Mahur* [and] to be able to make up my own patterns towards the ending of *gushe*-s. [Although staff notation was supplied,] Mr. Toraj would much rather that we sing with feeling and emotions than worrying about the precision of notes.

Student B: Mr. Kiaras regarded the *avaz* as being a more difficult form to perform, probably because it is more . . . associated with improvisation. To sing an *avaz* well would require a deep knowledge of Persian music [and being] familiar enough with a *gushe* (its defining characteristics, and preferably through studying different versions of it) to extract and play with its melodic material. For this reason, I feel unprepared at my present stage to sing an *avaz*, and have hence chosen to confine my improvisation ventures to ornaments and cadences.

It would seem that Student A was more willing to risk improvisation ("It did not take me very long . . . to be able to make up my own patterns") than the cautious Student B ("confine my improvisation ventures to ornaments and cadences"). A more careful reading, however, shows that both felt most comfortable extemporizing at cadences ("the ending of *gushe*-s"). Indeed, their exam performances were not so far apart, although Student A did take her teacher's comment about emotional expression rather seriously.

As in the case of the *mbira* students cited above, we see that there is considerable individual variation in the willingness to experiment and be creative when learning a new tradition. This variation arises both from students' personalities and teachers' methods and instructions.

Korean Percussion

Over the years, aspects of the related traditions *samulnori* and *nongak* (or *p'ungmul*) have been taught at SOAS primarily by Keith Howard and Nathan Hesselink, respectively. Many students, having watched performances, begin their lessons thinking that improvisation is a major part of these genres. As with Debussy and gamelan, it is easy for a newcomer, unable to penetrate the musical grammar and also deceived by the absence of notation in performance, to come to such a conclusion. Such people are then astounded to find that the pieces are virtually fixed. This leads a few improvisation-minded students to some initial disappointment, until they are fully absorbed into the learning process.

Central Javanese Gamelan

Andy Channing is a professional *pelatih* (gamelan teacher), instructing several ensembles around England. Over the years SOAS has had four Javanese and Balinese gamelan instructors (including myself), all non-natives; Andy has been in charge for several years now.

He intentionally avoids showing beginning students any notation for as long as possible, which is usually until early in the second term. By that point they have discovered from reading that notation exists, and they are also finding it difficult to hold their entire learned repertoire in long-term memory without the aid of notation.

Andy never has occasion to mention improvisation. He does introduce some legal variants in drumming patterns, *bonang* (horizontal pot gong set) elaborations and so forth, but at the level of our ensemble there is little need to go further. I have suggested that students might try devising new *sekaran* (cadential phrase) patterns for use in *bonang imbal* (interlocking patterns between two *bonang*), but not much else is within their capabilities. The student whose query gave me the title for this chapter was actually rather exceptional in his immediate thirst for improvisation: most students are having enough trouble keeping up with the basics without begging to be creative.

Andy also belongs to the Alpha Beta Gamelan, an ensemble dedicated to performing compositions for gamelan by its members and others. These new pieces, such as Andy's "Clear Blue Volcano," may diverge wildly from traditional gamelan style. We plan to introduce at least one such piece to the SOAS gamelan next year.

More than most world music ensembles, surely, gamelan groups tend to invite compositional activity. This fact, cleverly positioned in my narrative, leads us naturally to consider that aspect of creativity.

THE QUESTION OF COMPOSITION

While our performance program was developing during the 1990s, there was no precedent within SOAS to justify teaching or even examining composition. For example, the Department of Art and Archaeology has no courses in creative arts—no sculpture, no painting—and since by definition SOAS focuses on Asia and Africa, there was no in-house Western composition program to serve as a justifying model. Some students may take courses in the (Western) music department at King's College London, where composition is taught, but as their own students cannot study composition until having acquired a grounding in traditional Western techniques such as species counterpoint, ours are subject to the same prerequisites; two years of *mbira* or Persian singing does not qualify them. So whether at SOAS or elsewhere, there was no formal framework to allow our students to compose for academic credit and evaluation.

But many of our students, even those who are happy to stay well within traditional limits during performance classes, would like the chance to express their creativity through compositional activity. The kinds of questions we lecturers are discussing are: Should we allow students to tackle composition projects involving Asian and African music? Should we *teach* them composition? If so, on what basis? What criteria would we use to evaluate a student composition? We recognize that the English national curriculum for music teaching in the schools requires experience of compositional activity;[5] how should we relate to this?

To many readers this will seem like a nonissue. For example, both Indonesians (in the context of conservatories or not) and outsiders have in recent decades produced numerous new works for gamelan, and it seems that Indonesian musicians in general have no objection to foreign compositional activity. To me, even after having examined only two students in composition, the matter is a very challenging one. Here are a few preliminary thoughts.

I am wondering whether composition in an ethnomusicology program might be structured in a logical progression of three stages. At stage one, I would want to start (as in most Western music programs) with pastiche: attempts to compose in the style of particular cultures, repertoires, and eras. This would, of course, require the lecturer to be able to explain the grammar of, say, *shakuhachi honkyoku* solo pieces, the nature of *kushaura* and *kutsinhira* in *mbira* music, the limitations imposed by *ladrang* form in gamelan, and so forth. In many cases this activity could allow for considerable freedom and thus partially satisfy a student's desire for creativity. But I think such pastiche composition would be a much more mechanical and uncreative activity in the case of Javanese gamelan—paradoxically so, given the vastly greater flexibility of gamelan performance. Actually, the combined force of the rules of *pathet*, the *dhongdhing* principle, and so forth, plus the fact that most elaborating instruments derive their parts by extremely standardized choice based on the basic melody, mean that it is difficult to feel very creative when devising a pastiche piece.

Stage two could be a controlled but significant advance on stage one, in which the procedures and parameters of the tradition are preserved but given novel contents: new fingering or blowing techniques for *shakuhachi;* new *ragas* for sitar that are nonetheless developed in traditional ways; for Javanese gamelan, new *gendèr* or *gérongan* melodic formulas, or new applications of *irama* metric expansion and contraction; and so forth. At this point students could feel that they are being truly original and creative.

As stage three, could we offer a course unit in *free* composition, requiring only some elements of one or more Asian or African traditions plus a clear description of the aims of each work? If your program is embedded in an anthropology department, the answer is almost certainly no; in a music department, presumably yes. At this stage, musical elements from different cultures may well be mixed. But how will we evaluate—that is, mark!—such endeavors? Will our criteria be primarily aesthetic, boiling down to individual lecturers' value judgments about the originality or beauty of a composition? To make pedagogical sense within an ethnomusicology program, where transmission of and respect for cultural knowledge and values are still paramount, would we focus on those matters and devalue the aesthetic? Or should there be a subtype of "applied" ethnomusicology that trains and encourages students to produce commercially viable compositions with exotic flavors?[6]

Some of our SOAS students and graduates have been creating sound tracks for radio or television dramas, music for commercials, and so forth. One Ph.D. student composed a set of new Javanese gamelan pieces for such purposes by drawing (misguidedly, I fear) on my "grammar" of one restricted and structurally very simple subgenre of gamelan pieces (Hughes 1988). The results would fall into my stage one "pastiche" category. But my grammar only provides generative rules for the skeletal melody: the other parts must be filled in by the musicians' performative knowledge. That is how the pieces were recorded: a number of United Kingdom–based game-lanists (including a Javanese or two) were gathered in a studio, given the cipher notation for the skeletal melody, and asked to perform. The results would doubtless have been perceived in Java as somewhat boring traditional pieces, but they served their commercial purposes in England. Still, the demands and evaluative criteria of the marketplace differ from those of the Western university music department or the Javanese music world. In providing a place for compositional creativity within an ethnomusicology program, which criteria do we apply?

APPROPRIATE CREATIVITY

What, then, is "appropriate creativity"? What does the typical student want, need, and expect in terms of opportunities to be creative, and what can a teacher reasonably provide in a given tradition?

First, we have seen that there is no "typical student." Some cling to certainty, some are eager to take risks; and some have their hands full just trying to get an acceptable sound out of their instrument, leaving little time or energy to cope with improvisation.

Likewise, traditions vary in the degree to which they require creativity, as noted frequently above. A *shakuhachi* player and a *sitar* player would be at distant ends of the continuum.

Finally, different teachers will adopt different approaches. This does not simply boil down to native versus non-native teachers. Dusadee only began his studies of Thai traditional music at age eleven, by which time he was already inclined to be somewhat questioning in his approach to the learning process. He and Sanju (tabla) are both highly analytical by nature, trained in the sciences, whereas Toraj (Persian singing) tends to favor direct imitation with minimum verbiage. Moreover, native instructors often find that they must become more explicit in teaching foreign students who lack both time and the appropriate cultural knowledge. Being explicit in turn requires the teachers to be more analytical themselves, to dredge out of their subconscious certain procedures and principles that they never before needed to articulate. Non-native teachers, meanwhile, generally found it necessary as learners to concretize things that natives absorbed subconsciously through immersion, and thus tend to be more explicit from the beginning of their performance teaching careers. (One motivation for the research behind my 1988 article was that I just wanted to figure out how to know what was legal to play! Having finally worked out some things that Javanese musicians take for granted, I tend to verbalize these principles in my teaching.) Others feel it is better to try to expose their students to a near-native learning context, resisting the temptation to try to explain, say, the nature of improvisation. In a sense Steve Jones has tried to find a middle way: stressing the importance of varying one's performance in *sizhu,* he then provides students with model recordings that can serve as a sort of semi-immersion model and hopes that they will intuit the possibilities for variation.

In sum, appropriate creativity is some meeting point of the needs of students, teachers, and the tradition itself. A good teacher must surely strive to be aware of the needs of the particular set of students in the class. I have seen talented and arguably committed students drop out of a performance class precisely because they could not foresee a point at which creativity could be given free rein. To stimulate appropriate creativity, the good teacher will also seize on "mistakes" to point out the ways in which these unprecedented moments of performance either fortuitously succeed or else fail to satisfy.

It seems indisputable that most students—certainly the good ones—crave an element of novelty. Some find this craving satisfied by the very process of learning the basics of a new music. But many want more. Being able to devise a new *sekaran,* or a new *palta,* or a new realization of a *sizhu* melody, can be immensely satisfying and a major stimulus to further learning. Other learners are beckoned by the seemingly larger challenge of composing an entire new piece—I say "seemingly," because this may in fact be a lesser feat than mastering the existing stylistic language.

It is also fair to say that if our students do not aspire to and achieve some degree of creativity, then world music ensembles lay themselves open to the potential charge of doing little more than producing bad copies of Zimbabwean (or Japanese, or Javanese, or Indian . . .) musicians. Surely creativity does have to be an ultimate goal. But as in any genre of any music, improvisation must be based on knowledge of the parameters of the genre; whether one then works within those parameters or challenges and expands them is another question.

NOTES

1. In this chapter I generally use the terms *teacher* and *instructor* to refer to teachers of performance, and *lecturer* to refer (in standard British fashion) to the academic staff (lecturers, senior lecturers, readers, and professors). Some individuals fulfill both roles. All undated quotations are from interviews from mid- to late 1999 or early 2000; some additions from early 2001 are so indicated. Students are identified with varying degrees of anonymity, at the suggestion of some of them and according to my own judgment.

2. Three of this group played at a departmental party in 2000, bemoaning the absence of another member deemed essential to the ensemble. I noted cheekily that, since they were just making it up anyhow, surely a missing drummer was not a problem. They were not amused: having learned their lesson, they now proudly stressed the carefully structured nature of their performance.

3. SOAS is grateful to the Princess for her ongoing support: gifting us with a set of Thai instruments, financing our performance teachers Dusadee and Jutamas Poprasit during their studies, and repeatedly bringing leading Thai musicians to SOAS to perform.

4. Chartwell says that in fact harmonies in thirds are ever more accepted in Shona music today; some Shona from urban, Westernized backgrounds might even perform in this way at the traditional *bira* ceremonies where this *mbira* style is most at home.

5. The national curriculum requires the teaching of three "key skills": listening, performing, and creation. Creation, that is, composition, may make sense for Western classical and popular musics, especially as the students are at least passively familiar with such styles, and their teachers are relatively qualified to teach this skill. But how to deal with the rest of the world's music? No answer is yet forthcoming.

6. On this last point, it must be acknowledged that compositions drawing on musical material from other cultures have surely been created throughout human history. It is only in recent decades, with our postcolonial awareness, that we are particularly concerned or guilty about such things. But I feel we are right to be concerned.

Afterword

Some Closing Thoughts
from the First Voice

INTERVIEW WITH MANTLE HOOD
BY RICARDO TRIMILLOS

The following exchange derives from a conversation in early October 2002 (forty-eight years to the month since the inception of the first ethnomusicology performing ensemble at UCLA) between Ki Mantle Hood (b. June 24, 1918), the earliest pioneer of the world music ensemble in U.S. academe, and Ricardo Trimillos. Mantle had been cleaning the swimming pool when his wife, Hazel, called him to the study and the conversation began. The exchange was a relaxed "talk story" by telephone that linked Ellicott City, Maryland, with Hawai'i, mentor with student. Mantle sat in his study late in the afternoon, observing a doe and her fawn in his backyard, as Trimillos from his lanai watched the late morning surf rolling into Waikiki. Always the consummate raconteur, Mantle Hood provides stories that entertain, inform, and challenge.

RICARDO TRIMILLOS: It is so appropriate for you to have the last word in an anthology on world music ensembles. Thanks for taking the time to chat.

MANTLE HOOD: Oh, there would never be a time I would enjoy more. I hope my comments are pertinent and appropriate. I try to be a very positive voice for things I have found that work.

RT: Your voice is an important one. Let's concentrate mostly on the UCLA years. When you started, did you see the study group as something extra or integral to ethnomusicology?

MH: No, it wasn't a "something." It was terribly personal in the beginning, Ric. I found playing gamelan in Holland for two years had opened up so much about Javanese and Balinese cultures. Of course, I was where resources were plentiful. I was doing a lot of reading and also researching. The more I played gamelan, the more I began to understand and appreciate these cultures. So I thought, what better way to get a student acquainted with another culture than to perform? That was the motivation throughout.

RT: What was the history of the first study groups at UCLA? How did they contribute to establishing ethnomusicology?

MH: The first study group? We started Javanese gamelan in October of 1954. We gave our first, I guess I'd call it performance-demonstration, in spring of 1955. I bought my first gamelan in Europe after I got my degree. When I came home to L.A. the first thing I did when we got settled was put a yellow piece of scrap paper on the bulletin board in the music department. I said, "Anyone interested in learning to play Javanese gamelan sign below." At that time it was housed in the upstairs bedroom of our small rental apartment.

The first Wednesday night probably about a dozen came. The second Wednesday night, it was probably in the twenties. By the third Wednesday night [chuckle] it was in the thirties. And I realized we had to take turns because I could only accommodate about, well, it was stretching it to say a dozen. So we started that way. After not too long, the department suggested I move it to the campus.

The second group was actually inspired by Robert Garfias. That was *gagaku* [Japanese court music]. The Tenrikyo [Shinto-derived sect] mother church was in Los Angeles. For the first eight months or so, we borrowed their instruments to play. And then finally with Robert, we went off to Japan and bought some remarkably fine instruments.

I guess I have another story. A young man who had been a UCLA graduate student at the same time I was had gone to get his degree in Belgium. After that he had a one-year appointment at Yale—a very bright guy. Well, after my first year at UCLA we had a get-together session in early summer in Santa Monica. He said, "You know what they're saying about you back East? They say there is a mad professor at UCLA sitting students down to pots and pans and beating on them in the name of music!"

Okay, that's the first part of the story. About six months later, the American Musicological Society had a meeting in Santa Monica. I gave a demonstration-performance on Javanese gamelan. From that time on, Ric, I had musicologists, not ethnomusicologists, coming up to me privately and saying, "Please save us one of your students for our faculty." That's a fact.

RT: How did the African ensembles get started?

MH: Well, that's another story. There's a story behind everything. They put me on the African Studies Committee. They also had me on the Middle Eastern Committee, every committee, because what I was doing was considered—exotic. One day the chancellor announced a luncheon meeting, because the vice chancellor of the University of Ghana would be coming. And in he walks, finally—he was an hour and a half late—a redheaded Irishman. I was off in a far corner near the door, because I really felt as though I didn't qualify to be there. He went rushing past everybody, came up to this "white-haired man," stuck his hand out, and said, "You must be Mantle Hood. I'm vice chancellor so-and-so; you're coming back to Africa with me!"

Later he told me that he had orders from [Ghanaian ethnomusicologist J. H. Kwabena] Nketia that I should be brought to Africa as soon as possible. So that's sort of how Africa got into the swim. I had drums made for UCLA. Finally came the pièce de résistance, the *fontomfrom* drums [royal drums of the Asante nation, a.k.a. Ashanti]. The set was the same size as the *Asante-hene*'s [paramount chief of the Asante]. Nobody else in Ghana was willing to buy it. They were afraid to have a set as big and fine as the royal drums.

RT: You have often pointed out that ethnomusicology provides an opening to understanding a culture that other disciplines do not. What are some of your personal experiences?

MH: Oh, I can tell you a good one [laugh]. You know, I made a film called *Atumpan: The Talking Drums of Ghana* [filmed in 1963, released in 1964]. The night we finished shooting, they gave me a big party at a nightclub. The man in charge was named Koko. Well, the music went on until the club closed. Koko announced that was no reason to stop the party. We partied on until 4 or 5, I don't remember exactly. Then he said, "Let's go have breakfast." Now wait 'til you hear the end. So he took us to the house. By then there were only three or four of us. Sure enough, they had laid out quite a big breakfast. Pretty soon more people began to arrive. Finally, I'm guessing, there might have been two dozen or so. Koko had me sit next to him. He began to address the group. Now, what was he saying? Well, they were plotting how to overthrow Nkrumah [Kwame Nkrumah, first president of an independent Ghana]! This went on for about a half an hour. He suddenly looked at me, slapped me on my knee, and said "Oh, don't mention this." I said, "No, I won't for sure!"

Anyhow, I think when you've been involved—as I was, and most of our students have been—with music, you're not looked at as an outsider as much. So in that capacity you pick up a lot of information.

Want another story? This is starting back in Java, the beginning of my fieldwork, in 1957–58. As you know, the Javanese language is pretty complicated. I had learned some Indonesian and found out that some Javanese didn't speak it. If I wanted to know their music and dance, and theater, and puppetry I had better learn Javanese. Well, there are multiple levels of language. I said, "I have just so many years to live; I'll settle for the politest form, High Javanese." And that's what I learned. Well, very quickly word spread around where I lived that my talking to cigarette vendors entirely in High Javanese was a sign of American democracy [chuckle]! So I had that role to play.

RT: You have been instrumental in bringing so many artist-teachers from abroad to teach in the United States. How did they contribute to your vision for ethnomusicology?

MH: Make no mistake. I was doing my damnedest to do what I could with the little I knew about each music in order to deepen interest in it. This was before all the artists came from wherever the music originated. For example, what I knew about gamelan before [Hardja] Susilo came and about Karnatic music before [the late Tanjore] Vishwanathan [Karnatak flute virtuoso and Ph.D. student at UCLA, later longtime adjunct professor at Wesleyan University] arrived was just a start. But we really didn't get off the ground until I had those people here to help me out.

This is a story about Vishwanathan and Bala [Balasaraswati, the late Bharata Natyam dance virtuoso]. You know Bala. Robert Brown had engineered a Fulbright for her brother Vishwanathan. On my way home from my first trip to Java, I went to India and visited Robert. I met Bala; Vishwa had already left for the States. She was in bed with some illness, I'm not sure what. I was taken up to her room. At that time Bala didn't speak any English. We kinda sat and admired one another. Finally she mumbled something to the maid. Pretty soon here came the maid back with a record, an old 78, and put it on the phonograph. Bala got out of bed and danced for me. Wow! was my reaction.

Then, finally, I understood that I was to be Vishwanathan's American guru, an important responsibility. From that bedroom visit on, we became very close. And the same with her daughter. Well, with the whole clan. I miss them.

RT: As an outgrowth from study groups, Americans are undertaking the creation of new music for ensembles like gamelan. How do you view this activity?

MH: Now this really goes back. Timidly and tentatively I wrote my first *gendhing* [gamelan composition] and put it in rehearsal with the Javanese gamelan—and destroyed it after that. I felt I was not privileged to write Javanese music. Then the next thing I knew, everybody was writing Javanese music [chuckle]. Finally I was invited in such terms to compose that I would have been insulting somebody if I didn't. So I said, "Okay, don't be stuffy, write some Javanese music." I also wrote a percussion quartet and used an absolutely Balinese *gender wayang* [quartet of metallophones that accompany shadow puppet theater] technique, a little piece called "Implosion." So, anyhow, I just want to say I got over my initial "stuffy" attitude that you shouldn't write Javanese or Balinese music.

However, I believe some composers are not sufficiently informed about either Javanese or Balinese music to write it. For example, Javanese gamelan—its spirit is improvisation. In contrast Balinese gamelan, not all of it but most of it, is pretty well worked out and rehearsed. So you should stay within the tenets of a tradition, no matter how refreshing or different you want to be. Unless you are trying to capture and keep those tenets, I feel you haven't really done the job.

It may be that composers take refuge in the thought that they are doing something different and original. I am not in a position to quarrel with that. But I do think there is a limit to what you should do. Or at least, let's say that the problem appears to be that people haven't delved deeply enough to capture the aesthetic that I think is simply germane and absolutely essential to a given tradition.

RT: Study groups have changed in their nature over the years. What is your opinion of them now, almost a half century after you began at UCLA?

MH: In those days I don't think there were many "exotica fans"—it was more than that. I'm thinking of many groups that were formed then. People who joined had a very sincere and genuine interest in knowing more about the culture. I think it was a very pure interest. Today, I'm not sure whether the word *pure* still obtains. Now I think it's a very mixed bag of interests. Well, it's not surprising, considering the degree to which the whole field has shifted and changed.

RT: Mantle, in closing, what has study through performance meant to you personally?

MH: Well it won't be a story [chuckle]. That would take a lot of spinning out, but I'm gonna make it real short. I guess the big lesson that I've tried to pull out of all of this is: know the culture by becoming part of it to the best of your ability. You know it through music; you know it through dance; you know it through rituals. In these ways you know it better than people who struggle with language, often a superficial struggle.

As you know, it's pretty well assumed by humanists that a knowledge of a foreign language opens up a lot of doors in another culture, right? Now, I have thought about that. I confessed to a group recently that I stumble around in six or eight foreign languages, and I'm not very happy about any of them. But . . . I believe musical languages have it over spoken languages in many ways, especially if the music you're involved with is a traditional music and true to its culture. It can't lie. It can't be translated. It can't be misunderstood. For the spoken word all those shortcomings are par for the course.

So anyhow, that's my final word, my last pitch.

RT: Thanks again for sharing your thoughts and your stories.

Like the final gong in gamelan, his afterword closes but does not end this conversation.

NOTE

Editor's note: Our original 1999 panel at the Society for Ethnomusicology meeting in Austin, Texas, was honored by Mantle Hood's presence and laudatory remarks.

Hood's apprenticeship with ethnomusicology pioneer Jaap Kunst in Holland, from 1952 to 1954, included gamelan study, further testimony of the debt our discipline owes to post–World War II developments in that country. During his subsequent tenure at UCLA in the 1950s and 1960s Hood laid the groundwork for many subsequent developments in the field. I thus enthusiastically welcomed Ricardo Trimillos's idea for an interview.

WORKS CITED

Abu-Lughod, Lila. 1991. "Writing Against Culture." In *Recapturing Anthropology: Working in the Present,* ed. Richard G. Fox, 137–62. Santa Fe, N.M.: School of American Research Press.

Adler, Israel. 1995. *The Study of Jewish Music: A Bibliographical Guide.* Jerusalem: Magnes Press.

Agawu, Kofi. 1995. *African Rhythm: A Northern Ewe Perspective.* Cambridge: Cambridge University Press.

Anderson, Benedict. 1991. *Imagined Communities: Reflections on the Origin and Spread of Nationalism.* London: Verso.

Anderson, William M., and Patricia Shehan Campbell. 1989. *Multicultural Perspectives in Music Education.* Reston, Va.: The Music Educators National Conference.

Apedoe, Netta. 1999. "The Oka Community." Unpublished poem.

Appadurai, Arjun. 1991. "Global Ethnoscapes: Notes and Queries for a Transnational Anthropology." In *Recapturing Anthropology: Working in the Present,* ed. Richard G. Fox, 191–210. Santa Fe, N.M.: School of American Research Press.

Armstrong, Robert Plant. 1971. *The Affecting Presence.* Chicago: University of Illinois Press.

Austern, Linda Phyllis. 1998. "'Forreine Conceites and Wandring Devises': The Exotic, the Erotic, and the Feminine." In *The Exotic in Western Music,* ed. Jonathan Bellman, 26–42. Boston: Northeastern University Press.

Avorgbedor, Daniel. 1987. "The Construction and Manipulation of Temporal Structures in Yeve Cult Music: A Multi-Dimensional Approach." *African Music* 6, no. 4: 4–18.

Balme, Christopher B. 1998. "Staging the Pacific: Framing Authenticity in Performance for Tourists at the Polynesian Cultural Center." *Theatre Journal* 50: 53–70.

Baraka, Amiri [LeRoi Jones]. 1968. "Jazz and the White Critic." In his *Black Music,* 11–20. New York: W. Morrow.

Barz, Gregory F., and Timothy J. Cooley, eds. 1997. *Shadows in the Field: New Perspectives for Fieldwork in Ethnomusicology.* New York: Oxford University Press.

Baxter, Les. Ca. 1955. *The Ritual of the Savage/Le Sacre du Sauvage.* Capitol LP T288.

Beaudry, Nicole. 1997. "The Challenges of Human Relations in Ethnographic Inquiry." In *Shadows in the Field: New Perspectives for Fieldwork in Ethnomusicology,* ed. Gregory F. Barz and Timothy J. Cooley, 63–83. New York: Oxford University Press.

Becker, Judith. 1980. *Traditional Music in Modern Java.* Honolulu: University of Hawai'i Press.

———. 1983. "One Perspective on Gamelan in America." *Asian Music* 15, no. 1: 82–89.

Becker, Judith, and Alan H. Feinstein, eds. 1984–88. *Karawitan: Source Readings in Javanese Gamelan and Vocal Music.* 3 vols. Ann Arbor: Center for South and Southeast Asian Studies, University of Michigan.

Benary, Barbara. 1983. "Directory of Gamelan in the United States." *Ear Magazine* (Sept.–Nov.): 34–35.

Beregovski, Moshe. 2001 [1937]. *Jewish Instrumental Folk Music.* Ed. and trans. Mark Slobin, Robert Rothstein, and Michael Alpert. Syracuse, N.Y.: Syracuse University Press. Originally published as *Evreiskaia Narodnaia Instrumental'naia Muzyka* (Kiev: Kabinet far Derlernen di Yiddish Sovetishe Literatur, Sprakh un Folklore Sektsye).

Berliner, Paul. 1993 [1978]. *The Soul of Mbira: Music and Traditions of the Shona People of Zimbabwe.* 2d ed. Berkeley: University of California Press.

———. 1994. *Thinking in Jazz: The Infinite Art of Improvisation.* Chicago: University of Chicago Press.

Blacking, John. 1972a. *How Musical Is Man?* Seattle: University of Washington Press.

———. 1972b. *Music, Culture, & Experience: Selected Papers.* Chicago: University of Chicago Press.

———. 1987. *'A Commonsense View of All Music': Reflections on Percy Grainger's Contribution to Ethnomusicology and Music Education.* Cambridge: Cambridge University Press.

Bohlman, Philip V. 1988. *The Study of Folk Music in the Modern World.* Bloomington: Indiana University Press.

Brand, Oscar. 1962. *The Ballad Mongers: Rise of the Modern Folk Song.* New York: Funk and Wagnalls.

Brett, Philip. 1994. "Eros and Orientalism in Britten's Operas." In *Queering the Pitch: The New Gay and Lesbian Musicology,* ed. Philip Brett, Elizabeth Wood, and Gary Thomas, 235–56. New York: Routledge.

Brinner, Benjamin Elon. 1995. *Knowing Music, Making Music: Javanese Gamelan and the Theory of Musical Competence and Interaction.* Chicago: University of Chicago Press.

Brunner, Diane D. 1998. *Between the Masks: Resisting the Politics of Essentialism.* Lanham, Md.: Rowman & Littlefield.

Cadar, Usopay. 1996. "The Maranao Kolintang *[sic]* Music and Its Journey in America." *Asian Music* 27, no. 2: 131–48.

Catra, I Nyoman. 2002. Personal communication with Sumarsam.

Charry, Eric. 2000. *Mande Music: Traditional and Modern Music of the Maninka and Mandinka of Western Africa.* Chicago: University of Chicago Press.

Chernoff, John Miller. 1979. *African Rhythm and African Sensibility: Aesthetics and Social Action in African Musical Idioms.* Chicago: University of Chicago Press.

Clifford, James. 1984. "Introduction: Partial Truths." In *Writing Culture: The Poetics and Politics of Ethnography,* ed. James Clifford and George E. Marcus, 1–26. Berkeley: University of California Press.

———. 1988. *The Predicament of Culture: Twentieth-Century Ethnography, Literature, and Art.* Cambridge, Mass.: Harvard University Press.

Conant, Faith. 1988. "Adjogbo in Lome: Music and Musical Terminology of the Ge." Master's thesis, Tufts University.

Cooley, Timothy J. 1997. "Casting Shadows in the Field: An Introduction." In *Shadows in the Field: New Perspectives for Fieldwork in Ethnomusicology,* ed. Gregory F. Barz and Timothy J. Cooley, 3–19. New York: Oxford University Press.

Coplan, David B. 1991. "Ethnomusicology and the Meaning of Tradition." In *Ethnomusicology and Modern Music History,* ed. Stephen Blum, Philip V. Bohlman, and Daniel M. Neuman, 35–48. Urbana: University of Illinois Press.

Cowan, Joan Bell. 1997. "Beginning Javanese Gamelan: A Community of Listeners." *The Orff Echo* 29, no. 3: 28–32.

Cruz, Gabriela. 1999. "Giacomo Meyerbeer's L'Africaine and the End of Grand Opera." Ph.D. diss., Princeton University.

Csikszentmihalyi, Mihaly. 1991. *Flow: The Psychology of Optimal Experience.* New York: Harper Perennial.

Cultural Center of the Philippines. 1994. "Rondalla." In *CCP Encyclopedia of Philippine Art,* vol. 6, *Philippine Music,* 144–46. Manila: Cultural Center of the Philippines.

Dalmayr, Fred. 1996. *Beyond Orientalism: Essays on Cross-Cultural Encounter.* Albany: State University of New York Press.

Danielson, Virginia. 1997. *The Voice of Egypt: Umm Kulthūm, Arabic Song, and Egyptian Society in the Twentieth Century.* Chicago: University of Chicago Press and Cairo: American University in Cairo Press.

Davis, Ruth. 1992. "The Effects of Notation on Performance Practice in Tunisian Art Music." *The World of Music* 34, no. 1: 85–114.

Diamond, Jody. 1983. "Gamelan Programs for Children from the Cross-Cultural to the Creative." *Ear Magazine* 8, no. 4: 27.

———. 1989. "Making Choices: American Gamelan in Composition and Education (From the Java Jive to 'Eine Kleine Gamelan Music')." In *Essays on Southeast Asian Performing Arts: Local Manifestations and Cross-Cultural Implications,* ed. Kathy Foley, 115–39. Berkeley: Regents of the University of California.

Doty, David B. 1983. "Reflections on Gamelan and Composition." *Ear Magazine* 8, no. 4: 15.

Down, A. Graham, ed. 1993. *Vision for Arts Education in the 21st Century.* Reston, Va.: The Music Educators National Conference.

Dumont, Jean-Paul. 1983. "The Visayan Male Barkada: Manly Behavior and Male Identity on a Philippine Island." *Philippine Studies* 41, no. 4: 401–36.

Durkheim, Emile. 1915. *The Elementary Forms of the Religious Life.* New York: Free Press.

Emerson, R., R. Fretz, and L. Shaw. 1972. *Writing Ethnographic Fieldnotes.* Chicago: University of Chicago Press.

Enriquez, Virgilio. 1985. "Kapwa: A Core Concept in Filipino Social Psychology." In *Sikolohiyang Pilipino,* ed. Allen Aganon and Ma. Assumpta David. Manila: National Bookstore.

"Ethnomusicology: Unique Institute Probes Eastern World Through Its Music." 1963. *Ebony Magazine* 18, no. 3: 61–63.

Euba, Akin. 1990. *Yoruba Drumming: The Dundun Tradition*. Bayreuth: Eckhard Breitinger.

Feld, Steven. 1983. "Sound Structure as Social Structure." *Ethnomusicology* 28, no. 3: 383–409.

———. 1990 [1982]. *Sound and Sentiment: Birds, Weeping, Poetics, and Song in Kaluli Expression*. 2d ed. Philadelphia: University of Pennsylvania Press.

———. 1995. "From Schizophonia to Schismogenesis: The Discourses and Practices of World Music and World Beat." In *The Traffic in Culture*, ed. George E. Marcus and Fred R. Meyers, 96–126. Berkeley: University of California Press.

Feldman, Walter Z. 1994. "Bulgareasca/Bulgarish/Bulgar: The Transformation of a Klezmer Dance Genre." *Ethnomusicology* 30, no. 1: 1–35.

Friedson, Steven. 1996. *Dancing Prophets: Musical Experience in Tumbuka Healing*. Chicago: University of Chicago Press.

Gadamer, Hans-Georg. 1975. *Truth and Method*. Garrett Barden and John Cumming, eds. New York: Seabury.

Gamelan Music of Java: An Introduction (VHS Video). 1983. Honolulu: East-West Center, 1983.

Gangelhoff, Christine. 2002. "Klezmer in Academia." D.M.A. thesis, University of Minnesota.

Gardner, Howard. 1999. *Intelligence Reframed: Multiple Intelligences for the 21st Century*. New York: Basic Books.

Geertz, Clifford. 1973. *The Interpretation of Cultures*. New York: Basic Books.

———. 1983. *Local Knowledge: Further Essays in Interpretive Anthropology*. New York: Basic Books.

Goldberg, Rose Lee. 1988 [1979]. *Performance Art: From Futurism to the Present*. 2d ed. New York: Harry N. Abrahams.

Goldenshteyn, German. 1999. Transcript of interview conducted during class at the New England Conservatory Summer Klezmer Institute, July 14, 1999. Trans. Michael Alpert, New England Conservatory, Boston.

Goldin, Max. 1989. *On Musical Connections Between Jews and the Neighboring Peoples of Eastern and Western Europe*. Ed. and trans. Robert A. Rothstein. Amherst: International Areas Study Program, University of Massachusetts.

Goldsworthy, David. 1997. "Teaching Gamelan in Australia: Some Perspective on Cross-Cultural Music Education." *International Journal of Music Education* 30: 3–14.

Gordon, Lillie. 2002. "Routes of the Violin." Honors thesis, College of William and Mary.

Gourlay, Kenneth A. 1982. "Towards a Humanizing Ethnomusicology." *Ethnomusicology* 26, no. 3: 411–20.

Gross, Kelly. 1999a. "Energy, Interaction, and the Sound Vortex: Performance of BaAka Song and Dance." Unpublished paper.

———. 1999b. Personal communication with Michelle Kisliuk.

Han, Kuo-huang. 1979. "The Modern Chinese Orchestra." *Asian Music* 11, no. 1: 1–43.

Haraway, Donna. 1991. "Situated Knowledges: The Science Question in Feminism and the Privilege of Partial Perspective." In *Simians, Cyborgs, and Women: The Reinvention of Nature,* ed. Donna Haraway, 183–201. New York: Routledge.

Harlow, Barbara, and Mia Carter, eds. 1999. *Imperialism and Orientalism: A Documentary Sourcebook.* Malden, Mass.: Blackwell Publishers.

Harnish, David. 1996. "Gamelan Sekar Jaya: Balinese Music in America." *Asian Music* 28, no. 1: 146–49.

———. 2001. "A Hermeneutical Arc in the Life of Balinese Musician, I Made Lebah." *The World of Music* 43, no. 1: 21–41.

Harris, Marvin. 1970. "Referential Ambiguity in the Calculus of Brazilian Racial Identity." In *Afro-American Anthropology,* ed. Norman E. Whitten Jr. and John F. Szwed, 75–86. New York: Free Press.

Hatch, Martin F., ed. 1996. "Kulintang/Kolintang." *Asian Music* 27, no. 2: 1–148.

Hebdige, Dick. 1979. *Subculture: The Meaning of Style.* London: Routledge.

———. 1987. *Cut 'N' Mix: Culture, Identity, and Caribbean Music.* London: Methuen.

Heider, Karl. 1976. *Ethnographic Film.* Austin: University of Texas Press.

Herbst, Edward. 1997. *Voices in Bali: Energies and Perceptions in Vocal Music and Dance Theater.* Hanover, N.H.: University Press of New England.

Hobsbawm, Eric. 1983. "Introduction: Inventing Traditions." In *The Invention of Tradition,* ed. Eric Hobsbawm and Terence Ranger, 1–14. Cambridge: Cambridge University Press.

Hood, Mantle. 1954. *The Nuclear Theme as a Determinant of Patet in Javanese Music.* Groningen: J. B. Wolters. Reprint New York: Da Capo Press, 1977.

———. 1957. "Training and Research Methods in Ethnomusicology." *Ethnomusicology Newsletter* 11 (Sept.): 2–8.

———. 1960. "The Challenge of Bi-Musicality." *Ethnomusicology* 4, no. 2: 55–59.

———. 1963a. "Music, the Unknown." In *Musicology,* ed. Frank Ll. Harrison, Mantle Hood, and Claude V. Palisca, 215–326. Englewood Cliffs, N.J.: Prentice-Hall.

———. 1963b. "The Enduring Tradition: Music and Theater in Java and Bali." In *Indonesia,* ed. Ruth McVey, 438–71. New Haven, Conn.: Human Relations Area File Press.

———. 1982 [1971]. *The Ethnomusicologist.* New York: McGraw-Hill. New ed. Kent, Ohio: Kent State University Press.

Hood, Mantle, and Susilo Hardja. 1967. *Music of the Venerable Dark Cloud.* Los Angeles: Institute of Ethnomusicology, UCLA.

Hughes, David W. 1988. "Deep Structure and Surface Structure in Javanese Music: A Grammar of *Gendhing Lampah.*" *Ethnomusicology* 32, no. 1: 23–74.

Idelsohn, Abraham Z. 1929. *Jewish Music in Its Historical Development.* New York: Henry Holt.

Jairazbhoy, Nazir A. 1980. "Improvisation, II: Asian Art Music." In *New Grove Dictionary of Music,* 6th ed., vol. 9: 52–56.

Jameson, Fredric. 1991. *Postmodernism or the Cultural Logic of Late Capitalism.* Durham, N.C.: Duke University Press.

Jameson, Fredric, and Masao Miyoshi, eds. 1998. *The Cultures of Globalization.* Durham, N.C.: Duke University Press.

Kaeppler, Adrienne L. 1994. "Music, Metaphor, and Understanding." *Ethnomusicology* 38, no. 3: 457–73.

Kagansky, Edward. 1999. Transcript of interview conducted during class at the New

England Conservatory Summer Klezmer Institute, July 13, 1999. Trans. Michael Alpert, New England Conservatory, Boston.

Kaptain, Laurence D. 1992. *"The Wood That Sings": The Marimba in Chiapas, Mexico.* Everett, Penn.: Honeyrock.

Karp, Ivan, and Steven D. Lavine, eds. 1991. *Exhibiting Cultures: The Poetics and Politics of Museum Display.* Washington, D.C.: Smithsonian Institution Press.

Keil, Charles. 1998. "Applied Ethnomusicology and Performance Studies." *Ethnomusicology* 42, no. 2: 303–21.

Keil, Charles, and Steven Feld. 1994. *Music Grooves.* Chicago: University of Chicago Press.

King, Anthony D. 1990. *Urbanism, Colonialism, and the World Economy: Cultural and Spatial Foundations of the World Urban System.* New York: Routledge.

Kingsbury, Henry. 1988. *Music, Talent, and Performance: A Conservatory Cultural System.* Philadelphia, Penn: Temple University Press.

Kirshenblatt-Gimblett, Barbara. 1991. "Objects of Ethnography." In *Exhibiting Cultures: The Poetics and Politics of Museum Display,* ed. Ivan Karp and Steven D. Lavine, 386–443. Washington: Smithsonian Institution Press.

———. 1995. "Confusing Pleasures." In *The Traffic in Culture: Refiguring Art and Anthropology,* ed. George E. Marcus and Fred R. Myers, 224–55. Berkeley: University of California Press.

———. 1998a. *Destination Culture: Tourism, Museums, and Heritage.* Berkeley: University of California Press.

———. 1998b. "Secrets of Encounters." In her *Destination Culture: Tourism, Museums, Heritage,* 249–56. Berkeley: University of California Press.

———. 1998c. "Sounds of Sensibility." *Judaism* 185, no. 47: 49–79.

Kisliuk, Michelle. 1991. "Confronting the Quintessential: Singing, Dancing, and Everyday Life Among Biaka Pygmies (Central African Republic)." Ph.D. diss., New York University.

———. 1997. "(Un)doing Fieldwork: Sharing Songs, Sharing Lives." In *Shadows in the Field: New Perspectives for Fieldwork in Ethnomusicology,* ed. Gregory F. Barz and Timothy J. Cooley, eds., 23–44. New York: Oxford University Press.

———. 1998a. "Musical Life in the Central African Republic." In *Garland Encyclopedia of World Music,* vol. 1, *Africa,* ed. Ruth M. Stone, 681–97. New York: Garland Publishing.

———. 1998b. *Seize the Dance! BaAka Musical Life and the Ethnography of Performance.* New York: Oxford University Press.

———. 2002. "The Poetics and Politics of Practice: Experience, Embodiment, and the Engagement of Scholarship." In *Performance Studies: Theories, Practices, Pedagogies,* ed. Nathan Stuckey and Cynthia Wimmer. Carbondale: Southern Illinois University Press.

Koetting, James. 1970. "Analysis and Notation of West African Drum Ensemble Music." In *Selected Reports* 1, no. 3: 115–46. Los Angeles: Institute of Ethnomusicology, UCLA.

Koning, Jos. 1980. "The Fieldworker as Performer: Fieldwork Objectives and Social Roles in County Clare, Ireland." *Ethnomusicology* 24, no. 3: 417–29.

Kunst, Jaap. 1973. *Music in Java.* E. L. Heins, ed. 2 vols. 3d, enlarged ed. The Hague: Martinus Nijhoff.

————. 1974. *Ethnomusicology*. The Hague: Martinus Nijhoff.

Labuta, Joseph A., and Deborah A. Smith. 1999. *Music Education: Historical Contexts and Perspectives*. Englewood Cliffs, N.J.: Prentice-Hall.

Ladzekpo, Kobla. 1971. "The Social Mechanics of Good Music: A Description of Dance Clubs Among the Anlo Ewe–Speaking People of Ghana." *African Music* 3, no. 1: 33–42.

————. 1989. "Agahu: Music Across Many Nations." In *African Musicology: Current Trends: A Festschrift Presented to J. H. Kwabena Nketia*, ed. Jacqueline Cogdell DjeDje and William G. Carter, vol. 2: 181–90. Los Angeles: African Studies Center and African Arts Magazine, UCLA.

Lakoff, George, and Mark Johnson. 1999. *Philosophy in the Flesh: The Embodied Mind and Its Challenge to Western Thought*. New York: Basic Books.

Lapuz, Lourdes. 1981. "The Adolescent." In *Being Filipino*, ed. Gilda Cordero-Fernando, 27–32. Quezon City, Philippines: GCF Books.

Layang Wuwulang Nut: Papathokané Unggah-Udhun lan Dawa Cendhèké Swara. Teteladan Saka Tanah Eropa [The Book of Instruction on Notation: Rules of the Register and Rhythm of Melodies. Example from Europe]. 1874. Batawi: Kantor Pangecapan Gupremen.

Lewis, Reina. 1996. *Gendering Orientalism: Race, Femininity and Representation*. London: Routledge.

Lieberman, Fredric [with Responses by E. Eugene Helm and Claude Palisca]. 1977. "Should Ethnomusicology Be Abolished?" *Journal of the College of Music Society* 17, no. 2: 226–34.

Lindsay, Jennifer. 1979. *Javanese Gamelan*. Kuala Lumpur: Oxford University Press.

Locke, David. 1978. "The Music of Atsiagbekor." Ph.D. diss., Wesleyan University.

————. 1982. "Principles of Cross Rhythm and Off-Beat Timing in Southern Ewe Dance Drumming." *Ethnomusicology* 26, no. 2: 217–46.

————. 1987. *Drum Gahu: A Systematic Method for an African Percussion Piece*. Crown Point, Ind.: White Cliffs Media Company.

————. 1990. *Drum Damba: Talking Drum Lessons*. Crown Point, Ind.: White Cliffs Media Company.

————. 1992. *Kpegisu: A War Drum of the Ewe*. Tempe, Ariz.: White Cliffs Media Company.

————. 1996. "Africa/Ewe, Mande, Dagbamba, Shona, BaAka." In *Worlds of Music*, ed. Jeff Titon, 71–143. 3d ed. New York: Schirmer Books.

Loeffler, James Benjamin. 1997. *A Gilgul Fun a Nigun: Jewish Musicians in New York, 1881–1945*. Cambridge, Mass.: Harvard College Library.

Lomax, Alan. 1968. *Folk Song Style and Culture*. New Brunswick, N.J.: Transaction Books.

London, Frank. 1998. "An Insider's View: How We Traveled from Obscurity to the Klezmer Establishment in Twenty Years." *Judaism* 185, no. 47: 40–43.

MacCannell, Dean. 1992. *Empty Meeting Grounds: The Tourist Papers*. New York: Routledge.

MacKenzie, John. 1995. *Orientalism: History, Theory, and the Arts*. Manchester: Manchester University Press.

Malm, William P. 1977. *Music Cultures of the Pacific, The Near East, and Asia*. Englewood Cliffs, N.J.: Prentice-Hall.

Marcus, Scott. 1989a. "Arab Music Theory in the Modern Period." Ph.D. diss., University of California at Los Angeles.

———. 1989b. "The Periodization of Arab Music Theory: Continuity and Change in the Definition of *Maqāmāt.*" *Pacific Review of Ethnomusicology* 5: 33–49.

———. 1992. "Modulation in Arab Music: Documenting Oral Concepts, Performance Rules and Strategies." *Ethnomusicology* 36, no. 2: 171–96.

McAllester, David P. 1963. "Ethnomusicology, the Field, and the Society." *Ethnomusicology* 7, no. 3: 182–86.

McDermott, Vincent, and Sumarsam. 1975. "Central Javanese Music: The Patet of Laras Sléndro and the Gendèr Barung." *Ethnomusicology* 14, no. 2: 233–44.

Mcleod, Norma, and Marcia Herndon. 1984. *Music as Culture.* Darby, Penn.: Norwood Editions.

McPhee, Colin. 1966. *Music in Bali: A Study in Form and Instrumental Organization.* New Haven, Conn.: Yale University Press.

Merriam, Alan P. 1963. *The Anthropology of Music.* Chicago: Northwestern University Press.

———. 1969. "Ethnomusicology Revisited." *Ethnomusicology* 13, no. 2: 213–29.

———. 1973. "The Bala Musician." In *The Traditional Artist in African Societies,* ed. Warren L. D'Azevedo, ed., 250–81. Bloomington: Indiana University Press.

———. 1975. "Ethnomusicology Today." *Current Musicology* 20: 50–66.

Moyle, Richard M. 1984. "Jumping to Conclusions." In *Problems & Solutions: Occasional Essays in Musicology Presented to Alice M. Moyle,* ed. J. Kassler and J. Stubington, 51–58. Sydney: Hale & Iremonger.

———. 1993. "Drone, Melody, and Decoration—Paradigm Lost." *Ethnomusicology* 37, no. 3: 387–405.

Murgiyanto, Sal. 1991. "Moving Between Unity and Diversity: Four Indonesian Choreographers." Ph.D. diss., New York University.

Narkong, Anant. 1992. "Aspects of Improvisation in Thai Classical Drumming." M.Phil. thesis, SOAS (University of London).

Netsky, Hankus. 1997. "Klezmer Music: Local Rumbles and Distant Echoes." Paper presented at the Society for Ethnomusicology Conference, Pittsburgh, Penn.

———. 1998a. "A Context For Transmission." Unpublished paper.

———. 1998b. "An Overview of Klezmer Music and Its Development in the U.S." *Judaism* 185, no. 47: 5–12.

———. 2000. "A Voice Beyond Piety." Unpublished paper.

Nettl, Bruno. 1956. *Music in Primitive Culture.* Cambridge, Mass.: Harvard University Press.

———. 1964. *Theory and Method in Ethnomusicology.* New York: Free Press of Glencoe.

———. 1965. *Folk and Traditional Music of the Western Continents.* Englewood, N.J.: Prentice-Hall.

———. 1983. *The Study of Ethnomusicology: Twenty-Nine Issues and Concepts.* Urbana: University of Illinois Press.

———. 1985. *The Western Impact on World Music: Change, Adaptation, and Survival.* New York: Schirmer Books.

———. 1995. *Heartland Excursions: Ethnomusicological Reflections on Schools of Music.* Urbana: University of Illinois Press.

Nettl, Bruno, and Melinda Russell, eds. 1998. *In the Course of Performance: Studies in the World of Musical Improvisation.* Chicago: University of Chicago Press.

Nketia, J. H. K. 1962. "The Problem of Meaning in African Music." *Ethnomusicology* 6, no. 1: 1–7.

Nooshin, Laudan. 1998. "The Song of the Nightingale: Processes of Improvisation in *Dastgah Segah* (Iranian Classical Music)." *British Journal of Ethnomusicology* 7: 69–116.

Nussbaum, Martha. 1997. *Cultivating Humanity, a Classical Defense of Reform in Liberal Education.* Cambridge, Mass.: Harvard University Press.

Orquesta Casino de la Playa. 1974. *Memorias de Cuba.* RCA LP CAMS-712.

Patten, Charlotte Kimball. 1905. "Amusements and Social Life: Philadelphia." In *The Russian Jew in the United States,* ed. Charles S. Bernheimer, 233–48. Philadelphia, Penn.: John Winston Co.

Pemberton, John. 1994. *On the Subject of Java.* Ithaca, N.Y.: Cornell University Press.

Powers, Harold. 1980a. "India, §II, 3. Performing practice: (ii) Improvisation." In *New Grove Dictionary of Music,* 6th ed., vol. 9: 107–13.

———. 1980b. "Mode, §V. Mode as a Musicological Concept." In *New Grove Dictionary of Music,* 6th ed., vol. 12: 422–50.

———. 1996. "A Canonical Museum of Imaginary Music." *Current Musicology* 60–61: 5–25.

Qureshi, Regula Burckhardt. 1992. "Whose Music? Sources and Contexts in Indic Musicology." In *Comparative Musicology and Anthropology of Music,* ed. Bruno Nettl and Philip V. Bohlman, 152–68. Chicago: University of Chicago Press.

Racy, Ali Jihad. 1977. "Musical Change and Commercial Recording in Egypt, 1904–1932." Ph.D. diss., University of Illinois.

———. 1978. "Arabian Music and the Effects of Commercial Recording." *The World of Music* 20, no. 1: 47–55.

———. 1988. "Sound and Society: The *Takht* Music of Early-Twentieth-Century Cairo." *Selected Reports in Ethnomusicology* 7: 139–70. Los Angeles: University of California Ethnomusicology Publications.

———. 1991. "Creativity and Ambience: An Ecstatic Feedback Model from Arab Music." *The World of Music* 33, no. 3: 7–28.

———. 1997. *Mystical Legacies: Ali Jihad Racy Performs Music of the Middle East.* Compact Disc Recording with Souhail Kaspar, Lyrichord LYCRD 7437.

———. 1998. "Improvisation, Ecstasy, and Performance Dynamics in Arabic Music." In *In The Course of Performance: Studies in the World of Musical Improvisation,* ed. Bruno Nettl and Melinda Russell, 95–112. Chicago: University of Chicago Press.

———. 2003. *Making Music in the Arab World: The Culture and Artistry of Ṭarab.* Cambridge: Cambridge University Press.

Rasmussen, Anne K. 1991. "Individuality and Social Change in the Music of Arab Americans." Ph.D. diss., University of California at Los Angeles.

———. 1996. "Theory and Practice at the 'Arabic Org': Digital Technology in Contemporary Arab Music Performance." *Popular Music* 15, no. 3: 345–65.

———. 1997a. *The Music of Arab Americans: A Retrospective Collection.* Compact Disc Recording with 20 pages of notes and photographs, Rounder CD 1122.

———. 1997b. "The Music of Arab Detroit: A Musical Mecca in the Midwest." In *Musics of Multicultural America: A Study of Twelve Musical Communities,* ed. Kip Lornell and Anne K. Rasmussen, 73–100. New York: Schirmer Books.

———. 2001a. "Middle Eastern Music." In *The Garland Encyclopedia of World Music*, vol. 3, *The United States and Canada*, ed. Ellen Koskoff, 1028–41. New York: Garland.

———. 2001b. "The Qur'ân in Indonesian Daily Life: The Public Project of Musical Oratory." *Ethnomusicology* 45, no. 1: 30–57.

Read, Cathleen. 1975. "A Study of Yamada-ryu Sokyoku and Its Repertory." Ph.D. diss., Wesleyan University.

Rice, Timothy. 1987. "Toward the Remodeling of Ethnomusicology." *Ethnomusicology* 31, no. 3: 469–88.

———. 1994. *May It Fill Your Soul: Experiencing Bulgarian Music*. Chicago: University of Chicago Press.

———. 1997. "Toward a Mediation of Field Methods and Field Experience in Ethnomusicology." In *Shadows in the Field: New Perspectives for Fieldwork in Ethnomusicology*, ed. Gregory F. Barz and Timothy J. Cooley, 101–20. New York: Oxford University Press.

Ricoeur, Paul. 1981. *Hermeneutics and Human Sciences: Essays on Language, Action, and Interpretation*. Ed. and trans. John B. Thompson. Cambridge: Cambridge University Press.

Roof, Judith, and Robyn Wiegman, eds. 1995. *Who Can Speak? Authority and Critical Identity*. Urbana: University of Illinois Press.

Rorty, Richard. 1972. *Philosophy and the Mirror of Nature*. Princeton, N.J.: Princeton University Press.

Rothstein, Robert. 1998. "Klezmer-loshn." *Judaism* 185, no. 47: 23–28.

Rouget, Gilbert. 1985. *Music and Trance: A Theory of the Relations Between Music and Religion*. Chicago: University of Chicago Press.

Rouhana, Charbel. 1997. *Salamat*. Compact Disc Recording, Voix de L'Orient VDLCD 653.

Rubin, Ruth. 1963. *Voices of a People: The Story of Yiddish Folksong*. New York: Thomas Yoseloff.

Said, Edward. 1978. *Orientalism*. New York: Vintage Books.

Salmen, Walter. 1991. *Juddishe Muzikanten und Tentzer*. Innsbruck: Henle Press.

Sapoznik, Henry. 1999. *Klezmer!* New York: Schirmer Books.

Schechner, Richard. 1985. "Restoration of Behavior." In his *Between Theatre and Anthropology*, 35–116. Philadelphia: University of Pennsylvania Press.

Schein, Louisa. 1999. "Performing Modernity." *Cultural Anthropology* 14, no. 3: 361–95.

Schonberg, Harold. 1963. *The Great Pianists*. New York: A Fireside Book.

Scott, Joan W. 1996. "The Evidence of Experience." *Critical Inquiry* 17, no. 4: 773–97.

Seeger, Anthony. 1987. *Why Suyá Sing: A Musical Anthropology of an Amazonian People*. Cambridge: Cambridge University Press.

———. 1994. "Whoever We Are Today, We Can Sing You A Song About It." In *Music and Black Ethnicity: The Caribbean and South America*, ed. Gerard H. Béhague, 1–16. New Brunswick, N.J.: University of Miami North-South Center.

Sendrey, Alfred. 1970. *The Music of the Jews in the Diaspora*. London: Thomas Yoseloff.

Shaheen, Simon. 1992. *Turath: Simon Shaheen Performs Masterworks of the Middle East*. Compact Disc Recording with notes by Ali Jihad Racy, CMP 3006.

El-Shawan, Salwa. 1979. "The Socio-Political Context of al-Mūsīḳa al-'Arabiyyah in Cairo, Egypt: Policies, Patronage, Institutions, and Musical Change (1922–1972)." *Asian Music* 20, no. 1: 86–128.

———. 1981. "*Al-Mūsīqa al-'Arabiyyah:* A Category of Urban Music in Cairo, Egypt, 1927–1977." Ph.D. diss., Columbia University.

———. 1984. "Traditional Arab Music Ensembles in Egypt since 1967: 'The Continuity of Tradition within a Contemporary Framework?'" *Ethnomusicology* 28, no. 2: 271–88.

Shelemay, Kay Kaufman. 1997. "The Ethnomusicologist, Ethnographic Method, and the Transmission of Tradition." In *Shadows in the Field: New Perspectives for Fieldwork in Ethnomusicology,* ed. Gregory F. Barz and Timothy J. Cooley, 189–204. New York: Oxford University Press.

———. 1998. *Let Jasmine Rain Down: Song and Remembrance among Syrian Jews.* Chicago: University of Chicago Press.

Shiloah, Amnon. 1992. *Jewish Musical Traditions.* Detroit: Wayne State University Press.

Silkstone, Francis. 1993. "Learning Thai Classical Music: Memorization and Improvisation." Ph.D. diss., SOAS (University of London).

Singleton, Brian. 1997. "Introduction: The Pursuit of Otherness for the Investigation of Self." *Theatre Research International* 22, no. 2: 93–97.

Sklar, Deidre. 1994. "Can Bodylore Be Brought to Its Senses?" *Journal of American Folklore* 107, no. 423: 9–22.

Slobin, Mark. 1982a. *Tenement Songs: The Popular Music of the Jewish Immigrants.* Urbana: University of Illinois Press.

———, ed. and trans. 1982b. *Old Jewish Folk Music: The Collections and Writings of Moshe Beregovski.* Philadelphia: University of Pennsylvania Press.

———. 1992. "Micromusics of the West: A Comparative Approach." *Ethnomusicology* 36, no. 1: 1–88.

———. 1993. *Subcultural Sounds: Micromusics of the West.* Hanover, N.H.: University Press of New England.

———. 1996. "From Multiculturalism to Convivencia." *Academic Forms* (online paper and discussion). Middletown: Wesleyan University.

———. 2000. *Fiddler on the Move: Exploring the Klezmer World.* Oxford: Oxford University Press.

———, ed. 2002. *American Klezmer, Its Roots and Offshoots.* Berkeley: University of California Press.

Smith, Barbara. 1987. "Variability, Change, and the Learning of Music." *Ethnomusicology* 31, no. 2: 201–20.

Solís, Ted. 1980. "*Muñecas de Chiapaneco:* The Economic Importance of Self-Image in the World of the Mexican Marimba." *Latin American Music Review* 1, no. 1: 34–46.

———. 1982. "The Marimba in Mexico City: Contemporary Contexts of a Traditional Regional Ensemble." Ph.D. diss., University of Illinois, Urbana.

———. 1994. *Puerto Rico in Polynesia: Traditional Jíbaro Music on Hawaiian Plantations.* Compact Disc/Monograph, Original Music OMCD 020.

———. 1995. "Jíbaro Image and the Ecology of Hawai'i Puerto Rican Musical Instruments." *Latin American Music Review* 16, no. 2: 123–53.

———. 1999. "'It's All From Records': The Musical 'Americanization' and 'Latinization' of Diasporic Puerto Ricans in Hawaii and California." Paper presented at the annual meeting of the Far West Popular Culture and Far West American Culture Associations, Las Vegas, Nev.

———. 2001. "'Let's Play One Seis Caliente': Coalescence and Selective Adaptation in a Diasporic Puerto Rican Musical Style." In *Essays on Music and Culture in Honor of Herbert Kellman*, 549–66. Tours: Klincksieck.

Sorrell, Neil. 1990. *A Guide to the Gamelan*. London: Faber and Faber.

Spivak, Gayatri C. 1988. "Can the Subaltern Speak?" In *Marxism and the Interpretation of Culture*, ed. Cary Nelson and Lawrence Grossberg, 271–313. Urbana: University of Illinois Press.

Stoller, Paul. 1989. *The Taste of Ethnographic Things: The Senses in Anthropology*. Philadelphia: University of Pennsylvania Press.

Stutschewsky, Joachim. 1959. *Ha-klezmarim: Todotehem, Orah-Hayehem Vi-yetsirotehem*. Jerusalem: Mosad Bialik.

Sudnow, David. 1979. *Ways of the Hand: The Organization of Improvised Conduct*. Cambridge, Mass.: Harvard University Press.

Sumarsam. 1979. "Learn to Play Gendèr." Unpublished paper.

———. 1986. "Gamelan Journeys and Experiences." In *Proceedings of the First International Gamelan Festival and Symposium* 86: 25–34. Vancouver, Canada: The Republic of Indonesia Expo.

———. 1992. "Historical Contexts and Theories of Javanese Music." Ph.D. diss., Cornell University.

———. 1995. *Gamelan: Cultural Interaction and Musical Development in Central Java*. Chicago: University of Chicago Press.

———. 1999. "Learning and Teaching Gender: Recounting My Experience." *Seleh Notes* 7, no. 1: 4–7.

Supanggah, Rahayu. 1992. "Some Thoughts on Learning to Play Gamelan." In *Festival of Indonesia Conference Summaries*, ed. Marc Perlman, 19–22. New York: Festival of Indonesia Foundation.

Susilo, Hardja. 1986. "Changing Strategies for the Cross-Cultural Karawitan Experience: A Quarter Century Perspective." In *Proceedings of the First International Gamelan Festival and Symposium* 86: 62–69. Vancouver, Canada: Republic of Indonesia Expo.

———. 1990. *Toward an Appreciation of Javanese Gamelan*. Program notes for East-West Center concerts, April 7 and 8, 1990. Honolulu: East-West Center Performing Arts Series.

Sutton, R. Anderson. 1991. *Traditions of Gamelan Music in Java: Musical Pluralism and Regional Identity*. Cambridge: Cambridge University Press.

———. 1992. "Individuality and Writing in Javanese Music Learning." In *Festival of Indonesia Conference Summaries*, ed. Marc Perlman, 17–18. New York: Festival of Indonesia Foundation.

———. 1993. *Variation in Central Javanese Gamelan Music: Dynamics of a Steady State*. DeKalb: Center for Southeast Asian Studies, Northern Illinois University.

———. 1998. "Do Javanese Gamelan Musicians Really Improvise?" In *In The Course of Performance: Studies in the World of Musical Improvisation*, ed. Bruno Nettl and Melinda Russell, 69–92. Chicago: University of Chicago Press.

Suyenaga, Joan. 1999. Personal communication with Ted Solís, Yogyakarta, Indonesia, June.

Tabak, Robert P. 1983. *The Transformation of Jewish Identity: The Philadelphia Experience, 1919–1945*. Ann Arbor, Mich.: University Microfilms.

Tenzer, Michael. 1998. *Balinese Music*, 2d ed. Singapore: Periplus Editions.

———. 2000. *Gamelan Gong Kebyar: The Art of Twentieth-Century Balinese Music.* Chicago: University of Chicago Press.

Tenzer, Michael, and Rachel Cooper. 1983. "Sekar Jaya: Learning from Traditional Bali." *Ear Magazine* 8, no. 4: 12.

Thomas, David. 2000. *Skull Wars*. New York: Basic Books.

Thrasher, Alan. 1985. "The Melodic Structure of Jiangnan Sizhu." *Ethnomusicology* 29, no. 2: 237–61.

Titon, Jeff Todd, ed. 1996. *Worlds of Music*. 3d ed. New York: Schirmer Books.

———. 1997. "Knowing Fieldwork." In *Shadows in the Field: New Perspectives for Fieldwork in Ethnomusicology*, ed. Gregory F. Barz and Timothy J. Cooley, 87–100. New York: Oxford University Press.

Todorov, Tzvetan. 1984. *Mikhail Bakhtin: The Dialogical Principle*. Trans. Wlad Godzich. Minneapolis: University of Minnesota Press.

Toop, David. 1995. *Ocean of Sound: Aether Talk, Ambient Sound, and Imaginary Worlds*. London: Serpent's Tail.

———. 1999. *Exotica: Fabricated Soundscapes in a Real World*. London: Serpent's Tail.

Torgovnik, Marianna. 1990. *Gone Primitive: Savage Intellects, Modern Lives*. Chicago: University of Chicago Press.

Trimillos, Ricardo Diosdado. 1965. "Some Social and Musical Aspects of the Music of the Taosug [sic] in Sulu, Philippines." Master's thesis, University of Hawai'i.

———. 1972. "Tradition and Repertoire in the Cultivated Music of the Tausug of Sulu, Philippines." Ph.D. diss., University of California at Los Angeles.

———. 1988a. "Das Filipinische Rondalla-Ensemble auf den Philippinen als Spiegel oder Bestandteil der Filipino-Geschichte." *Jahrbuch für Musikalische Volks- und Völkerkunde* 13: 59–71.

———. 1988b. "Halau, Hochschule, Maystro, and Ryu: Cultural Approaches to Music Learning and Teaching." *International Journal of Music Education* 14: 32–43.

———. 1990. "Formal Instruction as Interface Between Theory and Practice in the Traditions of Hawai'i, Japan, and the Philippines." In *Atti del XIV Congresso della Società Internazionale di Musicologia*, 191–99. Torino, Italy: EDT.

———. 1995. "More Than Art: The Politics of Performance in International Cultural Exchange." In *Looking Out: Perspectives on Dance and Criticism in a Multicultural World*, ed. David Gere, 23–39. New York: Schirmer.

Tsui, Ying-fai. 2002. "The Modern Chinese Orchestra." In *Garland Encyclopedia of World Music*, vol. 7, *East Asia: China, Japan, and Korea*, ed. Robert C. Provine, Yoshihiko Tokumaru, and J. Lawrence Witzleben, 227–32. New York: Routledge.

Turnbull, Colin M. 1960. *The Forest People: A Study of the Pygmies of the Congo*. New York: Simon and Schuster.

Turner, Bryan. 1994. *Orientalism, Postmodernism, and Globalism*. London: Routledge.

Turner, Victor. 1969. *The Ritual Process: Structure and Anti-Structure*. Ithaca, N.Y.: Cornell University Press.

———. 1982. "Dramatic Ritual/Ritual Drama: Performative and Reflexive Anthropology." In his *From Ritual to Theater: The Human Seriousness of Play*, 89–101. New York: Performing Arts Journal Publications.

Veloso, Caetano. 1991. "Caricature and Conqueror: Pride and Shame." *New York Times*, Oct. 26, 1991, 34, 41.

Volk, Terese M. 1998. *Music, Education, and Multiculturalism: Foundations and Principles*. New York: Oxford University Press.

Wallulis, Jerald. 1990. *The Hermeneutics of Life History*. Evanston, Ill.: Northwestern University Press.

Wax, Rosalie H. 1971. *Doing Fieldwork*. Chicago: University of Chicago Press.

"'Whither Ethnomusicology?' The Scopes and Aims of Ethnomusicology." 1959. *Ethnomusicology* 3, no. 2: 99–105.

Widaryanto, F. X. 1984. "Teaching Javanese Dance: Lessons from an American Journey." In *Aesthetic Tradition and Cultural Transition in Java and Bali*, ed. Stephanie Morgan and Laurie Jo Sears, 209–19. Madison: Center for Southeast Asian Studies, University of Wisconsin.

Winslow, Richard [1967?]. "World Music." *Wesleyan Alumnae Magazine.* 3–9.

Witzleben, J. Lawrence. 1983. "Cantonese Instrumental Music in Hong Kong: An Overview with Special Reference to the Role of the Gou Wuh (Gao Hu)." Master's thesis, University of Hawai'i at Manoa.

———. 1995. *"Silk and Bamboo" Music in Shanghai: The Jiangnan Sizhu Instrumental Ensemble Tradition*. Kent, Ohio: Kent State University Press.

Woodly, Deva. 1999. "The Dance." Unpublished poem.

Yegenoglu, Myeda. 1998. *Colonial Fantasies: Towards a Feminist Reading of Orientalism*. Cambridge: Cambridge University Press.

Zborowski, Mark, and Elizabeth Herzog. 1952. *Life Is with People: The Culture of the Shtetl*. New York: Shocken Books.

Gage Averill is Professor of Music and Chair of the Music Department at NYU, where he also directs the ethnomusicology program. He is the author of *Four Parts, No Waiting: A Social History of American Barbershop Harmony* (Oxford University Press, 2003) and *A Day for the Hunter, a Day for the Prey: Popular Music and Power in Haiti* (University of Chicago Press, 1997) and a coeditor of *Making and Selling Culture* (Wesleyan University Press, 1996). He is currently editing a series of twelve CDs for Rounder Records called *The Alan and Elizabeth Lomax Expedition in Haiti, 1936–37.*

Kelly Gross is a graduate student in the Critical and Comparative Studies in Music program at the University of Virginia. A classical pianist, she has also participated in the university's African Drumming and Dance Ensemble since 1997. Her current research focuses on gender, vocality, and embodiment in film music.

David Harnish is Associate Professor of Ethnomusicology at Bowling Green State University and directs the Balinese ensemble Gamelan Kusuma Sari. He holds graduate degrees from the University of Hawai'i and the University of California at Los Angeles. He has published on music in Bali, Lombok, and Midwest Latino cultures and has recorded Indonesian and jazz performances with four different labels.

Ki Mantle Hood established performance as integral to ethnomusicology at the University of California at Los Angeles when he joined the faculty in 1954. In 1960 he founded the UCLA Institute of Ethnomusicology and served as Director until 1974. He has held positions at Yale, Harvard, West Virginia University, and the University of Maryland, Baltimore County. He holds an M.A. in composition from UCLA and a Ph.D. *cum laude* from the

University of Amsterdam. Versatile and innovative, he has published widely, directed documentary films, produced many recordings, organized gamelan groups, written historical fiction, and investigated chaos theory. Among his many honors is the first doctorate *honoris causa* awarded to an ethnomusicologist, by the University of Cologne, Germany, in 2003, and the title *Ki*, bestowed by the Republic of Indonesia in 1986. He is currently completing an autobiography.

David W. Hughes is Senior Lecturer in Ethnomusicology and Head of the Department of Music, School of Oriental and African Studies, University of London. His research and publications relate primarily to Japan (folk song, Okinawan music, music archaeology), Indonesia (street musicians of Central Java), oral mnemonics in comparative perspective, and musical grammars. He is a founder and former editor of the *British Journal of Ethnomusicology*.

Michelle Kisliuk holds a Ph.D. in Performance Studies from New York University and is a member of the faculty in Critical and Comparative Studies in Music at the University of Virginia. Her publications have focused on performance ethnography and critical aesthetics, with a research specialty in Central Africa. Her book *Seize the Dance!: BaAka Musical Life and the Ethnography of Performance* (Oxford University Press, 1998) won the ASCAP Deems Taylor Special Recognition Award in 1999.

David Locke holds a Ph.D. from Wesleyan University and is Associate Professor of Music at Tufts University, where he teaches world music, ethnomusicology, and the performance of African dance and music. He is the author of numerous written and audiovisual works that document and analyze performance traditions and music cultures of Africa, including three books on the repertories in the Ewe and Dagbamba musical heritage.

Scott Marcus, Associate Professor of Music (Ethnomusicology) at the University of California at Santa Barbara, is the author of numerous articles on Arab *maqām* and on *birahā* folk music of North India. He coedited the Middle East volume of the *Garland Encyclopedia of World Music* (Routledge, 1998).

Hankus Netsky is an instructor in jazz and contemporary improvisation at the New England Conservatory of Music and is the founder and director of the Klezmer Conservatory Band. He holds a Ph.D. in ethnomusicology from Wesleyan University.

Ali Jihad Racy is Professor of Ethnomusicology at the University of California at Los Angeles. He has conducted field research in Lebanon, Egypt, and the Arabian Gulf and earned his Ph.D. at the University of Illinois. A well-known composer and performer of Arab music, he has released a number of recordings, including *Taqāsīm: Improvisation in Arab Music, Ancient Egypt,* and *Mystical Legacies.* One of his compositions was released on the Kronos Quartet recording *Caravan*. He is the author of *Making Music in the Arab World: The Culture and Artistry of Tarab* (Cambridge University Press, 2003).

Anne K. Rasmussen is Associate Professor of Music and Ethnomusicology at the College of William and Mary, where she also directs a Middle Eastern music ensemble. Her publications and compact disc recordings have focused on politics and gender in the culture of Quranic recitation and Islamic musical arts in Indonesia, the musical life of Arab Americans, and musical multiculturalism in the United States. She is a coeditor of *Musics of Multicultural America: A Study of Twelve Musical Communities* (Schirmer, 1997).

Ted Solís is Professor of Music in the School of Music, Arizona State University, where his ethnomusicology courses include the Marimba Maderas de Comitán and Javanese gamelan ensembles. He holds graduate degrees from the Universities of Hawai'i and Illinois. His publications and recordings deal with Puerto Rican diasporic, Hindustani, and Mexican marimba musics.

Sumarsam is an Adjunct Professor of Music at Wesleyan University, teaching performance, history, and theory of gamelan. He holds an M.A. in ethnomusicology from Wesleyan University and a Ph.D. from Cornell University. He is the author of several articles on gamelan. His book *Gamelan: Cultural Interaction and Musical Development in Central Java* was published by the University of Chicago Press in 1995. As a gamelan musician and a keen amateur *dhalang* (puppeteer) of Javanese *wayang kulit* (shadow puppet theater), he performs, conducts workshops, and lectures throughout the world.

Hardja Susilo is a retired Associate Professor in Ethnomusicology at the University of Hawai'i, where he initiated the Javanese gamelan program in 1971. He initially came to the United States in 1958 as a student of ethnomusicology, and he was the first native gamelan teacher at the University of California at Los Angeles. He received the coveted Hadiah Seni (Art Award) from the Indonesian government for his contributions in *karawitan* (gamelan performing arts) in 1993.

Ricardo D. Trimillos is Professor of Ethnomusicology and Chair of the Asian Studies program at the University of Hawai'i at Manoa. His interests include issues of identity, gender, performance practice, and education related to multiculturalism. His research areas include the Philippines, Japan, and Hawai'i. He has studied at the University of Hawai'i (M.A.), the Ateneo de Manila, the University of Cologne, and the University of California at Los Angeles (Ph.D.). Asian musics he performs include Philippine *rondalla* and *kulintang* and Japanese *koto, gagaku,* and *kabuki* percussion.

Roger Vetter is Associate Professor of Music at Grinnell College and holds graduate degrees from the Universities of Hawai'i and Wisconsin. He has published on musics of Central Java and Ghana, and directs the Grinnell College Javanese Music and Dance Ensemble.

J. Lawrence Witzleben is a Professor in the Music Department of the Chinese University of Hong Kong, where he teaches courses in ethnomusicology, Chinese music, and world music and directs the Chinese and Javanese ensembles. His book *"Silk and Bamboo" Music in Shanghai: The Jiangnan Sizhu Instrumental Ensemble Tradition* (Kent State University Press, 1995) won the 1996 Alan Merriam prize for best monograph in the field of ethnomusicology. He coedited the East Asia volume of the *Garland Encyclopedia of World Music* (Routledge, 2002).

Compositor:	BookMatters, Berkeley
Indexer:	Pat Deminna
Text:	10/12 Baskerville
Display:	Baskerville